THE GREENWOOD ENCYCLOPEDIA OF

LOVE, COURTSHIP,

& Sexuality THROUGH HISTORY

THE GREENWOOD ENCYCLOPEDIA OF LOVE, COURTSHIP, AND SEXUALITY THROUGH HISTORY

The Ancient World, Volume 1
James W. Howell

The Medieval Era, Volume 2
William E. Burns

The Early Modern Period, Volume 3
Victoria L. Mondelli and Cherrie A. Gottsleben, with the assistance of Kristen Pederson Chew

The Colonial and Revolutionary Age, Volume 4
Merril D. Smith

The Nineteenth Century, Volume 5
Susan Mumm

The Modern World, Volume 6
James T. Sears

THE GREENWOOD ENCYCLOPEDIA OF
LOVE, COURTSHIP,
& Sexuality THROUGH HISTORY

THE NINETEENTH CENTURY
Volume 5

Edited by
SUSAN MUMM

GREENWOOD PRESS
Westport, Connecticut • London

To Ian,
with thanks for
everything.

Library of Congress Cataloging-in-Publication Data

The Greenwood encyclopedia of love, courtship, and sexuality through history /
volume editors, James W. Howell ... [et al.].
  p. cm.
  Includes bibliographical references and index.
  Contents: v. 1. The ancient world / James W. Howell, editor—v. 2. The medieval era / William
E. Burns, editor—v. 3. The early modern period / Victoria L. Mondelli and Cherrie A. Gottsleben,
editors—v. 4. The colonial and revolutionary age / Merril D. Smith, editor—v. 5. The nineteenth
century / Susan Mumm, editor—v. 6. The modern world / James T. Sears, editor.
  ISBN-13: 978–0–313–33359–0 (set : alk. paper)—ISBN-13: 978–0–313–33583–9 (vol. 1 : alk.
paper)—ISBN-13: 978–0–313–33519–8 (vol. 2 : alk. paper)—ISBN-13: 978–0–313–33653–9 (vol. 3 :
alk. paper)—ISBN-13: 978–0–313–33360–6 (vol. 4 : alk. paper)—ISBN-13: 978–0–313–33405–4
(vol. 5 : alk. paper)—ISBN-13: 978–0–313–33646–1 (vol. 6 : alk. paper)
  1. Sex—History—Encyclopedias. 2. Love—History—Encyclopedias. 3. Courtship—History—
Encyclopedias. I. Howell, James W. II. Title.
  HQ21.G67125 2008
  306.703–dc22   2007023728

British Library Cataloguing in Publication Data is available.

Library of Congress Catalog Card Number: 2007023728
ISBN-13:   978–0–313–33359–0 (set code)
           978–0–313–33583–9 (Vol. 1)
           978–0–313–33519–8 (Vol. 2)
           978–0–313–33653–9 (Vol. 3)
           978–0–313–33360–6 (Vol. 4)
           978–0–313–33405–4 (Vol. 5)
           978–0–313–33646–1 (Vol. 6)

First published in 2008

Greenwood Press, 88 Post Road West, Westport, CT 06881
An imprint of Greenwood Publishing Group, Inc.
www.greenwood.com

Printed in the United States of America

(∞)™

The paper used in this book complies with the
Permanent Paper Standard issued by the National
Information Standards Organization (Z39.48–1984).

10 9 8 7 6 5 4 3 2 1

Contents

List of Entries   vii

Set Preface   ix

Preface   xi

Acknowledgments   xiii

Introduction   xv

Guide to Related Topics   xix

Chronology of Selected Events   xxi

The Encyclopedia   1

Bibliography   267

Index   269

About the Editor and Contributors   273

List of Entries

Abortion
Acton, William
Adolescence
Adultery and Fornication
Age of Consent
Agriculture
Alcohol
Anthropology and Sexuality

Bastardy. See Illegitimacy
Beauty
Besant, Annie Wood (1847–1933)
Bestiality
Bigamy
Birth Control
Bradlaugh, Charles (1833–1891)
Brain
Broadsides. See Newspapers and
    Broadsides
Brontë, Charlotte (1816–1855)
Burton, Richard Francis
    (1821–1890)
Butler, Josephine (1828–1906)

Censorship
Child Abuse
Childbirth. See Pregnancy and
    Childbirth
Child Prostitution
China
Christianity
Circumcision and Clitoridectomy
Clitoridectomy. See Circumcision
    and Clitoridectomy
Cohabitation
Collins, Wilkie (1824–1889)
Comic Opera. See Gilbert and
    Sullivan (Comic Opera)

Comstock, Anthony (1844–1915)
Contagious Diseases Acts
Courtship

Dance/Dances
Divorce
Domestic Violence

Ellis, Havelock (1859–1939)
Erotica. See Pornography and
    Erotica
Etty, William (1787–1849)
Evolution

Fashion
Feminism
Fetishism
Flagellation
Fornication. See Adultery and
    Fornication
Foundlings
Free-Love Communities
The French System. See
    Prostitution, Regulated

Gender Roles
German Literature. See Literature,
    German
Gilbert and Sullivan (Comic
    Opera)
Gothic Fiction
Grand, Sarah (1854–1943)
Gynecological Manuals

Haddo, Lord. See Nude Models
Hardy, Thomas (1840–1928)
Harems
Hermaphrodites
Hinduism, Marriage in

Hirschfeld, Magnus (1868–1935)
Homosexuality
Hopkins, Gerard Manley
    (1844–1889)
Hopkins, Jane Ellice (1836–1904)
Hutchinson, Johnathan
    (1828–1913)

Illegitimacy
Imperialism
Islam and Homosexuality
Intersex. See Hermaphrodites

Kellogg, John Harvey (1852–1943)
Krafft-Ebing, Richard von
    (1840–1902)

Law
Lesbianism
Linton, Eliza Lynn (1822–1898)
Literature, German
Lock Hospitals. See Penitentiaries
    and Lock Hospitals
Love at First Sight
Love in Marriage

Madness
Malthus, Thomas Robert
    (1766–1834)
Marriage
Marriage, Irregular
Masochism. See Sadism and
    Masochism
Masturbation
Menstruation
Mental Illness. See Madness
Midwives. See Physicians and
    Midwives
Murder and Sex Crimes

Music Halls
My Secret Life. *See* "Walter"

Native Americans
Necrophilia
Newspapers and Broadsides
Novels, Romantic
Novels, Sensation
Nude Models

Orgasm
Orientalism
Ottoman Women

Painting
Passionlessness. *See* Sexlessness
Patmore, Coventry Kersey
   Dighton (1823–1896)
Penitentiaries and Lock Hospitals
Photographs
Physicians and Midwives
Polygamy, African
Polygamy, American
Popular Science. *See* Science,
   Popular

Pornography and Erotica
Pregnancy and Childbirth
Prostitution
Prostitution, Regulated

Queen Victoria (1819–1901)

Race
Romantic Friendship
Romantic Love
Romantic Novels. *See* Novels,
   Romantic

Sadism and Masochism
Science, Popular
Sensation Novels. *See* Novels,
   Sensation
Servants
Sex Crimes. *See* Murder and Sex
   Crimes
Sex Education
Sexlessness
Sex Manuals
Sexology

Sexual Pleasure. *See* Orgasm
Slander, English Law
Social Purity
Spermatorrhoea
Spinsters
Stoker, Bram (1847–1912)
Swinburne, Algernon Charles
   (1837–1909)

Theater
Trollope, Anthony (1815–1882)

Victoria, Queen of
   Great Britain. *See*
   Queen Victoria
Virginity
Virgin Mary

"Walter"
White Slavery
Widowhood
Women in the Media
Woodhull, Victoria Claflin
   (1838–1927)

Set Preface

Sex and love are part of the very fabric of daily life—universal concepts that permeate every human society and are central to how each society views and understands itself. However, the way sex and love are expressed or perceived varies from culture to culture, and, within a particular society, attitudes toward sex and love evolve over time alongside the culture from which they arose. To capture the multicultural and chronological dimensions of these vital concepts, the six-volume *The Greenwood Encyclopedia of Love, Courtship, and Sexuality through History* explores the array of ideas, attitudes, and practices that have constituted sex and love around the world and across the centuries.

Each volume of alphabetically arranged entries was edited by an expert in the field who has drawn upon the expertise of contributors from many related disciplines to carefully analyze views toward sex and love among many cultures within a specified time period. Students and interested general readers will find in this work a host of current, informative, and engaging entries to help them compare and contrast different perceptions and practices across time and space. Entries cover such topics as customs and practices; institutions; legislation; religious beliefs; art and literature; and important ideas, innovations, and individuals. Users of this encyclopedia will, for instance, be able to learn how marriage in ancient Rome differed from marriage in Victorian England or in colonial America; how prostitution was viewed in medieval Europe and in the contemporaneous Islamic societies of Africa and the Middle East; and how or even if celibacy was practiced in eighteenth-century India, ancient Greece, or early modern Europe.

Edited by James W. Howell, Volume 1, *The Ancient World*, explores love and sexuality in the great societies of Europe, Africa, and Asia in the period before around 300 CE. Entries include Marriage, Homosexuality, Temple Prostitution, and Sex in Art. Volume 2, *The Medieval Era*, by William E. Burns examines sex and love in Europe, East Asia, India, the Middle East, Africa, and pre-Columbian Mesoamerica in the period between around 300 and 1400. Entries in this volume include Arthurian Legend, Concubinage, Eunuchs, Krishna, Seclusion of Women, *Thousand and One Nights*, and Virginity.

Volume 3, *The Early Modern Period*, edited by Victoria L. Mondelli and Cherrie Ann Gottsleben, with the assistance of Kristen Pederson Chew, focuses on sex and love in Europe, India, China, the Middle East, Africa, and the Americas in the fifteenth and sixteenth centuries. Some important entries in this volume are Bastardy, Confucianism, Dowries, Sex Toys, Suttee, and William Shakespeare. Edited by Merril D. Smith, Volume 4, *The Colonial and Revolutionary Age*, looks at love and sexuality in western Europe, eastern Asia, India, the Middle East, Africa, and the Americas in the seventeenth and eighteenth centuries. The volume offers entries such as Bestiality, Castration, Berdache, Harems, Pueblo Indians, and Yoshiwara.

Volume 5, *The Nineteenth Century*, edited by Susan Mumm, explores sex and love in the Victorian period, primarily in Europe and the United States, but also in India, Asia, and the Middle East. Entries in this volume include Birth Control, Courtship, Fetishism, Native Americans, and Ottoman Women. Edited by James T. Sears, Volume 6, *The Modern World*, explores major topics in sex and sexuality from around the world in the twentieth and twenty-first centuries. Entries include AIDS/HIV, Domestic and Relationship Violence, Internet Pornography, Politics and Sex, Premarital Sex, Television, and the Women's Movement.

Each volume is illustrated and several cross-references to entries are provided. The entries conclude with a list of additional information resources, including the most useful books, journal articles, and Web sites currently available. Other important features of the encyclopedia include chronologies of important dates and events; guides to related topics that allow readers to trace broad themes across the entries; bibliographies of important general and standard works; and useful appendices, such as lists of Chinese dynasties and selections of important films and Web sites. Finally, detailed subject indexes help users gain easy access to the wealth of information on sex, love, and culture provided by this encyclopedia.

Preface

The Greenwood Encyclopedia of Love, Courtship, and Sexuality through History: The Nineteenth Century provides an introduction to key themes and topics relating to love and sex in the nineteenth century. Although it is obviously impossible for a single volume to cover all aspects of nineteenth-century thinking and behavior about these topics, the *Encyclopedia* endeavors in 122 entries to identify the most important areas of recent historical inquiry. Entries have been discriminately chosen to demonstrate the range of topics rather than attempting to discuss every possible subject. This *Encyclopedia* does not pretend to be exhaustive; it functions as a "first stop," allowing readers to gain information about topics new to them. The volume is wide-ranging but predominantly western in its orientation, reflecting the weight of current scholarship and the expert contributors available at the time of its creation. The contributors—more than sixty of them—are highly regarded specialists in the fields about which they wrote, and all gave their time and expertise generously to the project. Authorship is indicated at the close of each entry.

This volume is intended to give students of the nineteenth century a solid grounding in the key themes of the subject. Most entries contain boldfaced cross-references to other entries in the book and all conclude with a list of additional information resources, including books, articles, and websites. Biography entries contain the life dates of the entry subject in the headword. In light of the desire to supply introductory information on a wide range of topics, most of the entries are general, though some deal in depth with a single topic. The varying length of the entries does not necessarily reflect the importance of the subject; oftentimes it signifies no more than whether a subject is the focus of much current scholarly interest or is experiencing a temporary lull in attention. The suggestions for further reading at the ends of entries make no claim to be exhaustive, but indicate what the author believed would prove the most immediately rewarding resources for those seeking additional information. Thus, English language works have been chosen in preference to others in many cases.

The *Encyclopedia* also includes an Introduction that provides a broad context for the entries, a general Bibliography of important or standard works on the topic, a Guide to Related Topics that allows readers to quickly and easily trace broad themes across the entries, and a detailed Subject Index to look up names and terms in the entries. Photographs also illustrate many of the entries.

Acknowledgments

The *Encyclopedia* is by necessity, a collaborative effort, and I owe a debt of gratitude to the many busy experts who agreed to write for it. I am especially grateful to Robert Darby for his helpful suggestions with regard to contents and additional contributors. Danielle Bertrand, my editorial assistant, displayed unnerving levels of organizational talent, and the book would never have reached completion without her intelligent and patient industry, and her wide-ranging knowledge of the period.

Introduction

Few ages have suffered like the nineteenth century from the prejudices, exaggerations, and sneering of those born too late to be part of it. This is particularly true of the manner in which later generations depicted the nineteenth century's thinking and behavior with regard to love and sex. Victorian views of love are dismissed as excessively sentimental, even saccharine, and as imbued with hypocrisy and deceit. But love gets off lightly in comparison with how Victorian sexual behavior and attitudes have fared. For much of the twentieth century, commentators on the nineteenth century infused their analyses with positive venom, accusing their forebears of hypocrisy, self-loathing, willful ignorance, and every imaginable bad motive. Since the 1980s, however, the historical discipline has been pulling back from its earlier overgeneralized, sensationalized, and crude focus on extreme cases. For the last forty years, we have been abandoning our preconceptions about nineteenth-century sexuality and have been rewarded by discovering that this secret world was far more diverse and ambiguous than we previously thought. Looking at the whole range of evidence, rather than extrapolating from selected oddities, has broadened our understanding. Novels, poems, plays, advice manuals, medical treatises, professional pronouncements, scientific theories, diaries, letters, legal and criminal proceedings, and religious pamphlets are only a few of the sources upon which historians interested in love, sex, and culture now draw. As the analysis of the evidence has become more sophisticated, the conclusions drawn have become more nuanced, subtle, and contingent.

Sex, especially in the nineteenth century, can be seen as almost the stereotype of the unspoken, and as the most closeted of subjects in an age of reticence. But this is only partly true. It is probably more accurate to describe it as a partially hidden world that was at the same time compulsively scrutinized and discussed by its inhabitants. Polite literature, for example, was far more constrained in its discussion of sexual mores than were writers on social, medical, and even religious matters. Novelists, in particular, chafed against the constraints placed on them. In his preface to *Pendennis*, William Makepeace Thackeray complained that these restrictions made accurate depiction of human nature in fiction impossible, arguing that eighteenth-century novels had been able to depict male sexuality in a way unthinkable in the following century.

> Even the gentlemen of our age ... we cannot show as they are, with the notorious foibles and selfishness of their lives and their education. Since the author of Tom Jones was buried, no writer of fiction among us has been permitted to depict to his utmost power a MAN. We

must drape him, and give him a certain conventional simper. Society will not tolerate the Natural in our Art.

Given our fascination with Victorian attitudes toward sexuality, it is easy to forget that their beliefs about love were also conflicted and ambiguous. This is partly because the emotion of love (when kept within limits) was very culturally acceptable. The nineteenth century expected a lot of love. The weight of expectations placed on the emotion is perhaps less strange to us because it is less dissimilar to the views of our own time, although these, of course, continue to evolve. The shock of the unfamiliar is much more muted than it is when comparing our attitudes toward sexuality. However, recent scholarship has begun to re-examine nineteenth-century beliefs about love and the part it played in people's lives.

The nineteenth century did place strict limits on the proper operation of love. It was assumed to be invariably heterosexual. The declaration of love was a male privilege; the woman's role was to wait for the avowal, concealing her own feelings, and then respond. The truest love was assumed to be an amalgam of spiritual union as well as social compatibility; physical attraction was desirable but not essential. Love was expected to flower within marriage or lead to marriage; once married, the bond was assumed to be life-long and to express itself in marriage through the complementary nature of the two sexes. Many believed that mutual love was a gift from God, bestowed only once in each life. This was a tremendous amount to ask of any human emotion, and we should not be surprised that when the *Daily Telegraph* posed the question "Is Marriage a Failure?" in 1888, the great majority of the 27,000 letters, mostly anonymous, that were received in response declared emphatically that it was.

The nineteenth century contained fascinating extremes in its views of love and sex. It was a century in which a titled woman could advise, in all seriousness, that books by male and female authors should not be shelved side-by-side, unless the authors were married to one another. At the other extreme, it was a society where the House of Lords could vigorously oppose attempts to raise the age of female consent to thirteen, on the grounds that this might interfere with their own or their sons' sexual pleasure in brutalizing children. We should not be surprised by these contradictions, or fall into the easy trap of simply labeling them as hypocritical. Such criticisms ignore human nature. People today, as in the past, quite comfortably hold contradictory beliefs or advocate irreconcilable practices without being aware of their inconsistency. It is a mistake to try to force those who inhabited the nineteenth century to think and behave more consistently or logically than we can do ourselves. For example, the Victorians both claimed that respectable women were essentially without sexual desire, while at the same time warning that discussions of sex were dangerous for women because "it is tolerably well known that … cold-blooded mortals among the fair sex are few and far between" (Saladin, 41–42). We can also be startled by a Victorian physician's offhand remark that many wives faked orgasm, a casual aside that shatters our assumptions about the nineteenth-century marriage bed with breathtaking conciseness (Mason 1994).

Writers on the history of sexuality or social practices have begun to re-evaluate the role of religion in shaping the behavior and beliefs of societies. The nineteenth century was long dismissed as "Puritan" or "evangelical," which became a quick and easy shorthand for condemning repression, prudery, and any way of thinking or behaving that did not appeal to our current sense of justice. An overly simplistic explanatory device serves no historian well, and this crudity of analysis narrowed the breadth of interpretation for a considerable time. However, as with other areas of research, modern interpretations of the role of religion in shaping sexuality are slowly becoming more informed and sensitive to nuance. We are beginning to realize how profoundly religion influenced sexual mores and ideas about love, even among the small minority of nineteenth-century people who openly rejected religion altogether. While they might declare themselves nonbelievers, it was almost impossible for individuals to divorce themselves from the underlying religious assumptions that permeated the society in which they lived. Attitudes toward sexuality and love developed in a society saturated with taken-for-granted religious beliefs that stretched imperceptibly into all areas of life. In the West, Christian teaching formed an often unspoken, sometimes unrealized, thread of continuity underlying both behavior and practice. Take for example, "Holy Matrimony," as marriage was called in the marriage service used in the Church of England during the nineteenth century. In this service, employed virtually without alteration since the 1660s, marriage was described as having three purposes, blending a mixture of sexual and affectional motives (although it is noteworthy that there is no mention of romantic love):

> First, It was ordained for the procreation of children, to be brought up in the fear and nurture of the Lord, and to the praise of his holy Name.
> Secondly, It was ordained for a remedy against sin, and to avoid fornication; that such persons as have not the gift of continency might marry, and keep themselves undefiled members of Christ's body.
> Thirdly, It was ordained for the mutual society, help, and comfort, that the one ought to have of the other, both in prosperity and adversity.

The service also warned against marriage based purely on physical attraction, warning that it was not to be undertaken "unadvisedly, lightly, or wantonly, to satisfy men's carnal lusts and appetites, like brute beasts that have no understanding." It was a "holy estate." This simple example shows how far our understanding of the most central concepts of sex, love, and marriage has altered since the nineteenth century.

A famous Victorian murder trial throws a suggestive light on the depth of the links between traditional Christianity and social thought. When Adelaide Bartlett, wife of the London grocer Edwin, was accused of his murder by poison, her defence hinged on her allegations about Edwin's peculiar theories about sex and marriage. She alleged that her husband thought (and attempted to teach her) that men should have two wives, one for companionship and one for "use." So repugnant was this to the Christian teaching of the time that it was the deceased Edwin who was censured by the disgusted judge, and his wife very probably got away with murder as a result. Another interesting aspect of the case is what it reveals about the linkages between sex and procreation. So inextricably was sex linked (at the very least) to the *possibility* of conception that a medical nurse testifying for the defence was able to claim that "union" took place only once in the Bartlett's marriage of several years. Cross-examination revealed that the nurse took it for granted that sex without contraception was the only authentic form of sex, and was thus the only one that counted as "union." Evidently the jury agreed.

Religion also intruded into a surprising area of nineteenth-century sexuality in both the United States and in Europe, that of erotica and pornographic literature. Pornography often appeared disguised in a religious topcoat, where righteous indignation apparently made the salacious depiction of immoral acts somewhat more acceptable. Convent and confessional pornography was a flourishing genre in the nineteenth century, and played on traditional anti-Catholicism, often concocting "authentic narratives" out of venerable anticlerical tales long in circulation among continental writers. The classic of the genre, *The Awful Disclosures of Maria Monk*, sold over 300,000 copies in the twenty-five years after its publication in 1835 and remained in print throughout the century. The book chronicles lurid fantasies of rape by priests, murdered infants, and imprisoned nuns. It had many imitators, some far more explicitly pornographic than *Maria Monk*. Confessional pornography, closely linked to its convent cousin, arose in a chaperonage culture, where middle- and upper-class women did not spend meaningful periods of time alone with men to whom they were not related. This made nineteenth-century opponents of the practice claim that sexual impropriety was almost inevitable in such a situation. Within the Church of England, the Anglo-Catholic movement therefore found itself facing the extraordinary accusation of "turning many a quiet place of worship into a Ritualistic brothel" (Saladin, 34).

While religion, or at least theology, showed little sign of change in its views of love and sex over the period, in other respects the nineteenth century was an era of unrelenting, fast paced, almost breathtaking change. Industrialization and urbanization meant that millions of people crowded together in large towns and cities, breaking down traditional social mores and greatly expanding their choices in love and marriage. Easier travel within and between countries allowed people whose grandparents had never ventured beyond their parish of birth to relocate virtually on a whim, and to experience regions and lands whose customs and beliefs were very different from their own. Few societies have experienced "the shock of the new" to the extent that our nineteenth century forebears did, and their response to the constant change they underwent did not leave their beliefs about love and sex untouched, although social conservatives made valiant efforts in this direction. We may look back and see the period as an era of stability and confidence, but those who lived through it experienced it as a series of challenges to all they knew and believed, as well as an era of dazzling technological innovation.

Another of the challenge faced by those who desire to really understand nineteenth-century attitudes toward sex and love, is that of abandoning their knowledge of more recent events. The most important example of this is the absence of Freudianism from the intellectual landscape. Sigmund Freud only began to publish in the 1890s and it took considerable time for his influence to spread, particularly into the English-speaking world. Freud's influence is a phenomenon of the twentieth century, not the nineteenth. Therefore, it is the historian's task to imaginatively project ourselves into a pre-Freudian world. While some of the influences on Freud are discussed in this *Encyclopedia*, such as Havelock Ellis, Freud himself belongs to the twentieth century.

FURTHER READING

Hartman, Mary. *Victorian Murderesses*. London: Robson, 1977; Mason, Michael. *The Making of Victorian Sexuality*. Oxford: Oxford University Press, 1994; "Order for the Solemnization of Marriage." *Book of Common Prayer*, 1662; Saladin [pseud. of William Stewart Ross]. *The Confessional Exposed: As it Exists in the Church of Rome and the Church of England*. London: W. Stewart, n.d.; Thackeray, William Makepeace. *The History of Pendennis*. London: Bradbury & Evans, 1849.

Guide to Related Topics

AUTHORS AND BOOKS
Brontë, Charlotte
Burton, Richard Francis
Collins, Wilkie
Gothic Fiction
Grand, Sarah
Hopkins, Gerard Manley
Linton, Eliza Lynn
Literature, German
Newspapers and Broadsides
Novels, Romantic
Novels, Sensation
Patmore, Coventry
Stoker, Bram
Swinburne, Algernon Charles
"Walter"
Women in the Media

ARTS
Beauty
Censorship
Dance and Dances
Etty, William
Fashion
Gilbert and Sullivan
  (Comic Opera)
Music Halls
Nude Models Public Funding
  Controversy (1859–1860)
Painting
Theater

BIRTH CONTROL
Abortion
Besant, Annie Wood
Birth Control
Bradlaugh, Charles

Malthus, Thomas Robert
Sex Education

CHILDREN
Adolescence
Age of Consent
Child Abuse
Child Prostitution
Foundlings
Illegitimacy

FETISHISMS
Bestiality
Fetishism
Flagellation
Necrophilia
Sadism and Masochism

HOMOSEXUALITY
Gender Roles
Homosexuality
Islam and Homosexuality
Lesbianism

INDIVIDUALS
Acton, William
Besant, Annie Wood
Bradlaugh, Charles
Brontë, Charlotte
Burton, Richard Francis
Butler, Josephine
Collins, Wilkie
Comstock, Anthony
Ellis, Havelock
Etty, William
Grand, Sarah
Hardy, Thomas

Hirschfeld, Magnus
Hopkins, Gerard Manley
Hopkins, Jane Ellice
Hutchinson, Johnathan
Kellogg, John Harvey
Krafft-Ebing, Richard von
Linton, Eliza Lynn
Malthus, Thomas Robert
Patmore, Coventry Kersey
  Dighton
Queen Victoria
Stoker, Bram
Swinburne, Algernon Charles
Trollope, Anthony
"Walter"
Woodhull, Victoria Chaflin

LAW
Age of Consent
Bigamy
Censorship
Contagious Diseases Act
Divorce
Law
Murder and Sex Crimes
Penitentiaries and Lock Hospitals
Slander (English Law)

MARRIAGE
Adultery and Fornication
Bigamy
Cohabitation
Courtship
Domestic Violence
Harems
Hinduism, Marriage in
Love in Marriage

Marriage
Marriage, Irregular
Polygamy (African)
Polygamy (American)
Spinsterhood
Widowhood

MEDICAL ISSUES AND RESEARCH
Abortion
Birth control
Brain
Circumcision and
   Clitoridectomy
Gynecological Manuals
Hermaphrodites
Masturbation
Menstruation
Physicians and Midwives
Pregnancy
Spermatorrhoea

**NON-WESTERN
CULTURES**
Anthropology
China
Empire

Hinduism, Marriage in
Homosexuality, in the Islamic
   World
Native Americans
Orientalism
Ottoman Women
Polygamy (African)
Race

PROSTITUTION
Acton, William
Child Prostitution
Penitentiaries and Lock Hospitals
Prostitution
Prostitution, regulated
Servants
White Slavery

SEXOLOGISTS
Ellis, Havelock
Hirschfeld, Magnus
Kraft-Ebing, Richard von
Sexology

WOMEN
Agriculture
Besant, Annie Wood

Birth Control
Brontë, Charlotte
Butler, Josephine
Circumcision and
   Clitoridectomy
Courtship
Divorce
Domestic Violence
Feminism
Gender Roles
Grand, Sarah
Gynecological Manuals
Hopkins, Jane Ellice
Lesbianism
Linton, Eliza Lynn
Menstruation
Ottoman Women
Physicians and Midwives
Pregnancy and
   Childbirth
Queen Victoria
Spinsters
Virginity
Virgin Mary
Widowhood
Women in the Media
Woodhull, Victoria Chaflin

Chronology of Selected Events

1753 Parliament passes Hardwicke's Marriage Act, making it impossible to contract a valid irregular marriage in England, thus reducing the number of clandestine marriages and making it easier for magistrates to regulate marriage.

1764 Horace Walpole publishes *The Castle of Otranto*, a novel that brings Gothic fiction into vogue in England, a trend that continues into the nineteenth century.

1798 Thomas Malthus publishes *An Essay on the Principle of Population as it Affects the Future Improvement of Society, with Remarks on the Speculations of Mr Godwin, M. Condorcet and other Writers*, in which Malthus argues that all creatures have the potential to grow much faster than their food supply (the first grows geometrically, the second arithmetically), and that the human species had the potential to double its numbers every twenty-five years.

1801 The Society for the Suppression of Vice and the Encouragement of Religion and Virtue is founded in London.

1802 The English Society for the Suppression of Vice is established.

1803 Parliament passes the Miscarriage of Women Act (known as Lord Ellenborough's Act), the first statutory prohibition of abortion in English Law; "prequickening" abortions (performed before the first fifteen to eighteen weeks of pregnancy) were felonies, while "postquickening" abortions were capital crimes.

1804 France's Napoleonic code revokes the revolutionary era principal of the equality of all children, whether born in wedlock or not.

1807 Thomas Bowdler and his sister Henrietta publish their highly popular *Family Shakespeare*, a censored edition of the works of William Shakespeare that removes all impious and sexual references from the plays; more than 10 percent of *Hamlet* is deleted and some whole plays, such as *Romeo and Juliet*, are excluded.

1812 Because of difficulties arising out of the differences in marriage law between England and Scotland, English judges declare that marriages contracted in England cannot be dissolved by the courts of other nations, a pronouncement that cause many English couples to commit unintentional bigamy by obtaining divorce abroad.

1821 Following the quickening distinction made in the British Miscarriage of Women Act in 1803, Connecticut becomes the first American state making postquickening abortion a felony.

1826 Richard Carlile publishes *Every Woman's Book*, one of the first sex manuals written for women.

1828 New York State declares postquickening abortion as felony and prequickening abortion a misdemeanor, but also sanctions abortions in cases where it is deemed necessary to save the life of the mother.

1835 The daguerrotype, the first practical photographic process, is invented; sexually explicit and pornographic photographs make their first appearance shortly thereafter.

1837   The parliamentary abolition of the death penalty causes a revision in the statutory treatment of abortions in Great Britain, with the quickening distinction of the 1803 statute dropped and all abortions now treated as felonies.

1839   American physician and anthropologist Samuel Morton publishes *Crania Americana* in which he concludes on the basis of skull size that Native Americans are less intelligent than Europeans or Asians.

1840   American gothic writer Edgar Allan Poe publishes his *Tales of the Grotesque and Arabesque.*

   Queen Victoria wears a white wedding dress for her marriage to Prince Albert, thus setting the fashion for brides to wear white as a symbol of their virginity.

1842   The U.S. Congress enacts the first federal legislation regulating obscenity by banning the importation of obscene images, including paintings and engravings.

1843   The British Theatres Act requires a government license for the performance of plays, thus continuing the practice of preventive censorship by which offending words or actions had to be removed from a play before it could be licensed.

1844   The Young Men's Christian Association (YMCA) is founded in London, but soon spreads to other countries.

1847   Charlotte Brontë publishes her novel, *Jane Eyre*; Emily Brontë publishes *Wuthering Heights.*

   Spain institutes the Madrid Regulations in an effort to control the spread of venereal disease.

1848   A community of Bible communists led by John Humphrey Noyes and practicing free love moves from Vermont to Oneida, New York, where it will become known to history as the Oneida Community.

   Charles Meigs, MD, publishes *Females and their Diseases* (1848), in which he notes that some women prefer to suffer from gynecological problems rather than submit to the indelicacy of having their bodies medically examined.

1849   Elizabeth Blackwell, the first woman medical doctor in the United States, graduates from medical school in New York.

1850   American novelist Nathaniel Hawthorne publishes *The Scarlet Letter.*

1851   Nathaniel Hawthorne publishes *The House of the Seven Gables.*

   A proponent of women's rights, British writer Eliza Lynn Linton publishes *Realities*, a shocking novel that in its (unpublished) original version advocates women's political and social rights and sexual freedom.

1852   The Church of Jesus Christ of Latter-Day Saints (Mormons) publicly proclaims plural marriage as an important tenet of its faith.

1854   Initial publication of *Angel in the House*, a long poem on marriage by the English poet Coventry Patmore.

   Pope Pius IX issues *Ineffabilis Deus*, which declares that the Virgin Mary was conceived without sin, a unique favor granted by God in advance of, but in recognition of, the merits of her son.

1855   The Young Women's Christian Association (YWCA) is founded in London, but, like the YMCA, soon develops a strong international presence.

1856   Championed by Indian social reformer Ishwar Chandra Vidyasagar, the Hindu Widows Remarriage Act is passed in an attempt to ameliorate the oppressive institution of widowhood among the upper castes in British India.

1857   Surgeon and venereologist William Acton, one of the most influential authorities on sexuality in Victorian Britain, publishes *The Functions and Disorders of the Reproductive Organs in Childhood, Youth, Adult Age and Advanced Life*, a popular work aimed more at the general public than at medical professionals.

   Parliament passes the Matrimonial Causes Act, which permits divorce through the law courts rather than through the slow and expensive process of obtaining a private act of Parliament; the act requires a husband only to prove his wife's adultery, but requires the wife to not only prove her husband's adultery but also his commission of incest, bigamy, cruelty, or desertion.

Parliament passes the Obscenity Publications Act, which allows magistrates to seize and destroy obscene material and thereby largely drives the pornography trade overseas; British law defines as obscene anything intended to "deprave and corrupt" its readers.

1859   Charles Darwin publishes *The Origin of Species*, thereby changing the way society views theories of evolution.

Surgeon William Acton publishes *Observations on Illegitimacy* (1859), the first English-language study of the subject.

Margaret J. M. Sweat publishes *Ethel's Love Life*, which deals with erotic relationships between women and is believed to be the first lesbian novel written in the United States.

1859–   George Hamilton-Gordon, Lord Haddo,
1860   Liberal Member of Parliament (MP) for Aberdeenshire and son of a former prime minister, initiates action in Parliament over the use of nude female models in British schools of art.

1860s   Abortion is prohibited throughout most of the United States.

1860   Wilkie Collins, a British writer of sensational fiction, publishes his novel *The Woman in White*.

1861   The British Parliament passes the Offences Against the Person Act, which continues to treat all abortions as felonies, confirms the age of consent as twelve, and declares having consensual sex with a girl under ten a felony and with a girl between the ages of ten and twelve a misdemeanor.

1862   In response to the Mormon practice of polygamy in Utah, the U.S. Congress criminalizes polygamy in U.S. territories.

Addressing what was seen as an important nineteenth-century social problem, the over-abundance of spinsters, English industrialist W. R. Greg publishes his influential article "Why are Women Redundant?"

1864   The British Parliament enacts the first of the Contagious Diseases (CD) Acts, which allow the police to detain any woman suspected of prostitution in fourteen naval and military towns, to examine her for venereal disease, and to detain her in a certified hospital if

found to be infected; this initial act is later amended and extended by acts passed in 1866 and 1869.

Herbert Spencer coins the term "survival of the fittest" to describe theories of evolution and natural selection.

Marion Sims, a southern doctor often regarded as the father of gynecology in the United States, publishes *Uterine Surgery*.

1866   Charles Bradlaugh co-founds the National Secular Society, which seeks the abolition of the blasphemy law, a statute that limits what can be legally printed and distributed in Britain.

The poet Algernon Charles Swinburne causes great public outrage with the publication of his first collection of poetry, *Poems and Ballads Series 1*, which was characterized by the frank sexuality of its subject matter.

1867   Parliament enacts the Agricultural Gangs Act, which, in answer to a growing outcry against agricultural fieldwork performed by females, restricts women and girls' employment in such labor to single-sex, licensed gangs supervised by a female gang master.

1868   British women's rights and antislavery activist Josephine Butler publishes *The Education and Employment of Women*.

1869   British philosopher and campaigner for women's rights J. S. Mill publishes *Subjection of Women*.

Eliza Lynn Linton publishes her antifeminist article "The Girl of the Period."

1870s   Birth control becomes one of the chief concerns of feminists and proponents of women's rights.

1871   Charles Darwin publishes *The Descent of Man, and Selection in Relation to Sex*, which applies theories of natural selection to human sexuality.

American women's rights activist Victoria Woodhull delivers her celebrated speech, "The Principles of Social Freedom," in which she dismissed marriage as "legal prostitution."

1873   The U.S. Congress passes the Comstock Law, named for antivice reformer Anthony Comstock, which prohibits sending through the mail any book considered "obscene, lewd, or lascivious."

American antivice reformer Anthony Comstock founds the New York Society for the Suppression of Vice.

Britain abolishes a father's automatic right to the custody of children in a divorce case; henceforth, child custody was agreed on a case-by-case basis in the separation contract drawn up on the dissolution of a marriage, with an increasing tendency to leave young children with their mother as the century progressed.

1877　Annie Wood Besant and Charles Bradlaugh publish a pamphlet on birth control, and act that leads to their arrest and prosecution for obscenity, a court case that became one of the most sensational trials in Victorian England.

1878　The U.S. Supreme Court rules that the taking of multiple wives (polygamy), which was permitted by the Church of Jesus Christ of Latter-Day Saints (Mormons), violates criminal laws prohibiting bigamy and thus is not defensible as an exercise of religious liberty.

The British antiwife beating activist Frances Power Cobbe publishes "Wife Torture in England," which creates a public scandal and leads eventually to changes in the law regarding a woman's rights.

1879　Jane Ellice Hopkins, a social purity crusader, publishes *Notes on Penitentiary Work* (1879), which, with Hopkins' later work, *Man and Woman: The Christian Ideal* (1884), argues for the establishment of a higher lever of male sexual chastity.

1881　France tightens its obscenity laws, prohibiting anything that might offend "public and religious morality and good taste."

1882　The British Parliament passes the Married Women's Property Act, which gives married women the same rights over their property as unmarried women, thus allowing a married woman to retain ownership of property that she might have received as a gift from a parent; prior to this act, such property automatically became the property of the husband.

1883　Richard Francis Burton publishes his translation of the sexually explicit Sanskrit work, the *Kama Sutra*.

Jane Ellice Hopkins and Bishop Lightfoot of Durham, leading figures in the social purity movement, establish the White Cross Army (WCA).

1884　British Marriage Law is amended to prevent women without a formal separation contract from being imprisoned by their husbands to compel them to resume cohabitation.

1885　The British Parliament passes the Criminal Law Amendment Act, which raises the age of consent from thirteen to sixteen; makes it a criminal offence to procure girls for prostitution through fraud, intimidation, or the administration of drugs; and allows for summary proceedings against brothels.

Richard Francis Burton publishes his translation of the *Arabian Nights*

British newspaper editor William Thomas Stead publishes a sensationalist series of articles entitled "The Maiden Tribute of Modern Babylon" in the *Pall Mall Gazette*; in the article, Stead alleges that girl children were being sold, purchased, and violated on the streets of London.

1886　Parliament repeals the Contagious Diseases Acts.

As part of a renaissance of Gothic fiction in the late Victorian period, Robert Louis Stevenson publishes *The Strange Case of Dr Jekyll and Mr Hyde*.

The term *homosexual* gains increasing currency after its frequent use by German neuropsychiatrist Richard von Krafft-Ebing in his *Psychopathia Sexualis*, which is published in this year; the term, first used in the German-speaking world, later is widely used everywhere in Europe to describe those who have sex with or are sexually attracted to people of their own sex.

1888　The British Libel Act reaffirms the government's ability to prosecute newspapers for reprinting blasphemy or obscenity; the reporting of divorce trials, although often scandalous and explicit, is exempt because it reflects courtroom testimony.

c. 1888　First publication of *My Secret Life*, a work detailing the sex life of an anonymous English gentleman known as "Walter"; the book, which was to be banned for 100 years, eventually encompasses eleven volumes.

1888–
1889   Occurring in the Whitechapel district of London, the "Jack-the-Ripper" murders will become the best known examples of sexual serial murder.

1889   *Venus in India* is published; it is one of the many popular pornographic works of the late nineteenth century set in an exotic part of the British empire.

1890   In the United States, the Church of Jesus Christ of Latter-Day Saints (Mormons) renounces the practice of polygamy.

1891   Scandalized by the Hindu practice of child marriage, the British administration in Bengal raises the age of consent from ten to twelve.

Oscar Wilde publishes *The Picture of Dorian Gray*.

Thomas Hardy publishes *Tess of the d'Urbervilles*, which, although very popular, is bitterly attacked for its frank depiction of sex.

1893   British feminist novelist Sarah Grand publishes *The Heavenly Twins*, a best-selling novel that includes a shockingly forthright portrayal of syphilis.

The Legitimation League is formed in London to press for the acknowledgment of bastard children, and to campaign for them to be given equal rights with legitimate children.

Parliament passes a second Married Women's Property Act to extend the rights given to women by the 1882 statute; married women now have full legal control of all the property of every kind that they owned at marriage or that they acquired after marriage either by inheritance or by their own earnings.

1895   The Indian Contagious Diseases Acts are repealed.

Popular British writer Oscar Wilde is tried for sodomy.

1896   Writing under the pseudonym Theodor Ramien, German sexologist Magnus Hirschfeld publishes the article "Sappho und Socrates, Wie erklärt sich die Liebe der Männer und Frauen zu Personen des eigenen Geschlechts" ("Sappho and Socrates, How Does One Explain the Love of Men and Women for People of their Own Sex"), which argues that same-sex sexuality should be viewed as natural and not be prohibited by law.

1897   British psychologist Henry Havelock Ellis publishes the first volume of his eventual seven-volume *Studies in the Psychology of Sex*, which explores almost all aspects of human sexuality, including homosexuality and transvestism.

Bram Stoker publishes *Dracula*.

American Lutheran minister Sylvanus Stall publishes his sex advice manuals *What a Young Boy Ought to Know*, which ran through several editions and translations, and *What a Young Girl Ought to Know*, the latter written jointly by Stall and physician Mary Wood-Allen.

1908   Incest is criminalized in England and Wales.

The Encyclopedia

A

ABORTION. Abortion is the premature birth of the fetus, which may be either spontaneous or induced. Estimates of the extent of spontaneous abortion suggest that it may occur as often as one in every five conceptions and sometimes so early that the **pregnancy** passes unnoticed by the woman involved. Induced abortion, by contrast, is the conscious act of terminating pregnancy, whether through ingesting abortifacients or through instrumental interference in pregnancy. How women feel about pregnancy is intimately related to the circumstances in which the sexual relationship occurred, and to their social position. A woman who is pregnant as a result of rape, for example, may not wish to carry a child to term. A woman who has a number of children already may wish to limit her family by resorting to abortion, while a woman pregnant out of wedlock may seek an abortion to prevent scandal and to retain her employment. Historical research makes it clear that women have sought abortion for a variety of reasons when sexual relationships resulted in unintended pregnancies.

The nineteenth century saw a rising concern about the rates of induced abortion in both Britain and America. The church had long had an interest in the life of the fetus, which was expressed in the canon and statute laws. That interest intensified after the child was said to have "quickened" in the mother's womb (usually around sixteen weeks: the time when the mother first feels the fetus move). Lord Ellenborough's 1803 act introduced abortion into statute law in England. Following ecclesiastical tradition, the act distinguished between abortion before and after quickening; while the former warranted the pillory or transportation, the latter was considered a capital offence. From 1821, a number of American states introduced legislation that made certain kinds of abortion, those after quickening, statutory offences. Since at least 1756, in both England and the United States, it had been legally acceptable to sacrifice an unborn child in order to save the life of the mother. The 1828 New York Criminal Code, Section 21, made this explicit by sanctioning abortion when "necessary to preserve the life of the woman, or shall be advised by two physicians to be necessary for that purpose." It was the politics of the medical profession and, in particular, their desire to control irregular practice that led to a tightening of the abortion law over the nineteenth century. The medical profession also wished to remove the "quickening" distinction, based on women's perception of their pregnancy, which they saw as an artificial distinction in a continuous process of development. Continual revisions of statute law led to the demise of the quickening distinction. By the 1860s, statutes in both England and the United States named the woman herself as specifically liable for prosecution for abortion.

The heightened concern regarding abortion during the nineteenth century resulted from its use as a method of **birth control**. Couples who sought to limit their families used abortion as a means to achieve that end. This presented some advantages: it obviated the need to resort to preventative methods for every act of intercourse since abortion was only necessary once pregnancy had occurred. The common act of "bringing on a period" might be less psychologically difficult for a woman than the publicly condemned use of "preventatives" (mechanical devices to prevent pregnancy that were associated with **prostitution**, such as condoms). Adherents of Roman Catholicism might be aware that their church maintained a distinction that regarded abortion after "ensoulment" as a more serious offence, until that distinction was dropped in 1869. Since the risks of the mother dying in childbirth were high, the dangers of abortion were regarded as acceptable.

Abortion provided the woman herself with a form of family limitation without the necessary cooperation of her partner, which other popular means, such as coitus interruptus (withdrawal), required. Court records suggest, however, that the decision to resort to abortion was often made by couples. The first step in attempting to abort might be vigorous exercise or gin and a hot bath. If this failed, a woman might resort to one of the range of commercial "cures," Madame Restall's "female monthly pills" being but one notorious example. Interference in the pregnancy through techniques such as douching and the introduction of slippery elm or a knitting needle into the mouth of the uterus often produced the desired result. Those with contacts and money could seek the help of a professional abortionist. Cases usually came to court only when something went wrong, and the woman died. Juries were often sympathetic to abortionists and were thus reluctant to convict them, since they frequently knew women who had needed the abortionists' services.

It is difficult to gauge the extent of a private and illegal act. The outpouring of discussion over abortion in the nineteenth century, however, suggests that it was widespread. Two factors were important in bringing a traditional practice into the public arena. The first was the professionalization of medicine: as medical men sought to establish their authority, they looked to the law to regulate the activities of their competitors. The second was the widespread desire to limit family size. A key transition occurred when the law overrode traditional reliance on women's immediate experience of fetal movement (quickening) as a meaningful stage of development. Doctors, rather than women, became the authorities on fetal development. The opinion of doctors, lawyers, and legislators, however, had little relevance to a woman facing an unwanted pregnancy. "Bringing on a period" became an urgent necessity: an act that women might attempt on their own, with the help of those in the neighborhood who had the necessary skills, or through professional abortionists who plied a lucrative trade. At a time of few reliable alternative methods for birth control, abortion played an essential part in regulating the unintended outcomes of sexual relationships.

Further Reading: Brookes, Barbara. *Abortion in England, 1900–1967*. Beckenham, UK: Croom Helm, 1988; Keown, John. *Abortion, Doctors and the Law: Some Aspects of the Legal Regulation of Abortion in England from 1803 to 1982*. Cambridge: Cambridge University Press, 1988; Mohr, James C. *Abortion in America: The Origins and Evolution of National Policy*. New York: Oxford University Press, 1978; Regan, Leslie J. *When Abortion Was a Crime: Women, Medicine and the Law in the United States, 1867–1973*. Berkeley: University of California Press, 1997.

Barbara Brookes

ACTON, WILLIAM. A surgeon and venereologist, William Acton is considered by many to be the most influential single authority on sexual matters in Victorian Britain. The second son of a Dorsetshire clergyman, he was apprenticed at St. Bartholomew's Hospital in 1831, and five years later went to Paris, where he studied venereology under Philippe Ricord, and absorbed the teachings of Claude-Francois Lallemand on spermatorrhoea. Returning to London in 1840, he became a member of the Royal College of Surgeons, and in 1842 a fellow of the Royal Medical and Chirurgical Society. He married in 1852 and had at least four children. After qualifying as a surgeon, Acton entered private practice as a specialist in venereal disease, and employed the mercury treatment refined by Ricord for syphilis. From there, it was a small step to the treatment of male sexual problems, particularly spermatorrhoea, with the urethral cauterization techniques devised by Lallemand. Acton made enough money from his medical practice to acquire a rural estate, where he pursued the life of a country gentleman. He died of heart disease in 1875 at the age of sixty-one.

Acton was a frequent contributor to medical journals and published three books: *A Practical Treatise on the Diseases of the Urinary and Generative Organs* (1842; 2nd ed., 1851), *Prostitution, Considered in Its Moral, Social and Sanitary Aspects* (1857; 2nd ed., 1870), and *The Functions and Disorders of the Reproductive Organs in Childhood, Youth, Adult Age and Advanced Life* (1857). The last of these, a shorter work aimed more at the general public than at the medical profession, went through six much-revised editions before the author's death and sold widely in both Britain and the United States. Beyond his medical practice, Acton was prominent in public debates on **prostitution** and was a vigorous supporter of the **Contagious Diseases Acts**. He took a keen interest in the prosecution of quacks (unlicensed practitioners) under the Medical Act of 1858, and helped hunt down smut as a member of the Society for the Suppression of Vice.

Acton's most notable contributions to Victorian sexual discourse were his intense anxiety about male sexuality, especially masturbation, and his comparatively relaxed attitude toward prostitution. Regarding any sexual activity as debilitating for males, he urged chastity in the young, moderation in the married, and continence in the aged. Although *Functions and Disorders* reads more like a tract on the virtues of purity than a medical text, Acton's views on masturbation were no more extreme than those of most of his contemporaries. He followed Lallemand in identifying the foreskin as the most significant risk factor for premature sexual arousal in boys, as well as masturbation and spermatorrhoea in men, and he proposed strict measures of cleanliness to guard against such dangers. "I am fully convinced that the excessive sensibility induced by a narrow foreskin … is often the cause of emissions, masturbation, or undue excitement of the sexual desires," he wrote. Although he did not recommend preventive circumcision (suggesting parental watchfulness, strenuous exercise, and rigorous cleanliness instead), Acton's description of the foreskin as "a source of serious mischief" prepared the ground for the next medical generation's more extreme measures.

Acton's research on prostitution and venereal disease had an important influence on the Contagious Diseases Acts of the 1860s. Since prostitution was inevitable among a civilized population, he argued that the only realistic option was to minimize its harm by supervision. He attributed the lower incidence of syphilis among soldiers in Europe to the continental system of surveillance, whereby the men were inspected each week and any found to be infected were required to reveal their sexual contacts, who were then examined in turn and sent to a hospital for treatment if found to be diseased. Although the Contagious Diseases Acts were deplored by moralists, who saw them as condoning fornication, and by a number of feminists who resented the way women had been singled out for blame and made liable for humiliating examinations, Acton believed that the acts had worked well and contributed to the decline of syphilis. So successful did he consider them that he made the fatal mistake of trying to get their scope extended from garrison towns to the whole population—an alarming suggestion that provoked a powerful moral backlash, the repeal of the acts, and a swathe of sexually repressive legislation that was partly justified by Acton's contention that sex was harmful to, and not necessary for, male health.

Further Reading: Baldwin, Peter. *Contagion and the State in Europe.* Cambridge: Cambridge University Press, 1999; Crozier, Ivan. "William Acton and the History of Sexuality: The Medical and Professional Context." *Journal of Victorian Culture* 5 (2000): 1–27; Marcus, Steven. *The Other Victorians: A Study of Sexuality and Pornography in Mid-Nineteenth Century England.* London: Weidenfield and Nicolson, 1966; Mason, Michael. *The Making of Victorian Sexuality.* Oxford: Oxford University Press, 1994; Lesley A. Hall, "William Acton." *Oxford Dictionary of National Biography*, Vol. 1, 2004.

Robert Darby

ADOLESCENCE. The history of adolescence is difficult to discover; we know more about attitudes toward adolescents than we do of the experiences of the young themselves. Both boys and girls in their teenage years were described as characteristically exhibiting selfishness, irresponsibility, lack of self-control, and irrationality. Because of the nineteenth century's high birthrates, populations were youthful all over the world. The 1881 census of England and Wales showed that 46 percent of the population was under the age of twenty. The term "adolescence" was not commonly used in the nineteenth century but it was popularized in 1904 by the research of an American, G. Stuart Hall, who published a two-volume study entitled *Adolescence: Its Psychology and Its Relations to Physiology, Anthropology, Sex, Crime, Religion, and Education* in that year. However, the concept of a distinct stage of life between childhood and adulthood was familiar to the Victorians, and received considerable attention from social and moral authorities after 1870. It was ordinarily termed "youth," and was considered to extend from puberty (or confirmation) until marriage or the early twenties. The physical changes of puberty came later in the nineteenth century for most children, because nutrition for the vast majority of people was less than optimal. Most working-class children did not reach their full height until the age of twenty.

In **law**, adolescence did not exist. The law recognized only two stages of life: childhood, which was deemed legally irresponsible, and adulthood, where adults were legally responsible for their actions and capable of being called to account for them. Adulthood meant being able to enter into a legally enforceable contract, and the age of full adulthood varied depending on the nature of the contract concerned. For example, the age at which marriage was legal without parental consent varied from the age of consent, and (for those with the right to vote) the age at which the franchise could be exercised.

The gradual reduction (although never full abolition) of child labor over the course of the nineteenth century created a gap in which the concept of youth, and particularly the problems of youth, could flower. The raising of the school leaving age contributed to this as well. Working-class children in Britain left school at the age of thirteen, and if the family was very poor, permission could be given for the child to leave full-time schooling at the age of ten or eleven. Middle-class boys in Britain were experiencing a prolonged period of irresponsibility in boarding schools and at university, while working-class boys were precociously independent in dead-end jobs. In North America, wealthier boys were more likely to attend fee-paying day schools but they too remained dependent into their late teens, while their working-class peers worked in stores and offices. This meant that family and working life were the formative influence for working-class youth, but school was more influential in the life of the middle-class adolescent.

Organizations developed to guide adolescents early in the nineteenth century. In Britain, the Youth Guardian Society was in operation before 1835. Its campaigns included warning youths of the moral effects of **alcohol**, advocating educational pursuits, "rational recreation," and temperance. It was joined by the Young Men's Christian Association (YWCA) in 1844, founded in London but spreading quickly abroad, and the Young Women's Christian Association (YWCA), founded in 1855 and also with a worldwide presence by the 1890s. Both stressed recreation and sociability in a morally positive atmosphere. They also provided economical lodgings for young arrivals in the big cities. Many other organizations with the goal of assisting youth with the transition to adulthood sprang up in the second half of the century, often with a religious origin. Virtually all of these were sex-segregated.

From the 1860s, the "youth problem" was frequently discussed in print. Issues that especially concerned commentators were those of "boy labor" and the "girl of the period." Boy labor was a set of concerns that focused around teenaged idleness and hooliganism, and the ways in which adolescent boys accepted low-paid, unskilled jobs with no future, which they changed relatively often. Two of the most common occupations for young males were errand boy and messenger. Boy laborers were normally fired when they reached adulthood and could demand man's wages. Trapped in low-wage jobs and too old to be apprenticed, it was feared that they would father another generation of poor families.

The youth problem was mostly a set of anxieties about boys. In young unskilled males, adolescence was seen as a time of potential deterioration of character. Their attitudes, values, and leisure were all causes for anxiety. The growth of a market in leisure meant that adolescents in employment could purchase amusements for themselves, without adult consent or supervision. The leisure time amusements of youth created much concern among adults. They were depicted as frequenting music halls, hanging about on street corners, reading low and sensational literature, or engaging in coarse courtship rituals. Promenading in the evenings was a universal phenomenon among both sexes. The "penny gaffe," a very cheap theatre, caused particular concern, largely because of its popularity with adolescents of the working classes. There were 100 penny gaffes in London in 1880. These catered mostly for youths, and were also attended by some young girls. They provided salacious songs of a very mild description but were not permitted to produce spoken plays, so full-fledged drama was not performed. Ballet was popular, as was physical comedy of any description.

In addition, historians have traced anxieties about street gangs to this period. In British and American cities, unemployed or underemployed young men gathered on the streets, and acquired the epithet of hooligan. Working-class parents were reluctant to discipline their sons and daughters in employment for fear that these financially independent young people would leave home. These concerns indicate anxiety about developments in urban living as well as class prejudice.

Masturbation was considered to be a particularly dangerous temptation for adolescents, and they were cautioned against eating flavorful food, as it was thought that a rich diet could provoke premature sexuality. In general, young unmarried people were considered to be fighting the hottest battles of their lives with their sexual impulses, given that they had no legitimate sexual outlets and that their income and

7

place in life was not yet secure. Courtships leading to marriage tended to be long, and were preceded by a lengthy period of walking out, which could cover most of adolescence itself. In parts of rural Germany, bundling was practiced as late as the 1860s, although it had been common in both Europe and the United States in the previous century. In urban areas, premarital **pregnancy** was shameful and young women's terror of pregnancy probably resulted in sexually abstemious lives among urban adolescents. In all of Europe, it appears that rural girls were more likely to allow premarital sex as part of courtship. In some country areas it was seen as a legitimate way to get a husband, or as a way of proving useful fertility before committing to marriage.

Girls were sexualized but were not considered sexual, with considerable anxiety expressed over their potential for good or evil. It was considered essential to keep all girls, as much as possible, ignorant of the facts of life. This theoretical ignorance was in direct contradiction with the legal situation. Until the Criminal Law Amendment Act of 1885, the age of consent was thirteen for working-class girls (it had been twelve until a decade earlier), and twenty-one for heiresses. Hall, the father of adolescent psychology, was to insist that adolescent girls were too vulnerable to be exposed to dangerous ideas, such as information about their own physiology. Teenaged girls were believed to be especially vulnerable because of **menstruation**. Doctors recommend that young girls avoid physical exercise for six months after their first period, and avoid intellectual and physical effort during menstruation thereafter. Hall and his colleagues argued that after puberty, girls should be encouraged to cultivate their health rather than their intellect. Some girls were removed from school, never to return, at menarche.

Factory girls were considered especially problematic, exposed as they were to the banter of experienced married women. It was thought that the mothers of tomorrow would be rendered unfit for their future duties by factory life and their lack of domestic skill. Upper-class girls remained financially dependent until marriage, with home-based activities and an assumption of purity and a role as domestic peacemakers. Virtue was equated with self-sacrifice to the wants and needs of others. Girls were expected to be positive moral influences on their brothers, whether younger or older. The angelic martyred young girls of fiction were popular fantasy roles. Perhaps bored young women enjoyed a fantasy of having their self-denial appreciated and recognized, even if they had to die to achieve it. Biographies of noble women and heroic men were the recommended reading.

"The girl of the period," a phrase coined by **Eliza Lynn Linton**, was an attack on modern young women, and expressed the opposite values to angelic nobility. Being "fast" was shorthand for being unfeminine: loud, vulgar, racy, selfish, and sexually suggestive. But the middle-class girl was a minority. Three-quarters of all British girls over fourteen were in the labor market, mostly as domestic **servants**, where decorum and restrained behavior were universally demanded. In the 1890s, "career novels" and serial stories began to appear, with fictions depicting glamorous and romantic young women doctors, secretaries, nurses, lawyers, and journalists. This literature was devoured by adolescent girls of all classes.

As psychology began to develop as a discipline in the late nineteenth century, much attention was paid to special problems of adolescents. People in this age group were seen as needing restraint put on their newly powerful impulses, particularly their interest in sex and sexual exploration. In the eyes of late Victorian theorists, modern civilization, and especially urban life, created premature sexuality in the young. They identified the four main problems of adolescence as its rebellion against authority, its lack of discipline, its precocious independence, and its high levels of emotion.

Further Reading: Dyhouse, Carol. *Girls Growing Up in Late Victorian and Edwardian England*. London: Routledge & Kegan Paul, 1981; Gillis, John R. *Youth and History: Tradition and Change in European Age Relations, 1770–Present*. New York: Academic Press, 1981; Hendrick, Henry. *Images of Youth*. Oxford: Clarendon, 1980; Nelson, Claudia and Lynne Vallone. *The Girl's Own: Cultural Histories of the Anglo-American Girl, 1830–1915*. Athens: University of Georgia Press, 1994; Springhall, John. *Coming of Age: Adolescence in Britain 1860–1960*. Dublin: Gill and Macmillan, 1986; Wegs, J. Robert. *Growing Up Working Class: Continuity and Change Among Viennese Youth, 1890–1930*. University Park: Pennsylvania State University Press, 1989.

Ian Merrilees

ADULTERY AND FORNICATION. In the nineteenth century, any heterosexual relationship outside of marriage was classed as either adultery or fornication. Fornication involved premarital sexual relations where the parties involved were unmarried, although in the Christian scriptures, the term had been employed to describe any form of illicit sexual activity. Adultery was used to describe extramarital sexual relationships where the parties were married, but not to each other. Christian theology demanded chastity before **marriage** and fidelity afterwards equally of both sexes, but the societal view of male promiscuity was generally lenient.

The term fornication was still in common use in the nineteenth century. It was employed broadly, and covered a wide variety of sexual contacts, from one-night stands to situations where couples engaged in long-term cohabitation without having married. In some environments, even rape victims were considered to have committed fornication. It was invariably a term of condemnation, and it was often assumed that fornicators were probably guilty of a wide variety of other moral offences, especially if they were from the working class.

Observers of nineteenth-century English life pointed out that as many as a half of working class and rural brides were pregnant on their wedding day, demonstrating that premarital sexual activity was common within recognized courtship and that loss of virginity did not make young women unmarriageable. Despite this relatively relaxed view toward what was technically fornication, detected adultery by working-class wives was rare and created a strong sense of shame in the community, suggesting that working people saw fornication as a much less serious offence than adultery. In the first half of the nineteenth century, English parents often brought successful legal actions for the seduction of their daughters, collecting substantial damages from the man involved. It was felt that these suits upheld public morality, as well as compensating the parents for the dishonor done to their hearth. Breach of promise cases were also employed to punish men who tempted marriageable women into fornication. Damages were awarded to women whose chances in the marriage market were believed to have been harmed, although not all had been seduced.

Adultery raised stronger emotions than fornication, morally as well as socially. While fornication risked the creation of children who might be unprotected by fathers, adultery was seen as attacking the very basis of marriage and of family stability. It had less excuse than fornication, because it was thought that the strength of sexual passion in those who were unmarried and without legitimate sexual outlets might lead to occasional moral lapses of this kind. With mutual consent, fornication could be considered victimless, although it was always regarded as sinful. On the other hand, adulterers were viewed as having no excuse for their sexual offenses, since they had a

Adultery discovered, in "Past and Present, Number 1," by Augustus Leopold Egg, 1858.
© Tate Gallery, London/Art Resource, NY.

partner to whom their loyalty (and in the terms of Christian teaching, their very bodies) belonged. There was always a victim, the spouse of the adulterer.

The violation of the sexual exclusivity expected of marriage was considered a serious offence both morally and legally. While in some countries adultery could be cited as the rationale for **divorce**, it is clear that far more people committed adultery than divorce statistics would indicate, suggesting that it could be tolerated within marriages. Some men condoned their wife's adultery, although this could result in his being seen as a weak husband and facing ridicule for his inability to control his wife's behavior. Wives were typically advised to ignore adultery on the part of their husbands, unless it was unusually flagrant: for example, moving the mistress into the family home, or spending an excessive proportion of the legitimate family's resources on a lover. Women with unfaithful husbands had few economic alternatives, and may well have chosen to ignore evidence of infidelity, while praying for his reform.

Many laws dealt only with adultery in married women, which was considered a more serious offence than male adultery, since it raised questions about the paternity of the children of the marriage. In the sixteenth and seventeenth centuries, adultery had (in theory at least) been punishable by death in parts of Europe and America, but the more common punishment was a church-imposed ritual of public humiliation and penance. By the start of the nineteenth century even the sanction of public repentance had largely died out, except for a few isolated areas of Scotland. In France, the Napoleonic Code still made provision for the imprisonment of female adulterers for periods of up to two years. In both France and Spain, it was excusable for a man to slay his wife and her lover but he needed to kill both in order to escape punishment for murder. Where divorce was possible, adultery was ordinarily the only justification for it. After 1857 divorce in England was possible for husbands on the grounds of their wife's adultery, while wives needed to prove adultery and another marital offence, such as incest.

Adultery is surprisingly well documented in the nineteenth century, thanks to the legal concept of "criminal conversation," or crim con, as it was commonly known. In England a man who wished to divorce his wife first had to sue her lover for a form of trespass against his property, or crim con, and collect damages from the man involved. A married woman had no right to give her body to another man, so the husband's right to his wife's body and to her society, as well as to his honor, were damaged by her adultery. Even a formally separated wife was expected to remain chaste and any lover she took could be sued by her estranged husband. No wife had the right to sue her husband's lover.

There is evidence that there was more sexual permissiveness among the elite, possibly because through much of the century their marriages remained more a matter of business than among the middle classes, who were increasingly coming to expect sexual fidelity as an expression of love. **Queen Victoria** and Prince Albert consciously strove to make the court more moral after their marriage in 1840, and other countries also experienced reduced toleration of adultery, perhaps because of the influence of renewed religious seriousness in the century. Much of the active censorship of plays and books in both Europe and North America was prompted by depictions of adulterous relationships, although these were invariably portrayed as ending miserably for all concerned.

Open adultery was vigorously condemned because it was an affront to community standards. Especially for women, its social implications were serious; involving the loss of contact with children, family estrangement, and social dishonor. Adulterous women were expected to disappear from society and were certainly avoided by respectable women, a tendency that grew stronger until the 1890s.

Further Reading: Frost, Ginger. *Promises Broken: Courtship, Class and Gender in Victorian England.* London: University Press of Virginia, 1995; Leckie, Barbara. *Culture and Adultery: The Novel, the Newspaper, and the Law, 1857–1914.* Philadelphia: University of Pennsylvania Press, 1999; Lieberman, Lisa. "Crimes of Reason, Crimes of Passion: Suicide and the Adulterous Woman in Nineteenth-Century France." *Journal of Family History* 24 (1999): 131–48; Phillips, Roderick. *Putting Asunder: A History of Divorce in Western Society.* Cambridge: Cambridge University Press, 1988; Stone, Lawrence. *Road to Divorce: England 1530–1987.* Oxford: Oxford University Press, 1990.

Susan Mumm

AGE OF CONSENT. Virtually all societies have traditionally viewed childhood as a separate stage of life and have proffered to children special safeguards and protections, including protection from sexual degradations and depredations. One means by which societies have tried to protect female children and their families is through age of consent laws. Such laws make it a crime for men to engage in sexual relations with a female under the designated age and are rooted in the notion that female children are too young and immature of mind and body to understand the nature and consequences of the sex act. A child who is too young to make an informed decision is too young to give a legal consent. For the better part of the nineteenth century, most societies set the age of consent somewhere between ten and thirteen years. This age was not arbitrarily chosen for it tended to coincide with female puberty, which was the age at which many cultures allowed a female to marry without parental permission. The age also corresponds to the female age of consent that is stipulated in the Bible and the Talmud, for cultures that adhere to those traditions.

It is not at all evident that age of consent laws were originally intended to create a blanket protection for female children from sexual abuse or depredations. For example, the early English statutes, which were titled "Ravishment of Ward," protected the female children of wealthy fathers from being kidnapped, and either seduced or sexually assaulted, by men who would then try to claim an inheritance based on marriage. Ravishment of Ward statutes prevented an interloper from establishing a lawful claim to a daughter's inheritance through a forcible marriage. Most likely, lawmakers in most societies intended for their age of consent laws to proscribe the abduction of heiresses. The purpose of these early statutes was to ensure the legitimate transmission of property of the landed elites, and not to protect the virtue and chastity of young girls. Gradually, lawmakers and judges in many cultures expanded these laws to embrace a broader range of female children.

In the Anglo-American legal tradition, the **law** designating the age of consent was officially known as the "carnal knowledge and abuse of a female child." Today it is more popularly referred to as statutory rape, a derisive term popularized in the nineteenth century to indicate that the act was rape only because some statute so designated it. Typically the carnal abuse of a female infant was prosecuted on par with rape, though judges and legal authorities were careful to draw distinctions between the two offences. Rape required proof of force and resistance as well as penetration, whereas the carnal knowledge and abuse of an infant required only proof of the penetration. Nineteenth-century age of consent laws were not gender neutral. They protected only female children and only from sexual relations with males. That is not to say that male children were wholly unprotected from sexual denigration. Young boys could be spared prosecution while their adult abusers were charged with criminal sodomy.

Age of consent laws apparently were quite necessary in the nineteenth century. Many cultures, East and West, had folkloric traditions that espoused the idea that sexual relations with a virginal female could cure venereal diseases such as syphilis and gonorrhea, for which there was no medical cure until the twentieth century. Men who had acquired one of these deadly diseases were all too eager to find a virginal female to cure them, and many felt that the only way to be certain that the female was truly pure sexually was to use a young child, and the younger the safer. On occasions, unscrupulous men and women prostituted female children to such desperate men who sought relief. It may also be observed that having sexual intercourse with a female so young was indeed a good way to ensure that one did not acquire such deadly diseases in the first place. Enforcement of carnal knowledge and abuse statutes in the nineteenth century thus was in part an effort to protect the health and safety of the public.

While consent is an issue that goes to the very heart and soul of any rape prosecution, nineteenth-century law deemed children under the age of consent as wholly incapable of assenting to sexual relations. For that reason, consent was not a defense to a charge of carnal knowledge and abuse of a female child. According to the letter of the law, sexual intercourse with a female under the age of volition was a crime, no matter if she assented to the act, nor if the male used no force in achieving the intercourse. The act alone established the crime: if there was penetration, then the crime was complete. One problem with prosecuting this offence in the nineteenth century was that most judges did not believe that a fully grown, mature male could actually penetrate a female child. This misconception was based on conventional nineteenth-century medical wisdom. Both judges and doctors believed that an adult male's genitalia would be too large to be able to pierce the vagina of an immature child. If there was no penetration, then there could be no carnal abuse as defined in the statutes. The law did not recognize intercrural sex, a kind of nonpenetrative sex between the female's legs, which was a common way that men satisfied themselves sexually with children, but without technically violating the statutory rape laws.

In the late nineteenth century, women's groups in Europe and America began a law reform campaign to agitate for the raising of the age of consent from ten or twelve to sixteen or eighteen years, and in some cases even twenty-one years. Though the reformers' efforts met with tremendous resistance from many male legislators, the reformers generally prevailed in getting the age raised. The unintended consequence of the reformers' success was that the new statutes made prosecutions more difficult. Where legislators did not impose barriers on statutory rape prosecutions in the new laws, judges often did in legal proceedings. For example, where earlier many courts had refused a "mistake as to age" defense, they began to allow it. Also, where marriage could not be a defense to a statutory rape charge previously, judges began to allow it as well. They also began to require some proof of the use of force on the part of the male and resistance on the part of the female and to scrutinize the female's behavior and actions more closely. In short, raising the age of consent for females, led judges and lawmakers to treat female children more akin to adult females than they had before when the ages were still quite young.

Further Reading: Laiou, Angeliki E., ed. *Consent and Coercion to Sex and Marriage in the Ancient and Medieval Societies.* Washington, DC: Dumbarton Oaks Research Library and Collection, 1993; Engelstein, Laura. "Gender and the Juridical Subject: Prostitution and Rape in Nineteenth-Century Russian Criminal Codes." *Journal of Modern History* 60 (1988): 458–95; Simpson, Antony E. "Vulnerability and the Age of Female Consent: Legal Innovation and its Effect on Prosecutions in Eighteenth-Century London." In *Sexual Underworlds of the Enlightenment*, edited by G. S. Rousseau and Roy Porter, 181–205. Chapel Hill: University of North Carolina Press, 1988.

Mary Block

AGRICULTURE.   During the nineteenth century, rural women's work, in particular fieldwork, became the target of both official and unofficial investigation. Women's work in agriculture was surveyed by Parliament in 1843, again in the 1860–1870s, and in the 1890s. Social commentators disseminated the findings of the local and the national press, and added to the available body of evidence through independent research. In the vast majority of cases, women and girl's employment was attacked as unfeminine and morally corrupting. The only dissenting voices were those of most farmers, a few partial men such as Arthur J. Munby (1828–1910), who disliked "rustic heroines … of the Dresden China kind" (Munby 1880, 218), and the feminists of Langham Place, London, who believed "If deprived of this resource, their condition would be wretched indeed, as there is absolutely no other honest employment open to them" (*The Englishwoman's Review*, April 1867).

The first major report on the subject, the *Reports of Special Assistant Poor Law Commissioners on the Employment of Women and Children in Agriculture* (1843), had little impact. Though the public outcry resulting from the publication of the *Sixth Report of the Medical Officer of the Privy Council* (1863) and *Sixth Report of the Children's Employment Commission* (1867), resulted in the Seventh Earl of Shaftesbury (1801–1885) campaigning successfully for the 1867 Agricultural Gangs Act (30 and 31 Vict. c. 130), which restricted women and girls' employment to single-sex, licensed gangs supervised by a female gang master. It also led to a Royal Commission report entitled *Reports from the Commissioners on the Employment of Children, Young Persons and Women in Agriculture* (1867–1870). Though the minutes of evidence suggest that there were instances of girls being "ruined," that is, assaulted, by gang masters, and of miscarriage due to working in the gangs, these more physical matters did not form the focus of the reports.

Although the *Sixth Report of the Medical Officer of the Privy Council* focused on the high levels of infant mortality in the southeastern districts of rural England, where agricultural gangs operated, what quickly came into question was the girls' and women's supposedly indecent dress and behavior, and their promiscuous mixing with men and boys. For instance, it was said in 1867 that "in the case of females, their dress as it is often worn or as arranged to avoid the wet, and the stooping nature of the work, are said to involve a certain amount of exposure, which excites the notice of the other sex" (BPP 1867, 77). In addition, their language and behavior were reportedly coarse to the degree "that a respectable person meeting a set of these girls and women cannot venture to speak to, scarcely to look at them, without the risk of being shocked by them" (BPP 1867, 77).

Field women earned a wage; they worked outside, beyond home, family and community, and they undertook hard physical labor. Their employers may have called it women's work, but it was far from being feminine. Their tough, practical clothes, tanned or dirty skin, bare arms, and powerful limbs crossed the boundaries of "**race**" as well as gender. As a result, they moved into the realm of alien, dark, sensual, sexual womanhood—were converted, in Charles Dickens's (1812–1870) words, "into demons" (Dickens, *All the Year Round* 1867, 588). Drawing on racial stereotypes, the *Economist* therefore claimed that the rural population of Britain was becoming degraded to the level of African peoples—not just immoral, but amoral—as a result of rural women's work.

At the time, rural society was increasingly associated with communal social relations, valorized as forming the basis of a superior Christian morality, a morality that was itself taken to reside at the heart of British national identity. The ideal home came to be seen as the country cottage on the village green, and the perfect rustic scene through most of the century was of a woman playing with her children, outside its rose-smothered door. Field women's polluting, fluid sexuality therefore stood in particularly marked contrast to the contained purity of the women who filled in as stock characters for this English pastoral. Where field women were criticized for the neglect of their still nursing infants, milkmaids for example were associated with the ideal of natural motherhood via the qualities of their workplace: clean, milky whiteness.

There was, however, a long-standing tradition, within seventeenth- to nineteenth-century bawdy songs, in which the rural female laborer was represented as a loose woman. Nineteenth-century songs such as "The Spotted Cow," drawn on by Thomas Hardy (1840–1928) in *The Woodlanders* (1887) and *Tess of the d'Urbervilles* (1891), circulated widely throughout England, and were sung by men and women of all classes in the town and country. It tells the tale of a man who meets "a charming maid" looking for her "spotted cow." He offers to help her, and in their search "We hugged and kissed each other/And love was all our tale." Now, "She runs and cries, 'ye generous swain, I've lost my spotted cow'" whenever he passes by. This captures a range of complex power relations. To enjoy the song, audiences would have had to take up the (elite) male narrator's point of view. The audience watches, while the narrator has the last word: this is a man who can choose to come again, when out walking or when he goes "to view the plough," while the maid must wait. In *Tess* the song is used to foreshadow Tess Durbeyfield's experiences with Alec D'Urberville. As a member of the local elite and bewitched by her sexuality he expects her, "a cottage girl" to accept his advances, and to be at his beck and call (Preston 1992, 318–26).

It is possible to argue that women's fieldwork was largely accepted before the 1860s, because women were economically crucial to English agriculture until at least the middle of the century. After this time, women's fieldwork began to be rejected by wealthier farmers, as new techniques and machinery, which could displace casual female labor, were introduced. The 1860s were a turning point in this respect. By the end of the nineteenth century, due to further changes in the sexual division of labor, rural women had lost most of their skilled and therefore best-paid farm work, while the value of their unpaid work at home had increased. This goes a long way to explaining why by 1892–1894, when the *Reports from the Royal Commission on Labour* were published, it was suggested that farmers could no longer get women to work for them. In the meantime, following the Elementary Education (Forster) Act of 1870 and Education (Mundella) Act of 1880, children aged five to thirteen were required to attend school, and attendance at elementary schools became free after the Education Act of 1891. At the height of the debate about women's and girls' work in agriculture, however, the arguments went beyond the economic; the debate was inflected by class, gender and race, and shaped by cultural understandings of how rural women were, or were supposed to be.

Further Reading: Davidoff, Leonore, L'Esperance, J., and Newby, Howard. "Landscape with Figures: Home and Community in English Society." In *The Rights and Wrongs of Women*, edited by Mitchell, J. and Oakley, A. Harmondsworth, England: Penguin, 1986; BPP. "Sixth Report of the Childrens Employment Commission." British Parliamentary Papers 1867: [3796] XVI; Dickens, Charles. *All the Year Round.* Vol. XVII, December 29, 1866–June 22, 1867, pp. 585–89; Ebbatson, Roger. *An Imaginary England: Nation, Landscape and Literature, 1840–1920.* Aldershot, England: Ashgate, 2005; *The Englishwoman's Review of Social and Industrial Questions.* April 1867; Howkins, Alun. *Reshaping Rural England: A Social History 1850–1925.* London: HarperCollins Academic, 1991; Munby, Arthur J. *Dorothy, A Country Story.* London: Kegan Paul & Co., 1881; Preston, Cathy L. " 'The Tying of the Garter': Representations of the Female Rural Labourer in 17th-, 18th- and 19th Century English Bawdy Songs." *The Journal of American Folklore* 105, no. 417 (Summer 1992): 315–41; Sayer, Karen. *Women of the Fields: Representations of Femininity in Nineteenth Century Rural Society.* Manchester: Manchester University Press, 1995.

Karen Sayer

ALCOHOL. The consumption of alcoholic beverages was one of the most-discussed themes in the sexual politics of the nineteenth century. Many social reformers, temperance advocates, and feminists identified male inebriation as a source of poverty, demoralization, and **domestic violence.** This rhetoric cast women in the role of passive victims, but female inebriates also drew attention as likely prostitutes or "degenerate" mothers who harmed their babies in the womb and neglected them after birth. Crusaders against vice targeted drinking establishments as both the cause and symptom of the ugliest aspects of city life. Condemnation of drunkenness sometimes took hypocritical forms, but even the White House went dry under First Lady "Lemonade Lucy" Hayes, wife of President Rutherford B. Hayes (1877–1881). Yet for many people—women as well as men—drinking expressed urban possibility, not urban danger. The new and exciting venues for commercialized leisure—such as the gin palace, the sidewalk café, the dance hall, and the amusement park—sold alcohol but also offered the pleasures of seeing and being seen. The consumption of alcohol, because it was already invested with so much gendered meaning, also presented important opportunities for gender experimentation, as when the New Woman played the "college boy"—propping up her feet, puffing a cigar, and drinking in public.

Moral panics over habitual drunkenness and its destructive effects on both women and men were not new, as William Hogarth's famous eighteenth-century engraving of "Gin Lane" demonstrates. Nineteenth-century discourse on alcohol broke with the past by seriously contemplating teetotal abstinence. Hogarth had paired the squalor of "Gin Lane" with a companion picture, showing the merry life of prosperous "Beer Street," but newly emerging theories constructed alcoholism as a disease (rather than just a bad habit of overindulgence), and suggested that some people, at least, could not drink in moderation. However, older views of drinking remained influential, however, including the belief in the health benefits of moderate consumption, arising out of a long history of relying on some form of alcohol as a medical remedy, and in some places, as a dietary staple.

What actually counted as drink, or as drunkenness, remained a matter of continuing debate. Inebriation was stereotypically a male vice, but many women believed that they were respectable because they drank in private, or because they consumed alcohol masked as patent medicine. Women in Denmark continued drinking beer as a "safe" indulgence, oblivious to changes in brewing technology which had made this beverage more intoxicating. Even in the United States, a stronghold of temperance activism, etiquette manuals continued to prescribe formal table settings with numerous glasses for various alcoholic beverages. Where you drank, and in whose company, was at least as important as what you drank.

The later decades of the nineteenth century mark a transition in the gender conventions surrounding what constituted respectable drinking in a public setting. Earlier in the century, the London barmaid drew international attention as a striking exception to the homosocial atmosphere of pubs or saloons elsewhere. Barmaids titillated male drinkers with the appearance of sexual availability, an impression that worked in the interests of pub owners and which formed part of the commercial appeal of the enterprise, along with the posh furniture and abundant mirrors which flattered the ego of the customer. In contrast, the Parisian sidewalk café came to offer a space where men and women could drink together. Gaslight permitted the cafés to stay open late. Edouard Manet's **painting** "Woman Reading in a Café" (1879) captures the liberating potential of a place where an unaccompanied woman could come and sit with her beer, read a newspaper, and gaze upon the life of the street.

Predictably, the decline of gender-segregated drinking provoked a new era of uncertainty. Some female café-goers were simply flâneurs enjoying what the city had to offer, but others were sex workers hoping to solicit clients, while others were indeed alcoholics, like the despairing woman in Edgar Degas'

The degredation of alcoholism, depicted in "Dans un cafe or L'absinthe. Ellen Andree and Marcellin Desboutin," by Edgar Degas, ca. 1875–1876. © Erich Lessing/Art Resource, NY.

painting "Absinthe" (1876). In the United States, the proliferation of "tea dances"—another heterosocial setting involving alcohol—confused contemporary observers. Women, far from advocating the cause of abstinence, seemed to be refashioning public spaces to enable them to join men in the act of consumption.

Further Reading: Bailey, Peter. "Parasexuality and Glamour: The Victorian Barmaid as Cultural Prototype." *Gender and History* 2, no. 2 (1990): 148–72; Eriksen, Sidsel. "Alcohol as a Gender Symbol." *Scandinavian Journal of History* 24, no. 1 (1999): 45–73; Herbert, Robert L. *Impressionism: Art, Leisure, and Parisian Society.* New Haven, CT: Yale University Press, 1988; Kirkby, Diane. *Barmaids: A History of Women's Work in Pubs.* Cambridge: Cambridge University Press, 1997; Murdock, Catherine Gilbert. *Domesticating Drink: Women, Men, and Alcohol in America, 1870–1940.* Baltimore: Johns Hopkins University Press, 1998.

Isaac Land

ANTHROPOLOGY AND SEXUALITY. Anthropology in the nineteenth century was mainly interested in physical and climatic explanations for the differences between **race**s and ethnology with historical explanations of cultural differences in behavior. Both fields were also interested in sexuality during this period. This interest was fuelled by the increasing contact of the West with other cultures by missionaries and colonialists.

The blurring of physical and sexual interests is well evidenced at the beginning of the century by the case of the "Hottentot Venus," Saarti Baartman, who was famed for her pronounced buttocks and elongated labia. Baartman, born in 1789, was a Khosian from South Africa. In 1810, her "exotic" body parts encouraged a British surgeon, William Dunlop, to take her to London in the hope that he could exhibit her to paying audiences. She was later sold to a French entrepreneur, who displayed her in Paris. Her fortunes in Paris were poor, and she is reported to have fallen into **prostitution** and alcoholism, dying in 1816. Baartman was dissected by Georges Cuvier (1817, 259–74). She was also given scientific notice by Henri de Blainville (1816, 183–90). Much of this interest centered on her sexual organs, and explicitly linked race with sexuality.

Such early anthropological interests in sexuality were soon organized into a more defined field of study, particularly in the period 1860–1900 (Eggan, 121). The two main areas of interest in sexuality were **homosexuality** and marriage, and the treatment of such issues by various cultures was considered to be a marker of the "civilization" of the culture, especially within English traditions.

British traveler and translator **Richard Francis Burton**'s interest in sodomy stemmed from 1845, when Charles Napier asked him about the rumors surrounding three brothels in Karachi, where boys instead of women were engaging in prostitution. Subsequent researches into homosexual culture in many countries enabled Burton to conclude that homosexual activity relied on geographical climate (Burton, 1886). In his famous "Terminal Essay" of his translation of *Book of a Thousand Nights and a Night,* Burton suggested the name "Sotadic Zone" for the area that included Asia Minor, Mesopotamia and Chaldæa, Afghanistan, Sind, the Punjab and Kashmir, Indo-China, **China**, Turkey, Japan, South Sea Islands, and the New World. This was the climatic zone which encouraged homosexual practices. "Within the Sotadic Zone the Vice is popular and endemic, held at worst to be a mere piccadillo, whilst the **race**s to the North and South of the limits here defined practice it only sporadically amid the opprobrium of their fellows who, as a rule, are physically incapable of performing the operation and look upon it with the liveliest disgust" (Burton, 207).

From Greek notions of pædophilia, Burton suggested that the physical cause for the practice was that "within the Sotadic Zone there is a blending of the masculine and feminine temperaments, a crisis which elsewhere occurs only sporadically" (Burton, 208). He cited Italian anthropologist, Paolo Mantegazza, on the physical cause for sodomy: "the nerves of the rectum and genitalia, in all cases closely connected, are abnormally so in the pathici who obtains, by intromission, the venereal organs which is usually sought through the sexual organs" (Burton, 209).

Burton noted that "[t]his prevalence of 'molities' astonishes the anthropologist, who is apt to consider pæderasty the growth of luxury and the especial product of great and civilized cities, unnecessary and therefore unknown to simple savagery where the births of both sexes are about equal and female infanticide is not practiced" (Burton, 240). He further suggested that outside the Sotadic zone homosexual practices were sporadic, not endemic.

The interest in sex psychology displayed by ethnologists can be illustrated by referring to the research of English ethnologist Herbert Bancroft on West Coast American cultures. Bancroft considered the range of Native American cultures from "wild tribes," through "primitive nations," to the "civilized nations" (as he categorized them, following E. B. Tylor and John Mclennan's conceptions of "primitive" cultures, using attitudes to various kinds of sexual practice as indicators of primitivity). On many occasions, Bancroft referred to same-sex practices in different ethnic groups. Unlike Burton's physical model, he addressed the treatments of these behaviors in their respective cultures.

Bancroft discussed the Hyperborean races of North America, which included Koniangas of the island of Kadiak, noting the lax morality of this culture. "Female chastity is deemed a thing of value only as men hold property in it. A young unmarried woman may live uncensored in the freest intercourse with the men." Further, Bancroft noted that "[s]odomy is common" (Bancroft, 81). He found that "the most repugnant of all their practices is that of male concubinage," and described how a Kadiak mother would select her "handsomest and most promising boy," and dress and rear him as a girl, "teaching him only domestic duties, keeping him at women's work, associating him only with women and girls, in order to render his effeminacy complete." Once this boy came of age, "he is married to some wealthy man, who regards such a companion as a great acquisition" (Bancroft 1875–1876, 82). This practice was not specific to the Kadiak tribes; Bancroft found male concubinage throughout the Aleutian Islands. He further noted that in California similar practices existed, and reported that when missionaries first arrived there, "they found men dressed up as women and performing women's duties, who were kept for unnatural purposes. From their youth, they were treated, instructed, and used as females, and even publicly married to the chiefs or great men" (Bancroft, 415).

When discussing marriage among the New Mexicans, Bancroft noted that the Sisibotaris, Ahemes, and Tepehuanes held chastity in "high esteem," and noted that both "their maidens and matrons are remarkably chaste." He considered the standard of morality elsewhere in New Mexico "low, especially with the Acaxées and Tahrs, whose incestuous connections and system of public brothels are notorious." Worst of all, "among some of these nations male concubinage prevails to a great extent; these loathsome semblances of humanity, whom to call beastly would be a slander upon beasts, dress themselves up in the clothes of women" (Bancroft, 585).

Bancroft noted the varying attitudes toward sodomy. The Nahua nation of Mexico, a "civilized" nation, hanged those who committed sodomy. "[I]n Tezuco, the punishment for unnatural crime was characteristically brutal. The active agent was bound to a stake and completely covered with ashes and so left to die; the entrails of the passive agent were drawn out through his anus, he was also then covered with ashes, and, wood being added, the pile was ignited." In Tlascala, the sodomite was not punished by **law**, "but was scouted by society, and treated with scorn and contempt by all who knew him." The Aztecs also detested sodomy, according to Bancroft's interpretation of the "severity of the laws enacted by the later sovereigns for the suppression of this revolting vice," and from the fact that a scout was appointed by the judicial authorities to search the provinces for offenders of this class (Bancroft, 467). In other parts of Mexico, unnatural vice was tolerated, if not actually permitted, although the Maya nations punished sodomy (Bancroft, 676–9). Bancroft's work followed John McLennan's thesis of promiscuity, which argued that promiscuous behavior was more common in "less civilized" cultures: the more civilized a culture, the stricter the sanctions against promiscuous sexuality (Mclennan).

Not all ethnographers held such precepts in their work. Edward Westermarck's critical *History of Human Marriage* (1891) made the author "the foremost opponent of the Morgan-McLennan-Tylor-Lubbock theory of original promiscuity" (Harris, 198). In later editions of his work, Westermarck addressed homosexuality from a culturally relativist perspective. This attention included incidental engagement in homosexual activity, for example, reporting that homosexual intercourse with a holy person in Morocco could entail supernatural benefits. He also noted, for instance, that "in the Sandwich Islands most of the people of the court remained unmarried, but homosexual practices and fornication were common among them." Elsewhere, Westermarck commented that "in the world generally, and in some countries particularly, homosexual practices are infinitely more frequent than incest."

Explaining other causes of homosexuality, Westermarck noted that "[w]e must not forget that a lack of desire, and even a positive feeling of aversion, may in certain circumstances be overcome. The sexual instinct is so powerful that when it cannot be gratified in the normal manner it may seek for abnormal gratification. Thus homosexual practices are often due to the absence of women, to say nothing of **masturbation** and **bestiality**" (Westermarck, 201). Again he argued that a "paucity of marriageable women, for example, may lead to celibacy, prostitution, or homosexual practices, as well as to polyandry" (Westermarck, 206). These researches were taken further in Westermarck's later book, *The Origin and Development of the Moral Ideas* (1906, 1908).

It was not only in Britain that anthropologists posited ideas on promiscuity and marriage that differed from the ideas of marriage and civilization of John McLennan, E. B. Tyler, and John Lubbock. The most original work in this vein was Hermann Ploss's *Das Weib in Natur- und Völkerkunde* [*Woman in Natural Science and Ethnology*] (1885). Ploss made an exhaustive study of the role of women in world cultures. These roles were social, familial, religious, and filial, as well as sexual. Some of the clearest indications of sexual roles come from the discussions of masturbation and tribadism (lesbianism), as well as those that involved sex with animals. Details of the masturbatory practices of women in countries such as Bali, Israel, Japan, and Africa were given explicitly, including attention to the use of different sex toys (Ploss 1899, 151). As some evidence of mutual masturbation was included in Ploss's account, it was a short move to the discussion of lesbianism. It was noted that lesbianism existed in ancient Greece, Rome and Egypt, as well as in the Orient, and that it could also be found practiced among contemporary Europeans (Ploss, 452). Ploss reported that "active" lesbians had "excessively developed clitorises," which would either be manipulated digitally or orally. Such observations, ranging over a large chronological and geographical scope, were used by sexologists to support the theory that homosexuality in women was universal and natural.

At the beginning of the twentieth century, German physician Iwan Bloch compiled *Beiträge zur Aetiologie der Psychopathia Sexualis* [*Theory of the Aetiology of Sexual Psychopathology*] (1902, 1903), which relied on a great number of reports of nineteenth-century anthropologists in order to argue that sexual experiences were situated in culture. While Bloch presented a predominantly acquired model for sexual perversions, this model was based on individual object choice made within specific cultural climates. This relativism, promulgated by anthropological and ethnographical research, was the basis for the new way of looking at sexuality in the twentieth century (Davidson, 252).

Further Reading: Bancroft, H. H. *Native Races of the Pacific States of North America.* New York: D. Appleton, 1875–1876; Bloch, Iwan. *Beiträge zur Aetiologie der Psychopathia Sexualis.* Dresden: H. R. Dohrn, 1902; Burton, Richard. *Book of a Thousand Nights and a Night. Terminal Essay.* London, Burton Club, 1886; Cuvier, Georges. "Extrait d'observations faites sur le cadavre d'une femme connue à Paris et à Londres sous le nom de Vénus Hottentotte" ["Extract of observations made of the cadaver of a woman known in Paris and London as the Hottentot Venus"]. *Mémoires de Muséum d'Histoire naturelle* 3 (1817): 259–74; Davidson, Arnold. "How to Do the History of Psychoanalysis: A Reading of Freud's Three Essays on the Theory of Sexuality." *Critical Inquiry* 13 (1987): 252–77; de Blainville, Henri. "Sur une femme e la race hottentote" ["On a woman of the Hottentot Race"]. *Bulletin des sciences par la société philomatique de Paris* 4 (1816): 183–90; Eggan, Fred. "One Hundred Years of Ethnology and Social Anthropology." In *One Hundred Years of Anthropology*, edited by J. O. Brew. Cambridge, Mass: Harvard, 1970; Harris, Marvin. *The Rise of Anthropological Theory.* London: Routledge & Kegan Paul, 1968; McLennan, John. *Primitive Marriage.* London: Macmillan, 1865; Ploss, Hermann. *Das Weib in der natur- und Völkerkunde.* Leipzig: T. Grieben, 1899; Schiebinger, Londa. *Nature's Body: Gender in the Making of Modern Science.* Boston: Beacon Press, 1995; Stocking, Greg. *Victorian Anthropology.* New York: Free Press, 1987; Westermarck, Edward. *History of Human Marriage.* London: Macmillan, 1925.

Ivan Crozier

B

BASTARDY.   *See* Illegitimacy

BEAUTY.   While often romanticized as a timeless and ahistorical "fact," ideas of beauty are in fact deeply rooted in social, cultural, and historical determinants. Dominant ideas of what constituted beauty changed during the nineteenth century, and can be seen to mirror some of the social and cultural changes in European and North American societies during this time. Victorian writing on human beauty tended to link aesthetics with sexuality, suggesting that the "purpose" of female beauty in particular was to attract a mate and reproduce.

While beauty is a phenomenon which can be attributed to both men and women, in the nineteenth century the word tended to be associated with femininity, with attractive men instead designated "handsome," or with the word "beauty" masculinized with the adjective "manly." In terms of discourse, women bore the burden of beauty: books analyzing the "scientific" basis of human beauty focused on the female form, while the "Beauty Books," featuring engravings of upper-class women, had no masculine parallel. While beauty was considered to add somewhat to a man's attractions, particularly as a sign of "good breeding," it was seen as essential for women. It was considered to be basic to their very purposes in life: to some writers, the ornamentation of the home and sweetening of men's lives, and according to scientific writings, the attraction of men, leading to reproduction. Indeed, many writers championed beauty as a "duty" of women.

Widespread belief in physiognomy, the idea that a person's character can be read from their facial features, both promoted and mirrored the popular belief that the face provided keys to personality. Qualities such as virtue, compassion, loving dependence, and spirituality were thought to be reflected in a beautiful female face. Thus, it was that ideals of female beauty echoed dominant ideals of female character. Female beauty was often described in terms of softness, smallness, weakness, delicacy, and fragility, relating to ideals of submission and dependence. In contrast, male beauty was thought to consist in strength, size, force, potency, and vigor, qualities that reflected normative masculinity. However, a changing trend can be traced throughout the century. In the early nineteenth century, **fashion** illustrations featured women with small, demure, fairly insipid facial features, often in passive poses. These models are replaced by the end of the century and in the Edwardian period with much larger, bolder, and livelier women, in active poses and with confident body language. This can be linked to the growing visibility of women in the public sphere, the agitation for women's rights, and the move toward more active physical lives for women.

The appearance of the skin was an important aspect of female beauty throughout the nineteenth century. Pale skin was seen to be an indispensable mark of beauty, and middle- and upper-class women went to a great deal of trouble to stay out of the sun and to try to bleach the skin with home-made cosmetics and advertised remedies. This obsession with paleness relates to both class and **race**. Paleness advertised the fact that a woman not only did not work outside, but was not obliged to walk for transport, and instead could afford to stay indoors and travel by carriage. It was thus a class marker that distinguished a "lady" from a working-class woman. The fashion for pale skin also demonstrates that ideas of beauty were greatly determined by race. "Swarthiness" (an olive or tanned complexion), was associated with the people of southern Europe and the Mediterranean, and considered unattractive. Facial features which were considered beautiful, such as an aquiline nose, blue eyes, and delicate lips, are also those found specifically in northern European people, excluding nonwhite people from this definition of beauty.

Hair was often referred to as a woman's "crowning glory," and was seen as an important aspect of her attractions. Hair was worn long and tied up, and was often supplemented with pads and false hair. As this was expensive and time-consuming, long and abundant hair was another marker of class. Small, white hands were also thought to be a sign of beauty. Since household labor such as washing and scrubbing tended to roughen and redden the hands, only women who had **servants** to perform these tasks could keep their hands in this condition.

Beauty products, such as lotions to soften the skin, had long been produced in the home. In the nineteenth century, such products began to be produced in mass and marketed. Although some soaps and shaving creams were marketed at men, these advertisements tended to emphasize efficiency rather than the enhancement of beauty. The use of cosmetics such as face powder, lip tint, and rouge were widely considered to be improper, and respectable women were not expected to use them. Toward the end of the century the use of cosmetics became more widespread and more acceptable, but ideas of beauty nonetheless emphasized concepts such as the "natural" and the "real."

The beauty of the female body, while also subject to change over the century, can nevertheless be described in a generalized fashion. While obesity was seen as unattractive, thinness was also thought to be unappealing. A certain degree of plumpness, or embonpoint, was the ideal for much of the century. The voluptuous female body, rather than the muscular or athletic body, also reflects a class bias, as it exemplifies physical idleness. Well-developed hips and breasts, highlighted by a slender waist, also hint at the maternal function, which was seen as women's basic purpose and duty.

Health was seen as basic to a man's attractiveness. This was again related to class, and the growing social dominance of the middle class. While a ruddy complexion and a stocky body were markers of physical work, and thus stigmatized, slenderness, and fragility were seen as effeminate and often associated with a decadent upper class. A strong, athletic body, toned by pursuits such as riding and hunting, was the ideal. Fashions in male beauty also changed over the century, most noticeably with regard to facial hair, which underwent various permutations over the period, proving that men were not immune to these pressures.

Toward the end of the century, good health increasingly became associated with female beauty, encouraged by fears of "racial degeneration" promoted by Social Darwinism. The idea that humankind, or more specifically "the Caucasian race," might be falling behind in a kind of contest for supremacy, a failure which blamed diverse elements such as increased urbanization, women's education and increasing liberation, a lack of nutritious food and physical exercise, and a general dependence on luxury. This anxiety led to increased scrutiny of women's health, and a demand for women in particular to take care of their bodies for the purpose of improving the quality of their offspring. Thus markers of health, such as red cheeks, clear skin, and a strong, athletic body came to be associated with female beauty. This trend was also intimately tied up with imperialism, women's production of healthy children, as future servants of the empire, being promoted as a patriotic duty.

Further Reading: Hartley, L. "A Science of Beauty? Femininity, Fitness and the Nineteenth-Century Physiognomic Tradition in Mid-Nineteenth Century Britain." *Women: A Cultural Review* 12 (2001): 19–34; Steele, Valerie. *Fashion and Eroticism: Ideals of Feminine Beauty from the Victorian Era to the Jazz Age.* New York: Oxford University Press, 1985.

Jessica Needle

BESANT, ANNIE WOOD (1847–1933). Annie Wood Besant was a fiery iconoclast who, through her impassioned writings and speeches, challenged the Victorian gods of respectability. Known as "Red Annie," Besant fought for the causes of secularism, women's rights, trade unionism, socialism, and most controversially, **birth control**. When she and her fellow secularist **Charles Bradlaugh** published in 1877 a birth control pamphlet, they were arrested and tried for obscenity, a court case that became one of the most sensational trials in Victorian England.

Annie Wood was born in a middle-class London family. After her father died in her girlhood, she was sent to Devon to live with a wealthy single woman, who provided for her a rigorous education. Passionately religious in her adolescence, Besant later recognized the sexual meaning of her fantasies of being the Bride of Christ. This religiosity impelled her to make in 1867 a disastrous marriage to an Anglican clergyman, Frank Besant. Ignorant of sex and shocked by the act on her wedding night, in her autobiography she blasted mothers who let their daughters, in the name of innocence, go blindly into marriage.

Using her loss of faith in Christianity as the excuse to separate from her husband, she left their provincial vicarage in 1873 to go to London to join a community of freethinkers. She supported herself by giving public lectures in radical forums and writing for the secularist journal, the *National Reformer*, which she soon coedited along with Charles Bradlaugh. Defying Mrs. Grundy with her militant atheism, Besant also challenged conventional Victorian morality with her condemnation of the patriarchal marriage **law**, in which she argued that couples should live together monogamously in free unions until the law was reformed. Her radical writings and speeches made her suspect of being personally immoral, especially in her intimate relationship with Bradlaugh, but she and Bradlaugh both always insisted that there was no impropriety in their relationship.

Besant achieved her greatest notoriety with the defense of birth control. Concerned with the plight of especially poor women who had to bear too many children, and wanting to test the limits of free speech, in 1877 she formed with Bradlaugh the Freethought Publishing Company to publish a manual on artificial contraception, *The Fruits of Philosophy*, by an American physician, Charles Knowlton. Besant and Bradlaugh were arrested on the charge of obscenity. Arguing her own case in court, Besant insisted that birth control would promote rather than subvert sexual morality, in that it would make early marriage possible and eliminate both **prostitution** and **masturbation**. Even more controversially, she asserted the value of (presumably

Annie Besant, 1897. Courtesy of the Library of Congress.

nonmasturbatory) sexual pleasure without fear of pregnancy, as essential for the health and well-being of both women and men.

Although the case of *The Queen v. Besant and Bradlaugh* ended with the conviction of the defendants, they were released on a technicality. Irrepressibly, Besant then wrote her own birth-control manual, *The Law of Population: Its Consequences and Its Bearing upon Human Conduct and Morals*. She was also instrumental in forming the Malthusian League, to promote the dissemination of knowledge about birth control. She was not again arrested for these actions, but in her personal life she was not so fortunate. Her estranged husband sued successfully for custody of their daughter, with the court ruling that Annie Besant was an immoral woman with whom no respectable lady would associate.

In 1889, Besant shocked her contemporaries by converting to Theosophy, an ecumenical esoteric religion founded in 1875 by the Russian Helena Blavatsky and the American Colonel Henry Olcott. Under the influence of Theosophy, Besant changed her views on sexuality and birth control. She accepted the theosophical doctrine that humans are evolving upward from physical toward higher spiritual beings, and that people should therefore be encouraged to control their carnal desires. One should have sexual intercourse only when absolutely necessary to have children, a goal that contraceptive practices would subvert.

Quickly rising to a position of leadership in the International Theosophical Society, Besant moved in 1893 to its headquarters in India, where she lived for the rest of her life. In India she became involved in social reform, working for greater sexual purity in India through the abolition of child marriage and the prohibition of prostitution. Her leadership of Theosophy did cause her, however, to become involved in a notorious sex scandal, when her close associate Charles Leadbeater was accused of pederasty, first in 1906 and again in 1913. Leadbeater defended himself with the argument that he was simply showing boys how to masturbate to save them from going to prostitutes. Although Besant condemned Leadbeater's actions and his views, she did in his defense argue that masturbation was not as bad as the practice of prostitution, which ruined women for life. She then shifted attention to the cause of Indian nationalism. In 1916, she founded the Home Rule for India League, and in 1917, had the extraordinary honor for a British woman to be elected President of the Indian National Congress.

Annie Besant was too controversial a figure in Victorian England to be accepted by other women's rights advocates, who commonly eschewed any discussion of sex. Besant's willingness to frankly discuss sexual matters, and especially her boldness in advocating birth control, pushed the boundaries of acceptable discourse, allowing more moderate reformers greater freedom of discussion and action. Her shocking pretheosophical pronouncements on the importance of sexual pleasure for women were, however, rhetorical rather than rooted in her feelings. Traumatized by sex in her marriage, she probably felt much more congruency when she as a theosophist returned to conventional Victorian morality in her defense of sexual self-control and denial of the importance of sexuality.

Further Reading: Anderson, Nancy Fix. "Bridging Cross-Cultural Feminisms: Annie Besant and Women's Rights in England and India, 1874–1933." *Women's History Review* 3

(1994): 563–80; Anderson, Nancy Fix. "'Not a Fit or Proper Person': Annie Besant's Struggle for Child Custody, 1878–79." In *Maternal Instincts: Visions of Motherhood and Sexuality in Britain, 1875–1925*, edited by Claudia Nelson and Ann Sumner Holmes. New York: St. Martin's Press, 1977; Nethercot, Arthur H. *The First Five Lives of Annie Besant*. Chicago: University of Chicago Press, 1960; Taylor, Anne. *Annie Besant: A Biography*. New York: Oxford University Press, 1992.

Nancy Fix Anderson

BESTIALITY. Bestiality is sexual activity between a human and an animal. Bestiality is a difficult issue to access historically—as the research of Jens Rydstrom shows in Sweden, it is mostly found in court records and in medical texts, at least until the end of the twentieth century, when various internet user-groups sprang up, continuing a long but small linage of those interested in animal erotica and pornography. Nevertheless, Alfred Kinsey's research in the 1940s suggested that animal erotism was a widespread phenomenon, and not as rare as general abhorrence toward the topic might suggest—regardless of the fact that there are not as many sources as would be found concerning other "perversions." In the nineteenth century, however, there are some hints about bestiality in the more official documentation that can shed light on the subject.

It is not surprising to learn that compared with other perversions there was little directly written about bestiality in many medical and sexological texts. Some early hints about bestiality come from forensic medical practitioners, who were concerned with the definition of bestiality, and wanted to separate it from other "unnatural acts," such as buggery, both of which came under the general heading of sodomy at this time. An instance of this can be found in the work of the German court physician, Johann Ludwig Casper. Likewise, French medical jurisprudent, Ambroise Tardieu briefly mentioned bestiality, but only in so far as the act was considered a criminal offence that could be forensically detected. Indeed, Tardieu discussed bestiality only insofar as to ascertain whether or not the act was physically possible. No psychological reasons for why people might want to have sex with dogs (the example he was giving) were entered into.

After this initial forensic attention to bestiality, a number of psychiatrists interested in explaining so-called sexual perversions addressed sex with animals. For instance, English psychiatrist, George Savage noted that "The chief characteristic of the moral insanity of pubescence is the uncontrolled sexual passion exhibiting itself in self-abuse, unrestrained sexual intercourse, even with near relations, and bestiality of the lowest description." Frank Lydston, from Chicago, noted that these types of perversion could be manifest as "(a) Those having a predilection (affinity) for their own sex; (b) those having a predilection for abnormal methods of gratification with the opposite sex; (c) those affected with bestiality." In other words, bestiality was acknowledged, but not expounded in detail. The most significant of these sexological writings about bestiality can be found in **Richard von Krafft-Ebing**'s *Psychopathia Sexualis*, which went through twelve editions between 1886 and 1902. Six cases of bestiality appeared in the last edition published during Krafft-Ebing's life. These included people who had sex with poultry, rabbits, dogs, pigs, cows, and horses. Often such sexual relations were found in the country, and were *faute de mieux*, but such was not always the case, with some of Krafft-Ebing's cases genuinely displaying preference for animal sex. Albert Moll, in his *Untersuchungen über die Libido Sexualis*, presented the case of a neurotic man who from the age of fifteen had been sexually excited by the sight of animals or by contact with them. He had repeatedly had connection with cows and mares; he was also

25

sexually excited by sheep, donkeys, and dogs, whether female or male; the normal sexual instinct was weak and he experienced very slight attraction to women. In the first years of the twentieth century, **Havelock Ellis** wrote about bestiality in his *Erotic Symbolism*, although he took a dim view of it: "Three conditions have favored the extreme prevalence of bestiality: (1) primitive conceptions of life which built up no great barrier between man and the other animals; (2) the extreme familiarity which necessarily exists between the peasant and his beasts, often combined with separation from women; (3) various folk-lore beliefs such as the efficacy of intercourse with animals as a cure for venereal disease, etc." Ellis noted that bestiality was very rarely found in towns, whereas he found it often in the country-side, where it resembled a form of **masturbation**—sexual gratification without the spiritual dimensions that Ellis advocated.

Bestiality was known in anthropological writings. Iwan Bloch, in his *Beiträge zur Ætiologie der Psychopathia Sexualis* (1902–1903), discussed it extensively, as did his nineteenth-century precursors, Hermann Ploss and Max Bartels in their vast ethnographic study of women, *Das Weib (1900)*. Likewise, rare traces of bestiality could be found in nineteenth-century literature, usually as a form of exoticism. For instance, Alfred de Musset's, *Gamiani, ou Une Nuit d'Excès* (1835) follows the insatiable sexual appetite of the protagonist through her relationships with a voyeur, with depraved monks, innumerable nuns, an innocent virgin, and a donkey of prodigious endowment. Musset's use of zoophilia in his text emphasized the unnatural nature of Gamiani's desires and her unquenchable desires. Bestiality does not seem to have been a general pornographic theme, unlike other "perversions."

As noted, bestiality was foremost a legal issue in the nineteenth century. It was raised in the Labouchère Law Amendment Act of 1885—an act that broadly dealt with sodomy, "indecent acts," bestiality, and changed the age of consent to sixteen from twelve—that there was any definite consensus on the legal status of the sodomite. This act meant that the ill-defined crime of "indecent acts," which could include mutual masturbation, fellatio, bestiality, and the like, were punishable if committed in public or private. Before this 1885 act, cases were still coming before the courts, such as that of John Dennett, who was sentenced to ten years imprisonment in 1870 for buggery with a pig. He said he was drunk and had gone to sleep in the pigpen. After his release in 1885, Dennett was sentenced to life in prison for buggery with a mare. Dennett claimed he was caught by a policeman when drunk, standing behind a horse in its stable with his trousers down. He could not explain how he came to be there. He was released in 1893. Such a case, while not wholly uncommon in Britain, elicited some comment from the Law Lords. With regard to bestiality as an unnatural crime, the common opinion among judges was that it was too harshly punished. In a letter to the Home Office, Mr. Justice Hawkins noted: "The crime of sodomy with mankind stands upon a different footing, and deserves in my opinion more serious consideration and even with regard to that abominable crime much I think may be said in favor of limiting the minimum punishment of 10 years P[rison] S[entence] to persons over a certain age." In other words, this is to bring bestiality also in line with the punishments sentenced after the 1885 act.

In short, while bestiality was considered to be a moral aberration, it was barely understood scientifically, and was a legal curiosity based on ethical standpoint and historical precedent. It was universally condemned, and before a flourish of sexological writing in the first part of the twentieth century, was not a topic of major significance.

Further Reading: Casper, Johann Ludwig. *A Handbook of the Practice of Forensic Medicine, Based upon Personal Experience*. London: New Sydenham Society, 1863; Dekker, Midas. *Dearest*

Pet: On Bestiality. London: Verso, 2000; Ellis, Havelock. "Erotic Symbolism." In *Studies in the Psychology of Sex.* Philadelphia: FA Davis and Co., 1906; Krafft-Ebing, Richard von. *Psychopathia Sexualis.* Burbank, CA: Bloat, 1999; Lydston, Frank. "A Lecture on Sexual Perversion, Satyriasis and Nymphomania." *Addresses and Essays.* 2nd ed. Louisville, KY: Renz and Henry, 1892; Ploss, Hermann, and Max Bartels. *Das Weib.* Leipzig: Grieben's Verlag, 1887; Rydstrom, Jens. *Sinners and Citizens: Bestiality and Homosexuality in Sweden, 1880–1950.* Chicago: University Press, 2003; Savage, George. "Moral Insanity." *Journal of Mental Science* 27 (1881): 147–55; Tardieu, Ambroise. *Étude Médico-Legale sur les Attentats aux Mœurs.* Paris: Ballie et fils, 1878.

Ivan Crozier

BIGAMY. Bigamy is the legal offence of marrying a person while already lawfully married to another. It was made a felony in Britain in the Bigamy Act of 1603, as part of a drive to make **divorce** and remarriage more difficult. Until Hardwicke's Marriage Act of 1753, marriage practices were confused and ambiguous, and it was possible for people to be sincerely unsure whether their marriage was valid or not. By the nineteenth century, while the requirements for a marriage in Britain were regularized and clear, legal divorces were very difficult to obtain and were affordable only by the very rich. Among the poor, wife sales served as a form of popular divorce, and those who were involved in them seem to have mistakenly believed that the procedure freed them to marry again. There were other forms of self-divorce practiced by working-class couples as well, and some saw themselves as legally able to contract a new union as a result.

Quantifying desertion and bigamy is very difficult, but recent scholarship suggests that bigamy was common in both Britain and the United States in the nineteenth century. Most cases of bigamy, by their very nature, went undetected and unprosecuted. However, exposed cases delighted the general public. Bigamy cases joined adultery and rape trials in popular pamphlets sold in large numbers as titillating sensational reading in the eighteenth and nineteenth centuries.

In a period when communication was poor and travel, especially abroad, was slow, many spouses disappeared, often during voyages at sea, and presumption of death after long absence could be mistaken. The **law** recognized this by refusing to prosecute for bigamy if a spouse had been missing for seven years or more at the time of the second marriage. Given the increasing mobility of the population in the nineteenth century, with ready movement between all parts of the United Kingdom, Europe, and North America, bigamy was often difficult to detect or prove. The chaotic nature of the American state laws governing marriage and divorce made marriage in the United States a somewhat fluid concept, with many escape clauses. Many deserted first wives chose not to prosecute their bigamous husbands, suggesting that they preferred life without them. The patchy records that survive suggest that far more men chose bigamy than women. There is also much more evidence for bigamy among the working class, whose access to divorce was extremely limited. Many historians see this as evidence of the enduring popularity of marriage, however irregularly contracted. It also suggests that working-class people were expecting a reasonable degree of happiness and harmony in their marriages and at times, were willing to act outside the law to achieve this.

Theoretically, the sentence for bigamy in English law was death, but this was never enforced; in 1790, it was changed to transportation for seven years. Because bigamy was notoriously hard to prove, many probable cases were never tried. However, if a case was clear-cut enough to come to trial, there was a good chance of being transported for bigamy in the early nineteenth century; sentences had become very light by the end of the period. However, if the bigamist had kept his new wife in ignorance of her legal position, claiming that he was free to contract a valid marriage, penalties tended to be much harsher than the average. The English statute of 1861 set the penalty for bigamy as penal servitude of not more than seven or less than three years or to imprisonment of not more than two years. The French Penal Code punished bigamy by forced labor. The U.S. Supreme Court ruled in 1878 that plurality of wives (**polygamy [American]**), as originally permitted by the Mormon religion, violated criminal laws prohibiting bigamy and was not defensible as an exercise of religious liberty. The Latter-day Saints renounced polygamy in 1890, although some fringe groups continued to practice it.

In Britain, the situation was complicated by the differences between Scottish and English law. Because the law of marriage in Scotland remained relaxed, allowing clandestine marriages that were no longer possible in England, a man could marry in Scotland and then contract a church marriage in England. This made him bigamous in Scottish law, but not in English law, which did not recognize his first contract of marriage. English people marrying in England and then divorcing in Scotland also raised questions with regard to bigamy if they then married new partners and returned to England. In 1812, the Lolly case provoked the judges to declare that a marriage contracted in England could not be dissolved by the courts of any other country, creating manifold opportunities for unintentional bigamy among those who cared (or could afford) to travel abroad to end their marriages. However, being able to prove bigamy made it at least possible for desperate wives to divorce their husbands. Only three women successfully petitioned for divorce between 1827 and 1857, and two of these divorces were on the grounds of bigamous adultery on the part of their husbands.

Probably the most common reason for a bigamous marriage in the nineteenth century was the abandonment of a first spouse, followed by remarriage. Given the impossibility of divorce for all but the very rich in the first half of the century, and the tremendous stigma attached to divorce throughout the period, bigamy probably appeared to many as an attractive solution to their desire to start afresh. Men, in particular, seem to have seen bigamy as part of a package which included moving to a new location, constructing a new identity and personal history, and starting a new life and new family. Other reasons for bigamous marriage were to conceal the shame of an extramarital pregnancy, or to satisfy the demands of a sweetheart for the social legitimation of a marriage ceremony. Until the 1857 Divorce Act, the separation from "bed and board" awarded by the Ecclesiastical Court meant that many separated individuals, unable to achieve a full divorce, must have been tempted to commit bigamy. In the United States, the variation in divorce laws from state to state combined with high personal mobility, created legal chaos, meaning that some people came to consider that a court appearance, even simply for the purposes of separation, enabled them to form a new marriage.

Bigamy was virtually always conducted as a form of serial monogamy, and the bigamous unions could last for decades. Bigamous couples seem to have been accepted by their communities provided that the first marriage had broken down for misconduct, that the children of the first union received financial support, and if the spouse of the bigamous was aware of their equivocal legal position at the time of the "marriage." Very few bigamists juggled two households unaware of each others' existence, for years, and this form of bigamy was always extremely rare.

The consequences of bigamy could be serious for others beside the bigamist. Even if the spouse was completely unaware of the bigamy of their partner, the marriage was invalid, exposing the spouse to shame, and leaving them without property rights.

Their children were declared bastards without right of inheritance. War widows who did not realize that their marriages were invalid due to bigamy were denied pension rights as well. While the law was reluctant to punish otherwise inoffensive bigamists harshly, the economic realities of the legal position could be a real punishment for their families.

Further Reading: Frost, Ginger. "Bigamy and Cohabitation in Victorian England." *Journal of Family History* 22 (1997): 286–307; Schwartzberg, Beverly. "A Lot of Them Did That: Desertion, Bigamy and Marital Fluidity in Late-Nineteenth-Century America." *Journal of Social History* 37 (2004): 573–600; Stone, Lawrence. *Road to Divorce: England 1530–1987*. Oxford: Oxford University Press, 1990.

Ian Merrilees

BIRTH CONTROL. The use and development of birth control in the West during the nineteenth century was shaped by religious beliefs about marriage and sexual behavior that prohibited birth control use, and by views about women's control over their bodies. These views shaped Victorians' understanding of human reproduction and sexuality and the production, distribution, and consumption of various forms or methods of birth control. At the same time, developments in medical science and technology improved the knowledge and control of human reproduction and sexuality. Into this amalgam of ideas has to be added the Victorian social and cultural concerns with propriety and decorum, and similar informal restraints in other societies.

The nineteenth century is notable for the development of contraceptive devices, as well as chemical agents such as spermicide. Also of significance during the century was the publicity that birth control received. In the early decades of the century, broad health reform movements included family planning, as a way to improve women's (and their offsprings') health. Ideas about sexual restraint influenced the practice of birth control, since abstinence was an effective component of any family planning regime. Not only Christian conservative moralists promoted sexual restraint; health reformers often championed sexual restraint as a requisite for good health. This was a reflection of Victorian ideals that privileged the intellectual and spiritual and disparaged the physical aspects of human life and social behavior. From the 1870s forward, birth control was consistently a major concern of feminists and the women's movement, although various feminists supported it in different ways and to different degrees. Outside the mass women's movement were groups such as the iconoclastic free lovers, who believed contraception was necessary for women to avoid the trap of marriage.

Various forms of birth control spread throughout western European countries during the century. Family planning through birth control was so effective in France in the first decades of the century that the phrase "French family" came to be a synonym for a family with two children (McLaren 1990). German medical practitioners and reformers met with success in promoting birth control. In England, the neo-Malthusians promoted and advocated birth control as a way to limit population growth and thereby poverty. Neo-Malthusians based their support of birth control on the arguments of Robert Malthus that were put forth in his *Essay on Population* (1798)—that the working class should practice "moral restraint" (delaying marriage and practicing abstinence) to ease population growth. One such neo-Malthusian in England was Francis Place, often credited with starting the birth control movement in the English-speaking world in the 1820s. Place recommended methods such as semen-absorbing sponges, as a way for the working class in industrial England to improve their standard of living. But as working-class communities continued to have the largest families, his entreaties were not effective with that social group. In the United States, neo-Malthusianism was coupled with socialist utopian thought in the publications of British-born Robert Dale Owen (*Moral Physiology* [1830]), and the feminist reformer and writer Frances "Fanny" Wright. Owen's book, considered the first American book on birth control, also recommended sponges as well as coitus interruptus and the condom, which became both practical and inexpensive with the vulcanization of rubber in the 1840s. In the United States, the neo-Malthusian Edward B. Foote promoted the use of cervical diaphragm, another significant technological innovation in the nineteenth century.

The privacy traditionally enshrouding birth control was breached in the nineteenth century by the publication of numerous medical and popular writings. These included works such as Charles Knowlton's *The Fruits of Philosophy* (1832) and Frederick Hollick's *The Marriage Guide* (1850), as well as pamphlets and advertisements touting various methods and devices to prevent conception. Opponents of birth control attempted to stem the tide of publicity and diffusion of information by making it illegal to produce, distribute, or consume materials about contraception or abortion, which were legally classified as obscene.

Medical and scientific works on contraception both promoted the latest knowledge about what were believed to be effective methods or devices and criticized unfounded traditional folk methods. An example of this was the work of the German gynecologist Friedrich Adolph Wilde, who had invented the cervical cap. Wilde promoted scientifically confirmed methods of prevention in *Das weibliche Gebär-unvermögen* (1838). In the United States, Charles Knowlton's *Fruits of Philosophy* (1832) was the first of numerous medical tracts on birth control that promulgated the cervical cap. Throughout Europe, birth control moved into the public sphere; in Amsterdam, Aletta Jacobs opened a birth control clinic in 1882.

By the end of the of the nineteenth century, urbanization, secularization, and changing views of gender and marriage were leading to the promotion of voluntary motherhood through birth control and laying the groundwork for the birth control movement of the twentieth century.

Further Reading: Brodie, Janet Farrell. *Contraception and Abortion in Nineteenth-Century America*. Ithaca, NY: Cornell University Press, 1994; Gordon, Linda. *The Moral Property of Women: A History of Birth Control Politics in America*, rev. ed. Urbana: University of Illinois Press, 2002; Himes, Norman Edwin. *Medical History of Contraception*. Baltimore: Williams and Wilkins, 1936; McLaren, Angus. *Birth Control in Nineteenth-Century England*. London: Croom Helm, 1978; McLaren, Angus. *A History of Contraception: From Antiquity to the Present Day*. Oxford: Blackwell, 1990; Noonan, John Thomas. *Contraception: A History of its Treatment by the Catholic Theologians and Canonists*. Cambridge, MA: Belknap Press of Harvard University Press, 1986; Reed, James. *From Private Vice to Public Virtue: The Birth Control Movement and American Society since 1830*. New York: Basic Books, 1978; Riddle, John M. *Eve's Herbs: A History of Contraception and Abortion in the West*. Cambridge, MA: Harvard University Press, 1997.

Jody Pennington

BRADLAUGH, CHARLES (1833–1891). Charles Bradlaugh was a British lecturer, editor, and free-thinker who contributed to the growing discourse on **birth control** in the nineteenth century. Born in a working-class area of London on September 26, 1833, Bradlaugh was the first of five children. His father was a poor solicitor's clerk and his mother a nursemaid, and he was sent out to work at the age of twelve. At first, his formative years were spent attending the Sunday school of the Church of England; however, he soon found himself listening to free-thought speakers in Bethnal Green, after being temporarily excluded from the church for questioning discrepancies in religious text. By the age of twenty-five, when he joined the British army in order to pay off his debts, Bradlaugh had converted to atheism and was a convinced free-thinker. After leaving the army and before devoting his life to voicing his beliefs, he worked for a solicitor, where he learnt a great deal about the **law**, which became an asset in the court proceedings he would later find himself enmeshed in. In nineteenth-century England, the modern movement of birth control was in its early stages, but faced opposition from the medical profession, the church and the average Victorian, with his predominantly puritan outlook. Therefore, it is not surprising that Bradlaugh, an atheist and promoter of radical ideas, would only later be recognized as one of the greatest figures to emerge from the working class in the nineteenth century.

Bradlaugh was known for his "inflexible will, ferocious appetite for work and rampant egotism," and was said to "radiate force" (Taylor 1992, 75). These qualities made him a natural and captivating orator when lecturing on the controversial issues of the century such as secularism, atheism, republicanism, and birth control. Apart from the lecture circuit, Bradlaugh was also heavily involved in pamphleteering and writing, tools employed to promote his ideas. In 1860, he became the editor of the *National Reformer*, a weekly secularist newspaper, which gained a small but radical readership. However, due to the illegality involved in publishing such ideas, Bradlaugh spent a lot of time fighting in the court system, in defense of publishing "blasphemy." In addition, he was also a member of many groups and societies such as the Reform League, the Land Law Reforms, and the Secularist Society. In 1858, he became the president of the London Secular Society and in 1866 he co-founded the National Secular Society, which placed the abolition of the blasphemy law, which limited what could be legally printed and distributed, as one of its main objectives.

His greatest achievement in disseminating information on birth control was accomplished with the help of **Annie Wood Besant** (1847–1933), another British social reformer, whom he first met in 1874. *The Fruits of Philosophy*, subtitled "The Private Companion of Young Married People" (1833), was a pamphlet written by an American physician and writer, Charles Knowlton (1800–1850). Knowlton was sentenced to three months of hard labor for this short book, which explored the concept of birth control, addressing both the question of controlling population, and giving actual physiological information to put his ideas into practice. Although Bradlaugh did not agree with everything that Knowlton had written, he decided to reprint the pamphlet in the hopes of helping to "extend freedom of the press to such writings" and also to change the "warped narrowness of the Victorian attitude towards sex" (Banks 1954, 26). The publication of this pamphlet and the trial that ensued would send ripples across Victorian England.

It has to be noted that fertility rates had already fallen by the time *Fruits of Philosophy* was republished; however, the trial that followed the publication of the pamphlet by Bradlaugh and Besant had a significant influence on the birth control movement in Britain. The Bradlaugh-Besant trial was one of the sensational trials of the century, and a staggering amount of publicity was given to the hearing by national, as well as local newspapers. Therefore, thousands of readers had access to their story, as newsprint chronicled their reasons behind publishing such "filth." Over the period of this "obscenity trial," Bradlaugh had time to defend his case by presenting information that justified birth control and gave a basis for the population question. Not only did newspapers cite his findings, they quoted sections of *Fruits of Philosophy*. Those who read the articles carefully were able to learn all about birth control as well as what Bradlaugh and Besant were trying to accomplish, and it was great publicity for the birth control cause. It was a point won against the "guarded reticence and exaggerated prudery which made sexual matters a forbidden topic of public discussion" (Banks, 26). In 1877, Bradlaugh and Besant were convicted for the printing of the pamphlet and sentenced to a large fine and imprisonment; they were later let off on a legal technicality. The pamphlet had its largest circulation in the 1870s and over 125,000 copies were sold, including imitation and bootleg copies, due to the booklet's new-found fame and popularity. Naturally this provoked a reaction and there was much concern for the state of public morality, for what was the deterrent to having sex if you had birth control? Nonetheless, a steady decline in birth rates did follow suit, as the middle classes "precipitated a sudden concerted effort to control reproduction through any possible means: delayed marriage, long periods of sexual abstinence, contraception and abortion" (Hauck 2003, 224).

In 1877, after the trial, Besant enlisted the help of Bradlaugh in the formation of the Malthusian League. The leagues principles were based on Thomas Malthus' work, An *Essay on the Principle of Population as it Affects the Future Improvement on Society*. Bradlaugh had an important role in the organization as part of the subcommittee, as a lecturer, and in promoting the idea that population limits were needed. He often spoke of his own experiences as a young boy, and of the poverty he had lived through and the suffering he had seen. Although they used lectures, tracts, the press, and the *National Reformer* to convey their beliefs about population control, due to their previous experiences with *The Fruits of Philosophy*, they avoided giving practical advice on contraception, in order to avoid imprisonment. Again, Bradlaugh was met with fierce opposition from a population that was ever more fearful of the effects of birth control and also by a wave of imperialism; many Victorians felt that people should be sent to live in the British colonies in order to alleviate overpopulation. Already by the 1870s, birth control was prevailing and becoming more widely available, as a few pharmacies stocked contraceptives such as condoms, diaphragms, and vaginal sponges.

Bradlaugh's political life came into being in 1880 when he was elected, after two subsequent failures, as the Member of Parliament for Northampton. He was a radical politician of the time who was seen as an "advocate of three doctrines hateful to the vast majority of Victorian Englishmen: Atheism, republicanism and birth control" (Arnstein 1957, 254). Bradlaugh's abilities as an orator made him a very active parliamentarian, however, as the century moved toward its end, the "ideological climate" was changing and he was no longer seen as being part of the "extreme left wing," but rather as an "old-fashioned radical." After 1880, he "withdrew from active concern with birth control propaganda." Bradlaugh died on January 30, 1891. Three thousand mourners attended his funeral, including Mahatma Gandhi.

Further Reading: Arnstein, Walter L. "The Bradlaugh Case: A Reappraisal." *Journal of the History of Ideas* 18 (1957): 254–69; Banks, J. A. and Oliver Banks. "The Bradlaugh-Besant Trial and the English Newspapers." *Population Studies* 8 (1954): 22–34; D'Arcy, F. "The Malthusian League and the Resistance to Birth Control Propaganda in Late Victorian Britain." *Population Studies* 31 (1977): 429–48; Taylor, Anne. *Annie Besant: A Biography*. Oxford: Oxford University Press, 1992; Hauck, Christina. "Abortion and the Individual Talent." *English Literary History* 70 (2003): 223–66.

Danielle Bertrand

BRAIN. Nineteenth-century science and medicine pursued the new idea of the human brain as the seat of the mind. Although the nature of the investigations changed throughout the century, science's unwavering assertion that brain size dictated intelligence became an important justification of hierarchies of sexual and racial superiority.

Phrenology, the first biologically based science explaining individual differences in personality and intellect, postulated that gross brain size dictated intellectual capacity. Phrenologists "read" external cranium contours and bumps to reveal the strengths and weaknesses of the character. As a popular cultural and scientific pastime, "head reading" stimulated public lectures, private readings, learned societies, and collections of human skulls and brains. Phrenology fell into disfavor by mid-century, but the correlation between intelligence and brain size remained central to the emerging sciences of human difference based on sex and **race**.

Starting at mid-century, medico-science systematically investigated normal and abnormal human pathologies, and slowly uncovered the locus of discrete functions in various brain lobes. Successes in cerebral localization initiated a craze for dissecting and weighing brains, as investigators searched for the link between brain size and intelligence. Although cultural taboos historically prohibited human dissection, immortalizing one's own brain and intelligence appealed to certain socio-cultural elites. Many prominent citizens and philanthropists willed their brains to science: medico-science publicly celebrated the dissection of the brains of such celebrities as Walt Whitman (1819–1892).

This sustained craze for measuring brains confirmed a sexual difference, as women's brains are, on average, 14 percent smaller. This finding became the scientific justification of gendered ideals of women's intellectual inferiority and their biologically ordained role of motherhood. Scientists asserted that the brain had a finite intellectual capacity and that educated, white, Anglo-Saxon males were guided by rational thought: their larger brains were well suited for intellectual development. Women, by contrast, were guided by emotions and suited to nurturing and motherhood. Women who developed their intelligence (through higher education and self-improvement) diverted precious intellectual capacity from their smaller brains and depleted the energy necessary for motherhood. Education imperiled women's precarious mental health, thought to be predisposed to nervous ailments, hysteria, and other brain diseases. Ideas of women's lesser intellectual capacity fit within science's Darwinian-inspired, value-laded hierarchy of racial **evolution** and worth, which classified "races" by cranial shape and capacity. Scientists equated women with others of low intellect ("savages," blacks, and white children) in the lower stages of primitive evolution. These racial and sexual hierarchies (based on intellectual capacity) justified white men protecting and dominating the inferior (nonwhites and women).

Although science and popular culture used generalizations about brain size to justify sexual and racial stereotypes, postmortem investigations often presented contradictory data. Eminent white men could possess small brains, while psychiatric patients, nonwhites, and women could have excessively large brains. Scientists dealt with these inconsistencies by continually modifying their measurement priorities and indices, rather than questioning the tenets of their scientific theories.

Further Reading: Russett, Cynthia Eagle. *Sexual Science: The Victorian Construction of Motherhood.* Cambridge, MA: Harvard University Press, 1989; Stepan, Nancy. *The Idea of Race in Science.* Hamden, CT: Archon, 1982.

Laurie Jacklin

BROADSIDES. *See* Newspapers and Broadsides

BRONTË, CHARLOTTE (1816–1855).   Charlotte Brontë is best remembered for her novel, *Jane Eyre*, published in 1847. Jane, an orphan, lives at Gateshead, in the charge of her wicked and unloving step-aunt. After a violent scene between her and her cousin John Reed, where he throws a book at her, making her bleed—"the cut bled, the pain was sharp"—she is taken up to the attic to be locked in as a punishment. The scene follows three different stages that can be analyzed in sexual terms: the ascent to the room, the stay itself, and the fainting at the end of the episode, which evokes the falling of the curtain in a novel fraught with theatrical metaphors.

First Jane makes it clear that she is out of herself, she "sees red," which is confirmed by her cousin calling her "mad cat," "rat," "bad animal," as if Jane were a budding Bertha Rochester, the mad woman in the attic, whose main sin is her exacerbated sexuality. Jane is carried upstairs to the red room by two **servants** who use some garters to tie her up in a scene that is reminiscent of **flagellation** in Victorian pornography, as Elaine Showalter convincingly argues: "Whipping girls to subdue the unruly flesh and the rebellious spirit was a routine punishment for the Victorians as well as a potent sexual fantasy" (Showalter 1978, 116). The scene also anticipates Rochester's taming of his mad wife (the night/mare) with a rope in the attic at Thornfield.

The red room, because of its highly symbolic color and seclusion (Mrs. Reed's inspection of the drawers evokes for John Maynard a solitary masturbatory activity), is a womb or a tomb where Jane undergoes the painful rite of passage that is necessary to become a woman. Rooms are dangerous places. The bed stands erect in the middle like the statue of the Commandeur in Don Juan or the character of Brocklehurst, the clergyman whose main interest is to "punish the body to save the soul … to mortify (in these girls) the lusts of the flesh." The whole room is a metaphor for a huge coffin and Jane's fear of seeing the ghost of her dead uncle appear is expressed in highly sexual terms: "My heart beat thick, my head grew hot; a sound filled my ears," which stresses the difficulty of becoming an adult. Hence, Jane's begging to be brought back to the nursery at the end of the chapter.

She almost literally dies of fear in the room and fainting appears as a strategy to escape an unbearable reality. Eva Figes has qualified fainting as the point of physical submission, but I would also argue that it is a kind of petite mort (i.e., **orgasm**), significantly uniting Eros and Thanatos in this highly symbolic red room.

Later in the novel, the garden scene stages the meeting between Mr. Rochester, the master of Thornfield, and the now-adult Jane, his ward's governess. It brings to light Jane's Victorian dilemma: she is caught between the demands of Victorian morality and her own feminine desire. Jane, who has been employed at Mr. Rochester's estate for some time, is walking alone in the garden at Thornfield. The garden is a refuge, a "bower of bliss." The whole scene is actually under the aegis of sensuality and abundance, as if it were an echo to Keats's "Ode to Autumn." All Jane's senses are touched in a synesthetic poetic description. Each natural element participates in the climax which reaches an almost unbearable intensity. The alliterations of S—"A SPLENDID Midsummer shone over England: skies so pure, suns so radiant" (the capitals are the author's)—reminiscent of the

Portrait of Charlotte Bronte from the frontispiece of *Jane Eyre*. Courtesy of the Library of Congress.

snake's hiss—hint at the ambiguous, treacherous nature of this Eden like place. As in Milton's Paradise, innocence goes hand-in-hand with temptation.

But the biblical roles are reversed here as it is Rochester/Adam who is the tempter. He intrudes upon Jane's solitude, emerging from this poetic vision and announcing his presence metonymically with his highly Freudian cigar whose fragrance Jane is quick to detect among the surrounding natural smells. Jane is as much under the spell of nature as under Rochester's: she is rooted to the spot, trapped between sensuous enjoyment and the fear it induces in her because of her deeply instilled sense of sin and guilt. The conflict is between her contemplative I and her active I, which challenges the first. Jane abides by the Victorian codes of morality and analyzes the impropriety of her situation: she is alone in a garden at night with a man, who is her master.

Like her cousin John Reed, though more gently, Rochester forces Jane to come out of her shelter to enjoy the evening with him: "no one can wish to go to bed while sunset is thus at meeting with moonlight," an eloquent metaphor that no doubt paves the way to a more human kind of fusion. Jane's efforts at avoiding Rochester are vain as he uses his authority—she never calls him anything but "master" (except at the very end)—conveyed through the repeated orders he gives her in a sado-masochistic relationship, an analysis Jane herself corroborates: "I drank yet knew the cup was poisoned."

At the end of the passage however, Jane's moral conscience is fully awake and she gradually emerges from her apathy. The voice is now the narrator's who conceptualizes the conflict. But Jane is doomed to fail because the contradiction is within her; her senses are not subdued. She is spell-bound and will never escape the enchanted garden.

Further Reading: Eagleton, Terry. *Myths of Power: A Marxist Analysis of the Brontës*. London: Macmillan, 1974; Maynard, John. *Charlotte Brontë and Sexuality*. Cambridge, MA: Cambridge University Press, 1984; Showalter, Elaine. *A Literature of their Own*. London: Virago Press, 1978.

Claire Bazin

BURTON, RICHARD FRANCIS (1821–1890). Richard Burton's interest in sexuality spanned his life as a soldier, adventurer, diplomat, writer, and translator. He is widely remembered as the author of travel and adventure books including *A Personal Narrative of a Pilgrimage to El-Medinah and Meccah* (1855–1856) and *First Footsteps in East Africa; or, An Exploration of Harar* (1856), but, he is also remembered as the controversial translator and editor of sexually explicit editions of Sanskrit and Arabic literature, including the *Kama Sutra* (1883) and *Arabian Nights* (1885–1888). Burton's forays into sexual literature offended some and entertained others, but there was an underlying seriousness of purpose in his attention to sexuality, which can broadly be described as libertarian.

Burton's libertarian agenda began with an attack on **censorship**, not only in publishing but also in public life, where he exposed and contested the monopoly over sexual discourse enjoyed by doctors, lawyers, priests, and a handful of other professionals. His early attempts at sexual expression had been hindered by military superiors and censorious editors and publishers. As a young soldier in India in the 1840s, he claimed to have been ordered to investigate the boy brothels of Karachi, but then to have been dismissed for doing so, or for doing so with too much enthusiasm (Burton 1885–1886, 205–6). Burton tried to smuggle sexual content into the travel books he wrote in the 1850s, 60s, and 70s, though once again his efforts and enthusiasms were often squashed. Typically, the "Brief Description of Certain Peculiar Customs" that he appended to *First Footsteps in East Africa* was removed by the publisher (Brodie 1967, 10). Occasionally, as in his ethnographic study of "Sindh and the Races that Inhabit the Valley of the Indus" (1851), Burton did find anthropological opportunities to discuss such sexual and erotic subjects as aphrodisiacs, courtesans, and marital sex. But, generally taboos on sexual discourse held firm, and this prompted Burton to creatively open new channels for expression. He co-founded the Anthropological Society of London and its journal *Anthropologia*, both in 1863, as outlets for more sexually explicit writing. He dodged and ridiculed obscenity laws by variously printing (rather than publishing); selling to private subscribers; founding and working through a cover organization, the Kama Shastra Society; and (thinly) veiling the identity of himself and his fellow translators and editors. In practice, however, Burton's part in putting out a string of erotic works was no secret. These works, translated, printed, and marketed in the 1880s and 1890s, included Sanskrit **sex manuals**, the *Kama Sutra of Vatsyayana* (1883) and *Ananga-Ranga or the Hindu Art of Love* (1885), and erotic works of Arabic literature and storytelling including the *Perfumed Garden* (1886) and *Arabian Nights* (1885). These books embroidered the "myth of the erotic East" (Kabbani 1986, 66), imaginatively underpinning British imperialism, but their subjects were not entirely Oriental(ist). In his attention to the erotic East, Burton implicitly commented on the less-than-erotic West.

One of Burton's aims was to show the British how they could become less-reserved lovers. *The Kama Sutra* (1883) focuses on sex between men and women, championing the sexual needs of the latter. Dane Kennedy (2005) argues that, despite incoherent and often unsympathetic ideas about women, Burton consistently contested the dominant Victorian view of the male as the sexual predator and the female as the passive and often passionless partner, and asserted that the women's sexual passions and powers should be taken more seriously than they were. He introduced the *Ananga-Ranga* as a kind of coded sex manual: a book to "prevent the separation of husband and wife ... by varying their pleasures in every conceivable way" (Burton 1885, vii). There is also a great variety of sexual activity and pleasure in Burton's *Arabian Nights*, not only between men and women, but also between members of the same sex. Burton supplemented the text with footnotes and appendices, including a "Terminal Essay on Pederasty" that drew together his lifetime of observation, reading and perhaps experience of "Sotadic" love, or love between men.

Portrait of Richard Burton, published in the *Illustrated London News*, 1887. Courtesy of the Library of Congress.

Burton intervened in contemporary sexuality politics. He spoke out against various provisions of the Criminal Law Amendment Act (1885), which increased the range of sexual offences for which men could be punished, including intercourse with younger females, and with males of any age, the latter within the provisions of the so-called Labouchere Amendment. Not simply intervening in debates about how sexual subjects should stand before the **law**, Burton contested the ways in which sexual subjectivities were understood. Replacing gender-blind prohibitions on sodomy with attention to even the lightest sexual intimacies between men, the Labouchere Amendment coded in law the new **sexology** that treated sexual acts between men as expressions of coherent, deviant identities rather than as isolated events (Foucault 1979; Halperin 2002). This seemed liberating to some men, who felt it described, explained and legitimated their condition and opened avenues for community formation and political action. But, to Burton it seemed dangerous, given to moral, medical, and legal scrutiny of those cast as deviant. So Burton continued to speak of pederasty rather than **homosexuality**, invoking the sexual culture of classical Greece in which young men took younger males as their premarital lovers. Referring to a once accepted, even ennobled sexual practice in an idealized civilization, he sought to dignify what he asserted was its modern counterpart. For Burton, pederasty was about civilization, taste, pleasure, and power. The Victorian pederast pretended toward an "excessive but otherwise normal sexual appetite," and an elite rather than deviant or abnormal social position (Halperin 2002, 114). Burton's take on pederasty and on libertine sexuality politics more generally reflected the social power he enjoyed and desired, particularly the power of Britain—and British men in particular—in the late-Victorian world.

Burton's interventions in sexual culture and politics had mixed results. Though he was of course unable to stop the Criminal Law Amendment Act, he did sow seeds of doubt on its prohibitions against intimacy between men, to put forward arguments that would finally help win the case against the provisions of the Labouchere Amendment eighty years later (in 1967, male homosexuality was partially decriminalized in England and Wales). For instance, when Kenneth Walker argued for reform in the 1960s, he explicitly echoed Burton, writing that "homosexuals should be the responsibility of the doctor and not of the judge" (Walker 1964, 20). Burton's refusal of modern sexology, with its binary division of sexuality, has proved equally unable to sway the majority within the West, though once again it has articulated the disquiet of a growing minority in western countries, and often a majority elsewhere, who reject the stark choice between homosexual and heterosexual identities (Phillips et al. 2000). Burton's challenges to censorship laws, and particularly to restrictive sexual discourse and repressive or inhibited sexual culture, have also taken time to bear fruit, but have also arguably helped to loosen restrictions on sexual expression and sexual life in Britain. Though Burton's libertarian ideas about sexuality emerged from his imperial career and reflected his imperial masculinity, many of these ideas have outgrown these origins, speaking creatively and productively to contemporary sexuality politics and sexologies.

Further Reading: Brodie, Fawn M. *The Devil Drives: A Life of Sir Richard Burton.* London: Eyre & Spottiswoode, 1967; Burton, Richard. *Personal Narrative of a Pilgrimage to El-Medinah and Meccah.* London: n.p., 55–56; Burton, Richard. *Ananga-Ranga; or, The Hindu Art of Love.* London: privately printed, 1885; Foucault, Michel. *History of Sexuality.* London: Allen Lane, 1979; Halperin, D. M. *How to Do the History of Homosexuality.* Chicago: University of Chicago Press, 2002; Kennedy, Dane. *The Highly Civilized Man: Richard Burton and the Victorian World.* Cambridge, MA: Harvard University Press, 2005; Phillips, Richard, with Diane Watt and David Shuttleton. *Decentring Sexualities: Politics and Representations Beyond the Metropolis.* London: Routledge, 2000; Phillips, Richard. "Travelling Sexualities: Richard Burton's Sotadic Zone." In *Writes of Passage: Reading Travel Writing*, edited by James Duncan and Derek Gregory, 70–91. London: Routledge, 1999; Said, Edward. *Orientalism: Western Representations of the Orient.* New York: Pantheon, 1978; Walker, K., ed. *Love, War and Fancy. The Customs and Manners of the East from Writings of the Arabian Nights.* London: William Kimber, 1964.

Richard Phillips

BUTLER, JOSEPHINE (1828–1906). Josephine Butler was born on April 13, 1828, to John Grey and Hannah Annett in Milfield Hill, Northumberland, England, the seventh of ten children. Her mother, a culturally enriched homemaker, was determined that her daughters would become educated. Her father was related to Earl Grey, a Whig, and prime minister. The three issues that she was most passionate about were subjects of discussion in her home: women's education, women's suffrage, and slavery in

Undated portrait of Josephine Butler. Courtesy of the Library of Congress.

any form (negro or white). Although she was too young to understand the problem of abolition, she was exposed to the rhetoric and process of critical thinking. The experience of growing up in a liberal milieu probably contributed to her later social justice concerns.

In 1839, she and her sister Hatty visited Ireland at the nadir of its economic problems. Peasants were so deprived of food and water that masses of them lay on the ground, too weak to move. The memory of that misery and a future tragic event in her life influenced her decision to better social conditions for the disadvantaged.

When she met her husband, George Butler, he was a student at Exeter in Oxford. Like Josephine, he had a liberal outlook and they had common interests. He had an unusual attitude for a man in the nineteenth century, because although women were expected to be weak and dependent, men controlling, he did not subscribe to that gendered division.

She became pregnant in the first year of their marriage but refused the services of a male physician, preferring instead her sister's support. Midwives were being denied access to medical education and Josephine was vocal in her protest of this "wicked custom." She saw no reason to endorse any system that was closed to women. She gave birth to four healthy children in five years, three boys and one girl, without complication.

The family moved to Cheltenham where George was appointed vice principal of a college. As the wife of a highly visible public servant, she was criticized because she freely expressed her political attitudes regarding abolition and the Civil War.

Her life was suddenly interrupted by a horrific event. Her only daughter, Eva, fell from a height to a stone floor and sustained a concussion, later dying. Josephine, plagued by grief, found her only escape in focusing on the hardships of others. Well aware of a sexual double standard from life and literature, informed by Elizabeth Gaskell's *Ruth*, the story of an unmarried young woman who suffered the extreme consequences of bearing an illegitimate child, she began to explore workhouses where women, like Ruth, lived. She met a young prostitute who related that she entered this sordid lifestyle at age thirteen.

Josephine, shocked that no laws protected children under fourteen, expressed her views in writing and speech making. She recognized that without education, women would never be able to better their lives. And aware that her privileged social and financial position could help her gain access to a male-dominated societal milieu, she was able to promote her philosophies. After moving to Liverpool in 1866, she visited the Brownlow Hill Workhouse where sick, homeless, unwed mothers and prostitutes lived. As an alternative to this dire environment, she decided to create a home where women could gain self-respect, nurse their ills, and learn beneficial skills. Her first resident was a woman who had been raped at fourteen and forced into a dismal life of **prostitution**.

Rather than focusing on religious concepts of sin, penitence, and forgiveness, Josephine stressed the positive rather than punitive aspects. She encouraged prayer but as hope and security rather than contrition. She met other women with similar goals such as Jane Cragg who operated nearby Benediction House. Together they gathered 1,500 signatures to petition parliament to allow women to vote. In 1867, Josephine joined another activist, Anne J. Clough, to advance the cause of education.

Subsequently, she involved herself in the North of England Council for the Higher Education of Women, and a campaign to influence Cambridge University to provide more opportunities for female students, which later led to the establishment of Newnham College.

In 1868, she published *The Education and Employment of Women*, followed by *Women's Work and Women's Culture*. Her ideals combined cultured, caring, and nurturing image of women with independence and ability to earn money. She believed that gentle, caring qualities, would preserve and protect the nation better than war and aggression.

While working with former prostitutes, she learned of a political and legal event that placed all women under police surveillance. The **Contagious Diseases Act**, introduced in the 1860s, was created to combat venereal disease, but only enforced on women. Any woman could be picked up by the police, held in jail until morning and then subjected to a gynecological examination. The misuse of this **law** resulted in highly subjective judgments. A woman who was alone or dressed in a seductive manner could be arrested simply because of the policeman's perception. No corresponding law affected men and no woman was safe from the scrutiny and power of local law enforcement people. Married women had been detained, outraged, humiliated, and embarrassed without recourse. Josephine spoke out publicly against these laws. She toured England and spoke to male working-class audiences. For a woman to speak in public was abnormal enough but to hear a woman talk about venereal disease or sex to an audience of men was unheard of. In the typical Victorian worldview, no honorable man would permit his wife to do such a thing. George, although concerned, supported her actions, despite threats to his future in academia.

She returned to the plight of young children involved in prostitution. Although she had collected stories from young prostitutes regarding their initiation, in order to prove that an organized system of white slavery existed, she needed to present evidence to the House of Parliament. Disguised as wealthy clients, Josephine and her son went to a brothel and offered money to buy young virgins. She made the acquaintance, and enlisted the help, of Rebecca Jarrett to learn exactly how these children were recruited. Girls as young as three had been sold by their parents to such establishments. Clients were often upper class, so-called respectable members of society, ironically the same men who were eager to "uphold the morals" by refusing to allow women access to equal opportunities for education and work. With the exposés published by the *Pall Mall Gazette* and the help of Catherine and Florence Booth, of the Salvation Army, they were able to influence Parliament to enact the Criminal Law Amendment Act that raised the age of consent from thirteen to sixteen, a small but important change. The Contagious Diseases Act was repealed in 1886, too late to save women in the United Kingdom and the British colonies who had been victimized, but nonetheless essential to prevent future outrages.

After George became ill, she nursed him and after he died, in 1892, she wrote two more books: *Recollections of George Butler* and *Personal Reminiscences of a Great Crusade*. In her final years, she edited a monthly paper, *Storm-Bell*, and remained a supporter of suffrage although too fragile to campaign vigorously. She died in 1906.

Further Reading: Jordan, Jane. *Josephine Butler*. London: John Murray, 2001. See http://www.spartacus.schoolnet.co.uk/Wbutler.htm; http://www.bbc.co.uk/history/historic_figures/butler_josephine.shtml; Jordan, Jane, and Ingrid Sharp, eds. *Josephine Butler and the Prostitution Campaigns: Diseases of the Body Politic*. London: Routledge, 2003.

Lana Thompson

C

CENSORSHIP. The growth of literacy and the proliferation of cheap printing in the age of the steam press meant that the control of information by several means, including censorship, was an important issue in the nineteenth century. The development of a mass readership in the century meant that the "reading public" became a reality, and there was great concern that libraries, cheap editions, and newspapers conveyed moral improvement in addition to entertainment. Even novels and other forms of fiction were considered to have an educational and recreational value. "Good" literature needed, as well as literary merit, to be perceived as serving the moral and intellectual wants of society. Censorship was considered necessary to ensure that the moral standards portrayed in literature and drama remained at a level that was socially acceptable. It was considered essential that the young, in particular, were protected from anything that fell below a high moral level. It was taken for granted that exposure to morally debased material, such as pornography, would have damaging moral and physiological effects. Sexually explicit or stimulating books would harden the conscience, leading to loss of shame and eventually, shameless behavior. Sexually suggestive material was thought to speed up physiological development, and result in premature sexualization, again resulting in the risk of immoral behavior. Those who took this line of reasoning to an extreme denounced the reading of novels and love stories of any kind, no matter how innocent.

The legal basis of censorship in Britain, France, and the United States in the nineteenth century was that of libel: seditious libel attacked the political status quo; blasphemous libel attacked the Christian religion; and obscene libel, the primary focus of this entry, was an attack on moral standards through the unacceptable sexualization of literature. Nineteenth-century expurgation and censorship was as deeply concerned with irreverence as with sexuality, and there were far more prosecutions for blasphemy than for obscenity. In one sense, prosecutions for blasphemy could also be seen as protecting moral standards, because it was universally assumed that if religion were undermined, one of the most terrible consequences of the loss of faith would be an outpouring of unbridled sexual expression.

In France, it was generally agreed that some literature was publishable, on the understanding that it was suitable only for men's reading, but censorship prior to publication was enforced sporadically and irregularly. In England and the United States, it was assumed that everything published should be fit for women to read, but the great majority of censorship was voluntary, and fell into the categories of expurgation and self-censorship. Far more important than formal censorship was "a new censorship of restraint and inhibition" (Weiner 1984, 93). Governments were increasingly able to allow public opinion to shape the limits of acceptability in print and the drama. The moral standard demanded of literature became stricter in all these countries as the century passed.

There was a difference between censorship and expurgation. Censorship preceded publication in most cases, and expurgation followed it. Censorship was imposed and expurgation was voluntary; in addition, many authors anticipated objections and removed "warm" passages, thus effectively censoring themselves prior to publication. As a result, censorship of novels on grounds of impurity or their engagement with sexual issues was relatively rare in nineteenth-century Britain and the United States. Booksellers and libraries refused to stock questionable books; reviewers denounced books whose moral tendencies appeared negative; and the general public demanded books that could be read aloud in the family circle. Considered purely in economic terms, for an author capable of pleasing the public taste, there was far more money to be made in purity than in pornography. Censorship was also applied to the theater, but it tended to be more severe than that applied to books.

The seal of the Society for the Suppression of Vice, founded in the United States in 1873. On the left, the purveyor of obscenity is being thrust into a cell; while on the right a Christian layman consigns infamous volumes to the flames. The Granger Collection, New York.

The nineteenth century was the great pinnacle of expurgation rather than of censorship proper. The classics were cleansed and foreign translations were "purified" throughout the century. The most famous of those who attempted to purify English literature in the nineteenth century was Thomas Bowdler and his sister Henrietta, who published the *Family Shakespeare* in 1807, with the intention of excluding all the parts of Shakespeare "unfit to be read aloud by a gentleman to a company of ladies" (Thomas: 186). In the case of Shakespeare, it meant that substantial portions (about 10%) of Hamlet were cut, and some plays, such as *Romeo and Juliet*, were excluded altogether. Such was the popularity of the *Family Shakespeare* (which ran to many editions and sold even better in the United States than in Britain) that the family name gave birth to the verb "bowdlerize."

While the Bowdlers removed all impious references from Shakespeare as well as the indelicacies and direct sexual references, they did attempt to keep the plays relatively intact. Competitors crowded into the field, many of whom were less concerned with literary integrity than the Bowdlers. By 1850, there were seven other expurgated versions of Shakespeare on the market, and in 1900, there were over forty. Later expurgators, becoming more prudish as the century passed, found themselves reduced to publishing extracts (often called "beauties") from Shakespeare rather than entire plays. Next to Shakespeare, Chaucer was the author most often edited in the cause of decorum. Even the Bible was expurgated in this century. Early American dictionaries were expurgated, omitting terms like "brothel" altogether. Noah Webster founded his fortunes on purified dictionaries, and bowdlerized a popular edition of the Bible specifically for the American market. This kind of literary censorship was not universally approved of at the time; reviewers of expurgated books sometimes accused bowdlerizers of prudery; however, they were equally likely to be attacked for not cutting enough.

Not all bowdlerized books were of early authors. Changing tastes meant that by the 1830s, the works of many of the eighteenth-century novelists were considered unfit for reading, including Laurence Sterne, Henry Fielding, and Tobias Smollett. All of these underwent expurgation in the nineteenth century. Even earlier, in the late 1790s, Sir Walter Scott tells the famous anecdote of an elderly lady of his acquaintance, who returning in old age to the literature of her youth, found it unreadable due to its indecency of language—an indecency she had been unaware of sixty years earlier, before society was "purified."

In 1801, the Society for the Suppression of Vice and the Encouragement of Religion and Virtue was founded in London. Part of their remit was to prosecute the publishers and sellers of obscene books and indecent prints. This meant that everything from snuff boxes with images of copulating couples on the lid to books giving accounts of **divorce** trials were included. In England, the legal definition of obscenity was given as any item intended to "depraved and corrupt" its readers. Most of the mainstream literatures were subjected to self-censorship by the author and the Society for the Suppression of Vice mostly prosecuted those who distributed pornography. As the violation of the **law** was so easily provable at this level, they won most of their cases. The 1857 Obscene Publications Act, passed as a result of public demand for more stringency, drove much of the pornography trade to the continent. It allowed magistrates to order the destruction of indecent material, thus destroying the potential profit. The 1857 act was aimed primarily at pornography, not at mainstream literature—simply shocking readers was not enough to justify a prosecution under the act. Ironically, religious zealots sometimes found themselves offending against the law in this period. The Protestant Electoral Union published an anti-Catholic work entitled *The Confessional Unmasked*, purporting to "expose" sexual improprieties between penitent and priest, and was successfully prosecuted for obscenity in 1868. Other enthusiasts also ran into trouble. **Birth control** propagandists **Annie Wood Besant** and **Charles Bradlaugh** were tried under the act in 1877. France made its obscenity laws more stringent in 1881, prohibiting anything that might offend "public and religious morality and good taste." Newspapers were relatively exempt, although in England, the Libel Act of 1888 reaffirmed that newspapers could be prosecuted for reprinting blasphemy or obscenity. Divorce trials, reported at length in the papers, although very scandalous and sometimes explicit, were exempt because they were reports of courtroom testimony.

Legal offenses aside, censorship was ordinarily informal and was enforced at all levels of the industry. Self-censorship by authors was widespread, removing references that could be considered immodest. The publisher could, and often did, object to passages that appeared too passionate: Charles Dickens, George Eliot, Thomas Hardy, and Anthony Trollope were only four of the best-known British authors compelled to revise passages in order to get their books accepted by a publisher. In the United States, Stephen Crane was one of the many authors who were forced to edit their novels in order to achieve publication. Thomas Hardy (who was obliged to bowdlerize himself on both sides of the Atlantic) shared the common view that American purity standards were considerably more rigid than in England. Gustave Flaubert was compelled to agree to deletions in the first edition of *Madame Bovary*, but even with purified language, the sympathetic portrayal of a bored wife's adultery shocked readers.

It was only in the final quarter of the nineteenth century that the later Victorians had to deal with obscenity in serious literature. One of the rare instances of the prosecution of a serious novel for obscenity was that of Henry Vizetelly for publishing English translations of several of Zola's works in the 1880s. By the 1880s, the Society for the Suppression of Vice had fallen into decline. It was replaced in 1886 with the National Vigilance Association, who concerned themselves with **photographs** and the theater in addition to books. It was the National Vigilance Association (NVA) that brought the prosecution in the Zola case. **Havelock Ellis**'s writings on **homosexuality** were unable to be published in Britain for more than a decade, and poets like Baudelaire in France and Whitman in Boston, found themselves banned.

The situation in the United States was different. Unlike the uniform national systems in Britain and France, states made their own laws dealing with obscenity, which were based on the English common law offence of "obscene libel." Some localities formulated their own codes as well, based on the same source, often banning mockery of religion at the same time. As in Britain, the general public seems to have provided solid support for the censorship of print materials (attempts to censor art produced some opposition), and they generally applauded the prosecution of those who overstepped the bounds of public decorum. **Social purity** and temperance associations played a prominent role in American censorship from the 1870s. Free-speech attacks on censorship appeared relatively late in the century, and did not become a dominant factor in the debate over **censorship** until well into the twentieth century.

The first federal legislation regulating obscenity in the United States was passed by Congress in 1842, when the Tariff Act banned the importation of obscene images, including **painting**s and engravings. This act was modified in 1873 to include print materials, when it became a part of the Comstock Law. Obscenity had been banned from the mails in America in 1865, because it had become clear that interstate mail-order distribution of illegal materials made the state laws ineffective. The antivice agitations of the Comstock era were thus built on a long tradition of state censorship.

Drama was treated somewhat differently than books, especially in Britain. Censorship of plays began in England in the time of Henry VII. Preventative censorship was enforced before any new play could be licensed for performance, and was carried out by the Lord Chamberlain's Office. However, owing to the public taste becoming steadily more prudish as the nineteenth century advanced, old plays that had been acceptable before 1800 found themselves purged of indecency in the following decades. Repressive censorship, which is censorship after performance in response to public complaints, was seldom required. Respectable middle-class audiences were very ready to hiss any reference or stage business that offended their sense of propriety.

The most famous expurgators of plays were the Bowdlers, who had amended Shakespeare for performance as well as reading at home. In 1812, James Plumptre published *The English Drama Purified*, which bowdlerized a number of non-Shakespearian plays. At this date, a play could be hissed off the stage for a line such as "there is only a poor gentlewoman in labor," and the expurgators were careful to remove such references. Even if all the words were decent in themselves, the Lord Chamberlain refused licenses to plays that dealt with morally questionable topics. Shelley's *The Cenci* (which suggested a possible incestuous relationship), while written in 1819, was never publicly staged in the nineteenth century, despite considerable acclaim for its literary style. More commonly, offensive passages were excised and the play was then licensed. An 1824 play was approved after the objectionable word "thighs" was removed.

The Theatres Act of 1843 continued the system of preventative censorship. Official approval was needed for stage directions and "business" as well as the words themselves; innocent words could be made suggestive by vulgar gestures. Less than one percent of plays at this time were refused a license, and these were usually the translations of foreign works. From 1865, new ballets were also required to apply for a license, owing to anxiety about foreign **dances**, such as the notorious can-can. Even in light theater entertainment, visual cues were monitored: opera girls were ordered to have their skirts lengthened in 1874. French drama was very popular in England, but French plays required the most censorship, often for situation rather than for language, although English dramatists begin to imitate these problem plays in the 1870s. A slight increase in censorship was discernable in the 1860s, and from the 1870s, concerns about moral issues began to override political or religious concerns, and it became an increasing struggle for the censors to enforce existing standards of decency on new productions. However, playwrights could overestimate the liberality of the theater-going public, and reviews that detected indecency could condemn a play to failure. From the 1870s, ex-prostitutes could be depicted on the English stage, but only if shown to be suffering and repentant.

However, the issue of precedent created problems for the Lord Chamberlain's office. As the decades passed, many plays, previously refused a license, ceased to seem shocking. It was difficult for a play, once refused a license, to get that decision reversed, even in very different times. In 1891, the dramatization of Alexandre Dumas's novel *La Dame aux Camélias* finally received a license, after forty years of refusals, dating from 1852. The difficulty was in permitting a play to have a practicing prostitute as heroine. (The novel, while disapproved of, was not censored in England.) Ibsen's *Ghosts* (dealing with hereditary syphilis) was refused a license in the same year. Once a license was given, it was not generally revoked, even if the play sparked complaints (e.g., the outcry over Arthur Pinero's *The Gay Lord Quex* in 1899, which offended the public because it depicted a married woman inviting her lover to her bedroom).

France also operated a system of censorship of drama and licensing of theaters throughout the nineteenth century, despite a brief lifting of restrictions during the revolutionary period. The Napoleonic code of censorship, enacted in 1799, was changed little by his successors. It was more concerned with political and religious censorship than with immorality. As in England, playwrights almost invariably self-censored in this respect. The legitimate drama was far more heavily scrutinized than the boulevard theaters, which were considered too vulgar for consideration. French provincial theaters specialized in highly moral and rather old-fashioned melodramas, which were of no concern to the censorship. Censorship of slightly suggestive scenes relaxed somewhat as the century progressed, and like England, "shocking" plays—especially sympathetic depictions of prostitutes—began to appear in the later part of the century. However, French drama of this period was always more daring than indigenous British productions.

It has been argued by a number of scholars that censorship of English drama had very little effect before 1885, because so few plays were classifiable as new English drama. Most were little more than watered-down, anglicized adaptations from the French. However, the new generation of playwrights, often influenced by the Norwegian, Henrik Ibsen, such as Arthur Pinero, Henry Arthur Jones, Oscar Wilde, and Bernard Shaw, all encountered problems with the Lord Chamberlain's office in the decade after 1885. They were trying to write plays that discussed social problems with a frankness previously unknown, and more disturbingly, to challenge cherished social values. In the 1880s and 1890s, a few plays that were refused licenses were produced as private performances, with audiences by invitation only. This permitted a production of Shelley's *Cenci* in 1886, of Ibsen's *Ghosts* in 1891, and allowed Shaw's *Mrs. Warren's Profession* (Mrs. Warren was a brothel keeper and former prostitute), published in 1898, to be performed in the early twentieth century. However, this stratagem of private production was rare, because theaters were reluctant to allow themselves to be used for such performances, fearing that their licenses would not be renewed by the Lord Chamberlain's office. By the century's end, the censorship of the drama was on the increase again (aggravated by complaints by reviewers and by interest groups, such as the National Vigilance Association), while dramatists were displaying every determination to continue their examination of social problems, especially those associated with marriage and sexuality.

Further Reading: Boyer, Paul S. *Purity in Print*. New York: Scribner, 1968; Conolly, L. W. *The Censorship of English Drama 1737–1824*. San Marino, CA: Huntington Library, 1976; Dennis, Donna I. "Obscenity Law and the Conditions of Freedom in the Nineteenth-Century United States." *Law and Social Inquiry* (2002): 369–99; Hemmings, F.W.J. *Theatre and State in France, 1760–1905*. Cambridge, MA: Cambridge University Press, 1994; Johnston, John. *The Lord Chamberlain's Blue Pencil*. London: Hodder & Stoughton, 1990; Stephens, John Russell. *The Censorship of English Drama 1824–1901*. Cambridge, MA: Cambridge University Press, 1980; Thomas, Donald. *A Long Time Burning: The History of Literary Censorship in England*. London: Routledge & Kegan Paul, 1969; Weiner, Joel. "Social Purity and Freedom of Expression." *Censorship: 500 Years of Conflict*, 91–102. Oxford: Oxford University Press, 1984.

Susan Mumm

CHILD ABUSE. The physical and sexual abuse of children became the focus of mass campaigns and legislative changes in the United States and Great Britain during the late nineteenth century. Within Victorian culture, childhood was viewed as a state of innocence requiring special protection from sexual knowledge. A range of euphemisms, including terms, such as "moral outrage," "corruption," and "immorality," were used to describe what we now refer to as child sexual abuse. Debates focused on the age at which a female was sufficiently developed—physically, mentally, socially, and morally—to consent to sexual intercourse. Feminist and child-welfare campaigners aimed to raise the age of consent for girls to at least sixteen.

From the 1830s onward, middle-class reformers voiced concerns about incest among the laboring poor, which they associated with overcrowded living conditions. In Britain, parliamentary inquiries into conditions in factories, mines, and agricultural gangs in the 1830s and 1840s depicted the workplace as a site of brutality and sexual danger for children. Subsequent legislation sought to transform children from workers into scholars, who could be educated to live moral lives. In the first half of the century, however, there was a tendency to view the children of the poor as precocious threats rather than victims. The first Societies for the Prevention of Cruelty to Children (SPCCs) were founded in the years after 1860 in the United States, Britain, and Europe to protect child victims, to prosecute cases of abuse and neglect, and to campaign on issues relating to child welfare.

In the 1870s, concerns focused on the problem and prevalence of "the white slave trade," a term which was used to refer to a wide range of concerns about the sexual exploitation of female youth. In 1885, British newspaper editor William Thomas Stead published a sensationalist series of articles in the *Pall Mall Gazette* ("The Maiden Tribute of Modern Babylon"), in which he alleged that girl children were being sold, purchased, and violated on the streets of London. The news spread quickly across the globe, and it led to orchestrated attempts by coalitions of social purity, feminist and child-welfare activists to introduce protective legislation. In England and Wales, the **age of consent** for females had been fixed at ten in 1576, although reference was sometimes made to an older common **law** precedent of twelve. This had been raised to thirteen in 1875, and Stead's initiative led to the introduction of the Criminal Law Amendment Act in 1885, which raised it to sixteen. Legislation in the United States and in the British colonies pursued similar trajectories. The female age of consent in New York City was raised from ten to sixteen in 1886 and to eighteen in 1916. In British India, concerns centered on the Hindu tradition of child marriage, viewed as a savage anachronism in relation to the imperial civilizing mission. The age of consent was raised from ten to twelve in Bengal in 1891, a result of compromises between traditionalist, nationalist, and reformist agendas. The protection of children from sexual abuse remained a point of focus until First World War (incest was finally criminalized in England and Wales in 1908).

While there is little to suggest that the rhetoric of **white slavery** should be interpreted literally to imply an organized transcontinental trade in child prostitutes, evidence of the sexual assault of children—by relatives, neighbors, employers, and other acquaintances—was provided in the criminal courts on a daily basis. Sexual abuse was prosecuted through charges of indecent assault, rape, or the unlawful carnal knowledge of a female under the age of consent. The number of charges increased in volume across the nineteenth century in England and in New York, reflecting publicity campaigns, the work of welfare societies, and legislative changes (Jackson 2000; Robertson 2005). In England, over two-thirds of cases that reached trial by jury resulted in conviction; this was significantly higher than the conviction rate for cases involving adult complainants (Jackson). By the end of the century, however, incest and abuse were still associated with the poor, and successful complaints tended to be made against men of low social class.

Across western nation states, the SPCCs scrutinized the homes of the poor rather than the rich. If incest occurred among the middle classes, it was unlikely to end up in court. In 1896, psychologist Sigmund Freud published *The Aetiology of Hysteria* (in German), which was based on casework with his wealthy Viennese clientele, and clearly linked adult neurosis among the bourgeoisie to childhood sexual trauma. Freud, however, abandoned this theory, suggesting that neurosis resulted from sexual fantasy rather than actual abuse; the reasons for his shift have been hotly debated.

Although the Victorian era saw an expansion in the number of children's homes run by philanthropic organizations to care for orphaned or destitute children, very few were willing to take victims of sexual abuse. In Britain, a small number of specialist homes catered for "fallen girls"; these included the Church of England homes in Leytonstone, England (founded 1865) and at The Mumbles, Wales (founded 1885). Child victims of sexual abuse were viewed ambivalently. While they invoked considerable sympathy, philanthropists assumed that they were tainted or contaminated by sexual knowledge. Victorian treatment involved the repression of past memories—children were forbidden to speak of previous lives—and a diet of fresh air, physical exercise, and religious instruction.

Throughout the nineteenth century, campaigns relating to the sexual abuse of youth focused overwhelmingly on girl children. Similarly, institutional care for boys did not distinguish between the sexual categories of the residents. Nevertheless, cases of indecent assault involving boys and men were occasionally prosecuted in the courts, although they were rarely reported in the press. The outlawing of sexual activity between males meant that an "age of consent" for boys was effectively constructed through the age of criminal responsibility, which was set at fourteen. In 1889, the Metropolitan Police were involved in the covering up of the Cleveland Street male brothel scandal, which revolved around post-office messenger boys, and implicated a number of high-profile figures. The silence surrounding the abuse of boy children was part of a wider endeavor to remove **homosexuality** from public view.

Thus, the sexual abuse of girl children was acknowledged and discussed by Victorians, leading to the raising of the age of consent and its treatment as a heinous crime in courts of law. Feminist, social-purity, and child-welfare activists turned it into a campaigning issue, ensuring its prominence on reform agendas. Yet debates consistently made use of sensational, lurid, and highly euphemistic language. This drew attention away from the actualities of female experience, and served to construct the victims of abuse as an outcast group because of their problematic status as "fallen" children.

Further Reading: Gordon, Linda. *Heroes of Their Own Lives: The Politics and History of Family Violence.* London: Virago, 1989; Jackson, Louise. *Child Sexual Abuse in Victorian England.* London: Routledge, 2000; Masson, Jeffrey. *The Assault on Truth: Freud's Suppression of the Seduction Theory.* Harmondsworth, England: Penguin, 1985; Robertson, Stephen. *Crimes against Children: Sexual Violence and Legal Culture in New York City, 1880–1960.* Chapel Hill: University of North Carolina Press, 2005.

Louise A. Jackson

CHILDBIRTH. *See* Pregnancy and Childbirth

CHILD PROSTITUTION. In both Britain and the United States, the idea of childhood as being distinct and requiring protection had been established by the end of the nineteenth century. An important aspect of this was its definition as sexually innocent. The involvement of children in commercial sex, sexual transactions for money or material goods, clearly negated this image of childhood innocence and meant that such children experienced a double stigma of being tainted and diseased, and of having unnatural knowledge of sexual behavior. Child prostitutes were not perceived as asexual, dependent, moral, or even as real children, but at the same time they were not seen as adults. However, if a child was perceived to be an unwilling abductee, then they retained their childlikeness, and could then be depicted as a victim of circumstances over which they had no control or responsibility.

The first national media panic about child prostitution was in England in 1885. It was instigated by a series of sensational articles in the *Pall Mall Gazette* entitled "The Maiden Tribute of Modern Babylon." The writer of the articles and editor of the paper, William Thomas Stead, claimed to have uncovered a trade in very young girls for brothels in London, and depicted children and young people involved in commercial sex as abducted and betrayed innocents. The Maiden Tribute articles and the events surrounding them provided the crucial force in Britain to ensure the passage of the Criminal Law Amendment Act 1885. This **law** increased the age of consent from thirteen to sixteen (previously raised from twelve in 1875), and augmented police powers to deal with vice. Thereafter, the balance between control and protection was to become an enduring feature of debates on child prostitution and youthful delinquency in general.

The late-nineteenth-century panic about child prostitution encouraged the establishment of numerous charitable organizations. Although concern had been expressed in this form since the 1830s, children's societies experienced their most visible and significant expansion later in the century. Through the work of these child protection societies, the rights of the child were newly legitimated, and the idea that children possessed a right to reasonable treatment and sexual integrity came of age. The work of such charities also operated to define and separate "delinquent" from "normal" children, and associated the concepts of dirt, independence, and in particular, sexual knowledge with the former. Loose networks of campaigning purity groups emphasized prevention or the usually institutional re-education of young girls. Children believed to have sexual experience, even as a result of abuse, were in some cases taken from their families and placed in institutions for children with "knowledge of evil."

Despite considerable disagreement between the various organizations, they did serve to highlight the sexual and physical abuse of children. They also used the campaigns against both adult and child prostitution to attack wider sexual behavior and moral standards. Indeed, at this time, conceptions of sexuality, childhood, social class, urbanization, and the state of the nation became closely related issues that shaped public and political debate and action. Child prostitution became a focus upon which these broader issues converged and were debated. Child prostitution was one of the phenomena, with for example, the Ripper murders of prostitutes in Whitechapel, which elicited the flowering of New Journalism with its sexualized and personalized public campaigns.

The prominence of the Maiden Tribute articles has presented historians with the question of the extent to which children and juveniles were involved in **prostitution** and, in the way in which this activity should be interpreted. Deborah Gorham observes that historians of the 1960s and 1970s tended to accept that juvenile prostitution was a serious problem and that Stead's articles offered a genuine story of horrifying sexual exploitation. More recently, historians have been more circumspect. Gorham accepts that many girls were engaged in prostitution in that period, but owing to economic necessity and were not passive victims as depicted by Stead. Louise Jackson, however, treats the claims of the prevalence of juvenile prostitution with skepticism, and, largely considers them to have been euphemistic descriptions of child sexual assault.

Judith Walkowitz offers a different perspective, concentrating on the way discourses around sexual danger were produced and disseminated in late Victorian society. Walkowitz describes the way in which W. T. Stead took an older melodramatic formula and sexual narrative to the level of social drama, in his form of New Journalism. In an era when women increasingly mounted the political stage in defense of women and children, discourses on sexual knowledge expanded and new definitions of sexual danger emerged, a prominent one being child prostitution. Unfortunately, as Walkowitz suggests, the Maiden Tribute articles and the way they shifted focus from prostitution to that of the innocent abducted child victim of sexual exploitation, operated to mystify the realities of child prostitution.

Further Reading: Brown, Alyson and David Barrett. *Knowledge of Evil: Child Prostitution and Child Sexual Abuse in Twentieth Century England.* Cullompton: Willan, 2002; Gorham, Deborah. "The 'Maiden Tribute of Modern Babylon' Re-Examined. Child Prostitution and the Idea of Childhood in Late-Victorian England." *Victorian Studies* 21 (1978): 353–79; Jackson, Louise. *Child Sexual Abuse in Victorian England.* London: Routledge, 2000; Walkowitz, Judith. *City of Dreadful Delight: Narratives of Sexual Danger in Late-Victorian London.* London: Virago, 1992.

Alyson Brown

CHINA. The Chinese Yin-Yang theory holds that the harmonious interaction of male and female principles is vital, and this formed the basis of an essentially open and positive attitude toward sexuality in ancient China. In general, the government authorities never strictly enforced the laws related to sexual matters throughout China's history before the twelfth century. During the Sung dynasty (960–1279), the government began, for the first time, to change its policy to control the sex life of the Chinese people, and China slowly became a sexually repressive country. By the time the dynasties of Ming (1368–1644) and Ch'ing (1644–1911) came to power, the government policy had been changed in ways that were conducive to great ignorance about sexuality. For example, it was prohibited for anyone to write or talk about the subject in public. The nineteenth century, coming in the period of the Ch'ing dynasty in China, does not have the distinctive parameters of the Victorian era, but through a different line of development, came to share some of its sexual attitudes.

From the Sung to the Ming dynasties, government-run and privately owned **prostitution** existed side by side in China. Early in the Ching dynasty, from 1651 CE to 1673 CE, the Manchu Emperors Shun-chih and K'ang-hsi gradually abolished both local and imperial governmental involvement in prostitution; thus, for most of the Ching dynasty, prostitution in China was a private enterprise. The private, commercial prostitution became more highly developed during the Ming and Ching dynasties. In this later era, the cities of Suzhou, Hangzhou, Nanjing, Yangzhou, Shanghai, Beijing, Tianjin, and Kuangzhou were all famous for their flourishing trade in prostitution.

Before this time, however, publication of sexually explicit material had been long prohibited. For example, the Emperor Kangxi (r. 1661–1722 CE) announced a ban on erotic literature. The government's list of banned books contained more than 150 titles, most of them erotic fictions. In later versions of the laws of the Great Ch'ing, there was a requirement that all copies of banned books, and the original wood blocks, be burned. Harsh punishments were prescribed for anyone who published, distributed, or possessed banned literature. Although there was a marked growth in the writing of homosexual fictions during this period, it did not mean that Ch'ing government approved of homosexuality. In 1740, the Ch'ing authorities elaborated for the first time in Chinese history a punishment for sodomy, even between consenting adults.

However, there were still erotic fictions published underground, such as *The Prayer Mat of Flesh* [*Jou Pu Tuan*] (attributed to the famous writer Yu Li although this is questioned) and *Yi-chun Xiang-zhi*. Both books were examples of classic erotic fictions published during the Ch'ing dynasty.

Yi-hun Xiang-zhi, written by Xin Yue Zhu Ren, is a novel of homosexual behavior. It is believed that this novel was written in the first half of the nineteenth century. The novel contains four volumes, each volume an independent story with five chapters, and containing a large number of descriptions of homosexual behavior and acts. Another work of homosexual fiction, *Bian Er Chai*, was written by the same author and its structure is similar. A third work of homosexual fiction, *Ping-hua Bao-jan*, by Chen Sen, was more widely disseminated and became relatively popular. It included considerable glorification of **homosexuality**, and spoke eloquently of the virtues of male same-sex love. His model of the hero was actually based on a real person, an outstanding scholar and a higher official of the Ching dynasty, Pi Yuan. In 1760, when Pi had passed the highest national examination and had become a "Chuang-Yuan" (the top scholar), his same-sex lover Mr. Li was known as "Mrs."

Another book titled *Tuan Shiu Pien* (*The Records of Cut-Sleeve*), edited during the Ch'ing dynasty by an anonymous author, recorded some fifty examples of famous homosexual cases in Chinese history. This perhaps was the only book specifically dealing with homosexuality in a nonfictional context in Chinese literature of this period. It was translated into Italian, English, and a number of other languages.

In terms of social realities, there is evidence of widespread practice of homosexuality during the Ch'ing dynasty. For example, three emperors, Chien Lung (r. 1736–1795), Hsien Fong (r. 1851–1861), and Tung Chih (r. 1862–1874), all had well documented homosexual relationships with their subordinates. Emperor Chien Lung's homosexual lover, Ho Shen (1750–1799), became a very powerful prime minister as a result of their same-sex love relationship.

It is noteworthy that during the periods of the Emperors Chien Lung and Chai Ching's (1736–1820 CE), an occupation called "shiahng gung" (or "shiahng gu") was very popular. "Shiahng gung" was a term that originally used to refer to male actors who played female characters. Later, it was used to refer to a male actor and a male homosexual's lover, that is, a male prostitute for male homosexuals who, in effect, was a he-woman, a drag queen hustler, a catamite, or a pederast. The place where such business was conducted was called "shiahng-gung tang-sze" or "shiahng-gu tang-sze." The shiahng gungs dressed, behaved, and talked like women. They wore perfume and make-up, moved like women, and infatuated many male homosexuals. There was also another outlet for male homosexuals. For example, in Nanjing there was a "Chao Tian Gong" (a Taoist temple), which was famous for providing young monks to entertain powerful and rich men with homosexual proclivities for a high fee.

There are also a number of accounts of young boys being passed off and sold as girls in the Ch'ing dynasty, because girls brought the seller a higher profit. In that time, the price for a girl was ten times the price paid for a boy. Often they were sold as children, and sometimes the deception was not discovered until they were old enough to be taken as concubines. Apparently, some families disguised their male children as females to protect them from harm. Those cases can be looked as a kind of transvestitism or the third sex, but ones driven more by familial desperation than by personal preference.

Further Reading: Bullough, Vern. *Sexual Variance in Society and History.* Chicago: University of Chicago Press, 1976; van Gulik, Robert. *Sexual Life in Ancient China: A Preliminary Survey of Chinese Sex and Society from ca. 1500 BC till 1644 AD.* Leiden: E. J. Brill, 1961; Ruan, Fang-fu. *Sex in China: Studies in Sexology in Chinese Culture.* New York: Plenum, 1991.

Fang-Fu Ruan

CHRISTIANITY. Christian teachings on love and sexuality displayed little variation between denominations and churches in the nineteenth century. Both Catholics and Protestants agreed on the great majority of issues related to these themes. This is not to claim that all Christians strictly obeyed these teachings at all times, but it remains true that moral theology was very similar across the Christian spectrum, and did not change appreciably over the century, however adherents may have behaved. There were, however, several controversies that helpfully illuminate Christian attitudes toward love and sex at this time. The issue of **divorce** and the possibility of a man marrying his deceased wife's sister were two of the most important.

The theological basis of Christian teaching with regard to love and sex was based on their understanding of the creation story in Genesis, and focused on the consequences of Adam and Eve's fall from grace. It was assumed that sex changed as a result of the Fall, because of their loss of moral innocence. However, sex was believed to be elevated and purified by monogamy. The thinking of St. Thomas Aquinas was influential in shaping ideas about sexuality. He defined impurity as the enjoyment of sexual pleasure in the wrong ways—through perversion, through lawlessness, or through excess. Later theologians were to argue that marriage hallowed sexual desire to such a degree that excess was not a sin.

The churches taught that both men and women should be chaste before marriage and faithful afterward. Chastity was not only possible but was commanded. Because traditional Christian teaching taught that premarital chastity was the proper standard for both sexes, many of those involved in the **social purity** movement and related movements were committed Christians, such as **Ellice Hopkins** and **Josephine Butler**. Although popular culture in the nineteenth century saw sexual impurity for women as a sin more serious than any other, this was not the teaching of Christianity. There was no moral sin which was beyond the reach of repentance for either sex, but the repentant sinner might have to live with the consequences of their misdeeds.

Sexual unchastity before marriage was termed fornication, and was punished where possible. In most Christian churches, public punishment for fornication ceased to be practiced by the outset of the nineteenth century. However, in the Scottish Presbyterian Church public repentance for sexual sin still prevailed, although it was becoming rare. Unless an illegitimate baby was born, fornication was difficult for the Kirk Sessions to prove, and the Presbyterian Church was reluctant to resort to public shame if there was no illegitimate child in the case. Seating fornicators on the "stool of repentance," a public rite of humiliation, was so shameful that it was feared women would commit infanticide to avoid being found out, and thus it fell into decline. Most other Christian churches had abandoned public reprimand of penitents by the nineteenth century, although excommunication was technically a possibility if a sinner remained obdurate and unrepentant. Very rarely was it resorted to, usually for sins that were considered more serious, such as repeated and unrepented blasphemy.

In the Victorian Church of England, parish priests in rural areas reported that up to a third or even a half of rural brides were visibly pregnant on their wedding day. Because all parishioners had the right to be married in church, priests had no way to protest against these obvious cases of premarital sexual activity. Some argued that although intercourse before engagement was still sinful, it was less so than fornication or adultery. In line with the cultural climate of the century, **masturbation** was considered abnormal, but it was not mentioned in the Bible, so the generally accepted opinion of its wickedness had no scriptural basis.

All Christian churches taught that marriage was the public union of one man with one woman, except for the American-based Church of Jesus Christ of Latter Day Saints (Mormons) who allowed **polygamy** (which they termed "plural marriage"), until it was prohibited by government edict in the late nineteenth century. Some Christian missionaries in Africa began to argue for permitting polygamy in societies where influential men had many wives. These tribal leaders were reluctant to convert to Christianity if it meant sending away their wives, and their followers would hesitate to convert if their leaders did not. The churches refused to sanction polygamy even in these special circumstances, thus slowing rates of conversion. The churches stressed three aspects of marriage: the raising of children, sexual fidelity, and its lifelong nature. While popular culture became increasingly insistent that romantic love was the only acceptable reason for marriage, Christian teaching continued to insist that romantic love, transitory by its nature, was not the basis of marriage, and that sexual fidelity was expected even after love died. The promises made at marriage were expected to endure until the death of one spouse, regardless of the happiness of the union. Marriage turned two into one, and that union was irrevocable.

Marriage was considered to be the best form of life for adults in the Protestant traditions. They argued that Jesus appeared indifferent to asceticism, but clearly recognized matrimony. Nineteenth-century Protestantism was very prone to seeing marriage as the "higher" life, combining, as it did, the possibility of children to be raised as Christians, with mutual comfort and support, and a sexual outlet within the sanctified environment of marriage. Not all churches saw marriage as a sacrament, although the Catholic Church did. **Homosexuality** (in those rare cases where it was discussed) was seen as a sin in all Christian churches, and this issue raised virtually no debate during the century.

Birth control was considered as sinful, tampering with God's will. No Christian church (except for a few fringe sects, mostly small communal groups in the United States) allowed any form of family limitation other than self-control. Artificial means of family limitation were not officially condoned by the major Protestant denominations until the twentieth century, and after that remained forbidden to Catholics. **Abortion** after quickening was seen as murder; its status in the early weeks of **pregnancy** was unclear in the early part of the century, but as scientific understanding of the fetus advanced, attitudes condemning abortion hardened.

Catholicism offered a "higher" alternative to marriage in the form of life-long celibacy as a priest or monk for men, or as a nun for women. Women who became nuns were the Brides of Christ, and many wore a wedding ring as a symbol of their mystical union. Widows and widowers were allowed to join these orders, indicating that virginity was not normally a requirement, although chastity was. Protestants, with the exception of some Anglicans, viewed monasticism and the celibate priesthood with suspicion, seeing it as a denial of God's will for men and women, which was believed to be marriage and children. Protestant clergy could marry, and their wives carried out important social and charitable functions, often assisting their husbands with their parish work.

Remarriage after the death of one's spouse was permitted to all Christians (other than Catholic celibates) except for priests in the Greek Orthodox tradition, who could marry before ordination, but were not allowed to remarry if their wives died. Christianity prohibited marriage within certain relationships and marriages within these limits (called the prohibited degrees) were considered invalid and could be annulled. The two main prohibitions were consanguinity (blood relationship) and affinity (relationship by marriage). The most controversial question involving remarriage was what became known as the deceased wife's sister question. Marriage to a dead wife's sister was within the church's forbidden degrees of affinity, and was illegal in England from 1835 until the early twentieth century. (Until 1835, such marriages were not illegal, but could be annulled at the demand of any party, not just at the request of the couple concerned.) Efforts were made to repeal the legislation throughout the nineteenth century, and couples who were affluent enough traveled abroad to marry. Because the English church was a state establishment, the clergy were outraged by parliamentary efforts to force them to perform marriages within the forbidden degrees. Concerns regarding marriage to a deceased wife's sister as a form of incest, or spinster sisters being unable to live with their married sisters, thus disrupting a popular living arrangement, were other objections to repealing the legislation. The reasoning against allowing such marriages could be elaborate:

> The morality of the marriage law in general consists in this, that the sexual instinct that belongs to human nature is to be never separated from but always … wrapped up and veiled in personal and faithful love; and the ground on which marriage between near kindred is essentially immoral is that between such [relations] a moral and personal love already exists, so that a desire for marriage could only be an animal passion. (Boyd 1980, 273)

The Catholic Church and the Eastern churches also prohibited marriage with certain degrees, based either on canon law or on their interpretation of Levitical law. However, Roman Catholics could apply for a dispensation to marry a deceased wife's sister.

Divorce was considered a serious sin, and most churches did not permit their members to divorce without a serious cause, although most churches made provision for separation, in cases of adultery and cruelty. In the nineteenth century, it was harder to get a divorce in England than in most of Europe or in many American states. From 1670, English law allowed formal separation through the church courts. Administered by the Anglican Church, this was called a *mensa et thoro*, "divorce from bed and board." Although called divorce, this was a form of officially recognized separation, and did not permit remarriage without further court action. The church did not sanction remarriage after *mensa et thoro*, regardless of circumstances. If remarriage was desired, the offended spouse had to bring an action for "criminal conversation" (in a civil court) to establish adultery. Armed with the verdict, the spouse then turned to the ecclesiastical courts for a separation and then turned to the secular arm again, petitioning the House of Lords to grant the divorce. This meant divorce was open only to the very rich, as all of these legal actions were very expensive. In 1857, the Court for Divorce and Matrimonial Causes, based in London, was established. It took divorce duties away from the church courts, and abolished formal separation from bed and board, thus ending the Anglican Church's role in divorce. Annulment was sometimes a possibility, but a case was required to be made and approved by clerical and legal authorities. This was called a *vinculo matrimonii*. In these cases, it was deemed that the marriage was not valid in canon law, so that it was void from the outset and in the eyes of church, had never really existed. A sentence of "divorce" in such cases could be obtained from the Ecclesiastical Court, saying that the marriage had never been valid, and allowing either party to marry with the blessing of the church.

Leaving legality for morality, adultery was the only justification for divorce recognized by the Christian churches for most of the nineteenth century, and then only within very strict limits. Most advised their adherents to forgive the erring spouse. Forgiven adultery was not considered to break the marriage bond, whether the offender was male or female. In an era when few women had careers or enough money to support their children without assistance, it was argued that easy divorce would make vulnerable women victims of fickle men. Although some American states allowed easier divorce, this was a civil arrangement, and was disapproved of by virtually all religious leaders. All Christian churches attempted to discipline those of their members who lived in defiance of Christian teaching on sexuality, especially those who divorced. Some churches refused communion to divorced persons, and all major traditions refused communion to divorced people who remarried, who were considered to be living in adultery, given that the original marriage was still considered religiously valid. In Britain in 1866, only twenty-three divorced people remarried, but this was considered a worrying flood by the Church of England, which remained adamantly opposed to the remarriage of the divorced. Later in the nineteenth century, some churches allowed the "innocent party" (the spouse who had not committed adultery) to remarry in a religious ceremony. In countries, such as England, with an established church, Anglican clergy were outraged when late-Victorian changes to the law compelled them to allow the innocent party to remarry in a church in certain dioceses. Only a small minority of dioceses permitted these remarriages to enjoy a religious sanction. In 1888, the Church of England reaffirmed its convictions on the indissolubility of marriage, but softened its position on the faithful spouse, saying that they should no longer be refused the sacrament.

Most Christian teaching on sexuality and love shows little sign of development over the nineteenth century; the real debate on these issues was to come in the following century. However, at the same time, social attitudes, especially toward divorce, were changing faster than religious teaching. This created a gradual breakdown of ecclesiastical control over social behavior during the nineteenth century, with the church relinquishing any real control over morals, but reluctant to admit the fact.

Further Reading: Boyd, Kenneth M. *Scottish Church Attitudes to Sex, Marriage and the Family 1850–1914*. Edinburgh: John Donald, 1980; Luckock, H. M. *The History of Marriage*. London: Longmans, 1894; Northcote, Hugh. *Christianity and Sex Problems*. Philadelphia: F. A. Davis, 1906; Stone, Laurence. *The Road to Divorce*. Oxford: Oxford University Press, 1992.

Susan Mumm

CIRCUMCISION AND CLITORIDECTOMY. Circumcision and clitoridectomy are among the most distinctive Victorian contributions to bodily management and health promotion. Both procedures were introduced to control disapproved behavior and to prevent or cure disease. But, while clitoridectomy enjoyed only brief and limited vogue in the 1860s, circumcision of male infants and boys was popular for nearly a century, and remains common in the United States.

Before the nineteenth century, men valued their foreskins as "the best of your property" and regarded circumcision with horror, but during the eighteenth century, surgeons started treating serious venereal infections of the penis by amputation of the diseased tissue. Since the sores were usually on the foreskin, this was analogous to circumcision, but it was done only in advanced cases of disease, and only if the men agreed to it. Such sores often caused phimosis by producing scabs, which fused the foreskin to the glans, again requiring treatment. Some surgeons treated the condition by amputating the foreskin, while others preferred conservative approaches, such as bathing and fomentations, and operated only if gangrene was present.

The fundamental reason for the establishment of preventive circumcision of boys (and, to a lesser extent, of girls) was the rise of medical anxiety about **masturbation**. The masturbation phobia transformed the normal fondling of the penis, observed in nearly all young boys, into a wicked and harmful vice which had to be stamped out. This led to the medical error whereby the normal phimotic condition of the juvenile penis was characterized as a pathological abnormality requiring urgent surgical correction. Nobody had worried about phimosis in childhood until masturbation became an issue, but once that was seen as a problem, phimosis also became a problem, because the "secretions" it was supposed to trap were thought to cause irritation, thus leading boys to scratch and handle their penis. The main reason advanced for circumcision in Britain from the 1840s onward was to cure phimosis, that is, to surgically "correct" the natural condition of the penis. Later claims that a tight foreskin caused, and circumcision could prevent, cancer, epilepsy, paralysis, whooping cough, convulsions, hernia, etc. were all based on the original misconception that infantile phimosis was pathological. Various theories were advanced as to the cause: first one was that the foreskin pressed on the glans and caused imbalances of nerve force; then that the "secretions" putrefied and generated disease poisons (zymotic theory); and finally, as germ theory took hold, that the foreskin trapped harmful bacteria. Even those who did not support circumcision believed that the infant foreskin had to be separated from the glans and forced to retract within a few weeks of birth. It was not until the 1930s that this dogma was questioned, and not until research by Douglas Gairdner in the 1940s that the error was dispelled.

Circumcision in childhood was first introduced by French and English doctors as a treatment for masturbation in the 1830s, and also recommended for spermatorrhoea (involuntary loss of semen) in adult men. Much of this was based on the theories of Claude-Francois Lallemand, whose work on the risks of seminal emissions was well known in the United States and popularized in Britain by **William Acton**. Circumcision was not routine at this stage or even common, and was performed by only a few overanxious or highly punitive parents. Circumcision became "routine" (i.e., performed without consent on healthy children showing no signs of disease or abnormality) and widespread among the middle and professional classes in the 1880s as a result of the combination of several factors. Prevention of masturbation remained the major selling point, but the practice received a boost from the claim that it provided significant protection against syphilis (first raised in the 1850s by **Jonathan Hutchinson**, but not popularized until the 1890s), and then, as fears of masturbation and syphilis declined, against various genital cancers. As the prestige of surgery rose, the conditions preventable or curable by circumcision expanded to include tuberculosis, bed-wetting, epilepsy, pimples, hip-joint disease, brass poisoning, and many others. Sometimes advocates needed to do no more than employ the word "hygiene," a term with both physical and moral connotations.

Although the justifications for clitoridectomy were similar to those offered for circumcision (cleanliness, deterrence of masturbation, control of nervous diseases), the practice remained rare and never became a routine precaution. Doctors generally held that women's lower sex drive meant they were less given to self-abuse than males, and thus that drastic surgery was rarely necessary. There are occasional reports of masturbating girls being subjected to involuntary clitoridectomy, but it was only in the late 1850s that a few doctors started to apply to women the theories of nervous disease, which already legitimized circumcision in boys. The most famous of these was the prominent London obstetrician, Isaac Baker Brown, who specialized in the surgical treatment of disorders, such as epilepsy, catalepsy, and hysteria induced by "irritation of the pudic nerve" (i.e., masturbation). Although he attracted considerable interest at first, his procedures fell rapidly into disfavor, and he was expelled from the Obstetrical Society in 1867. While his critics condemned clitoridectomy as a "questionable, compromising, unpublishable mutilation," which would ruin the women's sex lives, leave them permanently maimed and cast an indelible slur on their honor, Brown defended himself by claiming that masturbation caused hysteria, epilepsy, mania, insanity, and death, and argued that clitoridectomy was no more mutilating than male circumcision, as proved by the subsequent pregnancy of several of his patients. His critics did not dissent from the proposition that masturbation could provoke the ills he mentioned, but they insisted that the practice was so rare in women that radical interventions of this kind were not necessary. Brown's disgrace put an end to clitoridectomy in Britain, and there are no reliable reports of its performance after the 1860s. Looking back on the controversy, his principal antagonist, Charles West, commented that "all right-minded men" were compelled to reject both the operation and its leading proponent, but that "happily we need not now dwell further on the subject, for all practitioners are agreed that the only indication for removal of the clitoris is furnished by the disease of the organ itself." It was a long time before doctors reached the same conclusion about the foreskin.

Clitoridectomy and other circumcision-like operation on girls and women had a longer career in United States, where there was also some attempt to apply the theories of Lewis Sayre—that many nervous diseases were caused by a tight or nonretractable foreskin—to women, and a number of doctors urged that girls also should have their clitoral hoods excised if there was any suspicion of adhesions of the accumulation of "secretions." In 1892, Dr. Robert Morris went to the extent of suggesting that all schoolgirls should be inspected to ensure that proper separation between prepuce and clitoris had occurred, confident that most of the girls would require surgery, and he added: "The separation of adhesive prepuces in young unmarried women should be done by female **physicians** anyway, and such physicians can be abundantly occupied with this sort of work." Although he was doing his best to expand the market for medical services, his suggestions were not widely taken up.

The age at which circumcision was done in Britain varied. It was often performed in infancy, but it was probably more common in early childhood, particularly just before a boy started school, as a precaution against picking up the habit of masturbation from his new mates. Many boys were not circumcised automatically, but because it was found that their foreskin was not easily retractable, or because they were caught masturbating. The style and technique of circumcision was never standardized, complications were common, and deaths were regularly reported. Doctors disagreed about the right technique, the amount of tissue to be excised, and the best ways to avoid bleeding and infection. Some urged the tightest possible job, others the minimum needed to free the glans, yet others a middle course. Many purpose-built devices were patented, the tendency of which was to make the operation more radical. In fact, English and American circumcision techniques turned out to be significantly more severe than most ritual or tribal varieties, involving the loss of considerably more penile tissue and often damage to the glans, particularly if the operation was performed before the foreskin's natural separation had taken place.

There are no reliable statistics on the circumcision rate in Britain, but it was overwhelmingly a middle- and upper-class phenomenon. Surveys of men born in the 1930s indicate an overall incidence of about 30 percent, but with a significant class differential: while almost 80 percent of boys at public schools might be cut, the rate might be as low as 5 or 10 percent among working class or rural communities. The keys to this difference lie in greater consumption of medical services by the rich, the uneven grip of the masturbation phobia, and the respectable obsession with "cleanliness." Although working-class mothers sometimes brought a toddler to hospital, complaining that he was "always playing with himself," the scare over masturbation was most heavily concentrated in the richer and better-educated classes, and it was a particular obsession at the public schools they attended. The better-off also enjoyed running water, baths, and the like, while the poor and working classes became the great unwashed; their foreskins were the final proof of how filthy they were. As George Orwell pointed out, the middle class believed that the working class smelled; the cleanliness of the circumcised boy was the visible proof of his access to the latest in medical care and his generally superior social status.

Further Reading: Dally, Ann. *Fantasy Surgery 1880–1930: With Special Reference to Sir William Arbuthnot Lane.* Amsterdam: Rodopi, 1996; Darby, Robert. *A Surgical Temptation: The Demonization of the Foreskin and the Rise of Circumcision in Britain.* Chicago: University of Chicago Press, 2005; Dunsmuir, W. D. and E. M. Gordon. "The History of Circumcision." *BJU International* 83 (1999): 1–12; Fleming, J. B. "Clitoridectomy: The Disastrous Downfall of Isaac Baker Brown FRCS (1867)." *Journal of Obstetrics and Gynaecology of the British Empire* 67 (1960): 1017–34; Gairdner, Douglas. "The Fate of the Foreskin: A Study of Circumcision." *British Medical Journal* (1949): 1433–37; Gollaher, David L. *Circumcision: A History of the World's Most Controversial Surgery.* New York: Basic Books, 2000; Hodges, Frederick. "A Short History of

Involuntary Sexual Mutilation in the United States." In *Sexual Mutilations: A Human Tragedy*, edited by C. D. George and M. Marilyn. New York: Plenum Press, 1997; Miller, Geoffrey. "Circumcision: Cultural-legal Analysis." *Virginia Journal of Social Policy and the Law* 9 (2002): 497–585; Morris, Robert T. "Is Evolution Trying to Do Away with the Clitoris?" *Transactions of the American Association of Obstetricians and Gynaecologists* 5 (1892): 288–302; Moscucci, Ornella. "Clitoridectomy, Circumcision and the Politics of Sexual Pleasure in Mid-Victorian Britain." In *Sexualities in Victorian Britain*, edited by H. M. Andrew and E. A. James. Bloomington: Indiana University Press, 1996; Parsons, Gail Pat. "Equal Treatment for All: American Medical Remedies for Male Sexual Problems, 1850–1900." *Journal of the History of Medicine and Allied Sciences* 32 (1977): 55–71; Sheehan, Elizabeth A. "Victorian Clitoridectomy: Isaac Baker Brown and His Harmless Operation." In *The Gender/Sexuality Reader: Culture, History, Political Economy*, edited by N. L. Roger and Micaela di Leonardo. London: Routledge, 1997; Szasz, Thomas. "Neonatal Circumcision: Symbol of the Birth of the Therapeutic State." *Journal of Medicine and Philosophy* 21 (1996): 137–48; Wallerstein, Edward. *Circumcision: An American Health Fallacy*. New York: Springer, 1980.

Robert Darby

CLITORIDECTOMY. *See* Circumcision and Clitoridectomy

COHABITATION. Cohabitation described the relationship between a man and a woman who lived together, but were not married to each other. Victorians also called these arrangements "living in sin" or "living as husband and wife." The latter phrase explains the anxiety and disapproval of many contemporaries; cohabitation mimicked marriage, but did not have its legal or religious sanction. In addition, cohabitation allowed regular sexual intercourse outside of marriage, and often resulted in illegitimate children. The number of cohabiting couples throughout the century probably never reached more than 10 percent of partnerships, even at its peak of popularity in the 1830s and 1840s. Nevertheless, many observers feared that it posed a strong challenge to marriage.

Rather than being rebellious, most Victorian cohabitants did so because they had no choice. Only a minority of unhappily married couples could divorce, even after the Matrimonial Causes Act of 1857, owing to limited grounds and high cost. Thus, separated spouses usually had to live with lovers or commit bigamy. Many of the most famous cohabitants of the nineteenth century were in this category, including Marian Evans (George Eliot) and George Henry Lewes, who lived together for twenty-four years, because Lewes could not divorce his wife. Other couples were too closely related by marriage or blood. The most notorious example of this was the controversy over marriage to a deceased wife's sister, which was illegal in England from 1835 to 1907. Middle-class couples caught in this dilemma married abroad, but working-class couples married illegally. At times, in addition, the couples were too far apart in class to consider marriage. Most of these couples involved a higher class man living with a working-class woman, a situation with great risks, but also great rewards, for the latter. **Wilkie Collins**, author of suspense novels, lived with a working-class woman named Martha Rudd for over twenty years. The daughter of agricultural laborers, Rudd had much better prospects as Collins's pseudo-wife, though, in the end, his estate was not large enough to support their three children after his death in 1889.

Only a minority of couples actively chose not to marry. The main group were the extremely poor, who saw no need to go through an expensive ceremony. Middle-class observers considered these couples an example of working-class pathology, and associated such moral "looseness" with alcoholism and crime. However, the choice not to marry was rational for many of them. Cohabitation clustered in professions that required travel and flexibility, including sailors, soldiers, tramping laborers, and traveling salesmen. In these cases, the couples had little reason to tie themselves together for life. For their part, cohabitants in the "criminal" classes needed freedom to leave, in case either partner was imprisoned, or, early in the century, transported.

A second group of couples who chose cohabitation were a small band of marital radicals, including socialists, feminists, and anarchists, who refused to marry for ideological reasons. Though their beliefs varied greatly, all of these groups shared two main critiques of marriage. First, they objected to the gender imbalance of the institution; both men and women complained that the marriage ceremony and laws treated women as chattels. Second, marital radicals disliked the indissolubility of marriage. They argued that no one could promise to love forever, and hence the marriage ceremony was a lie. They further insisted that marriage was a relationship, and when the relationship died, the marriage was over. Though these couples were few, their cultural impact was greater than their numbers. Many of the critiques of marriage influenced later movements to reform the laws of divorce and illegitimacy.

The experience of cohabitation differed socially. The middle class had the most notorious couples, but the vast majority of cohabitants were from the working class. The latter had little to lose in property for their children, and working-class women were not invariably "ruined" by sexual nonconformity. This was particularly true in the first half of the nineteenth century, when the numbers of cohabitants and illegitimate births rose. Even after the decline of open cohabitation after 1850, though, couples probably cohabited and "passed" as married. Most working-class couples lived together because they had no choice, just as in the middle class, and these couples often received sympathy and support, rather than censure, from their neighbors.

All the same, in all classes, women cohabitants had more difficulties than men. Though few middle-class women faced total isolation, they were unable to go about in society freely, unlike their male partners. In addition, men had a strong economic advantage, and cohabitants had no automatic inheritance rights, nor did their children. An unmarried mother also had a heavier responsibility for any child born to the union. As a result, men tended to be more in favor of extramarital partnerships than women. Often, when couples "chose" to remain unmarried, the man was the holdout against marriage. Ironically, despite their theoretical freedom, most cohabitants mirrored the **gender roles** of married couples, with men demanding obedience and women insisting that the man provide for any children. In addition, though cohabitants had not pledged life-long fidelity, the most frequent reason for violence between them was sexual jealousy. Cohabitation in practice, then, was less of a threat to marriage than contemporaries feared.

The attitude of the state toward cohabiting relationships was more complex than the **law** indicated as well. In theory, the civil law defined marriage strictly, based on the Hardwick Marriage Act of 1753. In practice, the civil and criminal courts were more flexible. For example, if a man left money to a long-time cohabitant, or gave her a bond for her support, the High Courts would enforce these provisions. The only exception was the instance in which the bond or contract was an inducement to get the woman to agree to live with the man, since those contracts promoted immorality. Otherwise, the courts allowed men to support any women with whom they had lived. Civil courts also permitted long-time cohabitants to sue for breach of promise, ignoring the dubiousness of some of these claims. In addition, the criminal courts were lenient to those who broke the marriage laws, particularly in the working class. Juries often acquitted men who had married their relatives, believing them ignorant of the law. Similarly, bigamists did not get long sentences unless they had committed fraud; an "honest" bigamist would usually get imprisoned for only a few days or weeks. In short, judges and juries tacitly accept the reality of extramarital unions and focused instead on enforcing the male obligation to provide for women and children.

As the state's reaction indicates, the "radicalism" of cohabitation in the nineteenth century was muted. Nevertheless, couples who chose to live together did expand the definition of marriage. Precisely because they did not differ from their married counterparts, these partnerships implicitly questioned the purpose and value of legal marriage. The expansion of cohabitation to a mass phenomenon, however, would not occur until the late twentieth century.

Further Reading: Bland, Lucy. *Banishing the Beast: Sexuality and the Early Feminists*. New York: The New Press, 1995; Frost, Ginger. "Bigamy and Cohabitation in Victorian England." *Journal of Family History* 22 (July 1997): 286–306; Gillis, John. *For Better, For Worse: British Marriages 1600 to the Present*. Oxford: Oxford University Press, 1986; Reay, Barry. *Microhistories: Demography, Society, and Culture in Rural England, 1800–1930*. Cambridge, MA: Cambridge University Press, 1996.

Ginger Frost

COLLINS, WILKIE (1824–1889). Wilkie Collins was a British writer who was one of the first writers of sensation fiction, a Victorian genre that relied heavily on secrets and mysterious, thrilling events which needed to be resolved by a detective figure, and is therefore often associated with detective fiction. Like other sensation-fiction novelists, such as Mary Elizabeth Braddon and Mrs. Henry Wood, Collins often used the figure of the fallen woman as a means to discuss Victorian issues of sexuality, morality, and love. Although Collins wrote twenty-seven novels and over fifty short stories, he is best remembered for his most famous novels written in the 1860s: *The Woman in White* (1860), *Armadale* (1866), and *The Moonstone* (1868). Collins continued to address issues of female sexuality and morality throughout his works.

Collins's *The Woman in White* was an immediate success with his readers because of its intricate plot and fairytale-like ending. The novel centers around the middle-class hero Walter Hartright's love for the upper-class Laura Fairlie, a woman betrothed to Sir Percival Glyde, who has squandered his fortunes and is relying on his marriage to Laura to resolve his financial difficulties. Glyde devises a plan whereby he switches Laura's identity with Anne Catherick, a woman who resembles Laura and who had been imprisoned in a mental hospital in London. When Anne dies, disguised as Laura, Hartright solves the mystery that Anne is the illegitimate daughter of Laura's father (hence the resemblance), and manages to rescue Laura and subsequently marries her after Glyde dies in a church fire, in which he was trying to burn the evidence that he was also an illegitimate child. The novel's plot is certainly complex, as is Collins's approach to Victorian issues of sexuality and love. While Collins does not portray any explicit seduction scenes, the novel does contain two illegitimate births, which underline the Victorian concern with sexuality. Although Collins acknowledged illegitimate children within the upper-class and aristocracy, he also emphasizes the social need to hide such sexual indiscretions. Thus, Glyde must destroy the church's register entry to bury the truth regarding his parents' premarital conception, and Anne is concealed in the asylum to protect Laura's father's memory and the family honor. However, the disclosure of Laura's family allows her and Hartright to marry because

Undated portrait of Wilkie Collins.
Courtesy of the Library of Congress.

they are finally on the same level socially. Although sexual acts and sexuality are not overt in the text, they certainly lie just beneath the surface as part of the novel's subtext.

Although Collins reused the mistaken or switched identity in several other of his most well-known novels, it was in some of his slightly less popular novels that he continued to explore the issue of illegitimacy and female sexuality. In *No Name* (1862), sisters Norah and Magdalen Vanstone are declared illegitimate after both their parents die shortly after they were married and before their father could change his will. Unlike the characters in *The Woman in White*, the girls do not try to hide their illegitimacy; instead Magdalen tries to find ways to regain her father's fortune, which had instead gone to his brother. Part of the acceptance of their illegitimacy is attributed to their new position in the lower class, whereby illegitimacy seems to be more acceptable. When Mr. and Mrs. Vanstone were alive and the family was part of the middle class, they saw the need to marry to justify the girls' social positions, again suggesting that the concern with legitimacy was more of a middle- and upper-class issue than a lower-class one.

Beyond addressing the issue of illegitimacy, the novel also engages with issues of female sexuality and power. Determined to regain her rightful inheritance, Magdalen decides to marry her feeble-minded cousin Noel who now possesses the money after his own father's death. Magdalen disguises herself as another woman (Susan Bygrave) and seduces Noel into marrying her. Effectively she transfers her sexuality into power in order to regain her inheritance, which, while initially successful, fails her when Noel learns her true identity and changes his will. Ultimately, Magdalen's misuse of her femininity backfires, and she never regains her father's money; instead, her sister Norah, who maintains her female innocence, marries George Bartram who has since inherited the money. Despite her actions, Magdalen then marries the middle-class Captain Kirke, thereby being readmitted into society through marriage and obtaining forgiveness for her abuse of her sexuality.

In some of his later novels, Collins was more explicit with regard to female sexuality and female scheming. *Armadale*, one of Collins's best-known works, deals with a complex plot of double and mistaken identities, which centers on an inheritance belonging to one of two Allan Armadales. Within the novel, there is also another plot dealing with Lydia Gwilt, one of Collins's most violent fallen women. Lydia was married to an Englishman named Waldron, but poisoned him when he began to suspect her of having an affair with Captain Manuel. Thus, Lydia is not only a fallen woman through her adulterous act, but also a murderess, which is subsequently covered up and she only serves two years in prison. Moreover, she commits bigamy when she marries Manuel after Waldron's death, another example of her transgression from acceptable female behavior.

Many years later, Lydia schemes to gain Armadale's inheritance by marrying him. When she learns this is not possible, she contrives to marry Midwinter, who was also born Allan Armadale and whom she loves, and then plans various ways for the first Armadale to die so that she can claim his money as being married to an Allan Armadale. In one of her attempts to kill Armadale, she accidentally poisons Midwinter with a deadly gas. While he survives, she leaves a written confession for him and then commits suicide. Although Lydia confesses to all her transgressions, Midwinter keeps them secret, maintaining her death was accidental. Thus, although she has transcended the gender boundaries of society and used her sexuality for malicious purposes, she escapes condemnation because of her suicide and Midwinter's cover-up. Again, Collins allows his fallen woman to escape social punishment, suggesting a sympathetic view of Lydia's actions and motivations.

Collins's sympathetic approach toward a sexualized female continued through his career, although his later novels became more contrived in his attempts to achieve this sympathy. In one of his last books, *The Evil Genius* (1886), Collins presents the reader with a fallen woman who does not need forgiveness from society, but rather transcends the triviality of society. Sydney Westerfield becomes governess for Kitty, the only daughter of Herbert and Catherine Linley. Inevitably, in a Collins's novel, Herbert and Sydney fall in love. Unable to deal with this marital infidelity, Catherine leaves her home with her mother and Kitty to flee to Scotland where she obtains a divorce. Kitty, however, is miserable because she is told her father is dead and the other children are not allowed to play with the child of divorced parents. Kitty's isolation demonstrates that while women could obtain divorces, the social effect of doing so was damaging to the entire family, indicating the importance of sexual fidelity in the Victorian period.

The only way to remedy this social transgression is for Catherine to remarry her original husband, which she does. Herbert and Catherine are reunited, and Sydney leaves the family by choice, suggesting she has chosen a more moral path than Herbert by leaving him. The novel ends with Sydney being employed by Captain Bennydeck, and the suggestion that they will marry. Again, Collins forgives his fallen woman and allows her to return to society. In the same way, Catherine, also a fallen woman because of her divorce, returns to society through her remarriage to Herbert. Although the novel's ending is contrived, it does emphasize Collins's sympathetic approach to the fallen woman.

Collins's forgiveness of misguided female sexuality and fallen women reoccurs throughout his novels; this attitude of forgiveness differed significantly from the opinions of most other Victorians. Sue Lonoff reasons that Collins's attitude was so different because he lived with a woman whom he never married, making him more sympathetic to the fallen woman (Lonoff 1980, 152). Collins's sympathy for the fallen woman can be traced back to his earliest novels, before other writers had dared to demonstrate the same compassion. Collins challenged views of female sexuality to demonstrate that forgiveness rather than exclusion was a more compassionate and civilized way to understand the sexualized woman.

Further Reading: Baker, William, Andrew Gasson, Graham Law, and Paul Lewis, ed. *The Public Face of Wilkie Collins: The Collected Letters.* London: Pickering & Chatto, 2005; Lonoff, Sue. *Wilkie Collins and His Victorian Readers: A Study in the Rhetoric of Authorship.* New York: AMS Press, 1980; Peters, Caroline. *The King of Inventors: A Life of Wilkie Collins.* London: Secher & Warburg, 1991; Taylor, Jenny Bourne. *In the Secret Theatre of Home: Wilkie Collins, Sensation Narrative and Nineteenth-Century Psychology.* London and New York: Routledge, 1988.

Amanda M. Caleb

COMIC OPERA. *See* Gilbert and Sullivan (Comic Opera)

COMSTOCK, ANTHONY (1844–1915). Anthony Comstock was an American antivice reformer. He was born in New Canaan, Connecticut, to farmers Thomas Anthony Comstock and Polly Lockwood. After an older brother died at Gettysburg, Comstock joined the Union Army to replace him. Discharged in 1865, Comstock moved to New York City to work as a dry goods clerk. Married to Margaret Hamilton, they had a child who died in infancy and later adopted a daughter.

Comstock had always been deeply offended by the tolerance of vice in American society. Army life had dismayed him as he watched officers tolerate lewd behavior among the troops, and living in New York City exposed Comstock to a full range of illicit and immoral activities. Incensed at the inability or unwillingness of government authorities to curb vice, he made it his mission to expose and root out evil.

Comstock argued that vice sapped the strength of the next generation, making it vulnerable to subversion by foreign immigrants who were flooding into the United States. Working with the Young Men's Christian Association, Comstock pushed New York City officials to enforce obscenity laws. One of his favorite tactics involved entrapping lawbreakers and turning them over to the police. A persuasive and self-righteous man, Comstock won the support of several wealthy benefactors who helped him establish the New York Society for the Suppression of Vice. Comstock served as secretary and principal investor of the society for the remainder of his life. In 1872, the society successfully lobbied Congress to pass the Act of the Suppression of Trade in, and Circulation of, Obscene Literature and Articles of Immoral Use, commonly known as the "Comstock Law." The U.S. Post Office appointed Comstock as a special agent to capture violators of the act. He remained in this post until his death.

Comstock took full advantage of his power. He targeted free love, illegitimate pregnancy, contraception, pornography, gambling, dime novels, and the performing arts. He prosecuted women's rights reformer, **Victoria Woodhull**, for publishing accounts of Rev. Henry Ward Beecher's adultery. He tried to block the performance in 1905 in New York of George Bernard Shaw's play about **prostitution**, *Mrs. Warren's Profession*. He sent socialist Emma Goldman to jail on several occasions for publicizing **birth control** methods, and would have imprisoned Planned Parenthood founder Margaret Sanger had she not gone into exile to avoid trial. In 1906, he arrested a bookkeeper and confiscated more than a thousand copies of the New York Art Students League catalog, which included several nude pictures. The Comstock Law represented a significant extension of government power in regulating the sexual beliefs and practices of Americans. It remained on the books long after Comstock died.

Further Reading: Beisel, Nicola. *Imperiled Innocents: Anthony Comstock and Family Reproduction in Victorian America*. Princeton, NJ: Princeton University Press, 1997; D'Emilio, John and Estelle B. Freedman. *Intimate Matters: A History of Sexuality in America*. New York: Harper and Row, 1988; Pivar, David. *Purity Crusade: Sexual Morality and Social Control, 1868–1900*. Westport, CT: Greenwood Press, 1973.

Caryn E. Neumann

CONTAGIOUS DISEASES ACTS. The first Contagious Diseases (CD) Act was passed by the British Parliament in 1864, and was amended and extended by the acts of 1866 and 1869. These acts allowed the police to detain any woman suspected of **prostitution** in fourteen naval and military towns, to examine her for venereal disease (VD), and to detain her in a certified hospital if found to be infected.

The spread of VD among enlisted men had long been a cause for concern; the Royal Commission on the Health of the Army in 1857 had recommended the creation of an army statistical department, which found that one in three sick cases in the army in 1864 were venereal in origin. VD was unusually prevalent in some of the port and garrison towns, most notably Plymouth and Portsmouth. Previous efforts to contain the disease had included periodic genital examination of soldiers, but the Commission

"Prostitutes wait for police doctor to be checked for venereal disease," by Christian Krohg, 1885–87. © The Granger Collection.

argued for its discontinuance on the grounds that it destroyed their self-respect and was not medically valuable. As Judith Walkowitz shows in her magisterial study of the acts, these reports and statistics threw fuel on the flames of a growing demand for regulation as the means of improving public health, stimulated by the ideas of influential writers like W. R. Greg and **William Acton**. Greg, in particular, argued that male sexual promiscuity was natural, and given delayed marriage, that prostitution was inevitable and unavoidable. The attendant hazards of VD meant that sanitary supervision of prostitutes was essential, even at the cost of their personal liberty. If the police were empowered to shoot a plague-ridden sufferer who broke through a cordon sanitaire, Greg argued, then they were also justified in detaining a syphilitic prostitute who "if not arrested, would spread infection all around her" (Walkowitz 1980, 44). Acton concurred in his 1857 treatise on prostitution, and rationalized the double standard and sexual exploitation of poor women by arguing that regulation would improve their health and living standards. By contrast, a committee set up by Florence Nightingale in 1862 to enquire into VD in the military, decided against regulation, and instead advocated improved sanitary conditions in barracks and the provision of "healthy, innocent and manly occupations."

The regulationists won the argument in Parliament. The first act in 1864, which was limited for three years, applied to eleven garrison and dock towns in southern England and Ireland, and empowered plainclothes members of the metropolitan police stationed in those towns to identify women who might be diseased prostitutes. The women were subjected to an internal cervical examination, either voluntarily or on the orders of a magistrate, and, if found to be suffering from a VD, were forcibly detained in a lock hospital for up to three months. Public opposition to this act was limited, emboldening its supporters, who argued for the act's extension on the grounds that prostitutes were easily able to escape from the regulated districts. A second act in 1866 increased the number of districts and introduced compulsory fortnightly examination of all known or presumed prostitutes, whose activities were to be closely monitored by a "well-organized system of medical police." Thus the acts introduced an overt system of control, which enshrined the double standard in **law**, and punished the woman alone for a situation that was often forced on her, as it was not on her male client, by economic necessity.

The supporters of the acts, who included aristocrats, local authorities, Anglican clergy and many doctors in addition to the police and military, campaigned to extend them even further, in order to form a regulatory system for the entire civilian population. The Simon Report (1868), however, argued conclusively that this would be too costly and impossible to enforce in large cities like London. The report could not, in any case, find evidence that the incidence of VD among the poor was as high as the campaigners claimed. The final extension of the CD Acts in 1869 was confined to increasing the number of military and naval districts; it also imposed a maximum of nine months detention in hospital. This act was to apply indefinitely.

There is little doubt that the vast majority of upper- and middle-class public opinion in 1869 was in full support of the acts. The "sanitary" arguments had been forcefully made and the acts affected the civil liberties of a class of women whom many believed were dissolute and depraved rather than desperate. The repeal of the acts was entirely the result of a courageous campaign that was dominated by **Josephine Butler**, who became the secretary of the newly formed Ladies National Association for Repeal of the Contagious Diseases Acts (LNA) in 1869. Butler had been taught by her evangelical father to hate the **white slavery** of prostitution and procurement, and had cared for needy prostitutes at her homes in Oxford and Liverpool. She believed that the CD Acts were "a deadly poison working through the wholesale, systematic, and now legalized, degradation of women." Her charismatic leadership, complete conviction, and devotion to the cause drove a campaign of pamphlet and letter writing, parliamentary lobbying, petition gathering, and nationwide speaking. Courage was needed, since convention decreed that it was unacceptable for a respectable woman to speak publicly on such a taboo subject. Having spoken to many of the victims of the acts, Butler became increasingly explicit and impassioned on the subject of the "instrumental rape" they had endured. The campaign aroused male hostility to the extent of putting her and fellow campaigners in physical danger at times, for example, at the Pontefract byelection in 1872.

A parallel men's campaign against the acts received support, in particular, from nonconformists and groups of working men. Repeal bills were regularly introduced by supportive parliamentarians from 1870 onward, and a Royal Commission was set up in 1871 to examine the operation of the acts that enlightened many MPs to their pernicious effects. James Stansfeld MP took over the leadership of the repeal campaign within Parliament in 1874, and was the chief architect of its increasing political success. By 1880, the tide had turned, with the election of a number of new Radical MPs opposed to the acts. Parliament voted to end the compulsory examination of women under the acts in 1883, and in 1886, the CD Acts were finally repealed.

The campaign against the CD Acts had significance far beyond this success. It politicized a generation of female campaigners, who went on to fight against the double standard in all its forms with the aim of creating sexual relations of equality between women and men. This was to be the most important ambition of British feminists in the period 1880–1910. Josephine Butler herself formed the British and Continental Federation for the Abolition of Government Regulation of Prostitution in 1875, and traveled regularly to the continent to protest about government complicity in prostitution through state brothels and the regulatory police. She exposed the traffic in young girls from England to Belgium in 1880, and was deeply involved in W. T. Stead's hard-hitting campaign against **child prostitution** in London in 1885. She challenged CD Acts in India that were repealed in 1895. Opponents of the CD Acts were foremost among those who campaigned to raise the age of consent from thirteen, and many also supported the "Purity" movement, although Butler herself rejected its methods. The CD Acts not only sparked nationwide resistance to the double standard, but provoked a feminist/civil libertarian debate on prostitution, women's rights, and sexual equality which continued into the twentieth century.

Further Reading: Bland, Lucy. *Banishing the Beast: English Feminism and Sexual Morality 1885–1914*. Harmondsworth: Penguin, 1995; Butler, Josephine E. *Personal Reminiscences of a Great Crusade*. London: Horace Marshall and Son, 1896; Jordan, Jane. *Josephine Butler*. London: John Murray, 2001; Walkowitz, Judith. *Prostitution and Victorian Society: Women, Class and the State*. Cambridge, MA: Cambridge University Press, 1980.

Helen Mathers

COURTSHIP. Unlike some countries in continental Europe, courtship in Britain and North America was not much impeded by chaperonage in the nineteenth century. Although some British heiresses were chaperoned very strictly in the earlier part of the century, the practice did not descend far down the social scale, and was considered old-fashioned by the 1880s. Amongst middle-class families, opportunities for young men and women to be alone together were limited, but could be contrived without too much difficulty. Middle-class couples did not ordinarily indulge in premarital sexual activity, but there is considerable evidence of growing physical intimacy as attachments deepened.

Undoubtedly, one of the main reasons for the great popularity of balls and musical evenings were the opportunities that these events provided for young men and women to mingle and converse without being overheard by their families. Although the advantages of dancing was obvious, given the opportunities for decorous physical contact in a crowded setting, even playing the piano in a quiet family evening could give rise to courtship opportunities. Young men with no previous demonstrable interest in music would eagerly volunteer to turn the pages if an attractive young woman were playing, because it allowed them to talk privately under cover of the music. Serious courtship was conducted openly, and by the point at which the father's consent was asked, the request to sanction an engagement would have surprised no one. Many of the novels of **Anthony Trollope** chronicle mid-Victorian courtship mores in meticulous detail. Some contemporary reviewers dismissed Trollope as an artist, because they believed his novels were too faithful to life to be interesting.

Engagements were ordinarily very short among those affluent enough to contemplate the expenses of a new household, often lasting only a month or two as wedding clothes were prepared and a house was furnished. The very wealthy also used this time to agree settlements on the future bride, to ensure her and her children's financial independence in case the husband died, or squandered his money. Less wealthy middle-class couples sometimes endured very long engagements, because of a belief that the husband should be able to offer his bride the same level of comfort as she had enjoyed in her father's home. There was also the thought that an unlimited number of children might arrive, and many fathers were unwilling to sanction an engagement until the man's income reached a certain level.

Among the working class, opportunities for courtship were both freer and more constrained. Women working as domestic **servants**, as a very high proportion of young unmarried woman did, would find almost no opportunities to get to know young marriageable men. Most were general servants, and worked alone with no male servants in the household. They were likely to have more contact with the men who delivered groceries or came to carry out work on the house, than with any others. Evidently, if the family for whom they worked included men, there might be seduction, but no courtship in the true sense, as he would never have contemplated marriage to a social inferior, whatever might have been promised in a moment of passion. Young men apprenticed to trades were commonly prohibited from marrying until the seven-year apprenticeship was complete.

On the other hand, factory workers and semiskilled working-class laborers had almost complete freedom in terms of courtship. Because of their limited homes, much courting was carried on in the street, in groups of young men and women "chaffing" each other. Middle-class observers misinterpreted this horseplay as shocking licentiousness, but most urban women seem to have strictly rationed their physical favors before marriage. The illegitimacy rates were far lower in London than in the countryside.

Courtships between working-class couples tended to be long, with well-established phases: "paying attentions," "walking out," and finally the promise of marriage. Working-class women were careful to introduce suitors to family and friends when available, as part of testing and confirming the seriousness of the young man's intentions. Engagements among the respectable poor could be very long, with both parties saving money for the household that they would establish. **Pregnancy** would result in a hasty marriage, and most **illegitimacy** seems to have been the result of a courtship gone wrong, and ending before its natural termination in marriage.

Further Reading: Barret-Ducrocq, Francoise. *Love in the Time of Victoria*. Harmondsworth: Penguin, 1992.

Susan Mumm

D

DANCE/DANCES. The history of social dancing in the nineteenth century reflects the enormous social changes that took place in an era of rapid industrialization and urbanization. At the beginning of the century, dancing took place predominantly within family and friendship networks. Group dances, such as the quadrille, with its complex dance steps and formalized and gendered social obligations (such as the bow at the start and end of a set, and the man taking the lead), were the most widespread form of dance in both Britain and America. By the end of the century, urbanization had created a thriving leisure industry with commercial dance halls (United States) and dancing rooms (United Kingdom) proliferating in cities across the United States and Great Britain. These provided public spaces for young, urban working-class men and women to socialize and dance to the sounds of the new ragtime music, such as Scott Joplin's hugely popular *Maple Leaf Rag* (1899). Although family, friendship, and cultural groups could and did hire halls for their own dances, the public halls enabled greater hetero and homosocialization between men and women outside these networks.

One of the key turning points in the social history of dancing came with the introduction of the waltz from Europe in the early decades of the century. It was considered scandalous, and attracted considerable comment owing to the unprecedented physical intimacy it permitted the dancing couple. From the mid-century, the waltz and its variations took over the ballroom. Dance manuals that targeted the emerging middle classes of Britain and America provided guides to social as well as dance etiquette. The manuals stressed that social graces and good breeding could be learned and showcased on the dance floor. Rules for acceptable behavior, dress, conversation, and complex codes of handkerchief, glove, fan, and parasol flirtation directed men and women on the art of "gentility" and heterosexual courtship: "young gentlemen are earnestly advised not to limit their conversation to remarks on the weather and the heat of the room" (Aldrich 1991, 102). The shift to "round dancing" in preference to group dancing represented a significant shift in cultural attitudes to social interaction between men and women, and was one of the key themes of antidance treatises, like Thomas Faulkner's *From the Ballroom to Hell* (1892), which emphasized (in lurid detail) the moral dangers of the waltz to young women: "her face is upturned, her bare arm is almost around his neck, her partly nude swelling breast heaves tumultuously against his, face to face they whirl on . . ." (Faulkner, 15). Antidance literature condemned dancing as detrimental to physical and moral health, as unchristian, and with the rise of commercial dance halls, as a waste of money. Scholars have noted that, as with many of the social reform movements of the

"Dancers at a ball," illustrated cover of *Jullien's Original Mazurka*, dedicated to Monsieur E. Coulon. © The Art Archive/Private Collection.

nineteenth century (temperance, anti**prostitution**), much of this surveillance was directed by the middle class at the working class—a trend that peaked in the dance-hall reform movement of progressive-era America (c. 1890–1914).

Indeed, much of what we know about the dance halls and the way they functioned as spaces for the urban working-class women (the majority of attendees were women aged between fifteen and twenty-one) and men to socialize and form sexual and/or romantic liaisons, is gathered from the reports of the dance-hall reformers or the eye-witness accounts of middle-class men "slumming" in red-light districts, such as the bowery in New York or Soho in London. For this reason, it is difficult to know the degree to which the descriptions of sexual liaisons, **prostitution**, **alcohol** consumption, and criminality, reflect the reality of dance-hall culture, or are themselves the products of middle-class anxieties about **race**, gender, and class. For example, contemporary "slummers" accounts of women who frequented the dance halls and pleasure gardens (United Kingdom) describe them as prostitutes, but as Kathy Peiss has argued, for urban working-class women, the dance halls provided the public spaces for their expression of a distinct sexual style. In one particularly fascinating account uncovered by historian George Chauncey for his groundbreaking book, *Gay New York*, a medical student visiting the bowery in 1890 relates how he was invited to a ball at Walhalla Hall on the Lower East Side, where he "discovered some five hundred same-sex male and female couples in attendance, 'waltzing sedately to the music of a good band'" (Chauncey 1994, 40–1). While the scholarship of Chauncey and Peiss has shed much needed light on the urban working-class and gay cultures of New York at the end of the nineteenth century, the social history of dance in broader urban and regional contexts remains to be written. Undoubtedly, future research will address this gap in the scholarship of nineteenth-century social life.

Further Reading: Aldrich, Elizabeth. *From the Ballroom to Hell: Grace and Folly in Nineteenth-Century Dance*. Evanston, IL: Northwestern University Press, 1991; Chauncey, George. *Gay New York*. New York: Basic Books, 1994; D'Emilio, John and Estelle B. Freedman. *Intimate Matters: A History of Sexuality in America*. New York: Harper & Row, 1988; Faulkner, Thomas A. *From the Ballroom to Hell*. Chicago: Henry Publishing Co., 1894; Koven, Seth. *Slumming: Sexual and Social Politics in Victorian London*. Princeton, NJ: Princeton University Press, 2004; Library of Congress Western Social Dance Collection http://memory.loc.gov/ammem/dihtml/; Peiss, Kathy Lee. *Cheap Amusements: Working Women and Leisure in Turn-of-the-Century New York*. Philadelphia: Temple University Press, 1986; Perry, Elisabeth I. "'The General Motherhood of the Commonwealth': Dance Hall Reform in the Progressive Era." *American Quarterly* 37, no. 5 (1985): 719–33; Schneider, Gretchen. "Using Nineteenth-Century American Social Dance Manuals." *Dance Research Journal* 14, no. 1/2 (1981–1982): 39–42; Victorian London website: http://www.victorianlondon.org/.

Sally Newman

DIVORCE. It was in the nineteenth century that most European and North American countries began their gradual relaxation of the **law**s governing divorce, although access to divorce as a solution to marital unhappiness was still very much restricted by the century's end.

In England, the law governing divorce was still largely that of the pre-Reformation church. Marriage was indissoluble, and only those who were both rich and powerful could divorce through a complex process involving the ecclesiastical courts and individual acts of Parliament. This meant that, by 1800, it was easier to get married in Britain and harder to divorce than in almost any other country. By the end of the century, England's divorce rate was the lowest in Europe, but it had the highest rate of legal separation, providing a vital safety valve for the unhappily married. Over the nineteenth century, a number of American states relaxed their laws regarding divorce, largely to discourage a growing trend toward illegal self-divorce. However, the American picture varied enormously from state to state. For example, it was almost impossible to divorce in New York State, and relatively easy in Indiana, while Virginia retained English common law practices. Although "fault" (normally adultery or extreme cruelty) remained central in the causes for divorce in the nineteenth century, and the numbers involved were very small, enormous public anxiety about the dangers of a growing divorce rate was expressed on both sides of the Atlantic.

When it came to divorce, Scotland was remarkably even-handed. It was probably the most liberal divorce law in Europe in the nineteenth century, except for 1792–1794 in revolutionary France, when ill-treatment and incompatibility were briefly recognized as causes, before divorce itself was abolished. In Scotland, divorce was allowed to both men and women on the grounds of adultery or desertion. However, collusion to obtain a divorce was prohibited. Women were not required to cite more causes than men, unlike England, and both sexes sought divorces in roughly equal proportions. Marriage was not considered to be a sacrament in presbyterian theology, and thus was regarded much more like a contract, which could be voided if the parties failed to fulfill it. The liberality of Scottish divorce law, which allowed divorce after forty days' residence, meant that, early in the nineteenth century, a number of unhappy English couples were tempted to divorce there. The Lolly case of 1811 changed this, when English judges decided that those who remarried in England after a Scottish divorce were guilty of **bigamy**, thus rendering Scottish divorces invalid for English subjects. (William Lolly, the unfortunate defendant in the test case, was sentenced to seven years transportation, although later pardoned.)

As only the very rich could end their marriages in a way that allowed legal remarriage, working-class people evolved a complex understanding of what marriage meant, including a kind of self-divorce. The most notorious form of self-divorce was wife sale, whereby a husband would "sell" his wife in the marketplace, ordinarily with her consent, to her lover or another man to whom she was willing to entrust herself. Although wife sale was obviously invalid in law, there was widespread belief in its efficacy, and both parties might remarry in ignorant confidence in their parish church. Because of this, a number of cases went to trial for bigamy, and the resulting legal proceedings provide evidence of the practice, which had virtually vanished by the 1890s. Far more working-class couples simply agreed to part, and some considered this binding enough to justify remarriage, again resulting in unintentional bigamy.

In England and Wales, the elaborate and expensive system of ecclesiastical separation followed by parliamentary divorce was ended in 1857, with the passage of the Matrimonial Causes (Divorce) Act. The act was opposed by many, who argued that men, thought to be naturally promiscuous, would use it excessively, removing support from their wives and children. It was claimed at the time that the new act would end the injustice in the rich having a legal remedy for marital breakdown that was closed to the poor, but the new act still required expensive legal action. The number of actions grew only slowly, and the poor could not take advantage of it. Under the Divorce act, the ecclesiastical court's role in divorce was ended, and men could divorce their wives for adultery alone. Wives had to prove adultery and another offence, such as cruelty or bigamy, in order to divorce their husbands, thus continuing to enshrine the sexual double standard in law.

Legal separation, either by a judicial or private contract of separation, became an increasingly popular alternative to divorce in England, and were employed by all social classes from professionals down to laborers. Cruelty, desertion, or adultery were the most common reasons, and applied equally to both sexes, although the relevant laws were revised to make them easier to prove as time passed. Formal separation, although it did not allow either party to remarry, did return women to the status of a single woman (*feme sole*), with control over her earnings and the right to live unmolested by her husband. This made legally separated wives "the first English wives to be legally fully independent persons—and the only ones until well after the Second World War" (Anderson 1999, 199). Separation meant that men were freed of the responsibility of their wife's debts. Alimony was normally awarded to the wife, based on a percentage of her husband's earnings. After 1873, when a father's automatic right to the children was abolished, child custody was agreed on a case-by-case basis in the separation contract itself, with an increasing tendency to leave young children with their mother as the century progressed. In 1884, further changes to the law meant that women without a formal separation contract could no longer be imprisoned by their husbands to compel them to resume cohabitation.

The Christian religion remained absolutely opposed to divorce throughout the century (*see* **Christianity**). Although a few denominations reluctantly permitted it on the grounds of adultery, none permitted divorced persons to remarry with the blessing of the church. Some Roman Catholics could seek an annulment, taking advantage of the wide range of conditions which could render a marriage invalid in canon law, but Protestants found declarations of nonvalidity much more difficult to obtain. Most Christians seem to have regarded marriage as a sacrament during this period, and saw the physical union of man and wife as spiritually indissoluble, meaning that a second marriage would be nothing more than adultery.

Those who decided to divorce normally faced considerable social punishment for their actions. While the very wealthy would find their social circles relatively unperturbed by divorce, the middle classes considered divorce extremely scandalous. Divorce could ruin a professional man's business, and middle-class women, who divorced, often passed themselves off as widows, to avoid being outcasts. A divorced woman had to behave with extreme decorum over a long period in order to gradually re-enter respectable society, and some doors would remain permanently shut to her. Women who were divorced on the grounds of their own adultery were often permanently excluded from society, although attitudes toward the "innocent party" became much more sympathetic as the century progressed. The children of divorced people were often considered as somehow tainted by their parent's behavior, and found it difficult to be accepted as acceptable marriage material by the families of their intended partners.

At the beginning of the century, women had no legal rights to the custody of their children, and their love for their children was a major motive for staying in an otherwise intolerable marriage. As time passed, determined campaigning gradually softened this stand. At first, women who were not divorced for adultery were allowed to keep infants, and gradually older children as well. However, women who divorced for adultery found it far harder to obtain custody of children, and were normally even prohibited from seeing them. Men's adultery made no difference in determining custody.

Overall, it is possible to detect a gradual relaxation of attitudes toward divorce over the course of the nineteenth century. However, this was not the result of social liberalization or of any desire to see people being able to freely end their marriages, but rather a desire to restrict self-divorce and a pressing need to remodel obsolete legal forms. As the change occurs, it is possible to identify a shift in the view of marriage as well—from an indissoluble sacrament and an unalterable status to a contract between freely consenting adults, which could be terminated in extreme circumstances.

Further Reading: Anderson, Olive. "State, Civil Society and Separation in Victorian Britain." *Past and Present* 163 (1999): 161–201; Leneman, Leah. "A Natural Foundation in Equity: Marriage and Divorce in Eighteenth and Nineteenth Century Scotland." *Scottish Economic & Social History* 20 (2000): 199–215; Phillips, Roderick. *Putting Asunder: A History of Divorce in Western Society.* Cambridge, MA: Cambridge University Press, 1988; Stone, Lawrence. *Road to Divorce: England 1530–1987.* Oxford: Oxford University Press, 1992; Thompson, E. P. "The Sale of Wives." In *Customs in Common.* New York: New Press, 1991, 404–66.

Ian Merrilees

DOMESTIC VIOLENCE. The phrase, domestic violence, is a modern term that describes violence or aggression, physical or psychological, enacted by one member of a family against another. It can be husband toward wife, parent toward child, or child against elder. In the nineteenth century, there were no commonly accepted understandings of the rights of women and children. Wives and offspring, in the strict legal sense, were chattel or property, and as such could be traded, sold, or abused without consequence. Slaves, **servants**, and prostitutes were often in a similar situation, with violence and abuse being a part of their daily lives. While the infamous "rule of thumb," which allowed a man to beat his wife with a stick no thicker than the circumference of his thumb is a legal fiction, many Victorians believed it to be one of the rights men enjoyed over their wives.

Regardless of the etymology of "rule of thumb," wife beating did exist, despite legislative attempts to curtail the practice. As early as the seventeenth century, documents from the Massachusetts Bay Colony stated that "no man shall strike his wife.... on penalty of such fine not exceeding ten pounds for one offense." In Maryland, in 1882, the punishment for spousal beating was forty lashes at the whipping post.

Some of the most sordid narratives regarding domestic violence can be found in the literature of the nineteenth century. In Charles Dickens's (1812–1870) *Oliver Twist*, the panorama of poverty and the working classes is dramatized through the story of Nancy, the mistress of a criminal, who is beaten and finally murdered by her lover. George Eliot's (1819–1880) novella, *Janet's Repentence*, focuses on the abuse of a lawyer's wife. Elizabeth Cleghorn Gaskell's (1810–1865) writings about the abuse that prostitutes and young women suffered was instrumental in **Josephine Butler**'s campaign to eradicate the survival problems of lower-class women. Thomas Hardy's *The Mayor of Casterbridge* (1886) begins with a drunken man who sells his wife to another man in a drinking house. The great publicist of nonfictional domestic violence was Frances

Power Cobbe, whose "Wife Torture in England" (1878) created a public scandal, and eventually led to changes in the **law**. Court records document those extreme cases that the authorities decided to prosecute, but then, as today, many cases of battering were never reported; hence, there is no way of knowing the actual extent of abuse.

More importantly, husbands, fathers, and male relatives believed that they had a right to "chastise" their wives and children by physical means. It appears that often, their wives agreed, as much as they might lament it. The origin of this belief comes from a variety of biblical sources, both in the Old and New Testaments. As a source of behavioral modeling and comportment, the Bible dictated gender relationships by naming the man as the head of the household. Statements, such as "submit yourself unto your husband," "the husband is the head of the wife," or "the husband shall rule over the wife," were claimed to justify men abusing their wives. Women were regarded as children or possessions, and expected to "mind" and "behave." Marriage vows subtly enforced this biased attitude, and used the word "obey" in the woman's pledge but not in the man's. In France, certain parts of the Civil Code conformed to a belief in woman's connection to sex and sin, derived from the creation myth and Eve's disobedience. According to one source, Napoleon wanted certain portions of this code to be read by women during marriage ceremonies so that they remained aware of their inferiority and the requirement that they be submissive to their husbands.

In England, a husband could beat his wife and hold her prisoner, provided he did so without cruelty. It is difficult to understand how this could be done without cruelty, but this right to imprisonment remained law until the 1890s. Since divorce was extremely uncommon, economic circumstances forced unhappy marriages to remain undissolved. During the lifetime of a marriage, conflicts could escalate to the point that "till death do us part" meant murder instead of death by natural cause, although wife murder usually led to prosecution, even if not conviction.

The reasons for marital violence were varied, and although poverty added to the stresses of family life, the upper classes were not immune. The apparent preponderance of domestic violence in the lower classes was because their lives were more transparent. They did not have the means to protect their privacy from public scrutiny and documentation.

It was not until 1878 that the English Parliament passed a law that allowed women to petition the courts for separation on grounds of assault. However, in the nineteenth century, there were few options available for women to survive without the support of a husband. Furthermore, if a woman had an income, her husband could request, through a judge, that it be garnished. No proof was necessary.

Sexual relations in marriage were likewise unbalanced. A man could use violence to force his wife to perform her conjugal duty. There was no such thing as rape in marriage as long as a man used force for what was defined as normal. A woman's infidelity in marriage threatened reproductive bloodlines and future distribution of property, if she produced a child from that union. A man's adultery was tacitly acceptable as long as he kept his mistress away from the home he shared with his wife. However, in France, if a man caught his wife in a sexual act and killed her and her partner, he was excused under the "red article" of the French Penal Code.

Some critics of gender inequality, such as Frances Power Cobbe, assumed that wife beating, wife torture, and wife murder did not occur in the upper classes, but J. W. Kaye pointed out that educated and refined men expressed their disregard for women in different ways.

The nineteenth century was an important time for changes in gender relationships within marriage. By the turn of the century, the nature of marriage was beginning to evolve from patriarchy to a more companionate character. Those changes advanced, aided by the entry of women into the labor force during World War I, and women's gradual political enfranchisement. Although domestic violence did not disappear, women's voices were given more agency, as their public presence was validated.

Further Reading: Arnaud-Duc, Nicole. "The Law's Contradictions." In *A History of Women: Emerging Feminism from Revolution to World War*, edited by G. Duby and M. Perot. Cambridge: Belknap Press, 1995; Bauer, Carol and Lawrence Ritt, "'A Husband Is a Beating Animal:' Frances Power Cobbe Confronts the Wife-Abuse Problem in Victorian England." *International Journal of Women's Studies* 99, no. 102 (1983): 99–118; Hammerton, A. James. *Cruelty and Companionship: Conflict in Nineteenth Century Married Life*. Oxford: Oxford University Press, 1992; Lawson, Kate and Lynn Shakinovsky. "Violence, Causality and the 'Shock of History.'" In *The Marked Body: Domestic Violence in Mid-Nineteenth-Century Literature*. Albany: SUNY, 2002.

Lana Thompson

E

ELLIS, HAVELOCK (1859–1939). Henry Havelock Ellis is remembered as the author of the seven-volume *Studies in the Psychology of Sex* (1897–1928), in which he studied almost all sexual "perversions" from **homosexuality** to transvestism to urolagnia, although he did not address paedophilia or klismaphila. His other contributions to the intellectual life of Britain in the modernist period include translations of various new scientific texts from German, Italian, and French, gathered together with a host of British texts and published in the widely selling *Contemporary Science Series*, which he edited for the Walter Scott Press. Some of his works include a translated book of Spanish poetry; a reprinted scholarly series of Elizabethan dramatists; a novel (and a translation of Emile Zola's Germinal); introductions to scores of literary and scholarly texts, from J. K. Huysmans's *A Rebours* to Bronislaw Malinowski's *The Sexual Lives of Savages*; reviews and original contributions to the *Journal of Mental Science* and other scientific periodicals; and literally hundreds of essays on topics as varied as the philosophy of Friedrich Nietzsche and the woman question. In other words, he was a dedicated polymath. Ellis's project was not, however, a disparate one. From his early involvement with a proto-Fabian movement, the Fellowship of the New Life, Ellis attempted to better society through education, and remained committed to the belief that if people had access to knowledge, they would be in a position to liberate themselves from the social control of religious dogma. It was this attitude, captured in his early work *The New Spirit*, which permeated his psychological studies of sexuality.

In *Studies in the Psychology of Sex*, Ellis attempted to give an overview of the manifestations of the sexual instinct. He did this first by focusing upon the so-called perversions. This focus was one that fitted with the aims of other sexologists of the period, who examined the protean forms of the sexual instinct (especially ones that were legally problematic, such as homosexuality and sadism), before establishing models of the "normal" instinct. As such, Ellis's initial contributions to sexual psychology addressed homosexuality, and he co-authored (with poet John Addington Symonds) the first medical textbook published on the subject in England: *Sexual Inversion* (1897; first published in Germany in 1896 as *Das konträre Geschlechtsgefühl*). This work, although adopting a psychological standpoint that some later historians considered to be homophobic, was written specifically to challenge the **law** on same-sex activity in Britain. These laws prohibited two men from committing acts of "gross indecency" in public or private—this did not have to include sodomy, which had been illegal since 1538, but could simply imply two men masturbating themselves in the same room. Ellis's work challenged the law by arguing that homosexuality was a natural phenomenon that had existed throughout history and in all cultures including the animal world. His reasoning suggested that homosexual desires were inborn, and therefore should not be thought of as vicious, and thus illegal. In other words, Ellis's text should be read as liberating, and his inclusion of a number of case histories of men and women who had not been convicted of sexual crimes or had not ended up in the asylum, meant that his text was read beyond sexological circles as a significant prohomosexual text.

Ellis's "scientific naturalist" standpoint, which he adopted throughout his sexological texts, was predicated on an idea of a sexual impulse that was polymorphous and instinctual. His contributions to understanding the sexual instinct, which had an arousal and a consummating phase that he termed tumescence and detumescent, suggested that it was a combination of a person's heredity, upbringing, and early-life experiences that would direct their sexual desires throughout their life. Such a conceptualization of sexual desire meant that all sexual phenomena could be explained, and could be understood as normal variations of the sexual impulse. This idea had a significant impact on Sigmund Freud's ideas of the sexual instinct, especially the first of his *Three Contributions to a Theory of Sex* (1905). Ellis's last major contribution to his *Studies, Sex in Relation to Society* (1910), took these psychological ideas further by addressing the social problems that sexuality raised, such as **birth control** and bodily attitudes, and argued that the centrally important issue that sexuality raised was the possibility of a loving and fulfilling relationship based on understanding between the parties. All his other sexual writings, despite being more voluminous, were studies in the variations of sexual desires so that these central, metaphysical principles could emerge.

Further Reading: Ellis, Havelock. *Studies in the Psychology of Sex*. Philadelphia: FA Davis and Co., 1898–1928; Ellis, Havelock. *My Life*. London: William Heineman, 1940; Crozier, Ivan. "The Medical Construction of Homosexuality and Its Relation to the Law in Nineteenth-Century England." *Medical History* 45 (2001): 61–82.

Ivan Crozier

EROTICA.   *See* Pornography and Erotica

ETTY, WILLIAM (1787–1849).   William Etty was born in the English city of York in 1787, an age when the demands of ideal art were to come into conflict with the interests of a commercial market. This can be seen not least in his struggle to conserve the old city of York, its walls, and its minster (cathedral). He joined the campaign to restore York Minster in 1829 after a destructive fire, keeping a close eye on the plans, and in 1831, protesting when the cathedral screen was to be removed, though he had just witnessed the more serious destruction of people in France at that time. No lover of the railway age, in which he lived, he wrote to a friend in 1840 that the new bells for the minster had not been hung, and only the squeak of the railway could be heard.

This desire to preserve traditional values in art and life during the accelerating commercialization of the "Age of Steam" can be seen in his attitude toward the classical subject of the nude, and in particular, the female nude. Etty reinforces her role in the discourse of ideal art, before she was to become ripe for commercial exploitation in the later nineteenth century. Etty copied the great works of classical antiquity, such as the Venus de Milo on his Grand Tour of Europe, and attempted to emulate this bold nakedness, as opposed to the modestly concealed nudity of many of his eighteenth-century predecessors' works, or the prudery of later Victorian artists who were to reintroduce the transparent drape—for equally transparent motives. Sadly for Etty, his motives were often misinterpreted, and his **paintings** reviled in the contemporary press.

In 2006, Manchester City Art Gallery put on display the large canvas "Ulysses and the Sirens." Exhibited with the work were extracts from the critical press of the time, 1837, which seem to encapsulate the various reactions to his work throughout his life. For example, the *Gentleman's Magazine* saw it as a "historical work of the first class," which "abounds with beauties of all kinds." *The Observer* of the same year had a very different judgment. The writer allowed that "the composition is fine" and the painting "beautiful," but believed that the subject "could not fail to produce the most unpleasant feelings. However cleverly treated such a subject could be, it is to be hoped that there are few who would nauseate their friends by placing it in their galleries." Etty had based his depiction on the poet Alexander Pope's translation of Homer's *Odyssey*, and it may be that the resultant abundance of bones and human carnage surrounding the apparently uncaring women disgusted the *Observer*'s critic. It is quite likely, though, that the depiction of the women themselves, seeming too human and too "real," contributed to his reaction. Born after the classical era of ideal "history" painting and before the new age of Realism, Etty's work fell uneasily between the two schools.

His realism seemed too extreme for the time. This can be seen in his drawing of a cast of the classical sculpture of the Venus de Medici being embraced by a naked female: the woman is unmistakably fleshy and curvaceous in form, as opposed to the cold lines of the statue. His contemporary biographer, Alexander Gilchrist, in 1855, quotes the poet Byron's lines in relation to Etty: "I've seen more lovely women, ripe and real/Than all the nonsense of the beau ideal." A contemporary painter, Daniel Maclise, praised Etty's sketches for having "the flavor of Nature in them" and Gilchrist cited Etty's own words that he only copied what he saw. Gilchrist defended Etty from the accusations of "unusual effects in his Studies which to many seemed unnatural"—not following the classical formula of his day—but have since been "borne out by the Calotype" (an early photographic process).

Gilchrist clearly wished to defend Etty's manner of depicting female nudes. In his own day and later, Etty's depiction has been criticized on the grounds of being tastelessly modern. The marks of contemporary stays (corsets) were said to be visible on the pink flesh of his buxom goddesses. Fashionable hairstyles were evidence to this. A reviewer of 1828 wrote of one of his naked set pieces: "One lady, though she has walked out of doors quite naked, has taken care to have her hair curled by Truefitt [a fashionable hairdresser] and wears a very handsome turban from Madame Maredan's" (a hat maker). By 1886, the pre-Raphaelite painter William Holman Hunt was calling Etty's nymphs "town models distorted by the modiste's art."

As with the French painter Edouard Manet's ironical nudes of the 1860s, it was the literalness of nakedness that had the power to disturb, all the more so when the

"The Bath." © The Art Archive/Garrick Club.

bodies seemed to be those of contemporary women. Respectable newspapers wrote of "dirty flesh" and "lascivious scenes." Etty was undaunted: "Though bruised, I trust I am not broken. I hear a consciousness of something bidding me not to despair of doing that which after-ages shall not let die." Gilchrist made an impassioned plea for the artist's "purity of heart" and a later biographer, William Camidge in 1890, defended his predilection for female nudes as a subject with the explanation that "he considered that God's most glorious work was woman in whom all human **beauty** has been concentrated."

There is no denying that to the modern reader, there seems to be a certain lascivious tone to Etty's exchanges with the painter John Constable. In 1828, Constable wrote to a friend about the painting *World Before the Flood* that "Etty has a revel rout of Satyrs and lady bums as usual," and Etty wrote to Constable in 1837: "A young figure is brought to me—who is very desirous of becoming a model—She is very much like the Antigone *and all in front memorably fine.*" Whichever quality possessed by the model strikes Etty, the moral theme she is meant to represent is what he hopes to capture, sometimes almost to the point of abstraction, as in *The Combat— Woman Pleading for the Vanquished, an Ideal Group.* The success of this large painting can be measured by the fact that it was exhibited at the Royal Academy of 1825, at the British Institution in 1826, twice at the Royal Scottish Academy (in 1831 and 1844), and was engraved in 1848. He was portraying what he used to call "some great moral on the heart" (here, the quality of Mercy) with posed studio models. "When I found that all the great painters of Antiquity had become great through painting Great Actions and the Human Form, I resolved to paint nothing else." Etty had drawn the classical sculptural group *The Laocoon* when he started training at the Royal Academy in 1807, and would have had access to the battling scenes portrayed in Greek reliefs, such as the Bassae and Parthenon friezes, deposited in the British Museum in the early years of the century. In France, he could have seen *The Intervention of the Sabine Women* (1799) by the neoclassical painter Jacques Louis David, where violence and peaceful intervention are represented by male and female nudes. Rather than the rigid linearity of the French classical school, Etty was more drawn to the color school of the Flemish artist Peter Paul Rubens and the Venetian Titian.

On exhibition in 1835, his painting *Venus and Her Satellites* aroused much indignation in the press: "This painter has fallen into an egregious error. He mistakes the use of nudity in painting and presents in the most gross and literal manner the unhappy models of the Royal Academy for the exquisite idealities in which Titian and other masters who have chosen similar subjects revelled" (*The Times*). *The Observer*'s critic wrote of "a brothel on fire," and that "several ladies" were deterred from going to see "other pictures of merit" to avoid the "offence and disgrace Mr. Etty has conferred on that quarter." In fact, Etty sold the painting to the Rev. Edward Pryce Owen.

Critics were receptive to *Cleopatra's Arrival in Sicilia* (1821): one wrote to the American writer Washington Irving, "Etty's Cleopatra is a splendid triumph of colour." The following year, however, the *Times*'s critic wrote: "we take this opportunity of advising Mr. Etty, who got some reputation for painting *Cleopatra's Galley*, not to be seduced into a style which can gratify only the most vicious taste. Naked figures, when painted with the purity of Raphael, may be endured: but nakedness without purity is offensive and indecent."

By 1843, portrayals of *Musidora* or *The Bather*, where a robust female nude is displayed in a woodland setting, had become more acceptable, and the various versions had no difficulty in attracting buyers. The recreation of ideal art in the genre of "history painting," which he had been striving for all his life, and the uneasy compromise with realism for which critics had attacked him, had reached a resolution. Etty's defense of his chosen subject matter of female nude can be summed up with the words quoted by his first biographer: "Finding God's most glorious work to be WOMAN, that all human beauty had been concentrated in her, I resolved to dedicate myself to painting—not the Draper's or Milliner's work—but God's most glorious work, more finely than had ever been done."

Further Reading: Gilchrist, Alexander. *Life of William Etty, R. A.* London: Bogue, 1855; Farr, Dennis. *William Etty.* London: Routledge and Kegan Paul, 1958.

Sara M. Dodd

EVOLUTION.   Evolution is the process by which organisms develop over a period of time as a species, acquiring traits that are then passed on to their offspring. While theories of evolution started at the beginning of the nineteenth century, the modern-day understanding of evolution is primarily attributed to Charles Darwin (1809–1882), and to a lesser extent to Alfred Russel Wallace (1823–1913). Evolutional theories impacted Victorian concepts of gender and sexuality in two specific ways: first, it was proposed that women were less evolved than men because of their physical and mental characteristics, and second, it was suggested that evolution impacted sexual selection, whereby mates chose each other based on the characteristics which they would pass on to their offspring. Such applications had social and political effects in both the Victorian period and the subsequent centuries.

One of the first theories of evolution was devised by Jean-Baptiste Lamarck (1744–1829), who argued that evolution was partly based on the passing down of traits acquired during an organism's lifetime, which, on this basic level, seems in line with Darwin and with modern theories of evolution. However, Lamarck argued that traits could be acquired in one generation that would be passed down to the next without the long developmental process. Although this theory was highly debated, social theorists found applications of Lamarckianism, as it was a means to explain social customs and their persistence. Thus, it was a means to explain why men worked and women took care of domestic duties, as this could be traced to previous generations. Although Lamarckianism was dismissed as a scientific theory by the end of the century, its contribution in understanding gender and society continued in relationship to Darwinism, whereby the gendered separate spheres of Victorian society could be justified.

The publication of Darwin's *The Origin of Species* in 1859 changed the way in which society viewed theories of evolution. Darwin proposed that the species as a whole evolved over time, and the traits they acquired over time would be passed on to future generations. The basis for his evolution theory was another theory called natural selection, whereby organisms must evolve in order to survive in their environments; those that do not or cannot adapt to their environment perish. This concept gave rise to the familiar phrase "survival of the fittest," which is often wrongly attributed to Darwin. It was actually coined in 1864 by Herbert Spencer (1820–1903). Although Darwin initially may have intended his theory to be applied to the human **race** as a whole, both he and his supporters applied his theory in regard to race and gender. With regard to gender, Darwinism was used in an attempt to demonstrate that men must be more evolved than women. Because men traditionally have had to fight in wars and hunt, they physically evolved into stronger humans. Moreover, because men had to plan a strategy for their wars, their **brain**s were arguably more evolved. Thus, the best place for women was where they did not need to physically or mentally strain themselves: the home.

Beyond this application of natural selection with regard to gender, *The Origin of Species* also addressed the issue of sexual selection. Darwin explained that sexual selection was the means by which organisms selected mates based on those which would help them to produce the most (and best) offspring. Significantly, Darwin noted that sexual selection "depends, not on a struggle for existence, but on a struggle between the males for possession of the females; the result is not death to the unsuccessful competitor, but few or no offspring" (Darwin 1981, 73). Darwin's wording again suggests that the male of a species is the stronger of the sexes, and it is he who competes for female attention. Moreover, claiming that a male competes to possess a female, again implies a natural domination of men over women. Not surprisingly, this theory was used in conjunction with ideas about natural selection to suggest the inferiority of women to men.

Darwin elaborated on his theory of evolution in 1871 with the publication of *The Descent of Man, and Selection in Relation to Sex*. While *The Origin of Species* discussed sexual selection primarily with regard to animals, *The Descent of Man* explicitly applied these theories to contemporary understandings of men and women. In this work, Darwin developed his idea as to how and why males choose their female mates, in addition to elaborating on his earlier presentation that women might not be as evolved as men. This is clearly stated in this later work, where he acknowledged not only the acceptable sexual differences between genders, but also the debatable physical differences which are not related to reproduction. Thus, Darwin argued for secondary sexual characteristics; "for instance, in the male possessing certain organs of sense or locomotion, of which the female is quite destitute, or in having them more highly developed, in order that he may readily find or reach her; or again, in the male having special organs of prehension so as to hold her securely" (Darwin, 253). In this passage, Darwin's argument is again in accordance with his earlier one in *The Origin of Species*, whereby female evolution is different from male evolution.

Moreover, Darwin reduced the sexual selection of women by men to female appearance, arguing that men select women for their **beauty**, which is the main trait passed down from women to women: "As women have long been selected for beauty, it is not surprising that some of the successive variations should have been transmitted in a limited manner; and consequently that women should have transmitted their beauty in a somewhat higher degree to their female than to their male offspring" (Darwin, 372). Again, Darwin implied that women evolved in a different manner from men, and suggested that their most important characteristic, and the one that they passed on to their daughters, was their beauty, as that was the means by which men selected them for procreation.

While Darwin's theories were based on his scientific studies of various animals during his time on the *Beagle*, the applications of these theories in mid-Victorian society affected the way in which women were viewed and treated. Conduct books and manners guides told women that they should behave in a certain manner to attract men, emphasizing Darwin's belief that women used their beauty to attract mates, inducing women to become complicit in this process. Moreover, because women were expected to be the weaker sex, they acted as such, further emphasizing the physical evolution of men that women lacked. This cyclical approach to gender was also evident in the understanding of female intelligence; women were not expected to be more intelligent than men, and since most did not pursue any education, this maintained the premise of their intellectual inferiority to men. Religious instruction also taught women to maintain this submissiveness to men, and while evolution theories are usually seen in opposition to religious teachings in the Victorian period, with regard to women, they seemed to have complimented each other. Through the religious teaching that women should be domestic angels, maintaining their beauty and their fragile forms, sexual selection theories were supported because women did appear to be less evolved.

Beyond the application of evolution to the differences between male and female development, sexual selection was used as a means to determine not only the future of a specific family, but the future of the human race as a whole. Darwin's cousin Francis Galton (1822–1911) used theories of sexual selection as a means to explain his theory of eugenics. Galton's theory was based on two suppositions: "first, that desirable physical and mental qualities were unevenly distributed throughout the population and, second, that those who had the desirable qualities could be identified and encouraged to multiply faster than the others" (Jones 1980, 99). Galton's application of eugenics meant that the more physically and mentally evolved, whom he considered were mostly middle class, would dominate society through selective reproduction. Ultimately, Galton envisioned a superior **race**, which eliminated the inferior members of society because they were left to reproduce with each other, an act that he assumed would not produce any offspring based on Darwin's theories. Galton's expectation was not only the elimination of the poor classes, but, to a lesser extent, the nonwhite races as well. This Victorian application of eugenics became a basis for both Hitler's argument for a "master race" and some applications of modern genetics.

The development and application of theories of evolution led to both scientific advancement and prejudiced views of gender, class, and race. Although evolution did unveil a theory of humankind's history, it also provided a scientific means to explain female inferiority. Similarly, although sexual selection scientifically explained why men were attracted to certain women, it also led to a view that women were inferior because of this; moreover, it led to theories of eugenics. Evolution in the Victorian period not only demonstrated the perceived and the actual differences between the sexes, but also suggested ways to select a mate to improve individual progeny and the race as a whole.

Further Reading: Darwin, Charles. *The Descent of Man, and Selection in Relation to Sex.* Princeton, NJ: Princeton University, 1981; Darwin, Charles. *The Origin of Species.* Oxford: Oxford University Press, 1996; Irvine, William. *Apes, Angels and Victorians: Darwin, Huxley and Evolution.* London: Weidenfeld and Nicolson, 1955; Jones, Greta. *Social Darwinism and English Thought: The Interaction between Biological and Social Theory.* Brighton: The Harvester Press, 1980; Shields, Stephanie A. "Functionalism, Darwinism, and the Psychology of Women: A Study in Social Myth." *American Psychologist* 30 (1975): 739–54.

Amanda M. Caleb

F

FASHION. While costume and codes of dress have always existed, many theorists and historians date the beginning of fashion, in the sense of a rapidly changing, market-driven system of clothing styles, from the nineteenth century, arguing that the emergence of fashion is inextricably linked with modernity. Of course, fashion is intimately connected with sexuality and eroticism. It is both determined by and determines what is seen as sexually attractive; it allows for bodily display and modification; and indulgence in the consumption of fashion can itself be an erotic experience.

Improved technology and the development of the factory system in the nineteenth century led to increased production of the raw materials of fashion, such as fabric, thread, and needles. While most clothes were still made at home or by seamstresses, dressmakers and tailors in the first half of the nineteenth century, from the 1860s, readymade or "off the rack" clothes were increasing in availability and popularity. The development of the sewing machine in the same decade meant that clothes could be produced more quickly and cheaply than ever before. However, fabrics varied widely in quality and cost, and skilled designers and dressmakers were expensive.

While theories explaining fashion as a phenomenon have varied over time, one of the explanations favored by fashion theorists is connected to clothing as a means of attracting sexual attention. Women's fashions over the century emphasized different areas of the body, but can be seen to significantly highlight various sexual characteristics. For example, the empire and neo-empire fashions of the early nineteenth century emphasized the bust, with a high waistline and a long, straight skirt that hinted at the shape of the legs. The huge crinoline hoops worn in the 1850s and 1860s made a feature of the waist by exaggerating the outswell of the hips, while the bustle, worn in the seventies and eighties, suggested protruding buttocks. Fashion played an important economic role in the lives of middle- and upper-class women, who depended on this aspect of display to accentuate their charms on the marriage market. Indeed, it was considered vital to a woman's role as a "lady" to keep up with fashion as far as her income would allow, and to be conspicuous or eccentric in dress was a serious fault.

Although men's fashion did not change so dramatically over the century, they were nevertheless distinctively Victorian. While the clothing of middle- and upper-class women was generally brightly colored, heavily ornamented with bows, ribbons, lace, and other embellishments, and fairly constrictive and discouraging of activity and movement, men's clothing was for the most part dark, plain, and allowed for more freedom of movement. Although this is a generalization, it is fair to say that in the nineteenth century, women bore the burden of fashionable display. Fashion also served to highlight and create gender differences, reflecting the perceived roles of men and women: women's clothing was frivolous, dainty, and decorative, while men's clothing was sober, sensible, and functional. This conformed to dominant theories of gender and the roles of men and women in the nineteenth century.

In addition to gender, an individual's class also affected his or her access to fashionable dress. Yet, although the magnificence or taste of an ensemble might reveal the class (or at least the income) of the wearer, specifically class-based costume died out over the course of the nineteenth century. Elements of fashionable dress, such as the crinoline hoop were worn by women from all classes, a fact which led to much anxiety about the possibility of social confusion. A "love of finery," it was argued, could lead working-class women into **prostitution**. Much was also written about the new status of high-class courtesans as leaders of fashion, especially after the 1860s. To look fashionable, some writers argued, was to look immoral.

This emphasis on the relationship of morality to fashion was the subject of many books and articles in the nineteenth century. Although, as noted earlier, women were expected to keep up with fashion, they were often criticized or denigrated for what was seen as vanity and narcissism. Changes in women's fashions were frequently the subject of satire, in magazines, such as *Punch* or the *Saturday Review*. Indeed, the very unpredictability and rapid change of women's fashion was seen as evidence of their innate foolishness and triviality. However, despite the fact that an excessive interest in fashion and appearance was seen as frivolous and superficial, a lack of interest in these things was maligned as dangerously "unfeminine." Women's participation in this sphere was thus fraught and contradictory.

One arena of clothing which developed during the nineteenth century was that of underclothes. While petticoats had been worn in various forms for centuries, the Victorian era saw the introduction of drawers for women, a precursor to modern underpants. These became increasingly adopted throughout the century, their use spreading to all classes. Although busks and corsets had long been worn by women of the upper classes, improvements in production made the corset cheaper and more accessible, and it became an indispensable part of almost every woman's wardrobe. The fashionable status and eventually universal adoption of the corset in turn affected the shape of women's clothing. The "hourglass" shape was fashionable throughout most of the century, giving way around the turn of the century to a shape which flattened and pushed back the stomach, thrusting out the buttocks, and smoothed out the bust. Throughout the century, women's underclothing became more and more elaborate and erotic, culminating around the turn of the century. Rich fabrics such as silk and lace were used in the most expensive items, suggesting that the wearing of this kind of underwear was at the least a privately sensuous experience.

Victorian fashion is often stereotyped as prudish or prim; yet, costumes for certain occasions revealed much of the outline of the body or even expanses of bare skin. Ballgowns, throughout the century, allowed for an erotic display of décolletage, certainly much more than would be permissible in any other setting. The arms, another body part that was eroticized during the period, were often completely bare in these gowns. At other times, tightness in dress allowed features such as the bust, legs or waist to be accentuated. While hemlines were more or less ankle length until the end of the century, crinoline cages, fashionable in the 1850s and 1860s, allowed glimpses of feet and ankles with their swinging motion. Women had a difficult duty: there was immense pressure upon them to look sexually attractive and fashionable enough to be noticeable. At the same time, it was imperative to appear modest and respectable, and not so fashionable as to be ahead of the current fashions, an advance which also made them immodestly conspicuous.

Further Reading: Cunnington, C. Willet and Phyllis Cunnington. *Handbook of English Costume in the Nineteenth Century*. London: Faber & Faber, 1959; Breward, Christopher. *The Culture of Fashion*. Manchester: Manchester University Press, 1995; Kuchta, David. *The Three-Piece Suit and Modern Masculinity: England, 1550–1850*. Berkeley: University of California Press, 2002; Steele, Valerie. *Fashion and Eroticism: Ideals of Feminine Beauty from the Victorian Era to the Jazz Age*. New York: Oxford University Press, 1985; Valverde, Mariana. "The Love of Finery: Fashion and the Fallen Woman in Nineteenth-Century Social Discourse." *Victorian Studies* 32 (1989): 168–88.

Jessica Needle

FEMINISM. At the beginning of the nineteenth century, the term feminism was yet to be coined, but "women's rights" served as a roughly comparable concept. In 1800, it rarely meant the demand for absolute equality with men; more ordinarily, it was understood to encompass women's right to education and to enjoy comparable civil rights with men, including their standing before the law, financial autonomy, and increasingly, the right to vote. It was tainted in the minds of almost everyone, with connotations of atheism, political extremism, and immorality, largely because the eighteenth century's most famous defender of the rights of women, Mary Wollstonecraft (1759–1797) was believed to be an atheist, dangerously republican in politics, and sexually immoral (she was notoriously not married to the father of her elder daughter). This popular association with Wollstonecraft's legacy meant that few women would admit to sympathy with the rights of women in the early part of the century, for fear of being condemned by association.

By mid-century, the image of a woman's rights sympathizer had shifted to some extent. They were now ridiculed as masculine, as "unfeminine," and as physically unattractive. Feminists were depicted as being primarily concerned with the right of women to have the vote. Advocates of women's rights to the vote, to education, or to equality in any sphere were caricatured as failures in the marriage market, and as sexually frustrated spinsters.

Education for women—especially higher education—was another area where feminism became increasingly active as time passed. Debates raged over whether girl's menstrual "weakness" meant that they were unfit for the rigors of sustained study, and studies of **brain** size were used by some opponents of women's education to demonstrate that they were incapable of intellectual competition with men. These were largely middle-class preoccupations. Working-class girls were educated for wifehood and motherhood, a trend that intensified in state schools on both sides of the Atlantic in the last twenty years of the century.

In the nineteenth century, femininity was defined by the church, by science, and by medical opinion. **Christianity** taught that chastity was the ideal for both sexes, but this was countered by arguments from some quarters that sex was medically necessary for men to enjoy full health. Women were often depicted as having less sexual desire than men (although this was disputed by some), although it was sometimes argued that prostitutes were a class of

Mary Wollstonecraft. © HIP/Art Resource, NY.

women whose desires were unnaturally heightened. Medical knowledge was so limited that it was still possible for some **physicians** to claim that rape could never result in pregnancy. The lack of sexual passion was considered to confer moral superiority, a concept that some late-Victorian feminists appropriated to argue for the superiority of women, claiming that sexual self-control was a sign of moral superiority. Other feminists disparaged the concept of passionlessness altogether, arguing that in a more natural society, men and women would experience desire equally.

Sexual issues became important in the women's movement from the 1880s onward. This trend developed from a feminist critique of the double standard, which was based on the underlying assumption that women were the sexual property of men. The moral reformers and feminists both rejected the sexual double standard, with its condoning of male promiscuity. Social purity activists aimed at nothing less than the complete moral transformation of society in the Western world. This linkage between feminism and sexually appropriate behavior problematized masculinity by claiming that men had an equal duty with women to remain sexually pure until marriage, and faithful afterward. The single sexual standard became a dominant theme in both feminist and **social purity** movements. This is unsurprising, given the significant overlap between activists and sympathizers in both movements. Motherhood became an important idea for some feminists, and women's capacity to bear children was seen as conveying a kind of superiority, sometimes of a physical kind, but more often depicted as spiritual. Employing the old idea of women as embodying nature and man culture, feminists subverted this (in a period when "civilized" society was increasing being viewed as decadent by social critics) to emphasize male unnaturalness.

As sexual politics evolved in the 1890s, the "new woman" became a much-discussed phenomenon. It was thought that for modern women, work was as important as for men, and that they were equally likely to find satisfaction in sexual contact. Although a minority interest, the new women tried to shape a feminism that was less moralistic and less tied to traditional beliefs about femininity. Despite the developments in thinking about women's rights and some social liberalization, most women were still distancing themselves from feminism at the century's end.

Further Reading: Bland, Lucy. *Banishing the Beast: Sexuality and the Early Feminists.* New York: The New Press, 1995; Dyhouse, Carol. *Girls Growing Up in Late Victorian and Edwardian England.* London: Routledge & Kegan Paul, 1981; Hall, Lesley A. *Sex, Gender and Social Change in Britain since 1880.* London: Macmillan, 2000; Russett, Cynthia Eagle. *Sexual Science: The Victorian Construction of Womanhood.* Cambridge, MA: Harvard University Press, 1989.

Susan Mumm

FETISHISM.   The fetish is a psychological concept that is used to explain the specific object of desire to which a person feels attracted. Alfred Binet began to develop a specific understanding of the fetish in the nineteenth century, when he encountered the researches of Jean-Martin Charcot and Valentine Magnan on sexual perversions (some of the cases of which had been of fetishists, although they were not thought of as such), but elaborated them in a two-part paper on fetishes that sought to solve the problem of "normal" love, even while explaining the specificity of certain perversions. Binet's theory of sexual fetishism derived from ideas about religious devotion—the word fetishism deriving from the Portugese *fetisso*, meaning an enchanted thing. In cases of sexual fetishism, it was an object that was particular for arousing the desire in each subject. This object could be an inanimate item, such as a nightcap, or could be a specific body part of an idolized person, such as red hair or a squint. The significant fact, however, was that this object was needed for the fetishistic subject to achieve sexual arousal.

Fetishism could take many different forms. For Binet, there were four common focuses: the eye, the hand, the hair, and scent. Other items could also act as "souvenirs" that triggered an erotic response by reminding the fetishist of a mental association. The key to understanding fetishism for Binet was the principle of association of ideas. As with other forms of hypnotic suggestion that had been developed in France immediately prior to Binet's research, the development of a sexual perversion relied upon a hereditary predisposition; hereditary factors "prepare the terrain," but they do not give the sexual impulsion its particular form. Rather, it is an "accident" that forges a particular association.

Binet was thus interested in uncovering a general sexual impulse that would explain different perversions. For Binet, there was a strong cultural factor pertaining to attraction. Different cultures have "fetishized" different traits, a notion suggested by Charles Darwin in *Descent of Man*, and by numerous anthropologists. This suggested that there were relative criteria for **beauty** that differed between cultures. However, more was needed than simply a focus on a specific beautiful trait. Rather, the making of perversion was caused by the deviations of the sexual selection instinct away from treating the object of one's desires as a whole person, and instead focusing on a single attribute that was raised above all other features as the desired symbol.

Without this kind of underlying theory of perversion, the work of sexologists Karl Westphal and **Richard von Krafft-Ebing** was reproached by Binet, as it did not explain the connection between the degenerate form and the specific desire. The inverted tastes and appearances of homosexual subjects that were announced by Westphal did not explain fully why an individual desires someone of the same sex; they merely demonstrated a degenerate predisposition, according to Binet. His claim went further: "Sexual inversion results ... from an agitating *accident* in the predisposed subject." This accident took place because of a "coincidence of two things, an immediately formed mental association, at an age when such associations are strong, and a child with a nervous system in disequilibrium, shows us the source of the obsession." This mental association in the predisposed child is strengthened when sexual experiences, especially **masturbation**, are combined with the focus upon stimulus (either real or in memory or imagination). In this case, the fetishistic state resembles that of the hypnotizable patient, where a patient can be suggested into profound changes in their conceptual life.

The difference between normal love and fetishism is one of degree: "The lover's fetishism is a tendency towards abstraction [of particular traits]. As such it is opposed to normal love, which addresses the totality of the [beloved] person." In other words, "Normal love is in harmony ... In sexual perversion, ... this harmony is disrupted." Such a disruption is caused when one focus is emphasized at the expense of all others.

Binet's theory had a significant impact on the work of sexologists. It allowed the move from the general idea—held by many—that there was some kind of predisposition toward perversion, deriving from degenerationist arguments, to a situation whereby perversions were but a specific *idée fixe*. This theory was enticing for a number of reasons: it would allow for a general description of the sexual impulse that could deviate in many different directions; it could explain cultural factors in the choice of a sexual object (or in the emphasis on a particular criterion for beauty). It also allowed some to think about a cure, as hypnotherapies more than other forms of psychiatry, posited that one could transplant a different erotic trigger in the mind of the fetishist to cure them of their perversions. The challenge for the "congenitalists" would be to account for Binet's model of fetishism by re-evaluating the respective roles of the predisposition and the accidental trigger.

Further Reading: Binet, Alfred. "Le Fétichisme dans l'Amour." *Revue Philosophique* 24 (1887): 143–67/252–74; Reed, Matt T. "Historicizing Inversion: Or, How to Make a Homosexual." *History of the Human Sciences* 14 (2001): 1 29.

Ivan Crozier

FLAGELLATION. While flagellation for punishment or as a part of religious rites is ancient, flagellation's role in sexual activity emerged comparatively recently. Renaissance writer Giovanni Pico della Mirandola noted a friend who had prostitutes flog him so that he could perform sexually. References to erotic flagellation appeared regularly thereafter, and featured prominently in Victorian erotic literature. Some brothels came to specialize in flagellation, and discussions and descriptions of flagellation even appeared in popular nineteenth-century magazines.

Medical literature soon corroborated the linkage between flagellation and sexual performance. German physician Johann Heinrich Meibom's oft-republished *On the Use of Rods in Venereal Matters and in the Office of the Loins and Reins* (1629) linked flagellation to male arousal. References to aging libertines who needed corporal punishment to maintain their ardor became common in erotic literature. Others attributed desires for flagellation to corporal punishment received as children by either their parents or school officials. As the character Snarl explains in Shadwell's play *The Virtuoso* (1676), "I was so us'd to't at Westminster School, I cou'd never leave it off since." This theory received medical corroboration in 1857, when **William Acton** linked childhood spanking to a sexual interest in spanking as an adult in *Functions and Disorders of the Reproductive System*. He also affirmed that spanking revived sexual function in old men. By the end of the eighteenth century, scenes of whipping, spanking, caning, and more elaborate forms of flagellation appeared regularly in erotic literature. Although only a minority of such books focused exclusively on flagellation [the *Merry Order of Saint Bridget* (1857), for example, described the practices of a secret female flagellation society without any mention of other sexual matters], flagellation made at least a brief appearance in most nineteenth-century British erotic literature—to the extent that commentators referred to it as *le vice anglaise*.

The number of brothels that specialized in flagellation attest to a substantial market for flagellation in Europe's major cities. These brothels required women to either flagellate, or be flagellated by, customers. Theresa Berkeley became famous for the elaborate scenes she arranged for her clientele in her London brothel. She offered them a wide selection of whips, canes, and other instruments, and a variety of specialized equipment, including the Berkeley Bench, a frame against which a man could be comfortably lashed and with openings so that his genitals could be stimulated by one woman while another flogged him. Despite the passage of laws against **prostitution**, flagellation brothels continued to operate and advertised their services in newspapers as massages or therapies for nervous maladies.

Several early sexologists noted this interest in flagellation, and interviewed practitioners. **Richard von Krafft-Ebing** applied the terms **sadism and masochism** to deriving sexual pleasure from either giving or receiving pain or cruelty, in the fifth edition of *Psychopathia Sexualis* in 1890. While Krafft-Ebing focused on case studies of people whose masochistic desires hindered their lives and labeled masochism a pathology, **Havelock Ellis** in *Love and Pain* (1903) noted several happily married couples that engaged in flagellation.

Discussions of flogging appeared in a number of Victorian periodicals, including the gentleman's magazines *The Rambler*, *The Gentleman's Magazine*, and *The Bon Ton*, which occasionally included stories on flagellation and repeated rumors of secret flagellation societies. In the late nineteenth century, several general interest magazines also devoted space to discussions of flagellation, including *The Family Herald*, *Society*, and *The Englishwoman's Domestic Magazine*. The latter opened its correspondence column to fetishists, and letters poured in from devotees of both flagellation and tight-laced corsets, which described their desires and fantasies.

As flagellation faded as a form of punishment from schools, navies, armies, and other institutions, erotic literature increasingly celebrated it. Widespread discussion of flagellation and other fetishist practices paved the way for the emergence of specialized fetishist periodicals and social organizations in the twentieth century.

Further Reading: Ian, Gibson. *The English Vice: Beating, Sex and Shame in Victorian England and After*. London: Duckworth, 1978; Marcus, Steven. *The Other Victorians: A Study of Sexuality and Pornography in Mid-Nineteenth-Century England*. New York: Basic Books, 1966; Peakman, Julie. *Mighty Lewd Books: The Development of Pornography in 18th Century England*. Houndsmills: Palgrave Macmillan, 2003; Sigel, Lisa Z. *Governing Pleasures: Pornography and Social Change in England, 1815–1914*. New Brunswick, NJ: Rutgers University Press, 2002.

Stephen K. Stein

FORNICATION. *See* Adultery and Fornication

FOUNDLINGS. A foundling is a child abandoned at birth or infancy. Christian care for foundlings or abandoned infants within monastic and conventual communities is known as the continental or the "Latin or Catholic" form of guardianship. Both ecclesiastical and civil authorities, intent on saving infants without parents, thought it best to institutionalize the unfortunates, isolating them in convents and monasteries for the rest of their lives. In Catholic countries, such as France, Spain, Portugal, Belgium, and the Italian city states, care for illegitimate children fell under the broader context of paths to salvation; this practice continued to the modern era.

Northern Europe took a different approach to foundlings. During the Reformation, churches and then states rigorously began to require marriage before childbearing. Society witnessed a rise in tandem of illegitimate childbearing and infant abandonment, and increasingly stigmatized women who conceived a child out of wedlock. A rift in the tradition of providing for the poor left foundlings, regarded as illegitimate, in a tenuous situation, particularly with the dissolution of the monasteries when traditional forms of care for foundlings disappeared. All such forms of institutional care were suspected as remnants of "popish" practices. Nonetheless, by necessity, the English ultimately turned to parish poor law asylums and private charities as repositories for foundlings.

As young people left their families and small villages, and moved to metropolitan London, the problem of infant abandonment increased. If mothers placed their babies in a privy or near a dung heap, townspeople understood that the infant had been abandoned to die. If the babies were "dropped" on a doorstep of a church, rectory, a wealthy home, or in a public building, then the mother clearly intended discovery. Passersby who retrieved abandoned infants from the streets took them to the ubiquitous parish rectories and later to poor law asylums.

To meet the needs of foundlings, a sea captain whose fortune accrued from the slave trade, Thomas Coram, promoted what he believed to be a humane solution. The inspiration for his initiative originated with witnessing large numbers of parentless children wandering in the streets of South London. Coram's philanthropic concerns were answered by his proposed and controversial solution, a foundling hospital. The project had a dubious future because English traditions opposed such "Romish practices," fearing that aid would induce improvidence. The opposition was so strong that Coram took almost nineteen years to fulfill his dream. Coram achieved his goal with the help of influential women. Further, tolerance for bastards among the elite, and concern for their domestic **servants**, inspired their support. The elite also regarded the proposed hospital as a long-term patriotic investment. Anticipating the age of Victoria and its penchant for efficiency, Coram also emphasized the institution's potential ability to prepare future colonists, rather than focusing on the hospital as an opportunity to save the spiritual and physical lives of London's foundlings, waifs, and strays.

In 1739, Coram received a royal charter from George II (r. 1727–1760) for the "Maintenance and Education of Exposed and Deserted Young Children," and in 1741, opened the doors to the London Foundling Hospital in Hatton Gardens. A large purpose-built residence hall with offices and apartments for house parents opened on Guildford Street in 1745. Initially, admission was on a first come, first serve basis. Mothers flocked to the Foundling Hospital, forcing governors of the charity to limit admissions because of inadequate funds.

In 1756, Parliament opened the doors of the Foundling Hospital to everyone. Of the 15,000 children brought to the institution in the next four years, over 10,000 died. This led to a scandal debated in the press as Foundling Hospital governors were widely accused of accepting infants for whom they could not provide. In the day before the development of infant formula, breast milk was the only form of nutrition that could assure the survival of the newborn. From this point forward, the institution never again served foundlings—that is, infants found in the streets, nor did it operate as a hospital, but it grew as an institution that accepted the infants of unwed mothers. Governors developed a calculus of respectability relating to the mother of the baby. Her reputation came under social scrutiny as administrators scanned for definitive traits of respectability. By 1780, governors instituted a standardized petition form that began screening the identities of all petitioners. In 1840, Secretary John Brownlow tightened up the standards for admission. London women knew that the Foundling Hospital had a stringent set of rules and regulations that required a thorough investigation of their character before their infant would or could be admitted to.

During the age of Victoria, women picked up an application at the gatehouse facing Great Ormond Street. The majority of the women who applied were illiterate; hence they required assistance in completing the petition form. They were advised to request the written support of at least three recommenders. If women met the profile, and their infant was between the age of six and twelve months, the secretary of the Foundling Hospital notified them of their hearing date and time. On Saturday morning at 10:00 AM, mothers appeared before a panel of governors, usually men who had served in the Holborn Law courts, without their infants. The men questioned the women regarding the circumstances of their pregnancies, delivery of their infant, and their current employment. Many women who appeared had delivered their babies at Queen Charlotte's Lying Hospital, where administrators found employment for them as wet nurses for respectable West End mothers. Finally, the secretary crosschecked the petitioner's testimony against those of her recommenders. If the governors admitted the infant, the mother, with her infant in arms, returned to the Foundling Hospital, gave the baby to a nurse mother, and left without hope of ever seeing their child again. While these measures appear draconian, the infant accepted at the Foundling Hospital had a considerably better chance at life than an infant abandoned in the streets of London. Nurse mothers ensured the child's survival to age five; educational and technological training were provided; and the Foundling Hospital governors ensured that the child would be placed with employers who ensured success later in life.

Over the course of the period of 1741–1907, the Foundling Hospital admitted 22,594 infants. Numbers fluctuated over time according to the admission policies and available spaces. Recorded applications annually averaged about 200 or more after 1760. Annual admission averages ranged around forty infants per year. In the late 1880s, applications began to decline. In 1925, the governors moved childcare services to Berkhampsted. The last year in which children were admitted to the Foundling Hospital was 1934.

Further Reading: Ball, Alan M. *And Now My Soul Is Hardened: Abandoned Children in Soviet Russia, 1918–1930.* Berkeley: University of California Press, 1994; Barret-Ducrocq, Françoise. *Love in the Time of Victoria: Sexuality and Desire among Working-class Men and Women in Nineteenth-Century London.* Translated by John Howe. 2nd ed. London: Penguin Books, 1991; Boswell, John. *The Kindness of Strangers: The Abandonment of Children in Western Europe from Late Antiquity to the Renaissance.* New York: Pantheon Books, 1988; Fildes, Valerie. *Breasts, Bottles and Babies a History of Infant Feeding.* Edinburgh: Edinburgh University Press, 1986; Fuchs, Rachel Ginnis. *Abandoned Children: Foundlings and Child Welfare in Nineteenth-Century France.* Albany: State University of New York Press, 1984; Gillis, John. "Servants, Sexual Relations, and the Risks of Illegitimacy in London, 1801–1900." *Feminist Studies* 5 (1979): 142–73; Hanawalt, Barbara. Growing Up in Medieval London: The Experience of Childhood in History. New York: Oxford University Press, 1993; Kertzer, David I. *Sacrificed for Honor: Italian Infant Abandonment and the Politics of Reproductive Control.* Boston: Beacon Press, 1993; McClure, Ruth. *Coram's Children: The London Foundling Hospital in the Eighteenth Century.* New Haven, CT: Yale University Press, 1980; Stone, Lawrence. *The Family, Sex and Marriage in England, 1500–1800.* New York: Harper and Row, 1979; Tilly, Louise A. et al. "Child Abandonment in European History: A Symposium." *Journal of Family History* 17 (1992): 1–23.

Jessica Ann Sheetz-Nguyen

FREE-LOVE COMMUNITIES. Communal societies in the United States in the nineteenth century inevitably confronted issues of family and marriage, and many ideas for transforming marriage emerged from the communitarian movement. Marriage became an issue in both religious and secular communities, in groups with tight organization and strong leadership as well as in communities that valued individual independence. By the 1850s, free love had become a distinctive movement in American society, criticizing the new standards of marriage emerging among the middle class. Communities from the 1850s onward often confronted free love as a distinct issue, and several communities—most importantly Modern Times and Berlin Heights—became identified with the broader free-love movement.

Believers in communal living often attempted to direct loyalties away from family ties and toward community purposes. This trend appeared with the Shakers, who demanded celibacy and the separation of children from parents. Other successful religious groups that attempted to alter the nuclear family included the Mormons, who originally practiced **polygamy, American**, and the Harmonists (1804–1905), led by George Rapp (1757–1847), who experimented with celibacy. Although the leaders of secular communities aimed to reform labor and the economy, marriage and family appeared as issues in these communities. These included groups inspired by British industrialist Robert Owen, beginning with New Harmony (1825–1827), and those that claimed affinity with the ideas of French social theorist Charles Fourier, beginning with Brook Farm (1841–1847).

The first community to embrace the term free love, and the one to make the most innovative departures from romantic marriage, was the Oneida community. Bible Communists, led by John Humphrey Noyes (1811–1886), began practicing life in common in 1837 in Putney, Vermont, but moved to Oneida, New York, by 1848. Oneida survived as a communal society until 1881. The community instituted complex marriage, the belief that all men were married to all women. This required frequent changes of sexual partners and the practice of male continence (intercourse without ejaculation) to conserve the male seed. Beginning in 1869, the community practiced selective breeding, known as stirpiculture. However, instability came from a variety of sources, including resistance to Noyes's leadership and controversies over the practice of complex marriage.

During the 1850s, free love acquired a distinctively secular meaning, one that would shape other communal societies. Josiah Warren (1798–1874) and Stephen Pearl Andrews (1812–1886) established Modern Times in 1853, located about 40 miles from New York City. Warren had already developed the idea of individual sovereignty, that each individual should claim complete responsibility for his or her own actions, assuming complete independence as long as this freedom did not violate the equivalent freedom of any other individual. Warren called upon other individual sovereigns to join him at Modern Times to solve problems of labor and economic equality. Andrews, however, applied individual sovereignty to marriage in the pages of the *New York Tribune*. Free love came to mean the recognition of the changing passion of the individual. Advocates might mean "free marriage," that is, marriage of love and passion. Or, they might go further and embrace "variety," in which an individual could exercise his or her sovereignty without regard to the bonds of marriage.

Soon people from nearby New York, attracted to the social and sexual implications of individual sovereignty, began to arrive at Modern Times. Speaking for free love, Thomas Nichols (1815–1901) and Mary Gove Nichols (1810–1884), both water-cure practitioners, claimed Modern Times as a center for free unions. Free love brought Warren into conflict with many community members, but in the spirit of individual sovereignty, the community continued to entertain highly controversial and often opposing views on marriage. Although Modern Times eventually lost its communal identity, it persisted into the late nineteenth century as an alternative community that attracted the eccentric and reform-minded.

Thomas and Mary Nichols retreated from the controversy at Modern Times in 1855, and in 1856, established the Memnonia community in Yellow Springs, Ohio. This new community brought together the practices of spiritualism, water cure and healthful living, and the doctrines of individual sovereignty. Although the community survived the initial opposition of Horace Mann, president of nearby Antioch College, by 1857, the community lost its free-love identity when the Nichols converted to Catholicism.

Networks of free lovers, or virtual communities, also existed throughout the nineteenth century. In the mid-1850s, the Nichols promoted the Progressive Union, a mailing list of people interested in free love. From mid to late 1850s, the radical newspaper *Social Revolutionist* served as the open diary of many free lovers who corresponded with James Patterson, the paper's editor. Traveling lecturers helped to strengthen the ties of committed free lovers, and spread ideas about the movement.

In the late nineteenth century, other newspapers, such as *Lucifer the Light Bearer*, also helped to create ties among widely spread free lovers, especially in the midwestern states.

The Social Revolutionist's editor and contributors moved from a virtual to a real community in 1857, when they helped establish a community at Berlin Heights, Ohio, which was based on free relations and was welcoming to a variety of views on the marriage question. Berlin Heights survived local hostility and thrived economically into the post-Civil War period. It was an open community that included individual households, group households, and a group home. The Berlin Heights group also established a community school and a cooperative grist mill.

The vast distances of the expanding American republic, and the mobility of westward-moving Americans, inevitably limited the opportunities for free lovers to practice their ideals. As the general communal movement declined in the late nineteenth century, so did the efforts to establish communities that included free love as a basis for community life.

Further Reading: Passet, Joanne E. *Sex Radicals and the Quest for Women's Equality*. Urbana: University of Illinois Press, 2003; Spurlock, John C. *Free Love: Marriage and Middle-Class Radicalism in America, 1825 to 1860*. New York: New York University Press, 1988.

John C. Spurlock

THE FRENCH SYSTEM. *See* Prostitution, Regulated

G

GENDER ROLES. Like sexuality, gender is not an objective category, but a relatively new, artificial concept that flexibly collects assorted social expectations for men and women. Gender roles as depicted in the nineteenth-century literature have their origin in the eighteenth century. The shock of the French Revolution meant increased psychological insecurity and a hardening of attitudes toward appropriate roles for the poor, the rich, men and women. Although women played an important role during the revolution, they were not rewarded by enlarged rights in society and politics. In the declaration of human rights women were not mentioned, forcing protofeminist writer Olympe de Gouges (1745–1793) to ask "Aren't women men?" Strictly demarcated gender roles may be seen as providing the middle class with security and social orientation in stormy times.

At the beginning of the nineteenth century, medical practitioners began to attribute special modern traits like cosmopolitanism, autonomy, and individualism into male physiology and physiognomy. Sometimes these typical attributes were defined by anatomy, because male genitals are outside the body, whereas female genitals are hidden organs. This was seen as symbolizing the dependence of women and their need to be hidden from the world outside the home. Masculinity and femininity became more rigid categories and increasing attention was given to defining and limiting appropriate characteristics for the sexes.

The scientific interpretation of gender roles developed into an important research field in the nineteenth century. Anthropologists, **physicians**, psychologists (and in the later nineteenth century) also criminologists, gynecologists, psychiatrists, and sexual scientists, investigated the bodies of both sexes. Scientists believed that the truth about men and women could be read out of their bodies, and that gender was inborn rather than socially constructed. Women in particular were placed at the center of this scrutiny. The different gender characteristics they emphasized resulted from a mixture of biology, determinism, and nature, and it was assumed that these characteristics were innate and universal. Most concluded that the man was intended for a varied and public life, whereas the woman's destiny was inside, bounded, and domestic. Men were imagined to be the natural possessors of energy, power, and backbone, while women were constructed as weak, pious, and unstable. In the sphere of activity, the gender scientists claimed that men were independent, ambitious, given to acquisition, and assertive. Women were imagined to be dependent, conservative, busy, given to small things, and full of love and benignity. The difference between the attributes of the sexes was linked to the principle of complementarity, which in turn accorded with the new ideals of marriage in the eighteenth and nineteenth centuries, that men and women should complete each other. Matrimony joined their disparate characteristics and functions and created a perfect whole. Alone, a human was imperfect. While the ideal sounded positive, in real life both genders did not have the same rights and were not equitable partners. Popularizers of these special gender roles wrote conduct books and pedagogic works for children, which asserted the "naturalness" of the gender roles they depicted. These nineteenth-century writings were mostly found in middle-class households and bolstered normative gender roles. Thus, the "traditional" gender roles and resultant expectations were set in stone for much of the European and American middle classes for decades to come.

Further Reading: Armstrong, Nancy and Leonard Tennenhouse, eds. *The Ideology of Conduct: Essays on Literature and the History of Sexuality.* New York: Methuen, 1987; Gallagher, Catherine and Thomas Laquer, eds. *The Making of the Modern Body; Sexuality and Society in the Nineteenth Century.* Berkeley: University of California Press, 1987; Gay, Peter. *The Tender Passion: The Bourgeois Experience, Victoria to Freud.* Oxford: Oxford University Press, 1986.

Ulrike Moser

GERMAN LITERATURE. *See* Literature, German

GILBERT AND SULLIVAN (Comic Opera). It may be a widespread assumption that nothing could be more foreign to the comic operas of W. S. Gilbert and Arthur Sullivan than references to sexual relationships, but it is possible that certain members of the audience may have detected a lewd innuendo at times. Did nobody ever smile during *Iolanthe* when the Fairy Queen wonders if Captain Shaw (Head of London's Metropolitan Fire Brigade) possesses a hose capable of quenching her great love, or when Strephon confesses he is a fairy down to the waist? Is it only a later, sophisticated, perhaps decadent audience that could hear a *double entendre* in Grosvenor's cautionary rhyme "Teasing Tom was a very bad boy/A great big squirt was his favourite toy" (*Patience*, Act 2)? In this last example, a sexual insinuation seems confirmed by the poem's moral: "The consequence was he was lost to*tally*/And married a girl in the *corps de bally*." There is no doubt, surely, that the popularity of St. James's Park as a haunt for prostitutes would have added spice to Lord Tolloller's comment on Iolanthe's assignation with an unidentified man: "I heard the minx remark/She'd meet him after dark/Inside St. James's Park/And give him one!"

There are a number of occasions when a decidedly sexual interest is shown by one character in another. Indicating the sentry, Private Willis, the Fairy Queen cries, "Do you suppose that I am insensible to the effect of manly **beauty**? Look at that man!" However, she lays great stress upon her crushing of these feelings—in other words, in displaying her sexual self-control. The song in which she invokes the real-life Captain Shaw, movingly describes a "type of true love kept under." Ironically, Captain Shaw was himself keeping true love under, as was revealed in court two years after the premiere of *Iolanthe* when Lord Colin Campbell accused him of having had an affair with his wife. Shaw admitted he had burned with love for her, but never declared himself.

Characters are aware of social contexts in which the erotic can intrude. In *Ruddigore*, Mad Margaret and Sir Despard Murgatroyd reassure the audience: "This is one of our blameless dances." In the *Mikado*, Nanki-Poo and Yum-Yum are fully aware of the moral dangers of kissing and, in their duet, kiss each other merely to make absolutely clear, by concrete example, that this is what they will never do in future. Of course, this duet is a tease; it is inevitably sexually loaded, and is one of the features of operetta that marks out new possibilities—here, humorous flirtation—for the musical stage. The Japanese setting should fool nobody; wherever they are set, the Gilbert and Sullivan comic operas are always about the social and political conditions of Britain.

Gilbert's young heroines are often conscious of their allure, as Yum-Yum makes clear in her song "The Sun Whose Rays." On the other hand, many have deplored his use of spinsters as figures of fun. However, Jane Stedman has argued that Gilbert's corpulent dames are used to satirize the value placed on youth and beauty in women as a conventional requisite for marriage, and they usually possess strength of character denied to his leading soprano characters. Moreover, they also have a part to play as sexual beings. When, in the context of the satire of artistic pretensions in *Patience*, Lady Jane announces "I am limp and I cling," the sexual dimension of the images of women in pre-Raphaelite **painting**s is made suddenly blatant by the thought of a clinging, fleshly Lady Jane.

In the same opera, the actions of the poet Reginald Bunthorne can be related directly to his sexual drive. He reveals to the audience that he has been playing the role of an aesthete, merely in order to be attractive to the women of the neighborhood who have fallen under the spell of the Aesthetic Movement. Yet, for Bunthorne, the aesthetic realm is opposed to the real world of flesh and blood and human desire, and he only occupies a place in the former domain so as to acquire a means of attaining the fleshly satisfaction for which he yearns. In such a manner, high-minded artifice and the realities of everyday life are bluntly juxtaposed.

In general, a nonromantic, even antiromantic, ethos prevails in these comic operas. Bunthorne, accepting that Jane will never leave him, comments that, after all she is "a fine figure of a woman." Marriage is often a solution to a problem: Private Willis, realizing that the Fairy Queen needs to marry to remain immortal, declares "I don't think much of the British soldier who wouldn't ill-convenience himself to save a female in distress." This is not to say that more conventional love pairs do not exist. We have only to think of Strephon and Phyllis, who are also given a love duet with conventional melodic intertwining. Nevertheless, such characters are rarely the focus point—and though Jack Point's death from love is moving in *Yeomen of the Guard*, in its own remarkable way, so is that of the lovesick little bird in the deliberately ridiculous "Tit Willow" from *Mikado*.

The antiromantic qualities, with their masculine connotations, may account for the numbers of men attracted to Gilbert and Sullivan. Also, it is not difficult to find a masculinity that resonates with ideas of camp behavior in the operas. Gay admirers are many, and Mark Savage staged a highly successful gay version of *H. M. S. Pinafore* in 2001. Gilbert himself was a contentedly married if undemonstrative husband, and very much a man's man—although he died as a consequence of rescuing a woman from drowning. Sullivan was the philanderer. He was closest to Mrs. Mary Frances Ronalds, who was living in London separated from her husband. Before this, there is evidence in the form of love letters to show Sullivan was conducting affairs with two sisters simultaneously.

Further Reading: Bradley, Ian, ed. *The Complete Annotated Gilbert and Sullivan*. Oxford: Oxford University Press, 1996; Stedman, Jane W. *W. S. Gilbert: A Classic Victorian and His Theatre*. Oxford: Oxford University Press, 1996.

Derek B. Scott

GOTHIC FICTION. Gothic fiction emerged in England when Horace Walpole published *The Castle of Otranto* (1764), continued in vogue through the early 1800s, and enjoyed a renaissance near the end of the nineteenth century. Walpole's novel established the genre's essential features, which would remain in place for the next 200 years. Gothic stories are usually framed narratives, and they sometimes include a number of tales within tales. Supernatural occurrences, whether genuine or contrived, may help to advance and complicate their plots. Gothic settings are alternately natural and man-made, open and confined, heartening and threatening. On the one hand, action takes place on mountains and in forests; on the other, it occurs in castles, abbeys, dungeons, and prisons. At the heart of Gothic fiction are often dark secrets, especially those involving identity and familial relationships, and the gradual elucidation of these mysteries contributes to the suspense that distinguishes the form.

Gothic fiction rose to its first peak of renown in the 1790s, when Ann Radcliffe became the leading author of the era with novels including *The Romance of the Forest* (1791), *The Mysteries of Udolpho* (1794), and *The Italian* (1797). Radcliffe's works were marked by their highly sensitive heroines, picturesque landscapes, and rational explanations of apparently otherworldly phenomena. Matthew "Monk" Lewis, whose phenomenally successful novel *The Monk* (1796) also contributed to the Gothic craze, wrote in a decidedly different fashion. His tale of a licentious cleric who pursues all manner of fleshly pleasures and ultimately sells his soul to the devil, serves as a counterpoint to Radcliffe's relatively restrained Gothicism. These two approaches have come to be known as feminine and masculine Gothic. The former emphasizes terror, the activation of the faculties through fear, while the latter stresses horror, the paralysis of the mind and body through shock.

In the nineteenth century, Gothic fiction continued to flourish. Foremost among minor Gothic works by major Romantic figures are Percy Bysshe Shelley's *Zastrozzi* (1810) and *St Irvyne* (1811) and Walter Scott's *The Bride of Lammermoor* (1819). Also noteworthy is John Polidori's *The Vampyre* (1819). The principal Gothic novels of the Romantic period are Mary Shelley's *Frankenstein* (1818), Charles Robert Maturin's *Melmoth the Wanderer* (1820), and James Hogg's *The Private Memoirs and Confessions of a Justified Sinner* (1824). Jane Austen both parodies and pays homage to the genre in *Northanger Abbey* (1818). Early- and mid-Victorian Gothic novels include **Charlotte Brontë**'s *Jane Eyre* (1847), Emily Brontë's *Wuthering Heights* (1847), and **Wilkie Collins**'s *The Woman in White* (1860). J. Sheridan Le Fanu contributed the novel *Uncle Silas* (1864) and the collection *In a Glass Darkly* (1872), which latter includes the influential vampire tale *Carmilla*. Charles Dickens, Elizabeth Gaskell, and George Eliot also wrote Gothic stories during this period. In the United States, Edgar Allan Poe and Nathaniel Hawthorne set high standards for Gothic short fiction and novels in the former's *Tales of the Grotesque and Arabesque* (1840) and the latter's *Young Goodman Brown* (1835), "Rappaccini's Daughter" (1844), *The Scarlet Letter* (1850), and *The House of the Seven Gables* (1851).

Gothic fiction again reached the heights of popularity and acclaim during the final decades of the nineteenth century, when a series of landmark works were published. Among the

Mysteries of Udolpho.

Unattributed 19th century engraving from Ann Radcliffe's Gothic romance "The Mysteries of Udolpho." © Mary Evans Picture Library.

most significant Gothic novels of this era are Robert Louis Stevenson's *The Strange Case of Dr Jekyll and Mr Hyde* (1886), Oscar Wilde's *The Picture of Dorian Gray* (1891), and **Bram Stoker**'s *Dracula* (1897). The period's Gothic short stories and collections of short fiction include Charlotte Perkins Gilman's *The Yellow Wallpaper* (1892) and Arthur Machen's *The Great God Pan and the Inmost Light* (1894).

Prominent within the topics of Gothic fiction are love and sexuality—often illicit love and forbidden sexuality. Early Gothic novels feature innocent maidens who are pursued by sadistic yet seductive villains and protected by valiant young heroes. Rape is an ever-present though seldom-realized threat in these texts, and this danger is sometimes complicated by that of incest, for the obscure genealogies of the characters make possible unnaturally close liaisons. Feminine Gothic fiction suggests rather than makes explicit aberrant sexuality, but masculine texts such as *The Monk* may depict rape, incest, and even **necrophilia**. In contrast to the works of the 1790s, nineteenth-century Gothic fiction is more subtle in its approach to romantic and sexual themes, often exploring them metaphorically. It is, however, also arguably more socially transgressive in its treatment of women's sexuality and **homosexuality**, perhaps in part because a number of Gothic writers were women and gay men.

Among Victorian Gothic novels, *Jane Eyre* may best acknowledge the power and peril of a woman's desire for love and sexual fulfillment. The motifs of fire and ice that run parallel throughout the novel signify passion and repression. Between these options—each of which holds risks—Jane must repeatedly choose. The passion-repression split and its hazards are also mirrored in the relationship between Bertha and Jane, Edward Rochester's first and second wives. These women function as doppelgangers who illustrate the bifurcated Victorian vision of female sexuality: according to contemporary mores, women were either pure or polluted, angels or whores. The ease with which a respectable lady might become a "fallen woman" is underscored by Jane's literal and figurative closeness to Bertha, and the hazardous link between these two characters is one of the novel's most Gothic and most noteworthy features. This type of connection is repeated in *Dracula*, which contrasts the modest Mina with the lusty Lucy. Mina is attacked by Dracula but recovers to become an unsullied wife and mother, while Lucy is transformed into a ravenous vampire and eventually slain in a rape-like staking scene.

Homosexuality is explored in a number of nineteenth-century Gothic texts, including *Carmilla*, *The Strange Case of Dr Jekyll and Mr Hyde*, and *The Picture of Dorian Gray*. These works are forward-thinking insofar as they depict same-sex love with some degree of sympathy, but conservative to the extent that such love is ultimately punished. Le Fanu's short story focuses on the close relationship between Carmilla, a female vampire, and her young victim, Laura. While intimate friendships between women were common in the nineteenth century, because the bond between Carmilla and Laura is not only erotic but also unhealthy and dangerous, it must end with the vampire's destruction. The relationship between Jekyll and Hyde is likewise suspect, and it serves as the central mystery of Stevenson's novel—one Jekyll's bachelor friend Utterson believes he has solved by concluding that Hyde is blackmailing Jekyll. His conclusion makes sense, for such blackmail cases became fairly common after the Labouchere Amendment (1885) criminalized homosexual sex between men. Breaking this law ultimately led to the imprisonment of Oscar Wilde, whose *The Picture of Dorian Gray*—a novel inspired by and modeled upon *Jekyll and Hyde* in which the preternaturally handsome Dorian ruins the lives and reputations of other young men in some unspeakable fashion—would eventually be used as evidence against its author at his 1895 trial for sodomy.

Further Reading: Hogle, Jerrold E., ed. *The Cambridge Companion to Gothic Fiction.* Cambridge: Cambridge University Press, 2002; Mulvey Roberts, Marie, ed. *The Handbook to Gothic Literature.* New York: New York University Press, 1998; Punter, David. *The Literature of Terror: A History of Gothic Fiction from 1765 to the Present Day.* 2nd ed. 2 vols. London: Longman, 1996.

Jamil M. Mustafa

GRAND, SARAH (1854–1943). Sarah Grand, a bestselling British novelist and feminist campaigner, was responsible for popularizing the term "The New Woman." Grand's writing centers on marriage and the relation between the sexes, and advocates a new form of sexual relation that had as its central concern questions of breeding and national health. She was one of the leading exponents of a maternalist agenda which, in the context of late nineteenth-century British fears of racial decline and imperial loss, developed as eugenic **feminism**. The central goal of eugenic feminists was the construction of a form of civic motherhood that sought political recognition for reproductive labor; applying new biological knowledge they argued that their contribution to nation and empire might be expanded if women assumed responsibility for the rational selection of reproductive partners.

Frances Elizabeth Bellenden Clarke, the fourth of five children, was born in 1854 in Donaghadee, Northern Ireland; her father was a naval lieutenant then serving in Northern Ireland and her mother, Margaret Bell Sherwood was the sister of the Lord of the Manor of Rysome Garth in Holderness, Yorkshire. The family moved to Scarborough when Grand was seven. In 1868, aged fourteen, Grand entered the Royal Navy School in Twickenham, followed by a finishing school. In 1871, aged sixteen, she married the thirty-nine-year-old Lieutenant-Colonel David Chambers McFall, Brigade-Surgeon of the Thirty-Fourth Foot, the Indian Border Regiment. Following the birth of their only child, David Archibald, Grand and McFall spent five years posted at military stations in the East. Grand's first novel, *Two Dear Little Feet* (1873) warned women of the ill-effects of ill-fitting boots and corsets, and thus, more generally, of the effects of vanity on health, emphasizing similarities between Chinese foot binding and Western women's **fashion**. This concern with health continued through her work, focusing on the choice of a reproductive partner. Her next novel, *Ideala*, initially rejected by publishers, was eventually taken up by Bentley, and went through three editions in the first year. With the proceeds, Grand left her husband, moving to Kensington and, now in her late thirties, her career as a writer took off. In addition to eight novels and three short story collections, Grand wrote numerous articles for the periodical press; she was also a popular lecturer, touring Britain and America during the 1890s. She served as president of the Writers' Suffrage League which, founded by Betty Hatton and Cecily Hamilton in June 1908, continued up to the First World War. During the last years of the suffrage campaign Grand served as President of the Tunbridge Wells branch of the Women's Constitutional Suffrage Society. She was also a member of the Rational Dress Society, the Pioneer Club and the National Council of Women. Following her move to Bath in 1920, she was the Mayoress six times and became involved with the National Council for Combating Venereal Disease (founded in 1914, the Council changed its name to The British Social Hygiene Council in 1926). From its inception it had close ties with the Eugenics Society.

Grand's most infamous novel, *The Heavenly Twins*, with its forthright treatment of syphilis, took Britain and United States by storm in 1893. Reviewed by all the major papers and periodicals in both countries, the book was reprinted in Britain six times in its first year of publication with Heinemann reporting a sale of 20,000 within a few weeks. More than five times as many copies were sold in the United States, where it made the overall bestsellers list for the 1890s, and was translated into Finnish and Russian. "As surely as *Tess of the D'urbervilles* swept all before it last year, so surely has Sarah Grand's *Heavenly Twins* provoked the greatest attention and comment this season. It is a most daringly original work ... Sarah Grand is a notable Woman's Righter, but her book is the one asked for at every hotel table in the kingdom" (from the cover of *Our Manifold Nature*, 1894). The novel explores the disastrous marriages of Evadne Frayling and Edith Beale to degenerate men, offering a forceful polemic against the sexual double standard, with Evadne refusing to consummate her marriage to Major George Colquhoun, an army surgeon. Emblematic of much of her fiction, *The Heavenly Twins* is punctuated with radical ideas—Evadne's abstinence from a sexual relationship after marriage for reasons of health and feminist politics, the importance of female education, cross-dressing, and the determination of one of the Heavenly Twins, Angelica, to lead a life of freedom. Once married, Angelica spends many of her nights wandering the streets dressed as a boy, and in the course of these wanderings she befriends a reclusive tenor. Alongside these radical ideas, Grand develops new concepts of duty. For example, when in a seemingly homoerotic encounter with a Tenor, Angelica falls into a river in a boating accident and reveals, to his great distress, her true sex. The Tenor catches pneumonia rescuing her, and his death catapults Angelica into a life of duty.

Grand was an essentialist feminist, fundamentally opposed to emphasizing men's and women's characteristics—which hostile contemporaries saw as the goal of the New Woman. In 1892, she wrote to her publisher John Blackwood "my own experience is that in every position women will be women. Womanhood is a constitutional condition which cannot be altered" (*Letters of Frances Elizabeth McFall*, National Library of Scotland). The entry of women into the public sphere and the political world would not eliminate femininity; indeed, Grand argued, it was on account of their femininity that women would be able to serve the nation. She embraced eugenic ideas and saw a crucial role for women in influencing morality, improving and regulating national health, and addressing population questions. Civilization was predicated on such fixed, or essential, sexual difference and the body of her work promotes eugenic love: the replacement of romance with the rational selection of a reproductive partner in order to better serve the state through breeding.

The Beth Book (1897), her bestseller follow-up to *The Heavenly Twins*, similarly contains cross-dressing scenes, but these are confined to childhood. *The Beth Book* offers an attack on the **Contagious Diseases Acts**. It is equally critical of effeminacy and medical help for the unfit. As Grand saw it, it was the duty of women to rewrite the novel and cure civilization of its love-madness. *Beth* concedes that novel-reading can be a vice, but insists on its capacity for moral influence and reform. Grand's didacticism tried her readers' patience. The notion of fiction as an educational treatise, or as a medicinal drug, was at odds with prevailing contemporary aesthetics. In 1896, Grand claimed that her aesthetics were in the ascendant: "in England, thanks to our efforts, the 'novel with a purpose' and the 'sex novel' are more powerful at the present time, especially for good, than any other social influence. We appreciate art, but not art for art's sake; art for man's sake is what we demand" (letter to Professor Viëter, Nizza, in Heilmann, vol. V). She devised a hierarchy of forms of love which she linked to the idea of evolutionary progress: love was conceived of as evolving from lower to higher forms, and seeks the ultimate good of the community to its own, and she argued forcefully against free love and passion. Love, for Grand, was linked with duty, sacrifice, care, and devotion to the happiness of others. In the *New Review* in 1894, Grand stated that young people "should learn the facts of life and be trained not to think anything about them, and this can only be done by early familiarity with the subject, and by removing all sentimentality from it" (680). Her late novels *Adnam's Orchard* (1912) and *The Winged Victory* (1916) centered on the importance of cultivating fit families and urged the supremacy of the middle class as breeding stock, urging the health benefits of living in the countryside, outside the degenerate spaces of the city.

At Grand's death in 1943, *The Times* remarked that her bestselling novel of 1893, *The Heavenly Twins* "may be said to mark something of an epoch in English fiction … Sarah Grand and other writers of the school widened the field of English fiction by freeing it from some of its former limitations as to subject and treatment." And the *Manchester Guardian* reported, "it is hard to realize now what a shock *The Heavenly Twins* gave the reading public of 1893 or how outraged were the nineties by her conception of the new woman—one of whose characteristics was to be that she had learned about sex before marriage" (Kersely 1983, 14).

Further Reading: Heilmann, Ann, ed. *The Late-Victorian Marriage Question: A Collection of Key New Woman Texts.* 5 vols. London: Routledge with Thoemmes Press, 1998; Heilmann, Ann and Stephanie Forward. *Sex, Social Purity and Sarah Grand.* London: Routledge, 2000; Kersely, Gillian. *Darling Madame: Sarah Grand & Devoted Friend.* London: Virago, 1983; Mott, Frank Luther. *Golden Multitudes—The Story of Best Sellers in the United States.* New York: Macmillin, 1947; Richardson, Angelique. *Love and Eugenics in the Late Nineteenth Century: Rational Reproduction and the New Woman.* Oxford: Oxford University Press, 2003.

Angelique Richardson

GYNECOLOGICAL MANUALS. Gynecology, the diagnosis and treatment of diseases specific to women and the reproductive organs, was a new study for doctors in the nineteenth century. Gynecological manuals were loose translations of ancient, seventeenth- and eighteenth-century midwifery manuals such as the Renaissance work *Der Rosengarten*, and usually written by women or written by men as told to by women. Jane Sharpe's (1671) *The Midwife's Book or the Whole Art of Midwifry Discovered* was the most comprehensive and trusted work on pregnancy, childbirth, and women's diseases.

Because the worldview of women's disorders in the nineteenth century was grounded in old beliefs that had gone unchallenged, medical men continued to believe that there was a correlation between the uterus and nervous disorders. Hysteria, the major diagnosis in women, was an example of such a disease. Much writing in gynecological manuals was imbued with beliefs rather than facts about female physiology.

However, the entire nature of medicine changed during this period. Gynecology and obstetrics were the most rapidly growing specialty in the United States, although the fields were not based on a strictly scientific body of evidence. In their practice of medicine, **physicians** viewed themselves as the protectors of morality and decency. They acted as counselors as well as medical practitioners, particularly when treating women's illnesses.

Marion Sims (1813–1883), a southern doctor, is regarded as the father of gynecology in the United States. He is best remembered for having developed a surgical technique to fix vesico-vaginal fistulas. His life as a physician was involved in experimenting and perfecting surgical techniques to treat the problems of women. After using instruments to open the cervix as a treatment for dysmenorrheal (painful **menstruation**), he wrote *Uterine Surgery* in 1864. It was later published as *Clinical Notes on Uterine Surgery*, as a text for medical students. When he was criticized by letters to the editor in the British medical journal, *Lancet*, he defended his position by stating that dysmenorrhea was a symptom of another problem, not an entity in itself. Sims's experiments were met with both praise and criticism. Because the majority of his patients were Negro slaves he was retrospectively accused of racism. In his defense, it can be said that these were the patients who had the most severe tears. His use of the speculum, an instrument shaped like two spoons, used to spread the vaginal walls was, highly controversial because of modesty concerns. At a time when men were supposed to perform a gynecological examination by touch rather than by sight, he was regarded as bold and arrogant.

Charles Meigs, M.D., the author of *Females and their Diseases* (1848), proudly wrote that there were women who preferred to suffer from their gynecological problems rather than undergoing the indelicacy of having their bodies examined. The British physician Robert Brudenell Carter, who wrote *On the Pathology and Treatment of Hysteria* (1853), did not approve of the speculum. He wrote that young single middle-class women had become so habituated to the constant use of the speculum that they degenerated to the level of a prostitute. He felt that there was moral evil in medical manipulations and that the remedy was worse than the disease. Allegedly he witnessed young unmarried women asking medical practitioners to examine their sexual organs.

Since "female problems" were more culturally than medically defined, it was difficult to separate science from cultural practice and belief. But, it was also difficult to control a growing number of invasive procedures. A tumor could block a cervix and it would be appropriate to remove the obstruction. On the other hand, there were many illnesses, particularly nervous disorders, that were attributed to abnormalities in the uterus, ovaries, clitoris, and cervix. S. Weir Mitchell (1829–1914) and his rest cure was the best-known promoter of neurasthenia, the culture-bound syndrome that affected women and required that they do nothing but domestic tasks. His essay, *Fat and Blood* explained his philosophy and treatment of hysteria and neurasthenia.

Augustus K. Gardner, a colleague of Sims, wrote *The Causes and Curative Treatment of Sterility* in 1856. He also wrote *Conjugal Sins against the Laws of Life and Health* (1870), which instructed parents against coitus interruptus which he referred to as conjugal onanism. He warned that any child conceived as a result of an encounter where the man withdrew his penis too soon and "soiled the conjugal bed with shameful maneuvers" would be defective.

Midwives, the traditional specialists who had formerly delivered babies and taken care of any gynecologic problems, were not allowed to take classes or matriculate in medical schools. To train or license midwives was not possible because it would allegedly decrease the number of cases where the new technologies of medicine, for example, the stethoscope and pelvimeter, would be used. The few women who had become physicians in the late part of the century went to women's medical colleges and were denied membership in both the American Medical Association and the British Medical Society.

A peculiar treatment known as uterine massage became a standard treatment for women suffering from nervous disorders, hysteria, or *furor uterinus*. This manual manipulation saved many from undergoing the mutilating surgeries of ovariectomy and **clitoridectomy** that were popular as cures for gynecological problems. Thure Brandt of Stockholm, Sweden wrote *Massage in Gynecology* in which he described internal, external, and combined methods. With the advent of the electrical vibrator, physicians could perform massage with an appliance rather than manually which saved them a great deal of energy. The massage was actually **masturbation** so that the woman could experience an **orgasm**, medically known as "hysterical paroxysm." On the other side,

William Heath Byford (1817–1890), a professor of gynecology at the University of Chicago, cautioned against excessive masturbation in his *Treatise on the Chronic Inflammation and Displacements of the Unimpregnated Uterus* (1864). He also touted opium as the treatment for delayed or absent menstrual periods, known as amenorrhea, but reversed his position in the revised edition of 1898.

With the advent of anesthesia, the demand for gynecological surgery grew. But anesthesia for obstetrical use was denied to many women because of religious prohibitions. The politics of religion weighed heavily against the rights of women for pain relief in childbirth and biblical quotes such as "in sorrow shalt thy bring forth children," were interpreted to mean that all women should suffer pain for the sin of one woman. Eve. Thomas Spencer Wells (1818–1897), a British naval surgeon, disregarded this caveat and was an advocate of the use of anesthesia for women in childbirth, as well as for abdominal surgery. He wrote *Diseases of the Ovaries* in 1872, in which he described the surgery for removal of the ovaries. The manual is illustrated with pictures of doctors wearing street clothing while operating, not at all uncommon before the adoption of sterile techniques in the operating room.

Nineteenth-century gynecological manuals were of two orientations. There was some valid scientific information based on experimentation, observation, and statistics emerging. But, there was also a fearful reticence to accept sexuality as normal and much ignorance about subjects such as masturbation and female orgasm, which were perpetuated by physicians.

Further Reading: Feibelman, Peter. *Natural Causes*. See Peter Feibelman, Novelist and Playwright at: www.fictionwriter.com/double.htm; Mayer, Oscar J. "Massage in Gynecology." *JAMA* (August 1894): 236–40. Medicinenet.com—www.medicinenet.com/script/main/art.asp? articlekey=8795; Jackson, Lee. Onanism. The Victorian Dictionary. www.victorianlondon.org/ sex/onanism.htmMcGregor; Kuhn, Deborah. *Sexual Surgery and the Origins of Gynecology*. New York: Garland, 1989; Mitchell, S. Weir. *Fat and Blood: An Essay on the Treatment of Certain Forms of Hysteria and Neurasthenia*. Philadelphia: Lippincott, 1907; Wetherington, Cora and Adele Roman, eds. NIH Drug Addiction Research and the Health of Women. U.S. Department of Health and Human Services at: www.nida.nih.gov/PDF/DARHW-exec.pdf.

Lana Thompson

H

HADDO, LORD. *See* Nude Models

HARDY, THOMAS (1840–1928). The British novelist and poet Thomas Hardy was preoccupied by the question of the sexual relation between men and women, which he termed in his preface to *The Woodlanders* "the immortal puzzle"; "given the man and the woman, how to find a basis for their sexual relation." This question runs through his novels, which scrutinize how to sustain the sexual relation in face of individual striving, sexual competition, and social and economic pressures. His explorations led him to consider a range of related questions, from alternative social arrangements of the family, to the very nature of femininity, bringing him into the thick of the late nineteenth-century "Woman Question."

In Hardy's first letter to his publisher in 1868 he wrote: "no fiction will considerably interest readers poor or rich unless the passion of love forms a prominent feature in the thread of the story" (British Library Macmillan Archives 54923 362F 1). The sexologist Havelock Ellis came closest among contemporaries in recognizing Hardy's overriding interest in the relations between the sexes: "he is less a story-teller than an artist who has intently studied certain phases of passion, and brings us a simple and faithful report of what he has found" (1896, 9).

Hardy's preoccupation with love and sex bears direct relation to shifts within the broader intellectual climate. The love-plot now appealed as much to the biologist as to the novelist. In the *Descent of Man and Selection in Relation to Sex*, Darwin justified a new and extensive focus on sexual relations, with Hardy citing Schopenhauer: "the final aim of all love intrigues, be they comic or tragic, is really of more importance than all other ends in human life … it is not the weal or woe of any one individual, but that of the human **race** to come, which is here at stake" (2nd ed., chap. 20 [1871; London: John Murray, 1874]). Hardy was one of Darwin's earliest admirers and writing in his wake, made biology one of the central concerns of his work. He copied into his notebook Zola's assertion that the novel had moved from the realm of art into those of "physiology and pathology." For Hardy, privileging biology had consequences for the romance narrative: as he wrote in the *New Review* in 1890: "life being a physiological fact, its honest portrayal must be largely concerned with, for one thing, the relations between the sexes and the substitution for such catastrophes as favor the false coloring best expressed by the regulation finish that 'they married and were happy ever after' of catastrophes upon the sexual relations as it is."

Hardy's preoccupation with biology fed his treatment of the sexes and, in particular, femininity, which in the second half of the nineteenth century was one of the main subjects of social and scientific debate. Darwin had argued for women's closer relation to animals in *The Descent of Man*, arguing that characteristics such as intuition, rapid perception, and possibly imitation, were more dominant in women than in European men. But he claimed that these traits were also typical of what Darwin termed the "lower races," and of an earlier and less civilized state of society. Hardy's fiction shows his engagement with these ideas but does not offer any final resolution. His women are unmistakably, palpably, embodied. Elfride, in *A Pair of Blue Eyes*, for example, is a "palpitating mobile creature"; she pouts and blushes, weeps and suffers from nervous disorder subsequent to unnecessary mental exertion. She was a favorite with Havelock Ellis. In a review of Hardy's work in the *Westminster Review*, Ellis declared "the pathetic figure of Elfride, with her eager and delicate instincts, her sweet hesitations, her clinging tenderness" to have "a charm for the memory, which no other of Mr. Hardy's heroines possesses in so great a degree." For Havelock Ellis, the chief merits of Hardy's heroines were their "instinct-led" natures.

While Hardy was undoubtedly influenced by the prevailing scientific view of women, his overall view seems more ambivalent. His women are certainly biological beings, but at times Hardy depicts them as held back by, rather than simple expressions of, their biological state. In *Jude the Obscure*, in contrast to Arabella Donn, who is "three parts animal" Sue Bridehead is ethereal and intellectual to the extent she causes Jude to wonder if she has a body at all. Here, Hardy is experimenting with forms of femininity that opposing intellectual currents were producing. Alongside Darwin, one of his main influences was J. S. Mill, the philosopher and campaigner for women's rights, whose views on liberty and individual freedom he championed. In his *Subjection of Women* (1869), Mill had exposed the social and political underpinnings of discourses on the natural: "what is now called the nature of women is an eminently artificial thing—the result of forced repression in some directions, unnatural stimulation in others" (238). In *The Well Beloved*, Hardy refers to "the rule that succeeding generations of women are seldom marked by cumulative progress, their advance as girls being lost in their recession as matrons; so that they move up and down the stream of intellectual development like flotsam in a tidal estuary. And this perhaps not by reason of their faults as individuals, but of their misfortune as child-rearers" (1897; Oxford, 1997, 161).

If Hardy's women are beholden to their biology, so too are his men. Jude's story is set in motion by biological drive which "seemed to care little for his reason and his will, nothing for his so-called elevated intentions, and moved him along, as a violent schoolmaster a schoolboy he has seized by the collar." At different times in their lives, Hardy's characters are driven, or circumscribed, by biology, but they are also striving for something more. Jude seeks a university education; Tess seeks to resist the sexual double standard, pursuing new joy with Angel after her seduction by Alec. Each seeks fulfillment. But central to their struggles are the complexities of the sexual relationship. D. H. Lawrence in his study of Hardy wrote "none care very much for money, or immediate self-preservation, and all of them are struggling hard to come into being. What exactly the struggle into being consists in, is the question. But move obviously from the Wessex novels, the first and chiefest factor is the struggle into love and the struggle with love; by love meaning the love of a man for a woman and a woman for a man. The via media to being, for man or woman, is love, and love alone.... The tale is about becoming complete." But though they may not care much for money, class intersects with love and sex in the novels, pulling the characters to and away from each other. *The Poor Man and the Lady* was the title of Hardy's first novel, which was subsequently destroyed. Class disparity recurs in the novels, pervading the sexual relations, for example, in *The Woodlanders* and *Tess of the D'Urbervilles*.

Hardy's engagement with the sex question also led him directly into the "Woman Question." A letter to Millicent Fawcett of 1906 objected that the stereotyped household should be "the unit of society," revealing the extent to which he had thought through the social consequences of alternative relations between men and women. He likewise engaged with the question of suffrage. In 1908, he wrote to Helen Ward, declining to be actively involved in the campaign for female suffrage, "I feel by no means sure that the majority of those who clamour for it realize what it may bring in its train ... I refer to such results as the probable break-up of the present marriage-system," adding "I do not myself consider that this would be necessarily a bad thing (I should not have written "Jude the Obscure" if I did) but I deem it better that women should take the step unstimulated from outside."

Ultimately, Hardy's men and women are victims of social and economic forces, as Jude remarks "that's what some women will fail to see, and instead of protesting against the conditions they protest against the man, the other victim" (*Jude*, 299–300). Perhaps the most illuminating remark on the question of sex occurs in Hardy's earliest novel, *Desperate Remedies* (1871): "in spite of a fashion which pervades the whole community at the present day—the habit of exclaiming that woman is not undeveloped man, but diverse, the fact remains that, after all, women are Mankind, and that in many of the sentiments of life the difference of sex is but a difference of degree" (1871; Penguin, 1998).

Further Reading: Ellis, Havelock. "Concerning *Jude the Obscure*." *Savoy*. October 1896; reprinted Ulysses Bookshop, 1931; Ellis, Havelock. "Thomas Hardy's Novels." *Westminster Review* 63 (1883): 334–64; Hardy, Florence [Thomas Hardy]. *The Life of Thomas Hardy*, 2 vols. London: Studio Editions, 1994; originally published 1928–1930; Hardy, Thomas. *The Literary Notebooks of Thomas Hardy*, edited by Lennart A. Björk. 2 vols. London and Basingstoke: Macmillan, 1985; Tilly, Arthur. "The New School of Fiction." *National Review* I (1883).

Angelique Richardson

HAREMS. As Ruth Bernard Yeazell remarks, "As imaginative projections ... harems tell us more about the Europeans who created them than they do about the domestic reality of the East" (Yeazell 2000, 8). The nineteenth-century fantasies of the harem thus reveal attitudes to gender, sexuality, **race**, and ethnicity; they are fantasies of power and domination, of racial difference translating into sexual difference. Beginning in the eighteenth century and gaining strength throughout the Victorian period, the cultural obsession with harems as imaginary spaces of eroticism and unrestrained sexuality had little to do with the reality. In traditional Arabic culture, the word harem refers both to the part of a dwelling which is reserved for the use of the women of the household, being out of bounds for males who are not relatives, and reserved for the women themselves. However, the harem existed in a much more lurid and sensational form in the nineteenth-century public imagination and it is vital to read these texts and images as fantasies. Whether romanticized or depicted as dens of depravity, the harem held an erotic charge that made it an essential part of any travel narrative of the East.

As figured in romances, **painting**s, pornography, and travel accounts, the nineteenth-century western idea of the harem centered around several elements. One obvious facet of the erotic appeal was the idea of many women to one man, a kind of sexual smorgasbord of compliant, sexually available women. The strong focus on monogamy in Victorian discourses of love and marriage made this apparent sanctioning of

"Fantasia in a harem," 19th century engraving of an Egyptian harem. © The Art Archive/Bibliothèque des Arts Décoratifs Paris/Dagli Orti.

unrestricted erotic variety an attractive fantasy. Unlike discourses of free love later in the century, the harem fantasy also provided the male consumer with women who were forcibly kept faithful, while he was able to pick and choose. An obvious imbalance of power between the genders also inflected this fantasy, as the women are forced to compete for the attention of the male. Although middle- and upper-class women of the nineteenth century competed, in a sense, on the marriage market, conventional discourses of gender enforced sexual passivity and reticence in women. As Ruth Bernard Yeazell notes, "for a man accustomed to the conventional order of attack and resistance, there was also something powerfully attractive in the idea of a prodigious number of women all hotly competing for his attention" (Yeazell, 108). Implications of same-sex desire between women also permeate many of these texts. This is seen to be affected by several factors: a lack of adequate male attention, the effect of the hot climate, which was thought to exacerbate sexual desire, and the inherently weak morality which was attributed to non-Christian cultures. This can be seen as yet another voyeuristic male fantasy, figuring same-sex desire as an inadequate substitute or prelude to heterosexual connection.

Another aspect of the imaginary harem is the challenge it is seen to provoke, as it cannot be viewed by the male visitor, or indeed by a female visitor, unless invited. It is thus taboo, out of reach, making entry into this space—even a vicarious entry, through the consumption of a text—a forbidden pleasure. There is also an element of bondage and domination, perhaps even of sadomasochism, in this fantasy of the harem. Although the word "harem" derives from the Arabic for "forbidden" or "sacred" (in Turkish, "sanctuary"), western interpretations have focused on the harem as a place of enclosure or imprisonment (Yeazell, 1–2). The overtones of captivity which color nineteenth-century fantasies of the harem place the consumer of such texts and images in a position of power, a voyeur who has penetrated this place of obsessive secrecy. This fantasy simultaneously disempowers the women who are imagined to populate this space, figuring them as passive objects rather than as active subjects.

105

Harems were a popular subject for Orientalist paintings, particularly in France and England, and usually focused on an implied or overt sexuality. While Eugène Delacroix and Jean-Auguste-Dominique Ingres are two of the most famous painters of this genre scene, there were many less celebrated artists who immortalized the fantasy of the harem, many of whom, like Ingres himself, never actually traveled to the East. As well, thousands of **photographs** and postcards were sold in the nineteenth century featuring scenes set up in photographers' studios to resemble harems—or at least, western fantasies of harems. Harems were thus aestheticized and consumed in both popular and high culture, as erotic and romantic images. This further disempowers the women depicted in harems scenes, whether visual or literary, as they become undifferentiated props rather than individual characters.

Further Reading: Alloula, Malek. *The Colonial Harem.* Manchester: Manchester University Press, 1986; Schick, Irvin C. *The Erotic Margin: Sexuality and Spatiality in Alteritist Discourse.* London: Verso, 1999; Yeazell, Ruth Bernard. *Harems of the Mind: Passages of Western Art and Literature.* New Haven, CT: Yale University Press, 2000.

Jessica Needle

HERMAPHRODITES. The term hermaphrodite has been replaced in medical and lay contexts with the term "intersex" since the 1990s. Hermaphrodite had always been a problematic word conjuring a mythical creature, Hermaphroditus, the figure from Greek mythology whose male body was merged by the gods with the female body of the nymph Salmacis. But, Hermaphroditus found no counterparts in the mortal human world. Nineteenth-century doctors searched for a person born with a perfect set of both male and female genital organs, but because they insisted on "perfection" in these organs, no one who fit this definition was ever found. This led some early medical authorities to believe that hermaphrodites did not exist in the human species. Earthworms, snails, and some reptiles could be hermaphrodites, these experts argued, but not humans. Nevertheless, people were born with ambiguous genitalia that allowed them flexibility in living variously as male and as female. Though their bodies did not fit the criteria exactly, these individuals were sometimes considered hermaphrodites.

Technically, the doctors were right; no humans were like hermaphroditic earthworms, possessing two perfect sets of external and internal reproductive organs, capable of reproducing as either female or male. But the claim that hermaphrodites did not exist encouraged nineteenth-century doctors and laypeople to insist on two and only two sexes, when not all bodies fit precisely into discrete male and female categories. True, most people had bodies with physical markers that were clearly male or female, but some had genitals, gonads, and genetic material sufficiently equivocal to make doctors and parents wonder to which sex they belonged.

Hermaphroditism, as a medical condition, was born in the nineteenth century. By the antebellum period in America, a new scientific, medical discourse dominated by professional **physicians** emerged. As scholars of medical history have pointed out, this was precisely the time when American physicians established themselves as a professional body. American doctors began attending medical schools in greater numbers, and they shared their cases with colleagues in newly instituted medical publications. Doctors wrote about a variety of cases involving unusual genital presentations, including elongated penises, urethral strictures, vaginal fistulas, and hypertrophied clitorises. Even the cases that did not specifically focus on hermaphroditism offered doctors the opportunity to compare one patient's presentation with another.

In making comparisons, doctors often referred to, and denied, hermaphroditic conditions.

Nineteenth-century doctors were intent on deciding patients' sex definitively, whether the patients were infants or adults who had already established their gender identity. In their zeal to achieve sexual certainty, doctors did not hesitate to judge their patients' gender performance as mistaken, if not deliberately fraudulent. There are dozens of examples in the medical literature in which patients sought advice for unrelated conditions and then had their ambiguous genitals "discovered" by a very interested doctor. By examining external organs as well as ascertaining tastes, manners, and habits, doctors sometimes labeled patients one sex when they had been living contentedly as the other. A doctor's encouragement to change genders in mid-life was not always appreciated, though sometimes the advice was heeded.

By the second half of the nineteenth century an irony had emerged in the medical reporting of the so-called hermaphrodites. Most doctors' accounts published in leading medical journals argued that hermaphrodites did not exist in the human species, and that all the so-called cases were simply patients whose proper sex, male or female, had been mistaken. Yet, incongruously, medical men clung to the term, further refining it to justify their pronouncements of one sex or the other. The classification schemes devised by European physicians became more detailed and ultimately, as European historian Alice Dreger has argued, centered on the gonads, both sets of which (testicles and ovaries) were required to label someone a true hermaphrodite. Since most believed such precise dualism was impossible, doctors had to figure out what combination of organs (along with what conduct) determined true sex. Despite surprisingly little medical agreement on exact criteria, it became the doctors' prerogative to proclaim sex, even if their assessments contradicted how their patients had lived their lives.

In deciding the sex of their patients, doctors sought happy endings, hoping to see their patients embrace at least one element of conventional sexual maturity: marriage. The early cases of interventionist surgery on genitalia were designed to make the genitals serve the doctors' perception of patients' sexual and marital requirements. Ensuring heterosexual sex, particularly intercourse, with or without accompanying sexual desire, became progressively more important for doctors, for when sexual inversion became the scientific explanation of **homosexuality** in the late nineteenth and early twentieth centuries, hermaphrodites were seen as in danger of coupling with their same sex.

The early cases of interventionist surgery were connected to the patients' perceived sexual needs as determined by the doctor in attendance (this remained true throughout the twentieth century and has been critiqued by current intersex activists). By the turn of the century, hermaphrodites became potential homosexuals or "inverts"; if some bodies could look both male and female, then would these patients be attracted to the "wrong" sex? Though the possibility of hermaphrodites being physically intimate with either sex had long been a concern for physicians, now doctors began to evaluate their patients' sexual inclinations in order to ensure surgically that potential sexual intercourse would be between two differently sexed bodies. If an indeterminately sexed patient, even one who seemed predominantly male, expressed sexual interest in men, for example, doctors advocated surgical intervention to make that person's genitals appeared female.

As time passed, medical (and therefore, legal) authorities became more and more certain of their ability to distinguish a person's actual sex and were increasingly able to impose a sexual conformation that suited their own prejudices against same-sex unions.

To uncover the hidden history of intersex is to expose implicit attitudes toward sexual normality and difference. What doctors began in earnest in the nineteenth century—the surgical "correction" of genitalia to match entrenched notions of normal bodies—became far more systematic and troubling later in the twentieth century. Today's intersex activists are trying to halt the unnecessary medical intervention that has occurred since the mid-nineteenth century.

Further Reading: Dreger, Alice. *Hermaphrodites and the Medical Invention of Sex*. London: Harvard University Press, 1998; Fausto-Sterling, Anne. *Sexing the Body: Gender Politics and the Construction of Sexuality*. New York: Basic Books, 2000; Kessler, Suzanne J. *Lessons from the Intersexed*. New Brunswick, NJ: Rutgers University Press, 1998; Laqueur, Thomas. *Making Sex: Body and Gender from the Greeks to Freud*. Cambridge, MA: Harvard University Press, 1990; Matta, Christina. "Ambiguous Bodies and Deviant Sexualities: Hermaphrodites, Homosexuality, and Surgery in the United States, 1850–1904." *Perspectives in Biology and Medicine* 48 (Winter 2005): 74–83; Reis, Elizabeth. "Impossible Hermaphrodites: Intersex in America, 1620–1960." *Journal of American History* (September 2005): 411–41.

Elizabeth Reis

HINDUISM, MARRIAGE IN. The nineteenth century witnessed the crucial beginnings in the modern transformation of Hindu marriage in India, driven by legal intervention, including judicial interpretations and legislative reform, and social reform. In their interpretation of Hindu marriage, the British Indian courts relied greatly on the authority of the *dharmasastras*, a large corpus of written texts that had evolved over at least 2,500 years. But, the *shastras* "did not lay down law, they taught righteousness to a population eager to acquire it" (Derrett 1978, 49). Given the diversity and nonprescriptive nature of the literature, as well as the influence of English notions of jurisprudence, the courts mediated new and controversial interpretations of marriage leading at least in part to the call for reform in the nineteenth century. Complicating the picture further was the lack of correspondence between the more celebrated/notorious picture of marriage with some basis in the *shastras* and the practice of the vast majority of the people, not only numerous lower and middle castes but also (in regions beyond north India) some of the brahmins and upper castes. Nor was the term "Hindu" located in the texts, it was derived from "Indus," an external reference to practices/people of the region.

Importantly, as the British understood the *shastras* as the source of traditional Hindu law and even looked to them for a definitive code, in the nineteenth century they validated a brahmanical system of marriage, which subscribed to highly restrictive notions of women's sexuality, over less inhibiting ones that had customary sanction. Under the brahmanical system, which extended well into the early twentieth century, marriage was a sacrament. Among the rituals that established it, the *saptapadi*, the seven steps taken by bride and groom around the sacred fire, were considered one of the most important, the seventh step completing the ceremony. References to marriage as a *sanskara*, that which makes a life complete, made it virtually obligatory for men and women, for the threefold purpose of religious duty, progeny, and conjugal love, the last receiving the least emphasis. The overriding and indissoluble character of marriage impinged disproportionately on the woman. The bride was transferred to the family of her husband quite completely, taking on a new identity and losing any substantial right of residence and maintenance in her natal home. "Her union with her husband was conceived as a condition of one body, and a widow was her husband's surviving half. Thus she was subordinate to those to whom he was subordinate. During marriage she was distinctly subordinate to her husband" (Derrett, 49). Significantly, it was with reference to a notion of marriage, which placed severe restrictions upon women's sexuality, that the British Indian courts designated the customary institutions of sexual **cohabitation** among matrilineal Hindus on the southwest coast as concubinage rather than marriage. In contrast, Anglo Hindu law recognized male polygamy/concubinage based on the ancient texts but disregarded the conditions they laid down to warrant it. These conditions were rigorous—where the wife could not, due to insanity disease or otherwise, properly conduct the obligations required of her status.

Remarriage of widowers was practiced widely, but widow remarriage, though sanctioned under certain conditions in the earlier texts, had disappeared entirely from the later *shastric* texts and from the social practice of Brahmins and several upper castes in the colonial period. However, there were no such constraints among the more numerous lower castes. The Hindu Widows Remarriage Act, 1856, championed most prominently by the well-known social reformer Ishwar Chandra Vidyasagar, sought to ameliorate the oppressive institution of widowhood among the upper castes. However, the act came to be used in adjudication of the disputes among groups that had previously admitted widow remarriage. As it deemed that widows who remarried would lose their rights over their deceased husband's property, it was used to deny lower-caste women their previously recognized claims. Also related to marriage, the custom of *sati*, self-immolation by widows on their husbands' funeral pyre, mentioned in some later *shastric* texts, was prohibited by the colonial state in 1829. In doing this, the state yielded to a powerful campaign led by the social reformer Raja Rammohan Roy. As in the case of widow remarriage there was intense opposition to the move, but interestingly both the proponents and the opposition rested their arguments on the authority of the *shastras*.

Child marriage, with consummation either before or not long after marriage, remained virtually undisturbed across the region for most of the nineteenth century. However, it did not enjoy uncontested *shastric* approval. In the late nineteenth century, the case of the death of a nine-year-old Bengali girl after she was forced to have sex with her thirty-five-year-old husband inflamed feelings on both sides and set up the

The marriage ceremony of Vasudeva and Devki with priest and ladies of the household from the Bhagavata Purana, 1760. © The Art Archive/British Library.

issue in sharp relief. Eventually the Age of Consent Act (1891) raised the **age of consent** for girls, prescribed in the Indian Penal Code (1860) from ten to twelve years, making an indirect intervention into the institution of child marriage. The liberal social reformer, Merwanji Malabari's campaign to prohibit child marriage came up against orthodox sections who defended the practice on cultural grounds, but also by liberals in favor of gradual reform through the spread of education.

The brahmanical system of Hindu marriage as reflected in the *shastras* was governed quite rigidly by norms of status, clan exogamy (marriage outside the clan), and caste endogamy (marriage within the subgroups). While marriage of girls upwards in the hierarchy was tolerated, the reverse was abhorred, as was the marriage of relatives by blood. However, there was considerable disjunction between the practices favored generally in the *shastras* and extant custom beyond north India. Most notable was the contrast to these norms provided almost universally in southern India, where Brahmin and non-Brahmin girls alike could and did marry close kin as close as cross-cousins, and among several social groups the mother's brother himself was the preferred bridegroom for a girl. Also, close distance marriage was practiced in contrast to rules of village exogamy in the north.

Reflecting the diversity of practices confronted by its authors, the *shastras* identified eight valid forms of marriage, but ordered them according to degrees of approval. Interestingly, they were described in terms of the manner in which a girl was given away. While the approved forms, *brahma, daiva, arsha,* and *prajapatya* were distinguished by the "gift of the daughter" (*kanyadana*) the not approved forms, *asura, gandharva, rakshasa, and paisacha,* involved the sale or violent capture of the girl or the motive of sexual attraction. Beginning in the nineteenth century and noted throughout the twentieth century, the *kanyadana* marriage received greater legal and social emphasis, reflected in the aspirations of several lower-status groups as well. However, the *asura* form of marriage, described as the sale of a girl through the payment of a bride price, was practiced by at least some among the Brahmins in southern India up until the early twentieth century. The very general adoption of the *kanyadana* forms is reflected most sharply in the shift from the widespread practice of paying a bride price at marriage in the nineteenth century to paying a dowry in the twentieth, but also in the spread of restrictive sexual norms concerning women in particular.

The concept of *stridhan* (women's separate property) is sometimes linked to *kanyadana* marriage, as the *brahma* and *daiva* forms required a bride to be adorned expensively in jewels. However, positive interpretations of *stridhan* brought within its scope gifts from father, mother, brother, husband and in laws, gifts at marriage, and a marriage fee on the occasion of the husband's subsequent marriage; under the *mitakshara*, one of two major strands in the *shastras*, inherited property from both male and female relatives were *stridhan*. Women were not to be denied the enjoyment and use of this property nor could their husband or male relatives assert power over it. Nevertheless there were constraints: women lost the right to acquire property during coverture. This meant that their earnings from their own labor was regarded the property of their husband and "[w]ifely initiative even in matters concerning *stridhan* was deprecated as 'bad form'" (Derrett 1978, 5). The concept of *stridhan* underwent significant changes through legal interpretation in the nineteenth century, furnishing in large measure the basis of the notion of dowry that was abolished by the Indian state in the twentieth century. A series of judgments between 1850 and 1930 sounded its death knell, excluding inherited property from its scope and reducing it to a limited estate.

Thus, the nineteenth century was marked by the first winds of reform of marriage that sought to loosen sexual norms concerning women. Legislation opened the doors to very slow changes in child marriage and enabled the prevention of sati. However, while the Hindu Widows Remarriage Act had limited impact, there are indications that restrictions against widow remarriage spread to the lower castes in their pursuit of social mobility in the twentieth century. Besides, while the notion of *stridhan*, legally battered in the nineteenth century has disappeared altogether, dowry has developed deep social roots.

Further Reading: Basu, Monmayee. *Hindu Women and Marriage Law: From Sacrament to Contract*. New Delhi: Oxford University Press, 2004; Derrett, J.D.M. *The Death of a Marriage Law: Epitaph for the Rishis*. New Delhi: Vikas Publishing House, 1978; Agnes, Flavia. "Women, Marriage and the Subordination of Rights." In *Subaltern Studies XI: Community, Gender and Violence*, edited by Partha Chatterjee and Pradip Jeganathan. London: C. Hurst and Co., 2000.

Praveena Kodoth

HIRSCHFELD, MAGNUS (1868–1935).   Born in Kolberg (Pomerania), Germany, Magnus Hirschfeld became one of the most prominent sexologists of the nineteenth and early twentieth centuries. Hirschfeld was instrumental in the propagation of the theory of the so-called "third sex" (*das dritte Geschlecht*), an intermediate stage of gender and sexuality between homosexuals and heterosexuals. Building on the work of Karl Heinrich Ulrichs (1825–1895), who is credited by some with the creation of the word "homosexual," Hirschfeld spent most of his life advocating for the rights of homosexual women and men, specifically, and for sexual reform, in general. He went on to found the *Wissenschaftlich-humanitäres Komitee* (Scientific-Humanitarian Committee) and the *Institut für Sexualwissenschaft* (Institute for Sexual Science) in Berlin.

Hirschfeld grew up in a well-known Jewish family. His father, Dr. Hermann Hirschfeld, was a physician and philanthropist who was revered by his community. The elder Hirschfeld's social conscience and medical approach influenced the younger Hirschfeld's own later work in science, and Hirschfeld held his father and his father's work in high regard (Wolff 1986, 25). The course of study, which led him to a medical degree in 1892, was not Hirschfeld's only academic experience. Before studying medicine, Hirschfeld had begun a course of study of philology and literature in Breslau, though he eventually became more committed to the idea of working in the same field as his father. Nonetheless, Hirschfeld's interest in language and writing stayed with him throughout the rest of his life (Wolff, 26, 28).

In 1896, Hirschfeld wrote an article (under a pseudonym, Theodor Ramien) that would signal a new focus in his life. Published by Max Spohr in Leipzig, *Sappho und Socrates, Wie erklärt sich die Liebe der Männer und Frauen zu Personen des eigenen Geschlechts* ("Sappho and Socrates, How Does One Explain the Love of Men and Women for People of Their Own Sex"), was Hirschfeld's first attempt at arguing that same-sex sexuality should be viewed as natural and certainly not prohibited by law. In this article, Hirschfeld began his lifelong work for public acceptance of homosexuals and "sexual variants."

Hirschfeld's theories of sexuality built on the work of psychiatrist and sex researcher, **Richard von Krafft-Ebing** (1840–1902), and Karl Ulrichs. Like Krafft-Ebing, Hirschfeld believed firmly that **homosexuality** and transvestism (a term and category that Hirschfeld is credited with creating) were not diseases, but rather sexual variants. Though he did not, at least at first, proclaim the equality of sexual variants with normative heterosexuality, Hirschfeld did view these variants as a kind of congenital defect that in no way affected the potential and capabilities of a person (Wolff, 36, 37). Preceding the work of American sex researcher Alfred Kinsey (1894–1956) and Kinsey's scale of human sexuality, Hirschfeld created his own scale of "quantity of desire" that had ten degrees of intensity, marking homosexuality, bisexuality, and heterosexuality as weak, moderate, or strong, according to where an individual's desire fell on his scale (Wolff, 34, 35).

On May 15, 1897, Hirschfeld, along with Max Spohr (who had published Hirschfeld's "Sappho and Socrates" article) and Edward Oberg, a German railway official, founded the Scientific-Humanitarian Committee. Soon joined by other men, this organization's primary concern was the abolishment of the German law that prohibited (male) same-sex eroticism, Paragraph 175. The Committee's first action was the January 1898 petition in the German *Reichstag* (Parliament) to do away with this law. Though this first attempt failed, petitions were introduced later with many more signatures, including those of such famous writers and intellectuals as Gerhard Hauptmann (1862–1946), Heinrich Zille (1858–1929), Heinrich Mann (1871–1950), Thomas Mann (1875–1955; later withdrawn), Frank Wedekind (1864–1918), and Rainer Maria Rilke (1875–1926).

In his fight against Paragraph 175, Hirschfeld made use of the publicity surrounding the suicides of many high-ranking officers, civil **servants**, and other prominent members of German society. At the turn of the twentieth century, Germany found itself in a climate of extreme homosexual suspicion; rumors circulated about the Kaiser, members of the Kaiser's social circle, and many members of the nobility. Hirschfeld often referred to this climate of blackmail and denunciation in his own struggles against discriminatory laws, claiming that prohibitions like Paragraph 175 cultivated such an environment (Wolff, 61).

In 1919, Hirschfeld created the Institute for Sexual Science in Berlin. The institute combined various branches of science in the pursuit of research on and about sex, sexuality, and sexual behaviors. Not only did the institute serve as a headquarters for academic inquiry, but it also offered testing for venereal disease, marriage and career counseling, family planning services, and library services. Hirschfeld's Institute eventually became the first announced target of the Nazis' destruction of "objectionable" books in May of 1933 (Steakley 1975, 103). The institute's library was burned and a bust of Hirschfeld was also thrown onto the fire, an incident that Hirschfeld himself witnessed in newsreels while on a lecture trip to Paris. Hirschfeld remained in exile in Paris and attempted to re-establish a sexual science institute there until his death in 1935.

During his lifetime, Hirschfeld contributed actively to the medical and scientific discourse on sexuality. He was an editor of and contributor to the *Jahrbücher für sexuelle Zwischenstufen* (*Yearbooks for Sexual Intermediates*, 1899–1923), in whose first issue Hirschfeld stated his hope that Paragraph 175 would not survive into the twentieth century. Starting in 1908, Hirschfeld edited *Die Zeitschrift für Sexualwissenschaft* (*The Journal for Sexual Science*). Hirschfeld's many other works include "*Was soll das Volk vom dritten Geschlecht wissen?*" ("What Should the People Know about the Third Sex?"; 1901), *Berlins Drittes Geschlecht* (*Berlin's Third Sex*, 1904), *Die Homosexualität des Mannes und des Weibes* (*Homosexuality of Men and Women*, 1914), and *Geschlechtskunde* (*Sexology*, 5 vols., 1928–1930). The work of Hirschfeld and the Institute of Sexual Science was most recently depicted in Rosa von Praunheim's 1999 film, *Der Einstein des Sex* (*The Einstein of Sex*).

Further Reading: Steakley, James D. *The Homosexual Emancipation Movement in Germany.* Salem, NH: Ayer, 1975; Wolff, Charlotte. *Magnus Hirschfeld: A Portrait of a Pioneer in Sexology.* London: Quartet, 1986.

Kyle E. Frackman

HOMOSEXUALITY.   It is generally accepted that in all societies and centuries people have engaged in sexual activities with other people of the same sex. The way these activities have been conceptualized and to what degree they have been considered part of normal sexuality or, in contrast, excluded from it has changed many times. The current use of the term "same-sex sexuality," which is supplanting homosexuality in Anglophone academic discourse, is an example of the endlessly shifting understanding of sexual practices different from what are considered those of the majority of people.

In 1869, when the word *homosexual* was coined in German by the Austro-Hungarian Karl Maria Kertbeny, one could already make out a number of conceptualizations of same-sex desire or practices, which complemented and extended the religious notion of sodomy. The nineteenth century was profoundly marked by legal and psycho-medical discourses on deviant sexuality brought about in large part by the after effects of the Enlightenment and the Industrial Revolution. Bénédict Morel's *Traité des dégénérescences* (1857) (Treatise on Degeneration) formed the foundation for later theories that associated all forms of deviant sexuality with hereditary decay. By linking physical stigmata to all mental disorders, Morel, like his fellow French medical doctor and forensic expert Auguste-Ambroise Tardieu, paved the way to the notion of same-sex desire as the obvious consequence of an inherited sexual pathology.

This notion achieved its logical conclusion in the view put forward by the German legal official Karl Heinrich Ulrichs who, in 1864, coined the term *Urning*, a reference to Aphrodite Uranus and the praise of Uranian pederasty in Plato's *Symposium*, to proclaim the existence of a third sex distinct from the male and female. According to Ulrichs, members of the third sex desired men because they harbored a female soul in a male body. As David F. Greenberg puts it, Ulrichs's "writings were the first in modern times to develop systematically the contention that same-sex love was caused by cross-sex identification, and that it was invariably congenital" (408). However, although Ulrichs's formulation concerned an alleged third sex, only the body lent itself to ambiguity; desire was clearly constructed as a bipolarized attraction between a "male self" and a "female self," albeit inverted in the case of the *Uranian*. Yet, despite its negative conceptualization of same-sex desire as an inborn mistake, this definition, in a way, could carry a highly positive connotation since it puts same-sex desire on an equal footing with opposite-sex desire, both being natural phenomena.

In 1869, Carl Westphal described same-sex desire as *conträre Sexualempfindung*, contrary sexual sensation. Westphal defined same-sex desire as deviant from what custom expected as desire—the attraction of opposites—and linked it with deviant sexual identity. Westphal's and Ulrichs's definitions of same-sex desire and transgender identification as pathology and not as vice must be read in the light of the legal situation in Germany during their time. In France, the Napoleonic code made no mention of same-sex activities after the French Revolution. Accordingly, it made no difference whether same-sex desire was a vice or a congenital illness, since in neither case could it constitute a cause for legal regulation. In contrast, Ulrichs and Westphal lived under the antisodomy laws existing first in Prussia and, in the aftermath of the Franco-Prussian war of 1871, in Germany. Both Ulrichs and Westphal, who might have wanted to define same-desire as pathological in the beginning in order to exempt it from these laws, concentrated on gender identity rather than on behavior.

In 1878, the Italian forensic doctor Arrigo Tamassia took a similar path to Westphal's in his attempt to name same-sex desire. While his translation of *conträr* as *inversione* was slightly off the mark, it emphasized homosexuality as a distorted gender identity. The French neurologists Jean-Martin Charcot and Valentin Magnan took up Tamassia's terminology and rendered it into French as *inversion du sens génital*, inversion of the genital sense. Yet, while the word *inversion* recalls the idea of contrary sexual sensation, Charcot and Magnan were actually at variance with Westphal and other German-speaking theorists who diagnosed same-sex desire as pathology distinct from other supposed perversions. The two French scientists instead fitted same-sex desire into a general theory of degeneration. By clinging to the concept of inversion they failed to differentiate preference for people of one's own sex (sexual orientation) from identification with the opposite gender (transgender identification). This changed with the growing currency of the term *homosexual*. Through references especially in the German neuropsychiatrist **Richard von Krafft-Ebing**'s *Psychopathia Sexualis* (1886), it became widely accepted, first in the German-speaking world and later on everywhere in Europe, to describe those who have sex with or are sexually attracted to people of their own sex.

Thus, the earlier contrast between prohibited immoral genital acts and deviant desire is increasingly replaced by a discourse where human identity itself becomes radically enmeshed in sexuality. The notion of homosexuality presupposed that individual identity was based on the anatomy of someone's sexual partner "independent of relative degrees of masculinity and femininity" (Halperin 1990, 9).

This theory of homosexuality and object choice was continued in Sigmund Freud's psychoanalysis, which, while avoiding any moral condemnation, nevertheless portrayed homosexuality as "a state of misdirected erotic energies resulting from childhood traumas and unfinished developmental processes" (Hall 2003, 36). He considered same-sex desire an arrested state of the normal development from a state of polymorphous sexuality toward the ideal, if imperfect, state of adult heterosexuality. In other words, a psychic accident occurs in the individual's **evolution** from primitive pansexuality to civilized heterosexuality. Because Freud did not view homosexuality as a hereditary illness or group inverts among the degenerates, his claims mark an important break from the tendency to pathologize homosexuality. Yet at the same time, Freud's Oedipus and castration complexes were profoundly heterocentric. Although he allowed for polymorphous sexuality in early childhood, the process of maturation should preferably lead to the ultimate goal of heterosexual desire, in which nonprocreative impulses have been largely repressed. Homosexuality was therefore partly congenital and acquired: congenital in that it was present in all human beings and acquired in that it has not been completely repressed. According to Joseph Bristow, Freud "contends these erotic behaviors and preferences [inversion, **fetishism**, **sadism and masochism**] have a constitutive role in all human sexuality, especially the reproductive heterosexuality that the sexologists were often at pains to differentiate from seemingly unnatural desires" (68).

The sexological construction of homosexuality as a hereditary pathology thus shifted toward a view that imagined homosexuality as some kind of failure in the acculturation of the child. In either interpretation, the patient's sexuality was considered deficient, an imperfect version of the adult heterosexual.

The nineteenth (and early twentieth) century made men and women come to recognize themselves as "subjects of desire" and "subjects of a sexuality" (Foucault).

If before same-sex desire was discussed in terms of deviant sexual acts, customarily referred to as sodomy or pederasty, for which the cure was to live in abstinence or to repent, now same-sex desire was defined in terms of either a potentially curable (American psychoanalysis) or probably incurable (Freud) pathology.

The way most people conceive of homosexuality today in the West, far from being a transhistorical and transcultural idea of sexual practice and identity, is rather the result of a complex evolution over the past 150 years. The Christian paradigm had represented sodomy as the manifestation of a person's sinful behavior and punished it by death both for its adulterous aspect and because it was a sin against the command to reproduce. The nineteenth century, conversely, attributed homosexuality to an essential biological/psychological predicament within the individual person. Contemporary constructions of same-sex sexuality are direct heirs to this gradually created belief in a *sexual identity*, carrying with it a partly religious and partly clinical baggage. This belief was especially essential to the identity-based politics of the lesbian and gay liberation movement in North America and Europe during the 1970s and 1980s. In the larger domain of contemporary queer politics these ideas are both maintained and questioned. *See also* Islam and Homosexuality.

Further Reading: Bristow, Joseph. *Sexuality*. New York: Routledge, 1997; Foucault, Michel. "An Introduction." In *The History of Sexuality*. vol. 1, edited by Robert Hurley. New York: Random, 1978; Greenberg, David F. *The Construction of Homosexuality*. Chicago: University of Chicago Press, 1988; Hall, Donald E. *Queer Theories*. New York: Palgrave Macmillan, 2003; Halperin, David. *One Hundred Years of Homosexuality*. New York: Routledge, 1990.

Max Kramer

HOPKINS, GERARD MANLEY (1844–1889). The British poet Gerard Manley Hopkins wrote a limited number of poems—never published in his lifetime—which mainly focus on the author's passionate quest for divine love. In a Victorian context, not encouraging sexual discourse especially when the desired lover is Christ, Hopkins broke down a number of barriers and sometimes offended the taste of the restricted number of friends who had access to his poetry. His verse is replete with sensuality, stressing physical encounter with the beloved rather than purely spiritual love, the standard theme of religious poetry of the period.

For Hopkins, love for Christ is the fire that impregnates his mind and gives birth to a poem—this is partly made explicit in his last poem "To R.B." and in his well-known statement that being in love with Christ is a necessary prerequisite to writing any poetry. Hopkins's use of an obvious sexual metaphor to conjure up an act of aesthetic creation sets the tone for all of the author's poetry: the poet is a womb that needs divine love to fertilize his imagination. It follows that Christ is the supreme lover endowed with great and dangerous strength that comes often in the sudden shape of a stallion, a firebird, or a cosmic suitor who leans over the balcony of heaven to kiss man. The poet, the earth-bound lover, desperately hurls his body toward the new-found physical presence of the divine. Whereas God's love for man is viewed by Hopkins as awesome, a titanic struggle leaving the soul vanquished and exhausted, Christ reaches out to the hearts of man, without violence. But, the relationship between the heroic lover and his human darling is strained because the lovers must bide their time before the wedding night. Thus, deprived of his inspirational source, Hopkins constantly fears aesthetic frigidity. The poet's yearning for consummation with his spouse, shut beyond the stars, is ultimately mingled with heartache and frustration ("To Seem the Stranger" and "I Wake and Feel").

Hopkins was a Roman Catholic priest and strictly orthodox, sanctioning sex between married partners only as a means of procreation (see "At the Wedding March"). In early poems, Hopkins equated "sex" with "sin" in a conventional Augustinian way (St. Augustine, like most fathers of the Church, castigated sex as unholy). The young poet expressed his social solitude and disenchantment with human love, which resulted in aesthetic barrenness and lack of creative power. In view of his mature religious love poetry—in the wake of his conversion to Catholicism—and his well-known admiration for soldiers, laborers, and male bodies in general, it is not surprising that some saw in his mature works a repressed homoerotic strain (e.g., "The Bugler's First Communion").

Yet Hopkins's poetry is "suprasexual," in that the author uses the erotic language of sex to express an intense and stressful love encounter with a supernatural being that is both absent and present, a presence–absence keenly felt by the poet's extraordinary senses. The divine lover appears in a flash, for example, in the imaginary shape of a falcon swooping at lightning speed or in a visionary spell. In "The Wreck of the Deutschland," the erotic union between human and divine is sealed dramatically when a shipwrecked woman, a nun, sees Christ "her lover" come to her (stanzas 25–28). This is followed by a feast and a birth (stanza 30); Hopkins remains consistent in his views that such a suprasexual act should be aesthetically and verbally fertile and beget words, whether in the form of a cry or a poem or both.

Set against the broader context of nineteenth-century religious verse, Hopkins's poems, with their barely veiled sexual language, appear striking and the author himself must have felt he was crossing the boundaries of Victorian taste. Reactions to his verse were generally hostile and he did not wish to be published, at least during his lifetime. But, he gave a new impetus and intensity to man's love affair with the divine, making it more concrete and vivid, breaking away from the romantic tradition of religious experience that took place on a spiritual, disembodied level. The Victorians' love for Christ was ebbing away and Hopkins believed they needed to be more excited lovers, instilling an unmistakable sense of urgency in his poetry. Going also beyond the traditional religious ethics of mystical bonding with God, Hopkins's verse rejects the mind-body duality and stresses a love bond that is holistic, the amorous encounter between the divine lover and his or her earthly beloved being both a physical and spiritual embrace.

Further Reading: Hopkins, Gerard Manley. "A Critical Edition of the Major Works." In *The Oxford Authors*, edited by Catherine Phillips. Oxford: Oxford University Press, 1986; Gleason, John B. "The Sexual Underthought in Hopkins's 'The Windhover'." *Victorian Poetry* 27, no. 2 (1989): 201–8.

Jean-Marie Lecomte

HOPKINS, JANE ELLICE (1836–1904).   Perhaps the most famous advocate of the single sexual standard in the nineteenth century, on her death in 1904 the York Conference of the National Union of Women Workers passed a resolution formally recording its admiration for the life and character of a woman whose "devoted and self-denying work [had] ... contributed to the quickening of the conscience of the country with regard to the care and legal protection of girls, as well as rousing attention to the necessity of an equal moral standard for both sexes" (cited in Barrett 1907, 248).

Ellice Hopkins was born on October 30, 1836, the youngest daughter of the Cambridge mathematician William Hopkins (1793–1866) and his second wife Caroline Boys (1799–1881). She entered public life during the late 1850s in a relatively conventional manner, leading bible classes and mothers' meetings. More radically, she evangelized local working-class men and established a mission hall at Barnwell, near Cambridge. On the death of her father in 1866 she moved to Brighton where, in order to assuage her grief, she immersed herself in the rescue of prostitutes. This was to alter the entire course of her life. Under the influence and encouragement of the medical specialist and sexual radical James Hinton (1822–1875), Hopkins established the Ladies' Association for the Care of Friendless Girls (LACFG) in 1878, funding its efforts through her own prescriptive writings on moral hygiene and penitentiary work. By the mid-1880s, the LACFG boasted branches in over a hundred British towns. Hopkins dramatically redefined the objectives and methods of late-Victorian rescue work so that it came to focus on a preventative as opposed to a curative and criminalizing approach to **prostitution**. She despised the palliative approaches of existing penitentiaries with their harsh regimes of sweated labor, shaven heads, and solitary incarceration. Instead, Hopkins emphasized preventative work with younger girls and the establishment of smaller rescue homes based upon a familial structure with a sound domestic education, plenty of physical exercise, and a good diet.

Her conviction of the need to strike at the causes of sexual sin rather than its results led Hopkins to argue passionately in *Notes on Penitentiary Work* (1879) and *Man and Woman: The Christian Ideal* (1884) for the necessity of an elevated standard of male sexual chastity. Indeed, it was her campaigning on male sexual purity during the 1880s and 1890s that established her reputation and profile in late-Victorian moral reform. She is best remembered for her work in the **social purity** movement through the White Cross Army (WCA), which she established in 1883 with Bishop Lightfoot of Durham. A grueling ten-year nationwide lecturing tour followed which, at times, took on revivalist proportions, where Hopkins addressed mass meetings of between 800 and 2,000 men on subjects as controversial as prostitution, **sex education**, and moral chastity. This was to earn her considerable opprobrium as well as respect within religious circles. Yet Bishop Lightfoot described her as having done "the work of ten men in ten years" (cited in Bristow 1977, 95) and her uncompromising attack on the apathy of the Anglican church toward the plight of the prostitute in *A Plea for the Wider Action of the Church of England in the Prevention of the Degradation of Women* (1879) eventually gained the enthusiastic backing of Archbishop Edward Benson in whose archiepiscopate two male purity societies, the WCA and the Church of England Purity Society were formed.

Hopkins was undoubtedly responsible for the mass popularization of male purity leagues in the late nineteenth century. In an evocative combination of chivalry and military heroism, her message was an explicitly class-ridden one. She suggested to working-class men, for example, that sexual chastity might form part of a wider demand for political and social liberty, whereas middle-class men were encouraged to join the WCA through the rhetoric of chivalrous duty and service to those less fortunate. The modern soldier of the WCA, she argued, fought upon the battlefield of sexual self-discipline where, if steadfast and valiant, he might rescue women from degradation through a life of heroic moral purity. In her most well-known pamphlet *True Manliness* (1883), Hopkins also forged strong links between sexual chastity and national progress in a discourse which drew upon Christian morality, popular medical scientific theory, and fears of imperial and racial degeneration. The influence of colonial bishops in countries such as Australia, New Zealand, India, the United States, and Trinidad among others ensured that the WCA, later renamed the White Cross Society, gained international momentum. In excess of two million of Hopkins's purity tracts were still in circulation in 1907.

Historical pronouncements on Hopkins's contribution to social and sexual reforms have proved somewhat inauspicious. She has been depicted variously as a mawkish spinster driven to rescue prostitutes by the desire to associate vicariously with sin, a prurient, reactionary leader of the late-Victorian social purity campaigns and the perpetrator of a massive legislative assault on the sexual practices of the working classes. She certainly evinced a not uncontroversial willingness to contemplate increased state intervention and legislation in the regulation of vice. She canvassed support for the Criminal Law Amendment Act of 1885, which raised the age of sexual consent from thirteen to sixteen years for example and, more notoriously, was instrumental in the passage of the Industrial Schools Amendment Act of 1880 which legislated for children know to be growing up in the company of suspected prostitutes to be removed and committed to certified industrial training schools. The latter earned her fierce criticism from personal rights activists and feminist contemporaries such as Elizabeth Wolstenholme Elmy and **Josephine Butler**, leader of the successful campaign to repeal the **Contagious Diseases Acts**. Yet, as a devout evangelical and High Churchwoman, Hopkins preached a gospel of social purity and transformation in which individual rights were of secondary importance to the collective good of the social body. Unlike her predecessor Butler, who had been unable to rouse the Church of England to action, such was its fear of public scandal, Hopkins proved herself an efficient political agitator of the religious establishment, effecting a virtual clerical *volte-face* in matters of sexual and moral reform. She was also responsible, through her oratorical skills, for the political mobilization of tens of thousands of respectable Christian women. Dominant interpretations of Hopkins's moral puritanism therefore belie the radical implications of her sexual agenda. She emerged as a contending force in the regulation of late-Victorian sexual morality, combining religious expectations of sexual chastity with feminist demands for the elimination of the sexual double standard and her influence in defining late-Victorian normative constructions of masculinity was substantial. Suffering from chronic sciatica and nervous exhaustion she retired from public life in 1888. She continued writing, however, and during her final years of ill health produced *The Power of Womanhood* (1899) and *The Story of Life* (1902), the latter a remarkable attempt at early sex education. She died on August 21, 1904 at her home in Brighton.

Further Reading: Barrett, Rosa. *Ellice Hopkins: A Memoir.* London: Wells Gardiner, 1907; Bristow, Edward J. *Vice and Vigilance. Purity Movements in Britain since 1700.* Dublin: Gill and McMillan Ltd., 1977; Morgan, Sue. *A Passion for Purity: Ellice Hopkins and the Politics of Gender in the Late-Victorian Church.* Bristol, UK: Centre for Comparative Studies in Religion and Gender, University of Bristol, 1999; Morgan, Sue. "Faith, Sex and Purity: The Religio-Feminist Theory of Ellice Hopkins." *Women's History Review* 9 (2000): 13–34; Mumm, Susan. "Ellice Hopkins and the Defaced Image of Christ." In *Transfiguring the Faith of Their Fathers: Women's Theology in Nineteenth-Century Britain*, edited by J. Melnyck, 165–86. New York: Garland, 1998.

Sue Morgan

HUTCHINSON, JONATHAN (1828–1913). Jonathan Hutchinson, surgeon and medical educator, was born in Selby, Yorkshire, as the second son of a Quaker flax merchant. He received his medical education at the York School of Medicine, as an apprentice to a local surgeon and later at St. Bartholomew's Hospital, London. He began his professional career as a reporter on the *Medical Times and Gazette* and took up private practice around the time of his marriage in 1856. Hutchinson then obtained a post as assistant surgeon at the London Hospital, which appointed him lecturer in surgery in 1862. By the time of his retirement in 1883 he held the title of emeritus professor, had been president of most of the London medical societies, and had received many honors both in Britain and overseas. He was knighted in 1908. Hutchinson is remembered as an outstanding general practitioner, as a specialist in ophthalmology, dermatology and syphilis, and as an influential teacher. He was a keen observer, an indefatigable note-taker, and a prolific author. He amassed a large collection of pathological drawings and specimens that were eventually housed in the Polyclinic, a post-graduate medical college he established in 1889 and are now held at the Institute of the History of Medicine, Johns Hopkins University.

Although Hutchinson gradually shed the supernatural elements of Quakerism, he retained its severe moral teachings. Even in an age when doctors were at the forefront of Victorian antisensualism, he was noted for his puritanical views on sex. Originally a supporter of the **Contagious Diseases Acts**, he came to agree with the purity campaigners that the solution to the twin evils of **prostitution** and venereal disease was not regulation but male chastity. In his brief stint as editor of the *British Medical Journal* (1869–1870), he argued that making "illicit intercourse" safer merely encouraged promiscuity and lowered the moral tone of society. He was equally opposed to contraception and the use of condoms as a prophylactic, asserting that such "disgusting" practices were "prejudicial to both moral and physical health." His objections to **masturbation** were so strong that he not only urged routine circumcision as a deterrent, but recommended castration in chronic cases.

Despite his reputation as an observer, Hutchinson could be erratic in his interpretation of data, and he found it difficult to change his mind once he had settled on an association. Striking examples of this tendency included his life-long convictions that leprosy was caused by eating rotten fish, and that the foreskin increased the risk of syphilis to such a degree that universal circumcision of male infants was necessary. Hutchinson accepted neither Hansen's discovery of the leprosy bacillus, nor Schaudinn's identification of *Treponema pallidum*, and he remained skeptical of germ theory. As Ernest Little (1867–1950) described him: "He was a tall, stooping, spare figure, wearing an unbeautiful straggling beard at a time when beards were obsolete. He was totally devoid of any sense of humor and like most humorless men, incredibly obstinate in clinging to his opinions long after they had been demonstrated to be untenable." To the end of his days he believed that a visible entity such as "filth" was the real key to disease.

Hutchinson's views on the association between syphilis and lack of circumcision were based on some dubious statistics collected in 1854, yet which remained the basis of the crusade for universal circumcision he waged during the 1890s. Although he believed that operation could prevent or cure many intractable diseases, especially masturbation, genital cancers, epilepsy, and syphilis, his aim was to control sexual behavior as much as to promote health. Circumcision was preferable to condoms or health checks because it would discourage premarital and extramarital sex, and the value of the operation would be enhanced by its effect in diminishing the sexual appetite. As he wrote in 1900: "The only function which the prepuce can be supposed to have is that of maintaining the penis in a condition susceptible of more acute sensation than would otherwise exist. It may be supposed to increase the pleasure of the act and the impulse to it. These are advantages, however, which in the present state of society can well be spared, and if in their loss some degree of increased sexual control should result, one should be thankful." It is ironic that while Hutchinson was preaching the health advantages of circumcision, his clinical reports showed that circumcision was itself a frequent vector of infection, especially of syphilis and tuberculosis, resulting in the death of many children. Although he is chiefly remembered as the author of "Hutchinson's triad"—three signs by which congenital syphilis could be recognized in infants— Hutchinson's most enduring contribution to Anglophone medicine probably lies in the tenacious suspicion that normal human anatomy is a health hazard.

Further Reading: Darby, Robert. "Where Doctors Differ: The Debate on Circumcision as a Preventive of Syphilis, 1855–1914." *Social History of Medicine* 16 (2003): 57–78; Hutchinson, Herbert. *Jonathan Hutchison: His Life and Letters.* London: Heinemann, 1946; *New Dictionary of National Biography*, vol. 29; Obituaries, *British Medical Journal* and *Lancet*, June 28, 1913; Royal College of Physicians, biographical note at http://www.aim25.ac.uk/cgi-bin/search2?coll_id= 7193&inst_id=8; http://www.whonamedit.com.

Robert Darby

I

ILLEGITIMACY. Illegitimacy, or bastardy as it was popularly known in the nineteenth century, was the state of being born out of legal marriage. Children born illegitimate suffered from severe social and legal disadvantages in most European countries. Their mothers could be penalized as well, although this was more variable over time and place. Bastardy rates are often used by historians to test a society's attitude toward sexual relationships outside of marriage, or as a measure of sexual laxness more generally.

Our understanding of the level of childbirth outside marriage becomes much more accurate in the nineteenth century, when national records began to be kept in Britain and some other European countries. American data for the same period was considerably more patchy, due to the relatively late imposition of formal registration of births. Illegitimacy rates varied greatly by time and place, peaking at about 6 percent in the mid-nineteenth century in much of Northern Europe, and then dropping again near the century's end.

Thomas Robert Malthus argued that the state could not afford to support illegitimacy, as it created undesirable population growth. Like many people in the early nineteenth century, he assumed bastards were feeble and likely to die, at least in part because their mothers were thought to be feeble-minded or lewd, both biologically undesirable characteristics. As the science of statistics developed, illegitimate birth rates became seen as a scientific measure of immorality. **William Acton**'s *Observations on Illegitimacy* (1859) was the first English language study of the subject, and set the tone for the remainder of the century.

Illegitimacy varied greatly by place. In the United Kingdom, rates were always lowest in London and its environs and higher in rural areas and in the north. But there were wide variations that have never been fully explained. On a local level, one village might have a high rate while another community only a few miles away could have a rate well below the average. In some parts of the United Kingdom, premarital sexual activity seems to have been a part of rural **courtship**, with as many as a third of brides pregnant on their wedding day. Any hitch in a courtship in these districts would result in an illegitimate birth. It has been suggested that in some parts of northern Europe, **pregnancy** on the wedding day was considered desirable among the poor, and the wedding was postponed until pregnancy occurred, as it proved the woman's fertility and potential to bear children who would later provide useful assistance with farm work.

The stigma associated with illegitimacy also displayed considerable variation. Few societies took shame to the extreme of Spanish America, whose "base-born" citizens found their situation so disabling that they would petition the Spanish crown to be made legally legitimate. This was an important step in an individual's rise in the social scale, although after the early 1800s there was less discrimination against those born out of wedlock. In Europe, there appear to have been more efforts to abort illegitimate children than children of marriage, suggesting that many women were made desperate enough by their situation to take such a grave risk. Infanticide was also a greater hazard for an illegitimate infant, although juries were extremely reluctant to convict on this charge. Not everyone shared the moral code of the establishment. There is good evidence that in England at least, rural people in many areas considered being detected in theft as far more shaming than bearing an illegitimate child.

For some reason, women of the **servant** class were considered particularly likely to bear an illegitimate baby; in Edinburgh, it was not uncommon to bar the windows on servants' rooms to prevent them from indulging in nocturnal adventures that might result in unwanted children. Some employers took this to the extreme of insisting on surveillance of female servants' sanitary napkins, in order to ensure that they were menstruating regularly. Women servants who got pregnant were dismissed without a character; their babies might be abandoned as **foundlings**, put into the orphanages that proliferated in the period, or sent to a baby farmer. Few could hope to support a child on a servant's wages, and fewer still could hope for a job where they would be able to live with their child. For servants as with other working-class women, illegitimate children were far more likely to be the result of a disrupted courtship than of promiscuity.

Legal legitimization of the illegitimate child was not possible in English **law**. It was felt that this would undesirably reduce the shame attached to the mother as a consequence of the birth of such a child. In Scotland, such a child would be legitimated retroactively if the parents later married. The Legitimation League was formed in London in 1893 to press for a way in which bastards could be acknowledged, and to campaign for them to be given equal rights with legitimate children. The debate over the rights of illegitimate children was slower to catch fire in the United States because of the patchiness of the information available. Nationally collated official statistics were not being collected by all states until well into the twentieth century.

An important issue linked to illegitimacy was the support of children born without legal fathers. France's Napoleonic code of 1804 revoked the revolutionary era's principal of the equality of all children, whether born in wedlock or not. It also prohibited women from asking for child support from the fathers of their children. In France, a distinction was made between acknowledged and unacknowledged bastards. The acknowledgment of an illegitimate child was voluntary, even by its mother, who could choose to renounce it. Unacknowledged children received no inheritance. If they were acknowledged, they would receive one-third of a legitimate child's portion.

In England, the support of illegitimate children was the responsibility of the father, in theory at least. In actual fact, given the difficulty of proving paternity, local parishes often shouldered the cost of rearing the infant. This meant that there was a tendency to move on pregnant unmarried women, because the baby would be entitled to support in the parish of its birth. Many single women found themselves giving birth in the workhouse, and some infants were reared in them until the age of nine, when they could be put out as apprentices.

Some historians have argued that rising bastardy rates show that women and men began seeking sexual pleasure more boldly, making high rates of illegitimacy evidence of a kind of early sexual revolution. Others have argued that high bastardy rates indicate periods in history when women were particularly powerless and vulnerable to sexual coercion. Still others see illegitimate babies as the result of normal courtship, ordinarily leading to marriage, going wrong for economic and cultural reasons beyond the control of those involved. It would not be until the twentieth century that a child born out of wedlock would start to enjoy the same financial and social life chances as a child of marriage.

Further Reading: Laslett, Peter, ed. *Bastardy and its Comparative History*. London: Edward Arnold, 1980; Reekie, Gail. *Measuring Immorality: Social Inquiry and the Problem of Illegitimacy*. Cambridge: Cambridge University Press, 1998; Twinam, Ann. *Public Lives, Private Secrets: Gender, Honor, Sexuality and Illegitimacy in Colonial Spanish America*. Stanford, CA: Stanford University Press, 1999.

Susan Mumm

IMPERIALISM. The term "imperialism" refers to the extension of a nation's power through territorial acquisition or economic and political domination over other nations. In the nineteenth century, the establishment and administration of imperial holdings by countries such as England, France, and Germany both influenced, and was influenced by, sexuality. Sex in the empire was a site of anxiety and regulation. Although nonwestern regions such as Asia and Africa had been imagined within western culture as spaces of unbridled sexuality for centuries, the expansion of political empire in the nineteenth century intensified this trend, creating unbalanced sexual relationships that can be seen as analogous to the unbalanced political relationships that form the basis of imperialism.

Ronald Hyam argues that "sexual dynamics crucially underpinned the whole operation of British Empire and Victorian expansion. Without the easy range of sexual opportunities which imperial systems provided, the long-term administration and exploitation of tropical territories, in nineteenth-century conditions, might well have been impossible" (Hyam 1990, 1). With decreasing sexual opportunity at home, empire provided travelers, soldiers, and bureaucrats with greater sexual opportunity. For some men the promise of sexual adventure may have added to the attraction of an imperial career, itself seen as an adventure as well as a duty. The status and power of a white man in a subjugated country was part of this increased opportunity, as these men could offer money, status, or protection to their sexual partners. However, sexuality was also a source of anxiety and tension for the rulers of the empire. Uncontrolled sexuality was seen to be the mark of the "savage" or the "native," not of the white European. By indulging in sexual experimentation or excess, colonizers were seen to be lowering the standard of white rule, undermining a discourse of European superiority that championed virtues such as restraint, self-discipline, propriety, and rationality. An understanding of "civilization," which condemned most forms of sexuality as degraded, immoral, and "savage" made sexual expression a betrayal of "racial superiority."

There was an abundance of legislation covering sexuality in the empire, originating both from local colonial governments and from home countries. What was "normal" and "proper" was defined against what was "deviant" and "immoral," thus constructing the sexuality and character not only of colonized people but of the colonizers, and indeed of the home nations which were defined through opposition. The attempt to control the sexuality, not only of the governed people but of the European imperial workers, is a sign of the anxiety that this issue evoked.

The gender imbalance in most colonies, where men greatly outnumbered women, was seen as a problem. The nineteenth-century cult of domesticity positioned women as a positive moral force, necessary to protect society by counteracting negative influences such as **alcohol**, **prostitution**, and gambling. On a more practical level, white women were needed to breed more "servants of empire," children to populate and eventually work in the colonies. While European women were encouraged to emigrate, there was always an imbalance in numbers. Interracial liaisons were viewed with especial ambivalence and anxiety as simultaneously a threat to, and a necessary aspect of, the smooth running of the empire. In some places, such as in British-controlled India, local prostitutes were provided to troops, whether traveling with them as camp-followers or annexed to a barracks. Also, unofficial prostitution was greatly encouraged by the arrival of soldiers and civilian workers.

Many men who emigrated to colonies and imperial outposts married or lived with local women and produced families. In some places, such as Canada, intermarriage with indigenous people women gave men an advantage, as it allowed them to socialize and trade with these groups. However, toward the end of the century there was increasing social pressure and even legal prohibition against mixed race relationships. Widespread beliefs about inheritance and **race** (widely seen in the nineteenth century as a scientific and biological category rather than a socially constructed one), posited that "miscegenation," the production of children by two people of different racial backgrounds, would lead to degraded and weakened people. Also, the imbalance of power between the colonizer and colonized needed a certain physical distance to maintain the symbolic distance necessary for the rhetoric of superiority to work; a sexual and domestic relationship between two people of different races questioned the truth of a discourse of race, which saw whites and nonwhites as deeply and fundamentally different.

In texts ranging from pornography to the romances of H. Rider Haggard, nonwhite women are depicted as beings ruled by overt, even aggressive sexual desire. Nonwhite women were dehumanized and objectified by racist imperial culture, and writers and artists exploited the opportunity that this provided, producing sexually titillating or even explicit work which would be unacceptable with a white female subject. For example, in H. Rider Haggard's romance *She* (1887), the queen Ayesha is revealed half-naked in a scene which would have rendered obscene a book set in England: "For a moment she stood still, her hands raised high above her head, and as she did so the white robe slipped from her down to her golden girdle, baring the blinding loveliness of her form" (Haggard, 110). Seen as essentially embodied rather than intellectual or spiritual beings, nonwhite women carried the representational burden of female sexuality in this period. There was a fraught and ambivalent, often condemnatory attitude toward female sexuality in the nineteenth century. Any displays of assertive female desire were perceived as unseemly or even frightening. There was a dominant discourse about middle-class women that characterized them as essentially passive and nonsexual, focused on procreation rather than sexual pleasure. As a result, nineteenth-century European culture projected female desire onto the Other, both in terms of class (as working-class women were seen to be unrestrainedly sexual), and of race. This projection not only allowed for the fantasy of the sexually voracious woman without disturbing the image of the demure, virtuous European wife and mother, it also functioned as a justification for the sexual exploitation of non-European women.

The climate is often blamed for the perceived libidinous nature of nonwhite people in these texts, as tropical heat was thought to encourage excessive sexual desire as well as the early onset of sexual maturity. In official discourse as well there is an underlying assumption that "native" people are basically depraved and overly sensual.

Differing ideas about the significance of clothing and covering up the body were interpreted as a lack of modesty and propriety. Indeed, Christian missionaries played a vital role in the imperial attempt to control the sexuality of colonized people. Encouraging the adoption of western-style clothing and attempting to imbue the concept of the unclothed body with shame, missionaries worked to change not only fundamental assumptions about modesty and propriety, but to change peoples' experience of their own bodies. Certain activities and attitudes that were considered normal and healthy in these cultures breached western understandings of normative sexuality, and were both socially condemned and legislated against.

Nonheterosexual activity was widely condemned by the imperial rulers, who imposed a European understanding of homosexuality onto examples of same-gender sexuality. At the same time, the empire was often interpreted as a space in which same-gender sexuality could be safely explored, outside of the pressures and expectations of "home." Many imperial rulers shared close, sensual relationships with other men, often sharing a home. Indeed, Sir **Richard Francis Burton**, a celebrated traveler, writer and translator, suggested that there existed what he termed the "sotadic zone," a geographical space wherein sex between men (or "pederasty" as it was then called) was socially acceptable and common. Notably, the posited zone contained many of the holdings of the British empire. Through this pseudoscientific thesis, sex between men is not only distanced from British sexual mores, it is made acceptable in other, non-British spaces.

The empire was a popular setting in nineteenth-century pornography, both in literary texts such as the late-century novels, A Night in a Moorish Harem (c. late 1890s) and Venus in India (1889), and in visual media such as engravings and, later, **photographs** and postcards. All these texts concentrate on elements seen as both erotic and aberrant to European mores, and thought to be everyday aspects of life in the empire: harems, public baths, slave markets, and so on. The perceived exoticism of the "Other" that empire provided gave these texts an added spice, but also served to reinforce the supposed alterity and deviance of these peoples. Indeed, in many of these texts the uneven power distribution between imperialist and subaltern is eroticized, with white men buying slaves and prostitutes in a demonstration of their economic power, and overcoming the resistance of unwilling women in an allegory of social and military might. Some texts, set in harems, reproduce in miniature the imperial mission, with the white protagonist "colonizing" various countries through his sexual possession of women of different nationalities. In these texts, race exists to add spice to sexual adventures, as the white protagonist plays the sexual connoisseur, sampling women of different ethnicities and judging their charms. Sexual dominance acts as a metaphor for the uneven political relationships of empire.

Indeed, the very gaze of the imperialist is a tool of power, and often this is a sexualized gaze. As well as scrutinizing and rewriting landscape, the nineteenth-century writer, painter, or photographer scrutinizes and analyzes the bodies and faces of colonized peoples. The body is imaginatively penetrated by the gaze of the imperialist. Consider this description, in the explorer H. M. Stanley's book In Darkest Africa, of a "Queen of the Pygmies" captured by one of his party: "She is of a light brown complexion, with broad round face, large eyes, and small but full lips ... I notice when her arms are held against the light, a whity-brown fell on them. Her skin has not that silky smoothness of touch common to the Zanzibaris, but altogether she is a very pleasing little creature" (Stanley 1890, 215–16). The tone is one of confidence amounting to arrogance, encoded with the assumption that the writer has both the ability and the right to judge and measure the nonwhite person. The "Queen" is allowed no agency or subjectivity in this narrative, and is dehumanized, as a mere passive object to be scrutinized. The violence of her capture, so casually accepted by the writer, is mirrored by the objectifying gaze. It is important to note that this is also a sexualizing gaze, which judges the woman's appearance by western standards of **beauty**. Part of the violence of this gaze is the way in which it reduces the nonwhite subject to nothing more than a body. There is no possibility of communication, or an attempt to interpret the woman through her actions; it is assumed that all that needs to be known about her can be "read" through her appearance. The relationship that this description sets up, of the white male subject and the nonwhite female object, is clearly one in which there is an imbalance of power.

The pressures of empire also had an effect on "home" countries, including aspects of sexuality. Anxiety about "racial degeneration" and the pressure to produce healthy offspring for the maintenance of empire led to a great deal of discussion centering around women and maternity. A discourse which posited the production of healthy children as not only a woman's role but as her duty placed women under a scrutinizing, disciplining gaze. There was increasing effort to control women's bodies. Homosexuality and sex outside of marriage, already considered as deviant by western societies, became seen as positive crimes against the empire, weakening the state and leading to degeneration.

Further Reading: Etherington, Norman, ed. *The Annotated She: A Critical Edition of H. Rider Haggard's Victorian Romance.* Bloomington: Indiana University Press, 1991; Hyam, Ronald. *Empire and Sexuality: The British Experience.* Manchester: Manchester University Press, 1990; Levine, Philippa. "Sexuality, Gender, and Empire." In *Gender and Empire,* edited by Philippa Levine. Oxford: Oxford University Press, 2004; McClintock, Anne. *Imperial Leather: Race, Gender and Sexuality in the Colonial Contest.* New York: Routledge, 1995; Schick, Irvin C. *The Erotic Margin: Sexuality and Spatiality in Alteritist Discourse.* London: Verso, 1999; Stanley, Henry M. *In Darkest Africa.* London: S. Low, Marston, Searle and Rivington, 1890.

Jessica Needle

ISLAM AND HOMOSEXUALITY. It may be argued that until the nineteenth century, the official western view of "sodomy" diverged only faintly from the public view that Muslim-majority cultures held on the same subject. In most of Europe and in most countries of North Africa and Islamic West Asia, anal sex between men was culturally condemned if not effectively proscribed, with the distinction, however, that Islamic cultures generally associated sexuality with the maintenance of the social order rather than with questions of individual religious morality, a Judeo-Christian hallmark. Yet since the Industrial Revolution, the perception of same-sex activity evolved very differently in Europe from the way it did in what was then called the "Orient." In the former, same-sex became the subject of medical and judicial study. Its importance was such that by the end of the nineteenth century, sexual object-choice in itself had become one of the principal parameters to define human identity, and the discourse on the sexual activity between men had spawned a new species, that of homosexuals, which comprehended both partners regardless of the role they might take in the sexual act. Needless to say, **homosexuality** was generally condemned.

Against this backdrop of legal and cultural practice many western homosexual archeologists, ethnologists, novelists, poets, and the like turned in imagination toward the Orient (and sometimes even went there) as the "fixed Other" which they encountered by way of colonial expansion, and which they used as a foil onto which they could project their racial and sexual fantasies. Here, unlike in Europe, there seemed to be a general recognition of male **beauty**, an atmosphere of sensuality was perceived as the norm, and homosexual gratification was easy to procure. According to Edward Said, "the Orient was a place where one could look for sexual experience unobtainable in Europe" (190). Said denounces the Orientalist thrust behind much of western nineteenth-century colonialist writing (even though in his seminal work, *Orientalism*, he leaves the question of homosexuality conspicuously untreated), whether be it in the form of fiction, travel literature, personal diaries, historical chronicles, or scholarly treatises. Along with the European imperialist enterprise, the Orient emerged as an intellectual construction that was the opposite of the civilized West, as a North African and mid-East cultural stereotype of sexual licentiousness in which homosexuality occupied a preeminent position. This is not to say though that only homosexuals were engaged in this enterprise. As Joseph Boone puts it: "Many heterosexually identified men have traveled to the Arabic Orient in pursuit of erotic fulfillment as well, but even these adventurers have had to confront the specter of male-male sex that lurks in their fantasies of a decadent and lawless East" (45). Among these adventurers one can find writers such as Flaubert, Oscar Wilde, Gide, E. M. Forster, and T. E. Lawrence; Orientalists such as Edward W. Lane or **Richard Francis Burton**, a painter such as Delacroix, or photographers such as Wilhelm von Gloeden, all of whom endowed their works with an Orientalist eroticism which often included homosexuality or other activities perceived as perversities by the West.

What lured many homosexual western artists, scholars, and adventurers to the Orient was the presumption that in Muslim-majority cultures men could readily have sex with other men without the fear of prosecution or cultural censure. Part of this Orientalist gaze did actually meet reality in the sense that in the Orient men could indeed engage in sexual activity with other men and avoid social condemnation. This was true, at least as long as long as they did not neglect their family obligations and assumed the penetrative role in the sexual act and their partners were boys, prostitutes, or effeminate men, that is, those who in the eyes of everybody were already nonmen. This permissiveness was partly linked to Islamic dogma: "Whereas Christianity reduces the sexual by sublimating or transcending it, Islam, while also wishing to transcend the sexual, sometimes by sublimating it, has always refused to reduce it and still less to destroy it" (Bouhdiba 1985, 100). The sexual anxieties of the Islamic world were reflected more by the pronounced segregation of sexes than by concerns with individual morality and the corruption of the flesh, and this helped to develop a literary tradition rich in same-sex descriptions. However, Europeans, trying to satisfy their own psycho-sexual fantasies in the repressive atmosphere of the nineteenth century, often transformed these traditions beyond recognition and created the impression of an unbridled sensual indulgence, which would permanently characterize the Oriental world. This suggests that the politics of imperialism were justified by relegating the Oriental to the role of the inferior and uncivilized being, as numerous scholars beginning with Said have highlighted. It is crucial to add that these politics also extended into the realm of the sexual where a culture that condoned and enjoyed what the West understood as a scientifically proved perverse and unnatural sexuality could only be seen as degraded or corrupt and "in need of European refinement" (Chari 2001, 282).

Further Reading: Boone, Joseph. "Vacation Cruises; or, The Homoerotics of Orientalism." In *Postcolonial, Queer*, edited by John C. Hawley. Albany: State Univsersity of New York Press,

2001; Bouhdiba, Abdelwahab. *Sexuality in Islam*. London: Routledge, 1985; Chari, Hema. "Colonial Fantasies and Postcolonial Identities: Elaboration of Postcolonial Masculinity and Homoerotic Desire." In *Postcolonial, Queer*, edited by John C. Hawley. Albany: State University of New York Press, 2001; Said, Edward. *Orientalism*. New York: Random House, 1979.

Max Kramer

INTERSEX.   *See* Hermaphrodites

K

KELLOGG, JOHN HARVEY (1852–1943). John Harvey Kellogg, an American health reformer, challenged the notion that meat consumption led to good health and increased sexual vigor among men. The most popular health reformer of the late nineteenth century and a proponent of Muscular Vegetarianism, Kellogg argued that the ideal man avoided illness and increased his strength by consuming a vegetable diet, refusing to brutalize his instincts by hunting, and sustaining his energy through sexual restraint.

Kellogg was born on February 26, 1852, in Tyrone, Michigan, to farmers and Seventh-day Adventists John Preston Kellogg and Anne Stanley. By 1856, the family had resettled in Battle Creek, Michigan. Originally planning a teaching career, Kellogg taught for a year at the age of sixteen in a district school in Hastings, Michigan. Convinced by this of his need for more formal education, he enrolled in 1872 in a teacher training program at Michigan State Normal College. Later that year, Adventist leaders, who had become aware of their need for professionally trained **physicians** if they were to criticize conventional medical practices, sent Kellogg to study at Russell Trall's Hygieo-Therapeutic College in Florence Heights, New Jersey. Kellogg received an M.D. in 1875 and joined the American Medical Association that same year. He did not directly attack traditional doctors but preferred to attempt to convert physicians to his way of thinking, often using chemical analyses to support his claims.

In 1876, Kellogg became the physician-in-chief of Michigan's Battle Creek Sanitarium, a position that he would hold for the next sixty-seven years. Under Kellogg, the sanitarium became a combination of health spa and clinic. Patients would be diagnosed and prescribed a regimen that included a systematic program of daily exercise, such as gymnastics or machine-aided activity, carried on vigorously enough to produce fatigue. Men were advised to change their habits of hygiene and dress. Kellogg advocated daily baths and a daily change of undergarments, as well as the use of porous fibers in clothing to allow better penetration of light and air.

Of all factors necessary to maintain health, Kellogg believed that a proper diet was the most important. Through his many writings, including the popular *Home Book of Modern Medicine*, Kellogg elaborated on his belief that the maintenance of mental, moral, and physical well-being required obedience to the natural laws of health. Digestive disorders were the most common of human illnesses, he argued, and no food came under more sustained attack than meat. According to Kellogg and other proponents of Muscular Vegetarianism, its free use lessened physical strength. Challenging age-old beliefs that meat consumption brought superior athletic performance,

John Harvey Kellogg, 1914. Courtesy of the Library of Congress.

Kellogg argued that men nourished at a vegetarian table were stronger, faster, and more energetic than carnivores.

Like many other nineteenth-century health reformers, Kellogg believed in the theory of spermatic economy. In *Plain Facts about Sexual Life*, he warned that all sexual excitement held danger since energy sent to the penis and testicles would draw strength away from the **brain** and other vital organs. To help men avoid stimulation, he provided a bland diet. Patients who left the sanitarium often had difficulty preparing grains and cereals to Kellogg's standards and, while most stopped following his dietary advice, others requested that he make his foods available for mail-order purchase. Best known for its cereals, Kellogg's food company remains in existence today, long after its founder died on December 14, 1943.

While Kellogg helped change American eating habits by providing one of the first convenience foods, his theories of manhood have not withstood the test of time. Unable to overcome age-old beliefs about the power of meat, he did not persuade large numbers of men to become vegetarian. His sexual theories also failed to attract a significant following. He is best remembered as a health reformer who challenged prevailing thought about men's health.

Further Reading: Butler, Mary et al. *The Battle Creek Idea: Dr. John Harvey Kellogg and the Battle Creek Sanitarium*. Battle Creek, MI: Heritage Publications, 1994; Schwartz, Richard W. *John Harvey Kellogg, M.D.* Nashville, TN: Southern Publishing Association, 1970; Whorton, James C. *Crusaders for Fitness: The History of American Health Reformers*. Princeton, NJ: Princeton University Press, 1982.

Caryn E. Neumann

KRAFFT-EBING, RICHARD VON (1840–1902).   One of the most important precursors of psychiatrist Sigmund Freud's (1856–1939) theories of sexuality, Richard von Krafft-Ebing, contributed to the classification of normal, abnormal, and perverse sexual behaviors as determining factors in bourgeois respectability and morality. A German-Austrian psychiatrist and one of the unknowing founders of modern **sexology**, Krafft-Ebing has been blamed by some for the confusion still connected to sexuality and sexual variations today. The system of classification that Krafft-Ebing developed in his most influential work, *Psychopathia Sexualis* (1886), became a widely known and comprehensive explanation of the cataloging of sexual abnormalities. He shared many of the beliefs of other medical professionals of his time, such as his belief that **masturbation** played an important role in sexual pathology, but he asserted that sexual abnormalities were generated in specific parts of the **brain**.

Born in Mannheim, Germany, and educated in Prague, Austro-Hungary, Krafft-Ebing studied medicine and psychiatry at the University of Heidelberg, in Germany.

After earning his medical degree in 1863, he completed a training period in an asylum and then set up his own private practice as a psychiatrist. Using his medical training in a different way, he also treated soldiers during the Franco-Prussian War (1870–1871). In 1872, he accepted a position as an adjunct professor of psychiatry at the University of Strassburg, though he left the following year for a longer stay as an adjunct professor of psychiatry at the University of Graz (1873–1889). While in Graz, Krafft-Ebing worked at a mental asylum (Feldhof) where he became superintendent and supervised medical students' clinical experiences with psychiatric patients. During this time, he was critical of the administration of public asylums and advocated a new form of mental hospital that would allow for the instruction of students of psychiatry as part of the proper treatment of psychiatric patients. In 1889, he moved on to the University of Vienna, where he held two different chairs in psychiatry. He continued to criticize the lack of psychiatric training with which most contemporary **physicians** were allowed to practice medicine.

Though he later changed his perspective on the various shades of normality, Krafft-Ebing made early distinctions in his work among perversion, perversity, and abnormality. He understood perversion as a "permanent constitutional disorder—be it inborn or acquired—that affected the whole personality." "Perversity" was "passing immoral conduct of normal persons." Abnormal sexual behavior was that which did not have the goal of coitus. Within his classification of perversions, Krafft-Ebing saw four main categories: "sadism, masochism, **fetishism**, and contrary sexual feeling" (Oosterhuis 2000, 47). Indeed, the first three categories are terms that Krafft-Ebing coined. Among other groups created by Krafft-Ebing in his taxonomy are zoophilia erotica, zooerasty, stercoracism, and pedophilia erotica. In his later work, he departed from these processes of individualized categorization and pathologization, preferring a "graded scale of health and illness, normal and abnormal" (Oosterhuis, 75).

An essential component of Krafft-Ebing's practice of psychiatry was the theory of degeneration. Becoming one of central Europe's greatest proponents of degeneration theory, he believed that family relations played a considerable role in the development of psychiatric pathologies. Neuroses and psychological conditions per se could not be attributed to heredity, but the presence of mental instability in a patient's family could indicate a predisposition to psychological abnormality. Mental and physical degeneration could also have visible indications such as brain lesions. In the end, degeneration would lead to a lesser ability or an inability to make morally sound judgments.

As with many other societal fears at the *fin de siècle*, increasing industrialization and urbanization in Europe were thought to cause or encourage sexual excess. Thus, there was a perceived threat that humans, whose sexuality was viewed completely differently from that of animals, could fall into the trap of their base sexuality. Indeed, Krafft-Ebing was of the opinion that human decency and morality had only been achieved through Christianity's long struggle with subhuman impulses. Nonetheless, his view of human sexuality was largely rooted in biology and has often been seen as a contrast to Freud's psychologically based theories.

Same-sex eroticism was seen by Krafft-Ebing and many of his contemporaries as an inversion of gender and sexual identity. That is, masculinity and femininity were inappropriately and incorrectly blended to form individuals who were sexually attracted to members of their own sex. In his opinion, individuals could be predisposed to same-sex attraction without exhibiting it. Therefore, he believed that **homosexuality** could be prevented. Indeed, "[he] advanced that hereditarily tainted boys and girls must not be admitted to boarding schools and warned against private tutors" and single-sex facilities like prisons and military schools (Oosterhuis, 245). He assigned his mostly male patients with same-sex affections to the broad category of contrary sexual feeling. Within that category, he granted that it was possible for individuals to have a normal gender identity and still be attracted to members of their own sex. Somewhat unusually, he placed same-sex love on the same level as different-sex love, acknowledging it to be morally valid.

Krafft-Ebing defined heterosexuality as an individual's sexual attraction for someone of another sex, although this classification was also utilized in his explanations of perversion. As noted earlier, his idea of sexual normality depended on the goal of the sexual activity; coitus and procreation was the normal objective. Krafft-Ebing's first heterosexuals were practitioners of fetishes who exhibited a "total indifference" toward coitus and hence qualified as perverse (Oosterhuis, 50).

Krafft-Ebing believed that individuals with psychological conditions that inhibited their moral judgment should not be convicted of crimes, but rather should receive medical treatment. He felt that, as a result of the insufficient training that physicians had received to prepare them to handle psychiatric patients, many people who actually needed psychiatric care were delivered to the criminal justice system. Krafft-Ebing was part of the developing psychiatric field, which advocated medical diagnoses and treatment in the place of what would have previously been purely legal solutions, for example, prison sentences.

Krafft-Ebing was a prolific author, writing hundreds of articles and nearly 100 books. He published work on psychiatric subjects, medical research, forensic topics, and social commentary. Possessing an international reputation as an accomplished clinical and forensic psychiatrist, Krafft-Ebing also served as editor and contributor to a variety of scholarly journals like the *Allgemeine Zeitschrift für Psychiatrie* (*General Journal for Psychiatry*), the *Jahrbücher für Psychiatrie und Neurologie* (*Yearbooks for Psychiatry and Neurology*), the *Jahrbuch für sexuelle Zwischenstufen* (*Yearbook for Sexual Intermediates*), and *Friedreichs Blätter für gerichtliche Medizin* (*Friedreich's Pages for Forensic Medicine*). Krafft-Ebing's other published works include his most famous study *Psychopathia Sexualis* (1886), *Lehrbuch der gerichtlichen Psychopathologie mit Berücksichtigung der Gesetzgebung von Österreich, Deutschland und Frankreich* (*Textbook of Forensic Psychopathology with Consideration of Legislation of Austria, Germany and France*, 1875), and *Lehrbuch der Psychiatrie auf klinischer Grundlage für practische Ärzte und Studierende* (*Textbook of Psychiatry with Clinical Foundation for Practical Physicians and Students*, 3 vols., 1879–1880).

Though they have been at least partly eclipsed by the popularity of Freud's findings and work, Krafft-Ebing's writings and research have had a lasting effect on the practice of psychiatry. Several of his theories, such as his work with transvestites and individuals who would later be called transgendered, preceded later categorizations and diagnoses of the twentieth century. Several everyday words in our sexual vocabularies can be traced to his work, for example **sadism and masochism**. Additionally, although Krafft-Ebing contrasted sexual variants with the drive toward reproduction, his work highlighted the many kinds of alternatives that still shape present-day views of sexuality.

Further Reading: Oosterhuis, Harry. *Stepchildren of Nature: Krafft-Ebing, Psychiatry, and the Making of Sexual Identity*. Chicago: University of Chicago Press, 2000.

Kyle E. Frackman

L

LAW. The dominant ideology of sexuality in the West during the nineteenth century required that sexual behavior be heterosexual, marital, and procreative. As a result, many of the laws that controlled or otherwise regulated sexual behavior attempted to channel it into marriage. The institution of marriage was strictly controlled, and divorce was either difficult or impossible to obtain. One commonly recognized ground for divorce, though, was adultery. Adultery was not only grounds for divorce, some jurisdictions allowed for justifiable homicide on the part of a husband who caught his wife in the act of adultery. Furthermore, the number of marriages a person could enter into at one time was limited in most western countries to one. In the United States, a system of informal marriage known as common-law marriage was fairly commonplace in rural areas in the early part of the century. Targeted by social reformers—secular and religious—the institution diminished by the end of the century.

As a result of the marital legal framework, fertility, abortion, and contraception were often illegal, or access to them was highly restricted. Controls on fertility were reinforced through the legal concept of "illegitimacy." Efforts to keep sexual behavior within the bounds of marriage led to a characteristic development of the nineteenth century, an array of formal and informal moral reform associations that served to control sexuality. In England, the Society for the Suppression of Vice was established in 1802 while in the United States the most (in)famous antivice organization, the New York Society for the Suppression of Vice, was formed in 1873 and led by **Anthony Comstock**. In many countries, vice societies or squads appeared in large cities, often empowered with legal authority, and attempted to curtail the distribution and consumption of contraceptive devices as well as commercial sexual behaviors such as pornography and **prostitution**.

One of the chief characteristics of social life during the century was a gradual increase in leisure time for the working and middle classes. This development led to an increased visibility of nonmarital sexual behavior among working-class youth in large cities as well as prostitution. Developments of medical knowledge about sexually transmitted diseases underscored efforts to control or prohibit prostitution. In Spain, the passage of the Madrid Regulations in 1847, prompted in part by concerns about venereal disease, while in England the **Contagious Diseases Acts** (1864–1869) attempted to stop the spread of sexually transmitted diseases by regulating prostitution. The extent and nature of regulation varied. Many of the growing urban areas in the United States officially prohibited but informally allowed prostitution to exist in certain parts of the city, such as Storyville in New Orleans or the Tenderloin in New York City.

Gay and lesbian subcultures emerged in the numerous cities during the urbanization of the modern period. In London, "molly" clubs provided gay men with a social space while numerous areas of Paris such as the Champs-Elysees and the Palais-Royal came to be recognized as places where men could meet men. Same-sex behavior became the object of scientific study and discourse during the latter decades of the century, often with repressive legal consequences, as antisodomy laws were enforced. In Germany, there was both a relatively successful homosexual emancipation movement and passage of repressive laws. Broadly, within the larger context of secularization that took place in the West during the latter part of the century, there were developments within medical knowledge that led to (sometimes pseudo-)scientific explanations of deviant sexual behavior. Such explanations were used to justify antisodomy laws governing homosexual behavior.

Repressive laws were often aimed at preventing sexual relationships between members of what were then perceived to be very distinct races. The issue of **race** is particularly complex in the Western world during the nineteenth century because of the existence of slavery in a number of countries during part of the century. On the one hand, as chattel property, slaves often had their sexual behavior controlled by their owners. After the abolition of slavery, prohibitions against interracial sexual behavior were codified in antimiscegenation laws in many countries.

Despite similar legal frameworks, there were considerable differences in the enforcement of and obedience to laws governing sexual behavior throughout the West. While it is possible to find similar legal restrictions and sanctions governing sexual behavior in countries across the world, it is important to remain mindful of the various legal systems and traditions within which these laws are found. Furthermore, the power of informal noncodified social norms to govern behavior varied between countries, and often within countries, as premodern rural communities often retained traditional values through the informal sanction of deviant behavior while urban areas often provided the anonymity and possibility of engaging in nonnormative sexual behavior.

Further Reading: Fout, John C. *Forbidden History: The State, Society, and the Regulation of Sexuality in Modern Europe: Essays from the Journal of the History of Sexuality.* Chicago: University of Chicago Press, 1992; Fout, John C. and Maura Shaw Tantillo. *American Sexual Politics: Sex, Gender, and Race since the Civil War.* Chicago: University of Chicago Press, 1993; Marcus, Steven. "The Other Victorians: A Study of Sexuality and Pornography in Mid-Nineteenth-Century England." *Studies in Sex and Society 1.* London: Weidenfeld and Nicolson, 1966; Ploscowe, Morris. *Sex and the Law.* New York: Prentice-Hall, 1951; Stone, Lawrence. *Road to Divorce: England 1530–1987.* Oxford: Oxford University Press, 1990; Weeks, Jeffrey. *Coming Out: Homosexual Politics in Britain from the Nineteenth Century to the Present.* London; New York: Quartet Books, 1977.

Jody Pennington

LESBIANISM. Lesbianism, in broad terms, is female **homosexuality**. Definitions of lesbianism, homosexuality, and other "sexual perversions" emerged throughout the nineteenth century. As new terminology was coined through the works of sexologists, the existence of the "lesbian" began to take shape toward the end of the century. However, it did so apart from the realities of what the true lesbian identity could have been, with definitions mostly based on medical and sexual studies formed in the context of the Victorian age. With so few sources left behind by women, and with the

"The two friends," by Gustave Courbet, 1867. © Erich Lessing/Art Resource, NY.

obvious secrecy involved in same-sex relationships, it is difficult to ascertain if a "lesbian identity" or "lesbian community" existed at all in this era. However, with the popularity of **romantic friendship**s between women, the emergence of the "New Woman," and research work preformed by sexologists, it is apparent that under the veil of the Victorian era, where sexual purity stood at the top of a high list of standards expected from women, **Queen Victoria** was wrong in saying that "ladies did no such thing."

Romantic friendships seem to have flourished in the nineteenth century, with many women, both single and married, maintaining very intimate relationships with one another. These relationships were fully accepted in nineteenth-century culture and were seen as a "guide to love" (Vicinus, xviii) before marriage. It is a matter of debate whether many, if any, women in romantic friendships engaged in sexual relations with each other; however, accounts from personal diaries do affirm that some women did enjoy a great deal of freedom under the guise of this common practice. Proof can also be found in novels such as Margaret J. M. Sweat's (1823–1908) *Ethel's Love Life* (1859), which dealt with erotic relationships between women. Sweat is believed to have written the first lesbian novel in the United States.

Throughout the nineteenth century, the lives of some women began to change and improve. With more opportunities for higher education, social mobility, and economic independence, women were able to stretch the confines of the private sphere. Through these changes, the notion of the "new woman" emerged, typically a western woman from the middle- and upper classes, who was able to enjoy economic freedom and avoid the pressures to marry and have children. With an escape from compulsory domesticity, it is thought that many new women found solace in relationships with other women, who may have better understood their new feminist ideals and growing political voices in involvement in the causes of abolitionism, the temperance movements, and other concerns of the time. The new woman and lesbians were therefore perceived by many as a threat to social order and as another vice created by industrialization and urbanization.

The family structure in the nineteenth century had the patriarch as the head of household and the main bread winner. This construct often stood in the way of women setting up a home together. However, some women were able to expand these boundaries and were able to enjoy life in the company of their female partners. At both ends of the social spectrum, possibilities for cohabitation existed. First, there were women who were economically independent, who did not need to take a husband in order to ensure their livelihood. This freedom was often practiced by "new women" whose radical approaches to home life mirrored their feminist and egalitarian political views. Within this context, new women often committed themselves to "Boston marriages," where two single women lived together in long-term relationships. This included the American founder of the settlement movement, Jane Addams, as well as the president of Bryn Mawr College, M. Carey Thomas. However, for the most part the social and familial structures discouraged such arrangements. And, even though some privileged women were able to live together, they were still constrained by their family responsibilities and by the loss of respectability associated with breaking the norm and challenging woman's place in society. The other group of women who, for at least some period of time, were able to enjoy cohabitation were unmarried working-class women. The necessity to pool their funds in order to secure accommodation, allowed romantic partners a freedom that would have been unknown to most middle- and upper-class women. It is likely that in most cases, women who were involved in intimate friendships saw them end when marriage, children, and new family commitments ensued.

Definitions of lesbianism and homosexuality emerged through the research and conclusions of sexologists throughout the era. Sexologists thrived "in an age that increasingly classified people by their sexual inclination" which as a result stigmatized people who were seen as deviant (Miller, 1995, XXiii). Medical manuals written in the mid-nineteenth century tended to pronounce on the appropriate limits of female friendship. For example, sexologists like **Richard von Krafft-Ebing**, a professor of psychology, spent the last part of the century cataloguing and classifying sexual pathologies. In 1886, he published *Psychopathis Sexualis* which included over 200 cases detailing sexual behavior. The German physician Karl Westphal wrote the history of a young lesbian and coined the phrase "contrary sexual feeling." **Havelock Ellis** wrote the first English book to deal with homosexual behavior and to deal with the subject of lesbianism "not as a disease or a crime." His book *Sexual Inversion* (1896) had six case studies of lesbianism. He believed that **feminism** and all-female environments, such as all female schools, could lead women toward same-sex relationships and noted the difference between "true inverts" and those for whom the "characteristic could be prevented." He also associated lesbians with having masculine traits but a woman's body and estimated that one in ten people were homosexuals. Sexologists have been blamed for "creating lesbianism as a deviant category and using it as an attack on the new woman and the feminist and reform movement" (Miller, 1995, 62).

The work accomplished by sexologists did give an insight into lesbianism in the nineteenth century. For example, studies had been made of another kind of women who enjoyed same-sex female relationships, the prostitute. Many doctors and sexologists of the time drew parallels between **prostitution** and lesbianism, claiming that one caused the other. This was accompanied by a rising fear that industrialization and urbanization was creating sexual perversions among other ills. In 1836, Alexandre-Jean-Baptiste Parent-Duchatelet published *De la Prostitution dans la Ville Paris* which gave evidence of same-sex relations between women in France. In his survey of Paris' regulated brothel district, Parent-Duchatelet discovered that as much as 25 percent of prostitutes had lesbian experiences (Miller, 2000, 70). Duchatelet blamed this fact on the behavior of men who frequented brothels. Krafft-Ebing supported Duchatelet's findings in his *Psychopathia Sexualis*, writing that prostitutes "disgusted with the intercourse with perversive and impotent men … seek compensation in the sympathic embrace of person of their own sex" (Miller, 2000, 75). However, he also thought that "homosexual behavior among women was almost purely situational and that practitioners would revert without fail to heterosexual behaviour" (Miller, 2000, 76). Many assumptions were made about lesbianism, and even though it remained a legal act throughout the century, it was seen as a deviant act belonging to the underclasses.

Further Reading: Cottingham, Laura. "Notes on Lesbian." *Art Journal* 4 (1996): 72–7; Diggs, Marylynne. "Romantic Friends or a Different Race of Creatures? The Representation of Lesbian Pathology in Nineteenth-Century America." *Feminist Studies* 21 (1995): 317–40; Miller, Heather Lee. "Sexologists Examine Lesbians and Prostitutes in the United States, 1840–1940." *NWSA Journal* 12 (2000): 67–91; Miller, Neil. *Out of the Past: Gay and Lesbian History from 1869 to the Present*. London: Vintage, 1995; Vicinus, Martha. *Lesbian Subjects*. Bloomington: Indiana University Press, 1996; Vicinus, Martha. "Lesbian Perversity and Victorian Marriage: The 1864 Codrington Divorce Trial." *The Journal of British Studies* 36 (1997): 70–98; Vicinus, Martha. *Intimate Friends: Women Who Loved Women, 1778–1928*. Chicago: The University of Chicago Press, 2004.

Danielle Bertrand

LINTON, ELIZA LYNN (1822–1898). Eliza Lynn Linton was a popular writer who made her reputation as a critic of women who sought emancipation from the domestic sphere. Warning that such women, whom she labeled "shrieking sisters" and "wild women," would cause such dire results as the fall of the British empire, Linton particularly focused on the moral consequences. The emancipation of women, she argued in her many novels and in hundreds of periodical articles, would lead Britain into a sexually decadent society marked by free love, the end of marriage, the blurring of sex differences, and lesbianism.

Given Linton's notoriety as a leading critic of women's emancipation in Victorian England, it is ironic that she began her career as a radical iconoclast who challenged conventional Victorian moral and social values. Born into a conservative Anglican vicar's family in the Lake District, as a young woman Eliza Lynn left her family to go by herself to London to make her living as a writer. Securing a position on the staff of the *Morning Chronicle*, she was the first woman in England to draw a regular salary as a journalist. She also wrote bold iconoclastic novels. In 1848, for example, she published *Amymone*, in which her heroine proudly defies conventional morality. Her most shocking novel was *Realities*, published in 1851, which in the (unpublished) original version, advocates not just women's political and social, but also sexual freedom. This controversial book was rejected by all the publishers she approached, including John Chapman, who said that as a publisher of works of free thought, he had to be particularly careful of morally suspect literature. She finally got a bowdlerized version published at her own expense.

Linton's early periodical articles tended to be more conventional, reflecting the tone of the journals. Even in *Household Words*, however, to which she was a frequent contributor in the 1850s, her writing caused the editor Charles Dickens to warn his subeditor about her submissions, because she tended to write too much about sexual matters. In the radical *English Republic*, she could express her views without censorship. In an 1851 essay on Mary Wollstonecraft, she praised the feminist's ideas and lifestyle, and criticized her only for giving in to conventional morality by marrying her lover before the birth of their baby.

In 1858, Eliza Lynn made a disastrous, short-lived, and probably unconsummated marriage to the radical artisan William James Linton. They separated in 1864, although to both their later frustrations, they did not get a divorce, because there were no grounds of infidelity. Resuming her independent life, Linton's writings shifted by the late 1860s from critic to defender of conventional morality. In what became her most sensational article, "The Girl of the Period," published in the *Saturday Review* in 1868, she accused young women from respectable families of imitating prostitutes with their use of make-up and their bold manners. This article set off a firestorm of controversy, and caused mothers to more carefully monitor their daughters' behavior.

Linton followed up "The Girl of the Period" with a series of pieces in the *Saturday Review* and elsewhere, condemning all varieties of female deviance, from the idle "lady" who neglects her maternal duties to, most vehemently, women's rights women. With strident attacks in her periodical articles, Linton expressed more ambivalence about women's emancipation in her novels. In her 1872 *Rebel of the Family*, the "rebel" is a sympathetic figure who wants to find a job rather than form a bad marriage. Her life of freedom and work leads her, however, to get involved with a group of women's rights women whom Linton explicitly describes as lesbian, and therefore dangerous. The rebel is saved from work, women's rights, and lesbianism by marriage to a manly man.

With the increased social and sexual freedom in the *fin de siècle*, Linton intensified her attacks on all forms of moral deviance. Even as she gently mocked Mrs. Grundy, she argued her importance, as a brake on a wagon careening downhill. Assuming the role of "Grundyometer," as Herbert Spencer sympathetically described her, she condemned higher education for women, arguing that women's colleges were nurseries of sexual immorality. Linton also condemned sports for women, and particularly decried bicycling, warning of the dangers of women falling off into the arms of strange men. Appalled at what she considered the sexual decadence of Oscar Wilde, she celebrated his downfall and, as she titled an 1895 *National Review* article, "the philistine's coming triumph." At the same time she condemned the new moralists, labeling them as "prurient prudes," who sought a single standard of morality for men and women.

With her impassioned condemnation of "mannish" women, Linton confused her contemporaries when she published in 1885 her life story, *The Autobiography of Christopher Kirkland*, portraying herself as a man. Condemning lesbianism, she had her most emotionally intimate relationships with women. Arguing that women needed religion to shore up moral sensibilities, she herself was a secularist. Linton nevertheless was a person of influence and respect in Victorian England who in her youth helped spark a debate on conventional morality and in her middle and later years became an important defender of that morality.

Further Reading: Anderson, Nancy Fix. *Woman against Women in Victorian England: A Life of Eliza Lynn Linton.* Indianapolis: Indiana University Press, 1987; Anderson, Nancy Fix. "Eliza Lynn Linton: *The Rebel in the Family* and other Novels." In *The New Nineteenth Century: Feminist Readings of Underread Victorian Fiction*, edited by Barbara Harman and Susan Meyer. New York: Garland Publishers, 1996; Meem, Deborah T. "Eliza Lynn Linton and the Rise of Lesbian Consciousness." *Journal of the History of Sexuality* 7 (1997): 537–60; Meem, Deborah T., ed. *The Rebel of the Family: Eliza Lynn Linton.* Orchard Park, NY: Broadview Press, 2002.

Nancy Fix Anderson

LITERATURE, GERMAN. In the long nineteenth century, German literature witnessed a tumultuous series of social, political, cultural, and economic developments.

The lands which would become Germany, in the unification of the German empire in 1871, experienced revolutions, rapid industrialization, increasing urbanization, and war. At the Congress of Vienna (1815) after Napoleon's defeat, the hundreds of German territories that had formed the Holy Roman Empire (dissolved in 1806) were consolidated into a German Confederation of thirty-nine states. In 1848, people in the German states, at large gatherings in cities like Berlin and Frankfurt, demanded freedom of the press, voting rights, and constitutional government, which led to the beginning of a revolution that eventually failed. A conservative Prussian-dominated German empire was formed after conflicts with Austria, France, and Denmark.

One of the pervasive issues of nineteenth-century German culture was the changing perception of gender relations and sexual behaviors. Homosexuality itself was not named as such until 1869, which left other terms with varying definitions such as "pederasty," "Uranian" or "Uranian love," and "sodomy." Even after **homosexuality**'s more or less clinical categorization in 1869, other terminologies persisted.

The literature of this period spans from the end of Classicism to the beginnings of Romanticism, to the "conservative" *Biedermaier* works and those of *Junges Deutschland* (Young Germany), to Realism, Naturalism, and onward to Modernism and the *fin de siècle*. Stereotypically, one may think of Victorian-age and nineteenth-century literature as rather sterile and perhaps monotonous, especially when one looks for works that make reference to sex or gender. An examination of German-language literature of this time period makes clear, however, that such an estimation is indeed unfounded. As one can see, sex and gender, in various senses of these complicated terms, were preoccupations of nineteenth-century German-language writers.

Romanticism, the most prevalent aesthetic movement of the nineteenth century, was an artistic current that cultivated a climate in which expressions of sexuality ("traditional" or otherwise) were more likely, if not slightly more acceptable. Moreover, rooted in the German literary movement of *Empfindsamkeit* (Emotionalism or Sentimentality) men were permitted to express affection for one another, as male friendships were perceived to be some of the strongest bonds present in nature, possessing or embodying a supreme spirituality.

Friedrich Schlegel (1772–1829) wrote one of the best-known Romantic novels and perhaps the prototypical German Romantic novel, *Lucinde* (1799), which treats Lucinde's love and marriage to Julius. This novel, which seems fragmentary, includes sections in which Julius, the protagonist, describes his own development and learning of *Männlichkeit* ("manliness" or "masculinity") and meets Lucinde, who personifies complete humanity. Schlegel portrays in *Lucinde* a brand of sexuality that encompasses emotional and physical love in addition to intellectual stimulation and connection. Schlegel's other work includes homoerotic poetry that is often left out of collections. Naturally, there were shocked reactions to Schlegel's work alongside supporters' encouragement not to allow private behaviors and emotions to be dictated by public and church censorship.

Heinrich von Kleist's drama "*Penthesilea*" (1807) delivers a different version of love, this one implemented through the introduction of Amazons. Penthesilea, Queen of the Amazons, and Achilles are mutually attracted, which leads to a struggle between their two versions of the sexes. Penthesilea comes from a homogeneous society of female control; Achilles resides in the classical utopia of the male ideal, Greece. Although in love, Penthesilea brutally slays Achilles, leading her to kill herself in her rage and sadness. She stabs herself with a dagger, an act resembling the penetrative arrow shots and removal of armor that killed the object of her sexual attraction.

Affected, like many others, by the adoration of "Classical" male **beauty** and Greek ideals, which had been fostered by Johann Joachim Winckelmann (1717–1768) and which waned by the middle of the century, poet August von Platen (1796–1835) became an example of an author who transgressed gender boundaries, too far for some. Platen's poetry was seen as overtly homoerotic by critics who included the writer and poet Heinrich Heine (1797–1856). Heine's criticism and mockery of Platen culminated in his *Die Bäder von Lucca* (*The Baths of Lucca*, 1829) in which Heine made reference to Platen's supposedly questionable sexuality. Heine's graphic criticism of Platen and his work was not well received, and Heine faced a great deal of public condemnation.

The construction and effects of male gender and sexuality play a different role in Georg Büchner's (1813–1837) fragmentary drama *Woyzeck* (published posthumously). Lacking a fixed order of scenes, Büchner's play begins with Franz Woyzeck, a weak man who hears voices, a servile barber to his captain, who insults him. To earn extra money, Woyzeck volunteers as a subject in medical experiments conducted by a physician who makes him eat only peas. His lover, Marie, is unfaithful to him with another soldier. The captain inspires Woyzeck's jealous rage, which leads him to stab Marie and eventually throw himself into the waters of a nearby pond. Despite its date, *Woyzeck* displays a rather pre-Expressionistic "conclusion," leading to the death of the main female figure. Similar to Kleist's *Penthesilea*, *Woyzeck* resolves gender confusion and transgression through violent, artificial deaths.

Gender behavior and social ideals were displayed in Jakob (1785–1863) and Wilhelm (1786–1859) Grimm's *Kinder- und Hausmärchen* (*Children's and Household Tales*, 1812, first edition). Often thought to be the painstaking transcriptions of the Grimms' travels around the German states to speak with elderly housemaids and storytellers (the "folk"), the fairy tales of the Grimms were actually gleaned from conversations the brothers had with women of their social circle, who related the tales of their nannies. Not only did the Grimms hear the stories from a source that is (still) not conventionally recognized, but the brothers also sculpted the tales into the versions that they wanted to publish. The tales were made supposedly more acceptable to children with supplementary Christian elements, less overtly erotic content, and embellishments that made the originally brief tales into more literary works. Among the crafted components of the tales are the gender features of the characters. Males filled the role of the capable, strong, and chivalrous or rescuing figure; females were either evil, in which case they were cunning, calculating, dark, and untamable, or good, in which case they were innocent, honest, obedient, and passive.

Literary contributions to women's efforts to obtain emancipation continued throughout the nineteenth century. At the start of the century, Karoline von Günderrode's (1780–1806) work was "a feminist confrontation with the age's poetic conventions" (Saul, 238). Also using a male pseudonym "Tian," Günderrode published poetry (e.g., *Gedichte und Phantasien*; *Poems and Fantasias*; 1804) and dramas (e.g., *Mahomet, der Prophet von Mekka* [Mohammed, Prophet of Mecca], 1805) as well as contributions to journals. In the latter half of the century, writer Louise Otto-Peters (1819–1895) advocated women's rights and education. She founded the *Frauen-Zeitung* (*Women's Newspaper*) in 1849 and was one of the founders of the *Allgemeiner Deutscher Frauenverein* (General German Women's League) in 1865. Otto-Peters also demonstrated a commitment to the common nineteenth-century theme of the *Volk* (folk, people), which she integrated into her conception of sexual roles and gender.

Around the turn of the twentieth century, the elements of Modernism began to captivate artists in the various media. More traditional forms of artistic expression were challenged and eventually mutated into other aesthetic styles. Gender and sexuality played sizeable roles in these artists' work. The "feminine" became ever more threatening, feared to be in danger of growing out of control. Psychological meanings were discovered and interpreted in artistic expressions; Austrian psychiatrist Sigmund Freud's (1856–1939) very influential and bestselling book *Traumdeutung* (*The Interpretation of Dreams*, 1900) popularized the notion of the unconscious and the importance of sexual(ized) readings of psychological problems.

Gender, sexuality, and youth are mixed in Frank Wedekind's (1864–1918) dark drama *Frühlings Erwachen* (Spring's Awakening, 1891). The adolescents in this play are sheltered by their surrounding adults from sexual truths. Wendla Bergmann, the main female figure, is protected from adulthood by her sensitive mother; Melchior Gabor and Moritz Stiefel, the two main male characters, have clandestine and incomplete communications about sex. Melchior and Wendla eventually have sex in the woods in a scene that displays a sadomasochistic pubescent sexuality. Wendla later dies from a failed abortion. Moritz experiences failure in school and commits suicide, later appearing to Melchior in a cemetery. Melchior is sent to a disciplinary reform school from which he escapes. Other scenes include one of **masturbation**, involving Hänschen Rilow, and (implied) homosexual love between Hänschen and Ernst Röbel. This drama caused a great deal of scandal for its frank depiction of adolescent curiosity and adult obliviousness.

Ever the controversial figure, Wedekind experimented with gender/sexual themes in later works as well, including his *Lulu* plays. The *Lulu* tragedy consists of two previously separate dramas: *Erdgeist* (Earth Spirit, 1895) and *Die Büchse der Pandora* (Pandora's Box, 1904). This work contributes to the (pre-)Expressionistic thread of Büchner's *Woyzeck* (mentioned earlier) in that a woman, namely Lulu, meets a violent death, an event that concludes the dramatic action. "Earth Spirit's" prologue introduces Lulu as a bestial, threatening figure, and over the course of both portions of the tragedy, Lulu indeed destroys any male who comes in her path. In her seductive designs, Lulu personifies female sexuality and the problematic *femme fatale* figure that appears often in *fin-de-siècle* German literature, art, and music. Lulu exposes a female eroticism that defies any notion that females should/could not enjoy their sexuality. The drama illustrates the supposed danger of female sexuality that has grown out of control. At the end of "Pandora's Box," Jack the Ripper is the final male presence that resolves the issue of Lulu's threatening nature. He murders Lulu and departs with a sense of accomplishment. Not only do the plays have one of the best-known lesbian characters in German literature, Gräfin Geschwitz (Countess Geschwitz), but they also served as the inspirational material for Alban Berg's opera *Lulu* and G. W. Pabst's film *Pandora's Box* (1929).

Another controversial work, Arthur Schnitzler's (1862–1931) drama *Reigen* (Hands Around or La Ronde, 1900), thematizes Viennese sexuality and had to be published by the author himself, as no publisher would accept it. Each of the ten scenes of this play portrays a sexual coupling of a character from the previous and following scenes in such a structure: AB-BC-CD-DE and so forth. The drama's characters comprise figures from multiple levels of Viennese society, from a soldier to a prostitute, from a maid to a count. Though he leaves homosexuality out of this drama, Schnitzler combines in this relatively short play the sexual values and the class implications of his contemporary society into a critique or frank commentary that inspired vehement opposition to his work.

One can see that sex and gender, to some extent, occupied the imaginations of German-language writers in the nineteenth century. The works that these writers produced received varied reactions. These authors often could not find publishers in their time who would accept their submissions; works by Kleist, Büchner, and Günderrode are among those that were "(re-)discovered" in the late-nineteenth and early-twentieth centuries. Thanks to continuing literary scholarship, such works that thematize sex and/or gender in some way or those that were written by women, who likely faced an uphill battle in the acceptance or publication of their work, are increasingly discussed and discovered.

Further Reading: Lorey, Christoph and John L. Plews, ed. *Queering the Canon: Defying Sights in German Literature and Culture.* Columbia, SC: Camden House, 1998; Saul, Nicholas. "Aesthetic Humanism (1790–1830)." In *The Cambridge History of German Literature*, edited by Helen Watanabe-O'Kelly. Cambridge: Cambridge University Press, 1997; Wellbery, David E., ed. *A New History of German Literature.* Cambridge, MA: Harvard University Press, 2004.

Kyle E. Frackman

LOCK HOSPITALS. *See* Penitentiaries and Lock Hospitals

LOVE AT FIRST SIGHT. In the nineteenth century, the phrase "love at first sight" anchored debates about the pitfalls and triumphs of instantaneous attraction. Accelerating the conventionally protracted narrative of courtship, "love at first sight" could signify either a dangerous or a liberating transgression of social rules. For those who saw danger, it represented a foolish, too-romantic desire and the essentially flawed epistemology of immediate attraction—an overemphasis on the visual and superficial. It thus signified a failure of the kinds of extended narratives novelists favored; the works of Jane Austen, Charlotte Brontë, and Charles Dickens, for example, clearly value long-term romantic negotiation over spontaneous "love." But for those who saw instantaneous attraction as liberation, love at first sight represented an authentic-because-intuitive evaluation of a potential mate—an ideal that still underwrites the concept's cultural currency.

Early in the century, love at first sight commonly signified misguided thinking. Essayist William Hazlitt's "On the Knowledge of Character" (1821) treats such love as a powerful erotic experience—fantasy made real—but not as a reliable means of gaining a true "knowledge of character." Through the 1830s, love at first sight was usually figured as a naïve pretence to knowledge. In "Love at First Sight; or the Fish Out of Water," an anonymous 1838 story in *Blackwood's Edinburgh Magazine*, such love simply creates farce when a bumbling university student discovers the imperfections of the woman he instantaneously loves. His likeness reappears in 1839 when a young **Charlotte Brontë** writes to a friend about a clergyman "fresh from Dublin University" who visits her family and asks her to marry him: "I have heard of love at first sight, but this beats all!" Brontë diagnoses youthful male "freshness" and Irish indiscretion, as well as a narrative flaw—a truncated story, a character undeveloped—unappealing to the future novelist.

By mid-century, however, the tide seems to have turned in favor of love at first sight. When Elizabeth Gaskell includes Brontë's letter in her 1857 *Life of Charlotte Brontë*, she commends the encounter as a "little adventure." Such an attitude is widely shared, especially in compact forms that could accommodate romantic spontaneity: short fiction, poetry, and narrative **painting**. Stories and essays celebrating love at first sight—with titles like "The First Time I Saw Her," "Falling in Love," and "Modern Love"—appeared in many major British and American periodicals from the 1840s to the 1880s. One representative story, satirist Horace Smith's 1850 "Love at First Sight," earnestly argues that a man "suddenly smitten" by a beautiful stranger is not "blind and

"Travelling first class—the meeting," by Abraham Solomon. © Fine Art Photographic Library, London/Art Resource, NY.

ignorant" but a "physiognimist" who finds a "sacred spell" in a woman's face. Such love was represented similarly in poetry, including Arthur Hugh Clough's mock-epic *The Bothie of Toper-Na-Fuosich* (1848) and Henry Austin Dobson's "Incognita" (1866). And founding Pre-Raphaelite poet-painter Dante Gabriel Rossetti often cited his namesake, Italian poet Dante Alighieri, and his famously intuited connection to his beloved Beatrice: Rossetti's 1859 painting *The Salutation of Beatrice* revels in such a narrative, and its appearance in the same year as Darwin's *Origin of the Species* testifies to love at first sight's place in broader cultural discourses about both the metaphysical and biological foundations of sexual attraction. In an 1886 essay on the topic, scientist-novelist Grant Allen argues that "Falling in Love" represents a form of Darwin's "universal selective process," and that "love at first sight" is simply the "divinest and deepest of human intuitions."

In these representations, the lover is almost always male and heterosexual, the woman almost always in public; and new technologies, as much as scientific theories, produce the conditions of instantaneous desire. One recurring setting for love at first sight was the railway, where the station's bustle and the compartment's enforced familiarity made intimacy between strangers newly available and problematic. In 1854, the painter Abraham Solomon exhibited at the Royal Academy his controversial *First Class—The Meeting: "And at First Meeting Loved,"* which depicts a young gentleman and lady thrillingly alone (her guardian sleeps beside her) in a train compartment. Clough's poem "Natura Naturans" (1849) similarly celebrates a railway encounter with a woman and a shared attraction that passes "From her to me, from me to her." Citing Charles Baudelaire's poem "À une passante" (1857), Walter Benjamin has described love at *last* sight in similarly modern, anonymous settings: "an unknown woman comes into the poet's field of vision ... The delight of the urban poet is love—not at first sight, but at last sight." Both loves share historical conditions and cultural concerns; but love at first sight, in its mid-to-late-century iteration, retains its specificity because it proposes that instantaneous desire can create meaningful, lasting couples. Returning to and revising an earlier Romantic faith in seen-and-intuited truth, Victorian lovers-at-first-sight, and their authors, more conspicuously devoted themselves to the mysterious acuity of sexual attraction and the comforting wonders it was imagined to produce.

Further Reading: Kern, Stephen. *The Culture of Love: Victorians to Moderns.* Cambridge, MA: Harvard University Press, 1992; Matthews, Christopher. "Love at First Sight: The Velocity of Victorian Heterosexuality." *Victorian Studies* 46, no. 3 (2004): 425–54; Soble, Alan. *The Structure of Love.* New Haven, CT: Yale University Press, 1990.

Christopher Matthews

LOVE IN MARRIAGE.   By the nineteenth century, marriage, affection, and sexual attraction were expected to go together: couples anticipated choosing their own partner and marrying for love. Nevertheless, the stereotype persists of Victorian marriage as dictated by prudence and parental influence. Revelations of the emotionally cold and sexually repressed marriage of high-profile Victorian men such as Ruskin contributed to an image of Victorian marriage as a rather frigid affair. The experience of most nineteenth-century couples was probably somewhere between the romantic ideals and the passionless stereotype. Many couples thinking about or embarking on married life would have to consider both their innermost personal desires for love, sex, and companionship along with the wishes of their family and together with practical questions of economy. As many nineteenth-century novels explored, marriage involved some tight negotiations between prudence and love, parental approval and sexual yearning as well as individual taste and the social expectations that were dictated by cultural norms.

The association of marriage with **romantic love** and sex was well established by the nineteenth century. In the dominant forms of Christianity of the time, marriage was perceived to be a consensual union of two individuals for the expression of sexuality and the rearing of children. The other side to this meant that, particularly in evangelical Christianity, marriage was closely linked to the family and ideals of domesticity. Nineteenth-century culture more generally perceived domestic life to be the foundation of public morality. As such, marriage was seen as an intensely private bond and a public institution for the regulation of sexuality and the cultivation of good habits and principles. The moral seriousness associated with marriage in Victorian culture does not mean that marriages were devoid of genuine passion. Many forms of Evangelical Christianity prescribed the sexual satisfaction of both partners in marriage and the evidence from advice books appears to demonstrate that sex and love within marriage were to be expected even if they were not to be talked about. Because of the association of marriage with domestic, private life wider evidence on love and intimacy in marriage is patchy and inconclusive. Nevertheless, studies based on private correspondence between middle-class men and women confirm that many emotionally intense courtships became sexually fulfilling marriages. Erotically charged letters between married couples temporarily separated are not too difficult to find (Tosh, 57–58).

On the surface, it would appear that marriage in the nineteenth century was undertaken voluntarily and for love. But, despite the emphasis on sexual and emotional compatibility, other factors did influence choices of who and when to marry. Decisions were affected by cultural norms and economic factors that varied according to class and location. One of the greatest factors influencing marriage patterns in the nineteenth century was the respectability of independence. The close association made between marriage, domesticity, and the family encouraged the newly married couple to set up their own independent household. This undoubtedly limited choice. The perceived immorality of marrying until one could support a family was an ideology that appears to have had a real impact on patterns of marriage. In Britain, working-class men tended to marry much younger than their professional counterparts. Working-class men started work at an earlier age while professional men would have to complete university and establish themselves in their career before independence was possible. For the middle classes and the aristocracy, matters of property and inheritance may have influenced the choice of marriage partner further. The novels of Trollope certainly create the impression that marriage in the upper classes was arranged, or at least approved, by parents for the settlement of property. Other evidence suggests that many important business networks were consolidated through marriage, although this may also be a reflection of the social circles that the nineteenth-century suitors moved in. Engels argued that marriage for love was more likely to occur in working-class relations because they did not have to consider the complexities of property and inheritance. Although this may be true, working-class communities had their own sets of norms that regulated sex, love, and marriage. For all classes, one's choice of partners was limited by social networks. Rarely did marriages cross too large a class boundary. Many studies have emphasized the growth of personal autonomy and the increasing importance of romantic love in the choice of marriage partner in the nineteenth century but, the need to cultivate independence, and the mechanisms for doing so (property, inheritance), demonstrate that parental opinions and social norms still held some sway.

Throughout the nineteenth century, evidence can be found for a belief in the ideal of companionate marriage in which both partners share emotional intimacy, sexual relations, and leisure. This took on a new emphasis in nineteenth-century Britain as the more permissive divorce laws gave public prominence to debates about the importance of marital affection. The details of divorce cases which were exposed in salacious detail in the newspapers of the day provided a forum for discussions on the need for genuine affection, passion, and understanding in marriage. Later in the century, changes to the Married Women's Property Act 1882, in partial recognition of women's legal personage, reflected a growing sense that, even in marriage, women retained their individuality. How did changes in the law affect marital love?

Such trends have been seen as evidence of the increasing prominence of companionate marriage in which relationships were based on love, shared responsibilities, and a unity of interests. Still, throughout the nineteenth century, marriages were rarely based on equality. Love and companionship were largely framed on the acceptance of different roles for men and women that were supposed to compliment each other: men provided economically for the family and women emotionally. Legally and culturally, patriarchal authority remained unchallenged.

Further Reading: Lystra, Karen. *Searching the Heart: Women, Men and Romantic Love in Nineteenth Century America*. New York: Oxford University Press, 1989; Mason, Michael. *The Making of Victorian Sexuality*. Oxford: Oxford University Press, 1994; Tosh, John. *A Man's Place: Masculinity and the Middle-Class Home in Victorian England*. New Haven, CT: Yale University Press, 1999; Ward, Peter. *Courtship, Love and Marriage in Nineteenth Century Canada*. Buffalo, Canada: McGill-Queen's University Press, 1990.

Donna Loftus

M

MADNESS.   Madness is the term used in the eighteenth and nineteenth centuries to describe the diagnostic term, mental illness, which was adopted later in the twentieth century. Madness in women was attributed to a malfunction of the uterus, and the word hysteria derived from the Greek *hustera*, for uterus. Menstruation itself was regarded as an abnormal condition because men did not menstruate, and men's bodies were assumed to be the ideal. A female body was unhealthy by nature because it differed from a man's. Allegedly, the uterus caused two kinds of problems: one in young women, because it needed to be impregnated, and the other in women over fifty, because it grieved its inability to bear children. All women were expected to suffer extreme anguish and mental problems at the end of their childbearing years. There were other so-called diagnoses that named the female reproductive organs as the cause, such as an "enlarged" clitoris, nymphomania, and chlorosis, a wasting, weakening condition. As surgical techniques were developed and the medical profession became more technological, women underwent mutilating procedures, in addition to being put in madhouses. Men were diagnosed with masturbatory insanity, and subjected to ornate restraints that were designed to prevent a man from handling his genitals. There were bed straps, mittens, muffs, and lock buckles that were attached to the restraints, only to be unlocked by the attendant. Strait jackets were used to prevent the individual from using his or her hands. The Utica crib was box-shaped, with a cover and rungs used to observe patients. It sat low to the floor, and was allegedly used to protect the patient and to keep him from wandering around. Since nocturnal emissions were also considered abnormal and referred to as **spermatorrhea**, devices were attached to the penis, such as a urethral ring or a toothed urethral ring, where spikes were pushed into the penile skin when an erection occurred. There was, of course, the very real tertiary syphilis that affected both men and women, which did cause actual lesions in the **brain** and dementia.

Demoniac possession, lunacy, and insanity were other terms used to describe mental aberrations with slightly different connotations. The first indicated witchcraft or a supernatural force, the second a mental deficiency or inability to reason, and the third became a legal rather than medical term. However, madness was the most dramatic, calling to mind a wild, unrestrained, state of mind with loss of emotional control and stability. Bertha, the first wife of Mr. Rochester, in **Charlotte Brontë**'s novel, *Jane Eyre*, is an excellent example of how nineteenth-century culture dealt with mental illness, if indeed Bertha was really ill.

The label, madness, also displayed gender bias, because any woman who was even slightly independent, or who questioned her position as subservient, wanted to do work other than domestic, or become educated, was apt to be locked up and declared mad. In addition, a woman who was not always receptive to her husband's sexual demands, or alternatively, experienced intense **orgasm**s was deemed abnormal and likely to be locked away.

Physicians were in a special position to control behavior because they had access to drugs, such as belladonna and chloroform which could cause women to appear disoriented and in need of institutionalization. One physician, S. Weir Mitchell, gained a reputation for curing women with his "rest cure." Writer Charlotte Perkins Gilman underwent the "rest cure" only to become more unhappy and depressed. She had been ambivalent about marriage originally, but after her child was born, probably experienced postpartum depression, known as nervous prostration in the nineteenth century. Her husband took her to Mitchell who agreed to treat her. However, the treatment was dire, consisting of complete isolation and enforced inactivity. After a month, she was sent home with the directive to live as domestic a life as possible, and have her child with her all the time. However, domesticity was depressing her, and once she recognized that her life would be better if she were to dedicate it to writing, she divorced her husband and gave him custody of their daughter. Her short story "The Yellow Wallpaper," is a semi-autobiographical account of a woman who goes mad through lack of intellectual and social stimulation.

Treatment for madness consisted of institutionalization, either in a private home like that of S. Weir Mitchell, or in a madhouse or asylum if one did not have adequate financial means. Water cures were used in a variety of applications. One treatment consisted of cold baths where patients were restrained in tubs and water flowed continuously. A harsher treatment, known as the "spread eagle cure," had an attendant at each limb stretching the stripped patient, while an attendant standing on a chair poured cold water over his head and chest. Electrotherapy using low voltage to treat the nervous system was popular. One example of the use of electricity for treatment was the electromechanical vibrator, used to treat hysteria. Ironically, although **masturbation** was regarded as a harmful and abnormal condition that needed to be eradicated, the physician "massaged the patient's clitoris" to cause a "hysterical paroxysm" (an orgasm) which cured the woman's mental problem.

Since much psychiatric illness was blamed on gynecological dysfunction, many treatments focused on the uterus, ovaries, external genitalia, or clitoris. Hot water was injected into the uterus, an electric current was applied to the uterus, or sometimes leaches were put on the cervix. Ovariotomy, a drastic surgical procedure, was first performed by Ephraim McDowell in 1809, for removal of a tumor. But, unfortunately in 1872, another surgeon recommended removal of healthy ovaries as a treatment for madness. This doctor, Robert Battey, also recommended clitoridectomy for a variety of female nervous disorders. Other mutilations performed on girls and women included red hot wires applied or silver nitrated used to cauterize the clitoris. Or, as a preventive measure, infibulations, sewing the labial lips closed to prevent the clitoris from being handled, was performed. Circumcision in men gained popularity as a treatment for masturbation, as it was generally accepted that masturbation led to insanity and death.

The association of sin with sexual desire prevented the nineteenth-century man or woman from feeling comfortable with the wide range of behaviors found in human sexuality. Physicians used phrases, such as "promiscuous intercourse," "seminal weakness," "inversion" (**homosexuality**) that hyperinflated and pathologized the normal expression of sexuality. Although the trend of the medical profession was to become more scientific and less religion based, the historic association of demonic possession and punishment for sin was difficult to eradicate. Patients themselves sometimes described their madness in terms of good and evil relating to their religious beliefs.

Toward the latter part of the nineteenth century, more humane methods of treating the mentally ill were developed, as drugs and various less-punitive therapies were introduced. At the Pennsylvania Hospital, where Quakers had supported the establishment of a mental ward, work and incentives to self-esteem were encouraged rather than inactivity. However, the stigma and severe loss of personhood that accompanied anyone diagnosed with madness remained a problem, and still exists, although to a lesser extent.

Further Reading: Brontë, Charlotte. *Jane Eyre*. London: Smith, Elder, 1847; Gamwell, Lynn, and Nancy Tomes. *Madness in America: Cultural and Medical Perceptions of Mental Illness Before 1914*. New York: Cornell University Press, 1995; Geller, Jeffrey L. and Maxine Harris. *Women of the Asylum*. New York: Anchor, 1994; Gollaher, David L. "From Ritual to Science: The Medical Transformation of Circumcision in America." *Journal of Social History* 28 (1994): 5–36; Maines, Rachel P. *The Technology of Orgasm: Hysteria, the Vibrator, and Women's Sexual Satisfaction*. Baltimore: Johns Hopkins, 2001; Robinson, William J. *Treatment of Sexual Impotence and Other Sexual Disorders in Men and Women*. New York: Critic and Guide Company, 1924; Shorter, Edward. *A History of Psychiatry*. New York: Wiley, 1997; Stengers, Jean and Anne van Neck. *Masturbation: The History of a Great Terror*. New York: Palgrave, 2001.

Lana Thompson

MALTHUS, THOMAS ROBERT (1766–1834). Thomas Malthus was a pivotal figure in the transition from eighteenth-century materialism and permissiveness to Victorian spirituality and antisensualism, though his work contained many disparate elements. His essays on population offered a fertile and potentially explosive mixture of ideas, with something to offend or please nearly every shade of political and moral opinion, in addition to inspiring later developments in both demography and biology. While his assumptions about the animal nature of man seemed very materialist, and outraged some early critics, they gave both Charles Darwin and Alfred Russell Wallace the mechanism that led them to the theory of **evolution** by natural selection. His insistence on the virtues of chastity, sobriety, and industry were appreciated by an age that applauded Samuel Smiles's tracts on duty, thrift, and self-help, while his pessimism about the speed and extent of human progress seemed alien to the spirit of both the Enlightenment and the optimism that animated "the workshop of the world." Malthus's law of population, his views on the poor laws, and his contributions to political economy, were all at the center of endless and often angry contention, as were his debates about sexual morality and reproduction.

Thomas was the second son of Daniel Malthus, a country gentleman with advanced views, an enthusiast for Enlightenment thought and a particular fan of both Rousseau and David Hume. It was possibly under the influence of *Emile*, the former's idealistic guide to childrearing, that Daniel had his son educated by a succession of private tutors (all of heterodox opinion) before sending him to Jesus College, Cambridge, where he studied Classics and Mathematics, graduating with honors in the latter. His father must have been both surprised and disappointed when Thomas, far from embracing the radical principles in which he had been reared, expressed the desire to be a clergyman, though as a good liberal he made no objections, and arranged for him to be appointed to a curacy near the family property. They remained in frequent contact and argued over the issues of the day, particularly the French Revolution—hailed by Malthus senior with Wordsworthian enthusiasm, regarded with skepticism by his conservative son. Daniel was particularly entranced by the optimistic vision of continuous human advance and social progress. Thomas disagreed, and in his search for a clinching argument against predictions of human perfectibility, he hit upon his law of population —all these utopian schemes must fail, he announced, because the more society improved, the greater would be the rate of population growth, leading inevitably to famine, disease, war, and a return to the bad old days. Daniel might have disagreed, but he was evidently proud of his contrarian son's debating skill, and urged him to set down his ideas and seek publication. The result in 1798 was *An Essay on the Principle of Population as it Affects the Future Improvement of Society, with Remarks on the Speculations of Mr Godwin, M. Condorcet and Other Writers.*

Malthus's argument was not, as many critics have falsely asserted, that human populations actually grew at a geometric ratio, while the food supply increased only arithmetically. What he proposed was that all "animate nature" had the potential to grow much faster than their food supply (the first geometric, the second arithmetical), and that the human species had the potential to double its numbers every twenty-five years. The fact that this did not happen was proof that checks to population growth were in operation, and Malthus defined these under two headings: positive (anything raising the death rate) and preventive (anything lowering the birth rate), more famously expressed in the alternatives of misery (famine, war, disease, industrial accidents, bad nursing, etc.) and vice. The details of the second category were not spelled out explicitly, but included "promiscuous intercourse, unnatural passions, violations of the marriage bed and improper arts to conceal the consequences of irregular connections" (1803, bk. 1, chap. 1). The last probably refers to **abortion** rather than contraception, since the latter was so unthinkable that when Condorcet hinted at it as a means to forestall excessive population growth, Malthus professed not to understand what was meant: "he alludes either to a promiscuous concubinage, which would prevent breeding, or to something else as unnatural." The fact that he did probably understand the allusion is shown by his following comment: "To remove the difficulty in this way will surely … be to destroy that virtue and purity of manners which the advocates of equality and of the perfectibility of man profess to be the end and object of their views" (1803, bk. 3, chap. 1). Such reticence might explain why one critic actually accused Malthus of favoring contraception, an error he sought to dispel in his Appendix to the 1817 edition: "I should always particularly reprobate any artificial and unnatural modes of checking population, both on account of their immorality and their tendency to remove a necessary spur to industry."

The aspect of the thesis that appealed most strongly to the nineteenth century was the assumption that both personal happiness and social stability depended on the rejection of vice. However, the radicals were quick to notice that the equation also implied that more vice meant less misery, suggesting that unnatural modes, such as contraception, might be just what the poor needed. The aspect of his case that appalled both religious conservatives (such as Coleridge and Robert Southey) and political progressives (such as William Hazlitt Godwin and later John Stuart Mill) was Malthus's insistence that the human sex drive came second only to the desire for food, and thus that "the passion between the sexes" would not abate and be largely replaced by spiritual communion as civilization advanced, in the manner postulated by Godwin and other high-minded rationalists. Checks to population growth would thus always be necessary. Malthus not only argued that there was no empirical evidence of any progress toward "the extinction of the passion between the sexes" and that it was certain to "remain in its present state" (1798, chap. 1), but that it would be a very bad thing for individuals and society if it did fade away:

> After the desire of food, the most powerful of our desires is the passion between the sexes ... Of the happiness spread over human life by this passion, very few are unconscious. Virtuous love, exalted by friendship, seems to be that sort of mixture of sensual and intellectual enjoyment, particularly suited to the nature of man, and most powerfully calculated to ... produce the most exquisite gratifications.... I am inclined to believe that there are not many of these plans [of life] formed which are not connected ... with the prospect of the gratification of this passion, and with the support of children arising from it. The evening meal, the warm house, and the comfortable fireside would lose half their interest, if we were to exclude the idea of some object of affection with whom they were to be shared. (1803, bk. 4, chap. 1)

Such eloquent praise of love is not the sort of sentiment usually associated with the man whose ideas led Carlyle to dub political economy the dismal science.

The vigorous reaction to the first essay encouraged Malthus to prepare a second edition that turned out to be a substantially new work (1803), though the basic argument did not alter. Although the first was, as Anthony Flew comments, "an occasional polemic designed to debunk utopian visions inspired by the French Revolution," the second was "a painstaking sociological treatise deploying a mass of detailed evidence." The change of emphasis was evident in the title, *An Essay on the Principle of Population; or, a View of its Past and Present Effects on Human Happiness; with an Inquiry into our Prospects Respecting the Future Removal or Mitigation of the Evils which it Occasions.* It was this version that went through four subsequent editions (1806, 1807, 1817, and 1826), as well as a *Summary View* prepared for the *Encyclopaedia Britannica,* and published as a separate booklet in 1830. The most important difference between the 1798 and the 1803 essays was the addition of "moral restraint" as a preventive check to population growth, defined as "a restraint from marriage from prudential motives, with a conduct strictly moral during the period of restraint" (1803, bk. 1, chap. 2). It suggested that the only virtuous (and thus happiness-producing) way to reduce population growth was by delayed marriage. It is apparent that Malthus could not imagine that married couples would (as the Victorian middle class later did) limit their family in order to enjoy a higher standard of living. He was very much a child of the eighteenth century in assuming that marriage meant plenty of sex, but also a Victorian in his assumption that sex meant reproduction.

Although the "law of population" was no law at all (as critics quickly noted, there was no reason why the food supply was limited to arithmetical increase), it was highly influential, setting the agenda for discussions of sexuality for much of the century, and spawning "left" and "right" trends. On the right were doctors, such as **William Acton**, with his insistence on absolute continence in the young and the single, to be followed by moderation in the married; and **Jonathan Hutchinson**, with his professional opinion that any form of contraception was both immoral and harmful to health. On the left were working-class radicals, beginning with Francis Place in *Illustrations and Proofs of the Principles of Population* (1822), who suggested that if married persons adopted

> such precautionary means as would, without being injurious to health, or destructive of female delicacy, prevent conception, a sufficient check might at once be given to the increase of population beyond the means of subsistence; vice and misery ... might be removed from society; and the object of Mr. Malthus, Mr. Godwin and every philanthropic person, be promoted by the increase of comfort, of intelligence and of moral conduct, in the mass of the population.

He was followed by the neo-Malthusians, advocating **birth control** for all, but especially as a means of avoiding unwanted children and raising working-class living standards. At their radical fringe was the remarkable (and in his day unmentionable) George Drysdale, who believed that Malthus was so correct about the delights of sex and the harm of too many children. Hence it followed that sexual abstinence must produce ill-health and mental misery, and that couples should be penalized for excess offspring. He became a passionate advocate of regular sexual activity, casual premarital liaisons, regular sex within marriage (at least twice a week), and contraception to guard against **pregnancy**. He was even daring enough to suggest regular use of condoms as a prophylactic against venereal disease (VD).

The fact that the radicals could extract such lessons from Malthus indicates the ambiguities of his legacy. As we have seen, he was never crudely antisex; he defended the passions against Godwin's unrealistic belief that they would weaken as society became more civilized, and endorsed them as a spur to effort, a molder of good character and a chief source of happiness. What was needed was not their extinction, but their "regulation and direction" under the guidance of reason. But his definition of moral restraint was stringent, and, as the following shows, he banned premarital sex entirely:

> The interval between the age of puberty and ... marriage must ... be passed in strict chastity; because the law of chastity cannot be violated without producing evil. The effect of anything like a promiscuous intercourse which prevents the birth of children is evidently to weaken the best affections of the heart, and ... degrade the female character. And any other intercourse would, without improper arts, bring as many children into the society as marriage, with a greater probability of their becoming a burden to it. (1803, bk. 4, chap. 2)

It was this aspect of his legacy that appealed to the few Victorians who genuinely were antisex, such as William Acton and Jonathan Hutchinson. If Malthus's insistence on "our obligation not to marry until we have a fair prospect of being able to support our children" (1803, bk. 4, chap. 1) could be seen as directed specifically at the poor while giving a free rein to the rich, his equally strong conviction that premarital sex was morally wrong applied to all, though the reason advanced related only to morality. Acton gave this argument a medical twist through his discovery that immoderate sexual indulgence of any kind was unhealthy, though especially risky in the young, meaning that while the married could indulge occasionally, the young must remain strictly continent. Despite the scientific gloss, Acton retained a good deal of Malthus's moral reasoning.

The echo is so strong that it suggests either that Acton had read Malthus, or that the views of the latter were in such common currency that it was impossible for an educated person not to pick them up. Malthusian echoes can also be found in the warnings of medical conservatives against the use of condoms in the war against syphilis. Malthus's moral views had been shaped by the teachings of William Paley (1743–1805), especially his *Principles of Moral and Political Philosophy* (1785), in which he argued that God had designed a world in which pleasure or pain was the reward or penalty attached to actions that were either conducive or detrimental to our virtue and happiness. This system of moral utilitarianism implied that sin would produce unhappiness, meaning that happiness was best achieved by a moral course, because sexual excess would lead to disease and too many children. The sensible thing from both a moral and practical point of view was restraint. However, the system relied on people reaping the wages of sin. If they could somehow avoid the consequences of excess by contraception to block pregnancy or prophylactics to protect themselves against venereal disease, the punishment for immoral behavior would vanish, and the system would break down. Thus in the 1860s, we find surgeons, such as Samuel Solly, opposing efforts to combat syphilis on the ground that it was a scourge specifically created by God to punish illicit sex, and Hutchinson objecting to schemes for the regulation of and health checks on prostitutes on the ground that it would reduce the penalties for fornication. In an influential article published in 1901, he attacked the use of prophylactics, such as condoms, because any measure which made "irregular sexual intercourse less dangerous" was "injurious to the sense of decency ... and detrimental to the moral conscience of a community." He preferred circumcision of male infants, because he believed that the damage it did to the penis would discourage pre- and extramarital sex. Both Solly and Hutchinson were extremists, but the medical profession as a whole remained violently opposed to both contraception and prophylactics throughout the nineteenth century and well into the twentieth, a situation usually justified on the basis of the same Malthusian reasoning.

Further Reading: Benn, Miriam J. *Predicaments of Love*. London: Pluto Press, 1992; Darby, Robert. *A Surgical Temptation: The Demonization of the Foreskin and the Rise of Circumcision in Britain*. Chicago and London: University of Chicago Press, 2005; Dolan, Brian, ed. *Malthus, Medicine and Morality: "Malthusianism" after 1798*. Amsterdam: Rodopi, 2000; Flew, Anthony, ed. *An Essay on the Principle of Population*. London: Penguin Classics, 1985; James, Patricia. *Population Malthus: His Life and Times*. London: Routledge, 1979; Mason, Michael. *The Making of Victorian Sexuality*. New York: Oxford University Press, 1994; Mason, Michael. *The Making of Victorian Sexual Attitudes*. New York: Oxford University Press, 1994; Winch, Donald, ed. *An Essay on the Principle of Population*. Cambridge: Cambridge Texts in the History of Political Thought, 1992.

Robert Darby

MARRIAGE. In the nineteenth-century West, marriage was considered the foundation of civilized life, allowing men and women to fulfill the law of God, the law of man, and natural law. Indissoluble wedlock was widely seen as the key to social stability, meaning that throughout the century, marriage was seen not as a private arrangement, but as a public institution, with a shifting combination of church and state control over it.

Until the sixteenth century, the only requirement for a valid Christian marriage was mutual consent. Marriage had been declared a sacrament by the Council of Trent in 1563, which also proclaimed that marriage was indissoluble, a view that had been held for centuries, but had not been formally promulgated before then. The council also formalized Roman Catholic marriage, demanding that a priest be present, that banns be read, and that there should be at least two witnesses, effectively giving the church control over marriage. Scotland maintained the practice of "contract marriage," that is, marriage by mutual consent alone, into the twentieth century, while England eradicated it in the 1750s. In countries which came under the influence of Protestant ideas after the Reformation, the idea of marriage as a sacrament was generally rejected, except for England, where the Anglican Church continued to see it as sacramental. However, even the most radically reformed states maintained that marriage was divinely ordained and holy in itself. Ordinary people seem to have considered marriage as a way of increasing the security and well being of the kinship network, and of ensuring their economic survival, in times when life and fortune could be very insecure.

During the eighteenth century, there had been a marked shift from the idea that marriage should primarily serve "interest factors," such as family aggrandizement, toward a reliance on mutual affection as the appropriate motivation for marriage, a change of emphasis most visible in those regions, such as Northern Europe and North America, where the influence of Romanticism was strongest. The nineteenth century, in both Europe and North America, saw a vigorous debate over the "marriage question." This centered around three hotly argued issues: the legitimate role of affection in marriage choice, gender equality and inequality, and class-based marriage practices. Over the period, there was increased consensus on the importance of love in the making of a marriage, although economic and social suitability remained important considerations. At the start of the century, there were still some who persisted in viewing marriage from the eighteenth-century perspective, especially among the wealthy. These people felt that a marriage should first of all satisfy the economic and social requirements of the family, and that it was properly employed to cement alliances between families. If a proposed match was suitable in these terms, then questions of personal affinity and affection could be considered. However, such views were soon being perceived as old fashioned, and marriage for money alone, although it certainly continued to happen, became less defensible as time passed. By the century's end, to marry for money was considered positively immoral if it were not also a marriage for love (although vast fortunes could cast a temporary haze of romance around the most unprepossessing). In all classes, increased emphasis on friendship and mutual esteem between husband and wife tended to increase gender equality within marriage, although this varied enormously.

At the start of the century, marriage was a religious institution in most Western countries. However, it was during this period that secular marriage began to emerge. All marriages in England were required to be religious until 1832. In France, secular marriage became legal in 1792, and the revolutionary government also temporarily legalized **divorce** by mutual consent. The founders of the United States brought secular ideas of marriage with them to the new world, and most states offered a choice of marriage by magistrate or clergy during the period. France imposed secular marriage on significant parts of Europe, such as Italy, in 1806. Most of southern Europe, including Portugal and Spain, moved to secular control of marriage much later in the century, in the 1860s and 1870s. However, purely secular marriage remained the choice of a minority where choice was possible. For example, in England in 1844, a mere 3 percent of marriages were nonreligious, and this had risen to only 18 percent in 1904. Even more revealingly, in the period when religious marriage was illegal in France, it appears from surviving records that about 80 percent of those marrying chose clandestine religious marriage. These statistics suggest that most people continued to see marriage as having religious meaning even as society became more secular, and when the state made such views officially disloyal. At the same time that marriage was slowly moving under secular control, legislation was being passed to increasingly protect the institution of marriage, a tendency that was particularly strong in English and German legal systems.

Marriage was considered the natural state for adults, with the assumption that almost all who could marry would probably do so at some point. The conventions of the period meant that a woman was expected to wait until her hand was requested in marriage by some man. Her choice in marriage was a negative one, the power to say no. But the theoretical power of refusal was augmented by many social devices that allowed women to indirectly express a preference, giving both sexes some agency in marriage choice. Failure to marry was considered shameful for women, because it was thought that they had failed in the business of a woman's life, unless they were wealthy enough to command respect regardless of their spinster status. Men who did not marry were assumed to have remained single from choice, and did not suffer social stigma as a result.

It was considered normal for a married woman to be financially dependent on her husband. Men had a legal obligation to support their wives in a manner suited to their own incomes, which meant that they were also responsible for their wife's debts. Her legal personhood disappeared at the moment of marriage in most jurisdictions, meaning that her possessions and money became the property of her husband. She had no right to undertake contracts or legal agreements in her own standing; if her pocket was picked while shopping, the thief would be charged with stealing from her husband's, because even her clothing was not her own possession in law. Of course, many married couples happily ignored the legal realities and continued to treat the wife's money as if it belonged to her. Married women in England regained their property rights in a series of acts passed in the 1870s and 1880s.

In rural areas, geographical endogamy remained a feature of marriage choice well into the nineteenth century in much of Europe. Rural laborers tended to marry someone from within their own parish or a neighboring one, seldom venturing further than a few miles in search of a partner. The more affluent had no such restrictions in marriage choice, although cousin marriage remained popular, suggesting that families socialized together regularly, and that women seeking friendship in marriage often chose a man they already knew well over a stranger. The other advantages of cousin marriage were the opportunities it provided to link properties or strengthen already-strong familial connections. Cousin marriage grew in popularity throughout the century in all social classes in throughout Europe, to the extent that by 1900, it was causing concern to some of the more radical eugenicists.

Disparity in social rank or standing was a severe hindrance to marriage throughout the century. It was considered disgraceful for a man to marry far below himself in the social scale, because it implied that his passions had proved stronger than his sense of family pride and social fitness. The great majority of men and women married within their own ranks. However, in theory at least, those few men who married below their own class were considered to raise their wife to their own standing. A woman who married "beneath herself," cut herself off from her own station and descended to that of her husband, experiencing instant downward social mobility. The social penalties for a woman marrying down the social scale were so severe that very few women did so. In general, women with independent incomes preferred to remain single if no suitable husband of their own class proposed. North America, with its more fluid social structures and its glorification of the "self-made man," displayed more social flexibility in marriage partners, although, even here, extreme disparities of background were viewed with caution. One exception to this was the increasing number of marriages between wealthy capitalists and the aristocracy, but here, each side could be seen as bringing something of equal value to the marital enterprise.

Middle-class commentators tended to assume that their working-class contemporaries married improvidently, carelessly, or for base material motives. Malthusian ideas stressed that working-class improvidence in marriage was an important factor in excessive population growth. **Thomas Robert Malthus** also argued that impulsive and early marriage could catapult people down the social scale, resulting in an increase in poverty and distress. In some central European countries, this pessimistic view of working-class marriage was taken to the point where the poor were required to prove that they had sufficient assets to support a family before a marriage would be approved by the local authorities.

While it is true that working-class parents had little influence over marriage choice, marriage seems to have remained a mixture of personal preference and prudential considerations among the poor, as it was with those above them in the social scale. In agricultural areas, a man who could not find a wife was severely handicapped in life, lacking the laboring assistance of a wife and children. In many areas, premarital cohabitation was common among the working class, although the arrival of children usually meant a speedy marriage, suggesting that marriage and childrearing were strongly linked in the popular understanding. Even in areas with a strong tradition of pre-marital sexual relations or cohabitation, disapproval of marital infidelity was marked.

The age at which marriage was contracted varied widely in the century, from under twenty for both sexes in some Russian rural areas, rising to nearly thirty for both sexes in urban northern Europe by the 1890s. However, regional variation remained enormous, as did the varying rates of permanent celibacy. The general trend was toward an increase in the age of marriage over the century, which may have been linked to rising expectations of material comfort and economic security. The "breadwinner theory," that the man should earn a family wage rendering him able to support his wife and children without the assistance of their paid labor, resulted in a need for more income before marriage was feasible.

The sexual double standard was enshrined in English law, because women could not divorce their husbands for adultery without another marital offense, such as incest or **bigamy**, while a woman was divorceable on the grounds of adultery alone. In the 200 years of parliamentary divorce in England, which ended in 1857, only 1 percent of divorces were awarded to women. Women were counseled to overlook sexual misdemeanors on the part of their husbands, in part because men were considered to be naturally promiscuous. While the right of women to sue for divorce varied somewhat between nations, it remained generally true that it was difficult or impossible for women in most jurisdictions to divorce their husbands without extreme cause. Women's financial dependence was also a factor in female condonation of male affairs, as was the strength of social pressure for women to be loving, forgiving, and endlessly forbearing with their husbands. Women who had affairs were considered depraved beyond belief, although this was relaxed slightly among the very wealthy, if great discretion was exercised in the conduct of the affair. Even among the aristocracy, however, a married woman detected in open sexual impropriety was almost certain to be denied any contact with her children for the remainder of her life.

People ordinarily assumed that marriage would be for life. Many considered it indissoluble by its very nature, although in practice, it was probably more accurate to consider it as extremely durable. Marriage breakdown and unhappiness, no matter how bitter, could not ordinarily be relieved by divorce. Divorce was rare and difficult in most countries throughout the century. In England, there were only one or two divorces a year between 1800 and 1857, when legal changes began to make it slightly more accessible. In France, only judicial separation was available between 1816 and 1884, when divorce was once more legalized (it had been briefly legal during the revolutionary period). In England, far more separations than divorces were awarded during the century. In the Catholic areas of Europe, including Spain, Italy, and Ireland, divorce was impossible during the first half of the century; it later became possible, but remained uncommon. Divorce carried considerable social stigma with it well beyond the end of the nineteenth century, but slowly grew more respectable at about the same time that marriage started to lose much of its prestige. *See also* Hinduism, Marriage in; Love in Marriage; Marriage, Irregular.

Further Reading: Kertzer, David I. and Marzio Barbagli, ed. *Family Life in the Long Nineteenth Century 1789–1913: The History of the European Family*. Vol. 2. New Haven, CT: Yale University Press, 2002; Phillips, Roderick. *Putting Asunder: A History of Divorce in Western Society*. Cambridge: Cambridge University Press, 1988; Stone, Lawrence. *Road to Divorce: England 1530–1987*. Oxford: Oxford University Press, 1990.

Susan Mumm

MARRIAGE, IRREGULAR. In the nineteenth century, marriage was considered to be a divine institution, a law of nature, and a law of society. It was imbued with considerable moral and political importance. In light of its social and religious significance, it was assumed on all sides that it should be solemnized with dignity and seriousness, and in a fashion that would increase the general public's reverence for the institution. In England in 1800, marriage by banns in the parish church was regular. The purposes of publishing the banns (they were announced from the pulpit before the sermon) included publicity, an opportunity for reflection on the part of those involved, and a chance for objections on the part of those with an interest in the matter. Marriage by license (in church, or later in the century, in a registrar's office) was regular; all other forms of marriage were considered irregular. They might be valid and —in certain places and circumstances—legal, but they were disapproved of and discouraged by officialdom.

The two major forms of irregular marriage still surviving in the nineteenth century were elopement and clandestine marriage. Elopement had two meanings: one was a private, runaway marriage, where one or both of the partners were under twenty-one; the other popular usage meant a married woman running off with her lover. A clandestine marriage was a ceremony conducted by a man who at least claimed to have the authority to perform marriages, and which (in England) followed the Book of Common Prayer. It violated canon law because of its secrecy, as it was performed without the three-week waiting period and publication of banns, and might involve minors without parental consent.

After 1753, it became impossible to contract a valid irregular marriage in England. Hardwicke's Marriage Act was passed that year, in order to reduce the chaotic nature of English marriage to a regularized system easily patrolled by officialdom, and regular marriage became the only acceptable form. Clandestine marriage rapidly declined as a result, and elopement to the Scottish border became the only option for a couple desiring to avoid the English regulations.

The Scottish law of both marriage and divorce was significantly different. As Hardwicke's Marriage Act of 1753 did not apply to Scotland, informal marriages remained legal, so that both contract and clandestine marriages were considered valid. Mutual consent was the only essential requirement for a legal marriage in Scotland, and remained so until 1949. Although public marriage in church with proper notice was considered the most respectable way of marrying, Scottish law required neither, which created considerable difficulties regarding proof, if one party later decided to deny the marriage. Even if the marriage was never made public, the spouse had full property rights. Furthermore, children born before a later marriage were legitimate after the marriage in Scotland, while illegitimate children in England remained illegitimate even if a marriage later took place.

After Hardwicke's Marriage Act of 1753, elopement was an expensive business for English people, because it involved travel to Scotland. A clandestine marriage in Scotland was considered valid, but irregular. The toll bar marriages, conducted traditionally by blacksmiths or toll keepers, lacked decorum and were not considered to protect women from later desertion in the same way that public marriage did. There was no residential qualification in Scotland until 1857, meaning that before that date, marriages could take place immediately upon arrival, a boon for runaway suitors. After 1857, the only requirements were that one or both parties were born in Scotland, or had been domiciled there, or had stayed there for three weeks. This caused a rapid decline in the number of English couples traveling there to marry. Even as late as 1893, the Scottish age of marriage for boys was fourteen, and twelve for girls.

Aristocratic elopements were heavily publicized, and probably gave the impression that elopement was far more common than was actually the case. One determined couple on the margins of European royalty married five times in five countries in 1836 to ensure the validity of their marriage. But the nineteenth century in England was a period dominated by regular marriage, usually in church, and the rapid decline of irregular forms, which continued to flourish over the border to the north.

Further Reading: Leneman, Leah. "A Natural Foundation in Equity: Marriage and Divorce in Eighteenth and Nineteenth Century Scotland." *Scottish Economic & Social History* 20 (2000): 199–215; Outhwaite, R. B. *Clandestine Marriage in England*. London: Hambledon, 1995; Stone, Lawrence. *Road to Divorce: England 1530–1987*. Oxford: Oxford University Press, 1992.

Ian Merrilees

MASOCHISM. *See* Sadism and Masochism

MASTURBATION. The fact that masturbation was physically harmful and morally unacceptable, was a cornerstone of Victorian medicine. Few doctors between John Hunter in the 1780s and **Havelock Ellis** in the early twentieth century questioned the eighteenth-century dogma that masturbation would induce organic and mental disease —even **madness**—in both men and women, and none doubted that it was the physician's role to do all he could to eradicate the practice. While the focus of eighteenth-century medical theory had been on elaborating the symptoms of masturbatory illness and identifying the signs by which the masturbator could be detected, their Victorian successors sought to explain the organic mechanisms by which masturbation caused harm, and to devise effective means to stop it. **William Acton** spoke for many in defining masturbation as "an habitual incontinence eminently productive of disease," and in explaining that the damage to health arose partly from the loss of semen and partly from the expenditure of nervous energy in the **orgasm**. The proposition that excessive loss of sperm would cause debility was ancient. The idea that the venereal orgasm was also (and probably more) risky, developed with the rising prominence of nerve force theory, the most important disease paradigm between the humoral system and the discovery of germs. Introduced by S. A. Tissot in the 1750s, this idea also accounted for the harm of masturbation by women. The trend of Victorian medical thinking was to stress the greater danger of losing nervous power, though this did not prevent the quacks and popular pamphleteers from continuing to preach the perils of seminal depletion.

The treatments devised for masturbation fell into two broad groups—depending on whether masturbation was regarded as a moral failing (arising from weak will), or a physiological problem caused by irritation in the genital region brought on by worms, eczema, uncleanliness, or a tight, long, or adherent foreskin. Remedies proposed by the first group (the doves) included such mild measures as wholesome reading, fresh air, tiring exercise, regular bathing, and religious devotions, while the hawks went for something stronger, involving physical and often surgical, interventions. Their tactics

"Sleep," by Philip Wilson Steer, 1894. © Tate Gallery, London/Art Resource, NY.

included straitjackets and chastity devices (for both boys and girls); blistering the penis or clitoris with hot metal, silver nitrate, or iodine; piercing the foreskin with a metal ring to inhibit erection; and circumcision. While the first four of these were probably recommended more often than applied, circumcision became common, and by the 1870s, it was generally agreed that this was the most efficient and reliable approach to the problem, particularly if done early as a preventive. There are occasional reports of further extreme measures, such as severing the main nerve of the penis or vagina, and **Jonathan Hutchinson** even recommended castration in chronic cases, but (as he regretted) such solutions were too radical for British public opinion. In the United States, however, infibulation was regularly employed, and castration of boys, particularly in orphanages and similar institutions, was far from unknown. Clitoridectomy was occasionally employed to treat masturbation in girls, but it was always a rare and controversial resort.

Masturbation was as much a moral as a medical issue. Writers on the subject were as avid on its threat to character as to health, and even the few doctors who remained sceptical of claims that it caused organic disease (such as James Paget) vehemently denounced "self-abuse" as a sin and vice. Preventing masturbation became a major element in the program of the British public schools to mould disciplined Christian gentlemen, and to this end floggings were common. Juvenile masturbation was also a prime target of the purity movement from the 1880s to the First World War, coinciding with the height of the syphilis scare and related anxiety over **prostitution**. It may now seem strange that a campaign against venereal disease should be so obsessed with solitary sex, but the practice was not then seen as a safe alternative to intercourse, but rather as a form of premature sexual arousal and slackening of self control that would lead boys to mistresses and prostitutes later on. Acton was frequently cited as authority for the view that so long as the tap of sexual interest was not turned on in the first place, strict male chastity was as realistic as it was desirable.

Further Reading: Darby, Robert. "Circumcision as a Preventive of Masturbation: A Review of the Historiography." *Journal of Social History* 36 (2003): 737–58; Gilbert, Arthur N.

"Doctor, Patient, and Onanist Diseases in the Nineteenth Century." *Journal of the History of Medicine and Allied Sciences* 30 (1975): 217–34; Hall, Lesley. "Forbidden by God, Despised by Men: Masturbation, Medical Warnings, Moral Panic and Manhood in Great Britain, 1850–1950." In *Forbidden History: The State, Society and the Regulation of Sexuality in Modern Europe*, edited by J. C. Fout. Chicago: University of Chicago Press, 1992; Hamowy, Ronald. "Medicine and the Crimination of Sin: 'Self-abuse' in 19th Century America." *Journal of Libertarian Studies* 1 (1977): 229–70; Hunt, Alan. "The Great Masturbation Panic and the Discourse of Moral Regulation in Nineteenth and Early Twentieth Century Britain." *Journal of the History of Sexuality* 8 (1998): 575–615.

Robert Darby

MENSTRUATION.   Menstruation is the normal physiological process that occurs in the human female when the uterus sheds its buildup of endometrial tissue. As the tissue sloughs off the inside of the uterus, it tears the blood vessels, which then bleed. The tissue and blood are expelled through the vagina for a period that varies from three to seven days every twenty-eight days. In all cultures, menstruation and sexual behavior are specifically linked, but in different ways.

There are prohibitions against sexual intercourse during menstruation in the fifteenth chapter of Leviticus in the Old Testament of the Bible, where the word "issue" is interpreted to mean menstruation. This created an assumption in the Judeo-Christian world that menstruation was somehow unclean, and by the nineteenth century, it became so shameful that few young girls were warned of this physiological event in advance of its arrival. In popular slang, it became known as "the curse," and some even thought it transmitted disease. In 1875, A.F.A. King stated that although conception was most likely during a woman's monthly flow, intercourse was dangerous and should be forbidden because menstrual blood was the "source of male gonorrhea."

In many preliterate societies, women were separated from men until they stopped bleeding, because menstrual blood was believed to be powerful enough to cause harm. There were beliefs, known as menstrual pollution, which held that poisoned wells, failed crops, plants withering on the vine, or food spoiling, were the result of the presence of a menstruating woman. One belief was that a man's penis would become contaminated if he had intercourse with a menstruating woman. In 1878, the *British Medical Journal* published a series of letters that perpetuated the myths regarding dangers of menstrual blood.

In educated nineteenth-century thought, menstruation was not viewed as abnormal because of beliefs derived from ancient Greek medicine. The humoral theory was the belief system at the time of Galen and Hippocrates, and remnants of it persisted until the early twentieth century. According to the theory, the human body was a microcosm of the earth, and it contained four liquids, or humors, that corresponded to the four elements in the universe. Blood, black bile, yellow bile and phlegm corresponded to fire, earth, wind, and water. Men and women differed because they had different amounts of these humors, but a balance was necessary for good health. When a woman menstruated, it was a signal that her body was ridding itself of an excess of blood. And, to model nature, the ancient practice of phlebotomy, or bleeding, was used as a treatment for many ills.

The persistence of these embedded cultural assumptions colored the attitudes of Victorian society toward menstruation. Young girls were not prepared for the possibility of pregnancy, because parents rarely discussed sexual matters with their children. Menstruation was referred to as being unwell, when referred to at all. The entire subject was clouded in mystery, partially because the relationship between ovulation, menstruation, pregnancy, and lactation had not yet been scientifically explained. If erotic literature of that century is a mirror of reality, often the sex partner or physician provided that information for the naïve pubescent girl. One example is given in Campbell's *The Amatory Experiences of a Surgeon* where a young man begins his sexual career after receiving his diploma from the Royal College of Surgeons. He is free to experiment and his first partner is Julia, the daughter of a wealthy merchant. He explains menstruation to her "without shocking her modesty," but then proceeds to deflower her and have sex with her. Menstruation is mentioned in erotica as either a reason to delay sexual relations or to demonstrate the power of passion over the power of menstrual pollution.

The ignorance associated with menstruation produced traumatic episodes in many young women. Rather than accept the change as a normal, natural part of life, they felt disgusted, and associated the monthly flow with decay and a punishment from God rather than a life-affirming process. Menstruation was considered an illness, the blood proof of some mysterious inner wound that relegated a woman's life to one of sorrow and disability.

Space was gendered, which meant that for one week out of every month a nonpregnant woman was relegated to domestic territory. The first commercially available sanitary napkin was sold in the 1890s in Germany, but it was not until the 1920s that sanitary napkins gained popularity in the United States. Rags were used and rewashed, or women simply bled into their thick clothing. Servants were required to remove menstrual blood from the floor, if a family was fortunate enough to afford them.

The greatest liability regarding sexuality and menstruation focused on a woman's inability to engage in academic study, because it was thought to damage her ability to reproduce and have children. In addition, the mental stress and nervous strain caused by intellectual work would allegedly interfere with her "weak nature," and cause harm. This was one of several rationales employed to justify denying women access to higher education. According to the writings of Edward H. Clarke, the unique period of growth that women experienced at puberty would be damaged if a female did anything other than concentrate on developing her reproductive system. The metaphor he used was that since one did not exercise when one was eating, likewise one did not perform **brain** work during the growth of the female reproductive system. However, in addition, after puberty, females were not to exercise their minds during their menstrual cycles or make the body do two things at one time. **John Harvey Kellogg**, the icon of misinformation regarding sexual matters, wrote that many young women injured themselves by excessive mental work during their periods. Other **physicians** showed statistical evidence that women who had college degrees had smaller families than uneducated ones, and attributed the smaller family size to damage from studying rather than educated women choosing to limit the number of children they produced.

A variety of suggestions to limit women's activities were promoted, usually by men in decision-making positions. Although universities and occupations eventually opened to women, the menstrual taboo continued to persist into the twentieth century, usually in the form of claiming that women were incapable of fulfilling political leadership roles because of their hormonal imbalances, which could influence their decisionmaking, and possibly compromise national security.

Further Reading: Anonymous. "The Feminist Chronicles 1970." See *The Feminist Majority Foundation* at: http://www.feminist.org/research/chronicles/fc1970.html; Bullough, Vern and

Martha Voght. In *Women, Menstruation and Nineteenth Century Medicine in Women and Health in America*, edited by J. W. Leavitt. Madison: University of Wisconsin, 1984: 28–38; Finley, Harry. "Pads." See *Museum of Menstruation* at: http://www.mum.org/collection.htm; Ripa, Yannick. *Women and Madness*. Minneapolis: University of Minnesota Press, 1991; Whelan, Elizabeth. "Attitudes Toward Menstruation." *Studies in Family Planning* 6, no. 4 (1975): 106–8.

Lana Thompson

MENTAL ILLNESS. *See* Madness

MIDWIVES. *See* Physicians and Midwives

MURDER AND SEX CRIMES. Nineteenth-century conceptualizations of murder and sexual crime witnessed a shift of emphasis away from a forensic discourse that focused upon the criminal act, to a medical (above all psychiatric) discourse, that centered on the criminal actor. As such, it gave rise to notions of "born" murderers, as well as to the concept of a special category of sexual predators who acted out inner compulsions beyond their control. The (sexual) serial killers who finally succeeded in capturing the popular imagination in the early decades of the twentieth century, and remain with us both as sources of terror and of cinematic entertainment, are the direct descendants of these nineteenth-century narratives.

Attempts to locate a propensity to crime, including murder, in the perpetrator's physiological or psychological difference, date from early in the century. The phrenological researches of the Austrian, Franz Joseph Gall (1758–1828) suggested that character traits, including the propensity for violence, could be mapped onto the topography of the **brain** and skull. The British psychiatrist, James Prichard (1786–1848), described a condition he called "moral insanity," whose sufferers, though perfectly rational in other respects, were unable to distinguish between moral and immoral acts. In France, the concept of "homicidal monomania," advanced by Jean Etienne Esquirol (1772–1840) and others drew much discussion early in the century. Once again it attempted to describe a class of deviant, in whom a compulsive urge to murder coincided with apparent rationality.

By the 1870s, the Italian, Cesare Lombroso (1835–1909), had formulated his theory that a large proportion of criminals were evolutionary throwbacks, whose primitive urges were at odds with the demands of modern civilization. While the theory covered many types of criminal activity, a propensity for violence and sexual voraciousness were considered key markers of a "delinquent man." Nevertheless, Lombroso also indicated that some murders should be regarded as "crimes of passion," whose perpetrators represented little danger to society at large. Murder could thus mark anthropological normality as much as abnormality. Outside Italy, Lombroso's theory was resisted in many of its particulars, but biological models of criminality—often making reference to the theory of degeneration that linked environmental influences, such as **alcohol** abuse and acquired sexual diseases to hereditary disposition—were gaining ground across Europe. In courtrooms, the appearance of psychiatric expert witnesses similarly became an increasingly common occurrence; implicitly, they suggested that the time honored category of (rational) motive no longer sufficed for the finding of an appropriate verdict. Sexologists, like the Austrian, **Richard von Krafft-Ebing** (1840–1902), began to compile case studies of sexually motivated killings, within the bounds of a much larger project of describing sexual deviancy that he believed was rooted in an ultimately physiological abnormality. His earliest publication on "lust murderers" stems from the late 1870s, and describes men whose sexual gratification depended on biting, killing, and/or eating their partners. Through Krafft-Ebing and those who followed his

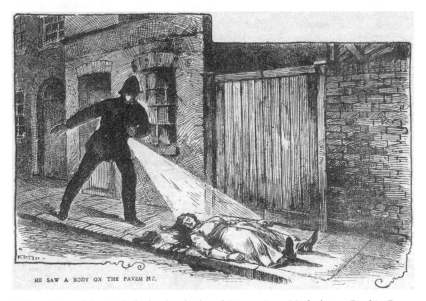

HE SAW A BODY ON THE PAVEMENT.

Police Constable Neil finds the body of Mary Ann Nichols in Buck's Row, Whitechapel, 1888. © Mary Evans Picture Library.

footsteps, the terms "sadism" and "masochism" entered the language of coroner's reports, courtrooms, and of the public at large.

Concurrent with these developments, there was a steady rise in the sophistication of investigative technologies, some of which specifically focused upon sexual crimes. Ballistics, fingerprinting and forensic toxicology were all developed in the course of the nineteenth century. Accusations of rape, and attempts to prosecute acts of "sodomy" (anal penetration between consensual or nonconsensual partners), precipitated a medical inquiry into what physical evidence could be regarded as conclusive. Both rape victims' vaginas and sodomites' anuses were subjected to examination and scholarly debate. The earliest treatments of the issue date back to the seventeenth century, and forensic examination flourished, in particular, in countries where it was a legal requirement for doctors to verify that the injuries found on a body were consistent with the supposed crime (e.g., Germany). In discussions of signs of sodomy, it became increasingly common toward the end of the century to comment not only on the physiological changes that the practice had produced, but to make statements about the psychological and physiological peculiarities associated with "sodomites" as an anthropological type. In actual trials, identification of a sodomitic anus proved fraught with uncertainties, and different doctors often failed to come to the same diagnosis. As for (vaginal) rape, here the discourse focused on those who had not had (or were not supposed to have had) sex before, for example, on the rape of unmarried women and children, and spelled out potential signs of intercourse that an examination might identify. Forensic investigation was thus itself medicalized alongside the emergence of medical models of criminal abnormality.

It is not easy to establish the point at which narratives of compulsive killers, rapists, and lust murderers made their way into popular culture during the nineteenth century, and this might have varied considerably from place to place. The evidence surrounding the Pierre Rivière killings in Normandy in 1835 (collected by Michel

Foucault and a number of his students) indicates that the rural witnesses and the provincial newsreaders of the period were familiar with the concepts of "mania," "genius" (a suspect category often regarded as closely related to other forms of abnormality), "fanaticism," and "delusion." At the same time, the commentators were in no agreement whether the killer's insanity was, or had been, corrigible via education; whether it was a symptom of a (Godless) age; what signs proved or disproved "**madness**," and whether it was a permanent or temporary state. Emile Zola's *La Bête Humaine*, first published in 1890, helped to popularize the idea that there existed a class of degenerate murderer who compulsively killed women when sexually aroused. The newspaper coverage surrounding the 1888/1889 Whitechapel murders that were destined to become synonymous with sexual serial murder, by contrast, reveals a relative dearth of medical and determinist language. The reports were dominated by minute descriptions of the investigative process, but could be astonishingly taciturn on the subject of motive. The idea that the perpetrator was a "lunatic," acting out of "maniacal fanaticism," was floated on occasion, but must be juxtaposed with theories that blamed a series of assailants or suspected "socialist Jews" to have embarked on a program of social vengeance. In many ways, it was the letters sent by "Jack" himself—whether genuine or penned by imposters—that went furthest in constructing a compulsive deviant who ate prostitutes' kidneys, and found them "very nise" [sic]. One might add that as late as 1898, the brutal killing of a Viennese prostitute, whose savagely mutilated body was found the day after Christmas, was not immediately emplotted in a narrative of "lust-murder." Despite the fact that the victim's liver had been removed by her killer, the newspapers speculated on a range of possible motives, including robbery. It was only after the forensic report was released, in which the medical authorities aired "sadism" as a likely motive, that this reading found a popular echo. At the century's end, determinist narratives of (lust) murder had just commenced their victory march through the public imagination in many parts of Europe. Within a few decades, they would be firmly entrenched.

Further Reading: Crozier, Ivan. "'All the Appearances Were Perfectly Natural': The Anus of the Sodomite in Nineteenth-Century Medical Discourse." In *Body Parts, Critical Explorations in Corporeality*, edited by C. Forth and I. Crozier. Lanham, MD: Lexington Books, 2005; Foucault, Michel, ed. *I, Pierre Riviere, Having Slaughtered My Mother, My Sister, and My Brother ..., a Case of Parricide in the Nineteenth Century*. Lincoln: University of Nebraska Press, 1982; Tomaselli, Sylvana and Roy Porter, ed. *Rape: An Historical and Social Enquiry*. Oxford: Blackwell, 1986; Vyleta, Daniel M. "The Cultural History of Crime." In *A Companion to Nineteenth-Century Europe 1789–1914*, edited by S. Berger. Oxford: Blackwell, 2006.

Dan Vyleta

MUSIC HALLS. There was considerable variety in music-hall audiences across the United Kingdom; for example, London had socially mixed halls in the West End and working-class halls in the suburbs, while halls in Glasgow were remarkable for the youthfulness of their audiences. The entertainment was equally varied, but though it contained ideologically subversive elements at times, it more typically upheld the values of the lower-middle-class male. Even some of the songs that appeared to have working-class subject positions can be seen as endorsing bourgeois "Victorian values." Nelly Power sang "The Boy in the Gallery" (Ware 1885) to an imaginary lover, a shoe repairer, who could only afford the cheapest of seats in the theater. It can be read as a tribute to a warm-heartedness toward working-class communities, or alternatively, as an example of how Victorian society encouraged people to accept their social station.

A lion comique at the Oxford London music halls, ca. 1890. Courtesy of the Library of Congress.

In the early period, 1850–1880, halls were diligently policed, and the **law** was sometimes used in a repressive manner. A hall could be closed if single women were seen entering without men, the assumption being that they were looking for business as prostitutes. It was more difficult to use the law to enforce moral rectitude where songs with a sexual theme were concerned. The "saucy" song with a sexual theme was part of music hall from its beginnings.

The difficulty for censors was that "suggestiveness" was something difficult to pinpoint or prove. In *"Jones's Sister"* (Sidney c. 1865), the singer makes the mistake of courting his friend's wife under the impression that she is his friend's sister. Since she makes no attempt to correct the mistake, is this a song about licentious behavior? Or, take, for example, a song written, composed, and sung by the *lion comique*, Arthur Lloyd, a song whose title is still a well-known saying today, "It's Naughty but It's Nice" (1873). Here is an excerpt: "I kiss'd her two times on the cheek, / I would have kiss'd her thrice, / But I whisper'd, ain't it naughty? / She said, Yes, but it's so nice." The words are innocent enough, but the implication that naughtiness is nice brings with it a moral threat. Another song plays upon fears of a moral threat to women and girls of respectable families. What men could pose a seductive danger in the hallowed middle-class home? For one, the piano tuner. We can only speculate about the parental reaction to the chorus of "The Tuner's Oppor-tuner-ty" (Adams–Coyne 1879). "At first he'd tune it gently, then he'd tune it strong, / Then he'd touch a short note, then he'd run along, / Then he'd go with a vengeance, enough to break the key, / At last he tuned whene'er he got an opportunity."

Censorship was also a blunt weapon when deployed against some performers. There is no doubt, for example, that it was the way in which Marie Lloyd (1870–1922) performed that had such an impact on her audience—the lack of bodily discipline seen in the gestures, winks, and knowing smiles that she employed to lend suggestiveness to apparently innocent music-hall songs, like "What's That For, Eh?" (Lytton–Le Brunn

1892). One may imagine how her famous wink may have been applied to her singing of "Oh Mr. Porter" (Thomas Le Brunn–George Le Brunn 1893), in which she finds herself being taken on to Crewe when she only intended to go as far as Birmingham. The device of innuendo is found in many of her best-known songs, such as "A Little of What You Fancy Does You Good" (Leigh–Arthurs) and "When I Take My Morning Promenade" (Mills–Scott). In the latter, she concedes that her dress shows her shape just a little bit, but that's "the little bit the boys admire." Her song "Twiggy Voo?" (Morton–Le Brunn 1892) is entirely about the role of innuendo in its diverse social contexts.

There is considerable scope for queer readings of music hall, especially in the travesty performances. Vesta Tilley made famous the song "Following in Father's Footsteps" (Rogers 1902), in which she declares: "He's just in front with a fine big gal, / So I thought I'd have one as well." Vesta Tilley's contract prohibited her from wearing her male garb when offstage. Vesta Victoria delighted in young *ingénue* roles, and conveyed with unknowing innocence the irony of "Our Lodger's Such a Nice Young Man" (Murray/Barclay 1897), assuring the audience that "mummy told me so."

Married life tends to be portrayed via the stereotype of the nagged husband, and sometimes worse: Gus Elen in "It's a Great Big Shame" (Bateman–Le Brunn) and Dan Leno in "Young Men Taken in and Done For" (King 1888), tell of husbands who, contrary to the Victorian norm in working-class domestic disputes, are beaten violently by their wives. Such examples are a caution against viewing art as a reflection of reality. A song that stands as the exception to tales of marital strife is Albert Chevalier's "My Old Dutch" (1892), one of the few music-hall songs to be praised by such moral campaigners as Mrs. Ormiston Chant. "Dutch" is an abbreviation of "Duchess of Fife," Cockney rhyming slang for "wife."

By the 1890s, halls were being bought up, touring circuits and chains of halls were being established, and managers were seeking to enhance profits by promoting respectability and catering for the family audience. Yet, saucy songs, of varying degrees of vulgarity, continue unabated in the Edwardian music hall, an example being "Has Anybody Seen My Tiddler?" (Mills and Carter 1910). Such songs clearly informed the repertoire of later variety artists, like George Formby, whose father (of the same name) was a music-hall entertainer.

Further Reading: Baker, Richard A. *Marie Lloyd: Queen of the Music-halls*. London: Robert Hale, 1990; Bratton, Jacqueline S., ed. *Music Hall: Performance and Style*. Milton Keynes: Open University Press, 1986.

Derek B. Scott

MY SECRET LIFE.   *See* "Walter"

N

NATIVE AMERICANS. Native Americans are usually defined as those people, who were encountered in North and South America at the time of the European conquests in the fifteenth century. They arrived in the western hemisphere about 25,000 years ago from Asia when the two continents were joined by a land bridge in the area of the Bering Sea. From there, they spread across North America to form various culture areas from the Eskimo in Alaska to the Aztec in the Valley of Mexico and south to the Inca in Peru. Since there are so many different groups, there is a wide range of cultural variation. However, they do share certain characteristics. Physically, they have black straight hair and an epicanthic eye fold. Their skin is darker than the European and lighter than the African tones. They were referred to as "redskins" by English-speaking explorers. Many of their sex and gender relationships were based on matrilocal residence and matrilineal inheritance lines. These kinship structures were difficult for Europeans to comprehend until anthropology, which also developed in the nineteenth century, studied and defined them.

Much of the information about Native American sexuality in the nineteenth century was derived from pioneers during the westward expansion movement. Their interpretations were later transmuted into a popular culture that idealized, demonized, or ridiculed what they observed of the natives' relationships. A few became romanticized paragons of virtue, such as Pocahontas, Sacajawea, and Tekakwitha.

Native Americans had prohibitions and rules about who could have sexual relations with whom, although they appeared to be "free" to the naïve and biased observer. Native Americans in the Caribbean were regarded as promiscuous: men lustful, women seductive and beastly, and in need of domestication. Their egalitarian social structure, misinterpreted by European standards of patriarchy and Christianity, was deemed deviant. Women were not subservient to men in the way that Europeans expected, and because of that misperception, they were not treated with respect.

Alaskan natives and people of the northwest coast of North America, among them, the Aleut, Inuit, Tlingit, Haida, Kwakiutl, Nootka, and Tsimshian were known for alleged sexual freedom, particularly prior to marriage. The Inuit practice interpreted as wife sharing or wife lending was actually crucial to the survival of the people living in a harsh environment where interdependency was the most important tool. Technically referred to as comarriage, two conjugal pairs would meet at a festival, and any one of the four could initiate the sexual alliance. It was usually between couples who lived in different residential areas and created bonds that provided a means of mutual access to resources. The comarriage also extended to their children who would be treated like siblings rather than what Western cultures call "cousins."

Native Americans in the northwest coast lived with extended rather than nuclear families. One man might have more than one wife and the concept of uncle or aunt was different from that in European culture. There are contradictory explanations for the custom. One claims that it demonstrates the male's dominant position in the social structure and expresses male control of all the women, while others stress the sexual freedom inherent in female roles. A man demonstrated his power in society by stealing wives from other men, and creating an extended household with many women and children. Sometimes, rival brothers would compete for dominance, but all depended on the support of their kin to make the situation viable. Both polygyny and polyandry were practiced, in addition to monogamous relationships. The apparent fluidity of these marriages was dependent on economic security and the ability of a man or woman to provide food and shelter to the children they produced.

The plains Indians, Native Americans who lived in the areas west of the Mississippi to the foothills of the Rocky Mountains, had a specific sex role for a man who felt compelled to adopt the gender role of a woman. The *berdache* or *man-woman* was a respected individual who often was said to have great spiritual power. While nineteenth-century European standards would have regarded him as abnormal, in Plains Indians society the berdache lived a respected life and could enjoy an elevated reputation. They were believed to be gifted in healing arts, crafts, social skills, and as matchmakers. Some married other men. Some, not all, were homosexual and some homosexuals did not choose to live as berdaches.

There were cross-gender females, known as *hwame* among the Mohave, *kwiraxame* among the Maricopa, and *tw!nnaek* among the Klamath. They were informed of their changed role in dreams, usually as children, and took wives. But two cross-gender females did not marry. Sometimes, a family that wanted a male child and did not have any would tie dried bear ovaries to a female child's belt to wear as protection against conception, and that girl would be raised as a boy. In both male and female cross-gender roles, there was no stigma involved. Sexual identity was not crucial to sexual behavior in the same way as with Amer-European beliefs and standards.

Among the Zuñi, a group of Pueblo Natives of New Mexico, male and female roles were separate. Marriage was casual and arranged easily. The boy would visit the girl's family, and if the girl were willing, the mother would prepare a nuptial bed for them that night. After a period of four days, if they decided to stay together, the girl would dress in her best clothing and carry a present of fine corn flour to his mother. Extramarital affairs were subjected to stringent social pressure by both sets of relatives. Nothing in Zuñi culture compares with western sexual jealousy in living relationships. However, sexual relations with a new partner after the death of a spouse were prohibited for a year because of a belief that the deceased will be jealous. After a year, the surviving spouse was expected to have sex with a stranger and give that person a gift to symbolize past danger and availability to remarry.

Unlike European culture, where a denial of sexual themes was practiced publicly, sexuality and fertility were expressed in Native American ceremonies. The relationship of humans to the earth, animals, and crops, particularly after sedentary **agriculture** and horticulture replaced hunting and gathering as the major food source, was crucial. Dancing and elaborate costumes punctuated these ceremonies. In South American Peruvian culture, there were races between men and women, where strength and sexual ability were clearly linked. The men ran naked, and each man could later have sexual intercourse with any woman they overtook.

Coming of age ceremonies were extremely important because they symbolized the young person's ability to enter the adult world. At menarche (a girl's first menstrual period), elaborate ceremonies marked this time in a girl's life, because it signaled that she would be fertile and capable of bearing new members to the society. Each Native American culture celebrated this event with a different ritual, but all regarded menarche with reverence, awe, and celebration. The mystery of a woman's body and the symbolic relationship of the womb to "mother earth" also played an important role in the stories and creation myths that people told, although there were male, female, and animal deities.

In most Native American cultures, menstrual huts were built to segregate menstruating women and women who had just given birth from the rest of the society. These residences were temporary and were used to prevent any harm to the spouses as a result of blood. The belief was that, since the blood was somehow related to procreation, a woman was dangerously powerful, and to have sexual relations or any other kind of contact would be dangerous.

Although the anthropologists of the nineteenth century provided insight using the concepts of race, language, culture, psychology, and prehistory, governments continued to disrespect the contracts and treaties they agreed to, slaughtered their tribes, forced them into hostile unnatural environments without their tools of survival, and exposed them to microbes against which they had no resistance. Indian reservations and the introduction of **alcohol** to what were left of Native American populations come close to destroying their culture.

Further Reading: Benedict, Ruth. *Patterns of Culture*. Boston: Houghton Mifflin, 1959; Blackwood, Evelyn. "Sexuality and Gender in Certain Native American Tribes: The Case of Cross-Gender Females." *Signs* 10 (1984): 27–42; Fogel-Chance, Nancy. "Fixing History: A Contemporary Examination of an Arctic Journal from the 1850s." *Ethnohistory* 49 (2002): 789–820; Green, Rayna. "Native American Women." *Signs* 6 (1980): 248–267; Haviland, William. *Anthropology*. Fort Worth, TX: Holt, Rinehart and Winston, 1974; Kroeber, Alfred. *Anthropology*. New York: Harcourt, Brace and Company, 1923. Lowe, Ben. "Body Images and the Politics of Beauty." In *Ideals of Feminine Beauty*, edited by Karen A. Callaghan. Westport, CT: Greenwood, 1994; Service, Elman. *Profiles in Ethnology*. New York: Harper and Row, 1963; Spencer, Robert et al. *The Native Americans*. New York: Harper and Row, 1977.

Lana Thompson

NECROPHILIA. The taboo of sexual attraction to the dead has been a feature of the Western cultural imagination since classical antiquity, when Achilles is said to have slept with Penthesileia after her death, and continues to occur in the form of a present-day fascination with sexual transgression, violence, and death. However, the nineteenth century, which saw the naming of sexual typologies in sociomedical discourse and the privileging of perverse sexual subject matter in literature and art, saw a particular efflorescence of European and Anglo-American representations of necrophilia (see Praz 1933; Downing 2003a). The term "necrophilia" (literally meaning "love of corpses") was coined by the Belgian alienist Joseph Guislain as one of a group of sexological categories, and was first used by E. Monneret in his *Treatise on General Pathology* (1861). It was given an entry by **Richard von Krafft-Ebing** in the first edition of his seminal *Psychopathia Sexualis* (1886), and filtered into the major European languages via subsequent translations of this work. However, the most frequently discussed criminal case of necrophilia in nineteenth-century Europe—that of the grave-robbing and corpse-desecrating French solider, le Sergeant Bertrand—occurred in 1849 before the establishment of the medicolegal term "necrophilia." For want of another label, Bertrand was charged with acts of "vampirism," and diagnosed to be suffering from "erotomania" (see Dansel 1991; Rosario 1997). Probably the first appearance of the term "necrophilia" in a literary work in any language was in Guy de Maupassant's story, "La Chevelure" ("The Head of Hair"), in 1884.

Representations of necrophilia in the nineteenth century run the gamut from subliminal and suggestive to explicit and extreme. "Subliminal" necrophilia, when the deadness of the object desired is expressed by the evocation of states which resemble it, is found in such themes as the sexual violation of an unconscious woman (Heinrich von Kleist's *Die Marquise von O*, 1808) or in the libidinal investment in cold, inanimate, pale statues (Théophile Gautier's *Spirite*, 1866). Other forms of sublimated or "gentle" necrophilia are found in the English Pre-Raphaelite **fashion** for **painting** idealized and highly aestheticized dying or dead women (e.g., John Everett Millais's "Ophelia" 1851–1852). These forms of representation are, for the most part, very traditionally gendered, with deadness adding a further, final layer of passivity to femininity (see Bronfen 1992).

Necrophilia has been understood in psychoanalytic discourse as the result of the failure of processes of mourning (see Jones 1933). The theme of the dead beloved who is reanimated by the strength of erotic memory and desire is common in nineteenth-century tales of the supernatural [e.g., Edgar Poe's "Ligeia" (1835) and "Morella" (1838) or Villiers de l'Isle-Adam's "Véra" (1874)]. In other cases, the dead being is transformed into a powerfully erotic figure, such as a sexualized vampire, in, for example, Gautier's *La Morte amoureuse* (1836) and **Bram Stoker**'s *Dracula* (1897). In these cases, the desire of the living subject is projected onto the dead other. The epigraph of Heinrich Heine's *Der Doktor Faustus* (1847) offers a particularly good insight into this phenomenon. It is voiced by a dead woman who has been called back into the world of the living by the strength of her partner's grief and desire. In the closing lines, the dead woman articulates effectively the attraction and frustration of necrophilic passion: "Die Toten sind unersättlich!/!" ("The dead can never be sated!").

Charles Baudelaire's *Les Fleurs du mal* (1855) features more sexually explicit representations of necrophilic desire. "Une martyre" recounts the reactions of a viewer standing before a painting of a decapitated female corpse. The poetic voice starts by describing the dead body in rapturous, erotic terms, before going on to imagine the sexual murder that led to the creation of the *tableau*. The decadent French female writer Rachilde (Maurguerite Vallette-Eymery) is responsible for one of the few full-length novelistic explorations of necrophilia in existence, *La Tour d'amour* (1899). This novel, written in a lyrical and dreamlike style, charts the relationship between a necrophiliac lighthouse keeper, who sates his lusts on the bodies of female shipwreck victims, and his young assistant, who, by the end of the novel, acknowledges his own necrophiliac tendencies. The novel is unusual in describing an isolated setting in which the young man's rite of passage is a perverse one, and necrophilia becomes the norm. In this way, it offers an alternative to the European *Bildungsroman*, which focuses on the ideals of social and sexual (re)production.

Further Reading: Bronfen, Elisabeth. *Over Her Dead Body*. Manchester: Manchester University Press, 1992; Dansel, Michel, *Le Sergeant Bertrand: portrait d'un nécrophile heureux*. Paris: Albin Michel, 1991; Dijkstra, Bram. *Idols of Perversity: Fantasies of Feminine Evil in fin-de-siècle Culture*. Oxford: Oxford University Press, 1986; Downing, Lisa. *Desiring the Dead: Necrophilia and Nineteenth-Century French Literature*. Oxford: Legenda, European Humanities Research Centre, 2003; Downing, Lisa. "Death and the Maidens: A Century of Necrophilia in Female Authored Textual Production." *French Cultural Studies* 14, no. 2 (2003). 157–68;

Epaulard, Alexis. *Nécrophilie, nécrosadisme, nécrophagie.* Lyon: Stock, 1901; Goodwin, Sarah Webster and Bronfen Elisabeth, ed. *Death and Representation.* Baltimore and London: Johns Hopkins University Press, 1993; Jones, Ernest. *On the Nightmare.* London: The Hogarth Press and the Institute of Psychoanalysis, 1931; Praz, Mario. *The Romantic Agony.* Oxford: Oxford University Press, 1933; Rosario, Vernon A. *The Erotic Imagination: French Histories of Perversity.* Oxford: Oxford University Press, 1997.

Lisa Downing

NEWSPAPERS AND BROADSIDES. Improvements in printing technology, coupled with increasing literacy, meant that newspapers and broadsides became vital sources of information and entertainment in the nineteenth century. Inevitably, one of the areas that these texts explored was sexuality, through subjects, such as **marriage**, adultery, **divorce**, "deviant" or criminal sexuality, and **prostitution**. Through articles like **law** court reports, editorial columns, and letters to the editor, newspapers explored, reflected, and constructed Victorian ideas of love and sexuality. They not only reported, but judged, assessed, and condemned certain modes of behavior.

Although the 1857 Divorce Act made divorce somewhat more accessible than it had hitherto been, adultery was still the only grounds upon which it could be obtained. In addition to this, once proven, adultery was sufficient grounds to grant a man a divorce from his wife. Women had to prove another marital offense, such as bigamy, cruelty, or desertion, in addition to adultery. These cases, often widely reported (and in great detail), gave newspapers and broadsides the opportunity to offer titillating details of sexual misconduct. Deliberations on the ideals of marriage, such as fidelity and loyalty, and the different roles of husband and wife allowed the newspapers to contribute to the construction of **gender roles**. Issues like the perceived differences between male and female sexuality and the propriety or impropriety of erotic desire were at the heart of these cases. Similarly, suits for breach of promise often involved intimate letters read out in court, which could then be reprinted. Cases such as these offered a kind of soap opera to the reading public. Since divorce was prohibitively expensive, it was accessible only to the wealthy, meaning that often the players in these real-life dramas were well-known aristocratic figures.

Criminal prosecutions also offered an opportunity for newspapers and broadsides to explore the limits of propriety, and to contribute to the discourse of normative sexuality. Incidences, such as the Cleveland Street scandal in 1889 and Oscar Wilde's trial for sodomy in 1895 were widely reported, and allowed for deliberation into the nature of masculinity, class, art, and sexuality. By describing **homosexuality** as "unnatural," "depraved," and "unmentionable," heterosexuality was implicitly set up as the norm—the natural and decent form of sexuality. The question of how much to print was ever present. While newspapers were consumed as a source of information, and were expected to provide this to their readers, there was also a great deal of anxiety about the potential for details of sexual misconduct to corrupt and deprave.

Different papers varied in tone, and some were more explicit in detail than others. Broadsides, more common in the first half of the century than in the second, were single pieces of paper, cheaply printed and sold on the streets or in public houses. The market for these papers was the poor and working class, not necessarily even the literate, as they would often be read out to a group. Newspapers, which consisted of several pages, varied from the cheap and sensational to the sober and respectable. Competition between papers sometimes centered around the level of sexually explicit detail provided, for example, during the Boulton and Park cross-dressing scandal of the 1870s, when the *Times* and the *Pall Mall Gazette* traded snide comments about obscenity and the necessity of providing the public with news. Other newspapers were openly political and partisan, and used the press to campaign for social change.

Indeed, press agitation was responsible in part for the formation of various laws relating to sexual activity. In 1885, William T. Stead, editor of the *Pall Mall Gazette*, published the infamous notorious piece of investigative journalism, "The Maiden Tribute of Modern Babylon," in which he proved that a young, virgin girl could be bought on the streets of London for as little as five pounds. This exposé of **child prostitution** landed Stead in jail, but led to the passing of the Criminal Law Amendment Act in 1885, which raised the **age of consent** for girls from thirteen to sixteen. However, the act also contained the infamous Labouchere Amendment, which criminalized male homosexual acts. Stead's writing inspired what was known as the "New Journalism" in the 1880s, a style that can be seen as the precursor of the "tabloid" press. Mixing salacious detail with moral outrage, this journalism was condemned by the establishment, but was nonetheless financially successful.

Part of the outrage generated by the "Maiden Tribute" scandal related to the matrix of class, sex, and power that was revealed by the exposé. The "white slave trade," as the trade in young virgins was known, demonstrated the social and economic repression of the poor and the huge power of the rich. Similarly, the story that came to be known as the Cleveland Street scandal was broken by a journalist writing for a radical weekly newspaper, the *North London Press*. This affair, which involved sex between members of the upper classes and teenage boys working for the Postal Service, ignited outrage at what was seen as the sexual exploitation of one class by another. The growing social and economic power of the middle class throughout the nineteenth century was shored up by a depiction of the upper classes as decadent and sexually promiscuous, as opposed to the hard working and moral middle class. Various scandals that centered on class were thus endlessly dissected and eagerly consumed.

Newspapers and broadsides thus simultaneously formed and reflected Victorian attitudes to sexuality, by reporting on sensational divorce cases and other instances of what was considered sexual transgression, such as homosexuality and prostitution. While these reports generally carried a condemnatory moral tone, they nevertheless provided prurient details to a curious public.

Further Reading: Cohen, William A. *Sex Scandal: The Private Parts of Victorian Fiction*. Durham, NC: Duke University Press, 1996; Garrigan, Kristine Ottesen. *Victorian Scandals: Representations of Gender and Class*. Athens: Ohio University Press, 1992; Leckie, Barbara. *Culture and Adultery: The Novel, the Newspaper and the Law 1857–1914*. Philadelphia: University of Pennsylvania Press, 1999; Mulpetre, Owen. *The Great Educator*. The W. T. Stead Resource Site at: www.attackingthedevil.co.uk.

Jessica Needle

NOVELS, ROMANTIC. Romantic literature, understood as expressive of or exciting sexual love or romance, is as old as literature itself. However, with the increasing urgency of the Woman Question, nineteenth-century romantic fiction shows a distinctive shift toward greater female sovereignty and the awakening of female sexuality. Moreover, cheaper publication methods and wider distribution techniques create an unprecedented, mostly female, mass readership. This protofeminist activity and the birth of mass fiction render the nineteenth-century romantic novel an important moment within the history of love, sex, and culture.

Romantic fiction flourishes throughout the nineteenth century. The novels of Walter Scott, Jane Austen, the Brontës, Charles Dickens, George Eliot, and Thomas

Hardy are all concerned with relations between the sexes. However, it is only in the second half of the century that love becomes almost exclusively the domain of the rising number of popular women writers.

Among the first generation of post-1850 women novelists, female characters modeled after **Coventry Patmore**'s *Angel in the House* (1854) and John Ruskin's domestic queens, in *Sesame and Lilies* (1865), prevail. In representations that would later be considered the epitome of Victorian male sexual stereotyping, women are described as pacific, altruistic, and uncompetitive, and the source of man's happiness. Women who did not conform to this model were attacked in print. Noteworthy among these is **Eliza Lynn Linton**'s attack on "The Girl of the Period" (1869), as coarse in language and manner, useless in domestic duty, embracing the ways of the *demi-monde*, and using her sexuality to enter materialistic unions. Linton's outlook is expressedly antifeminist, and her novels often end in the heroine's death as she fails to uphold the Ruskinian ideal, as in *Lizzie Lorton of Greyrigg* (1866), and *The Atonement of Leam Dundas* (1877). Linton's novels *The One Too Many* (1894) and *In Haste and at Leisure* (1895) disparage the Girton girl and the politically minded woman. Mrs. Humphry Ward's romantic novels express similar attitudes. Celebrated for their complex religious outlook, their subterranean emotional drama is rather one-dimensional. Ward became the President of the British Anti-Suffrage League in 1908. She portrayed misguided femininity in *Delia Blanchflower* (1915), in which a financially independent heiress eventually accepts the role as her guardian's submissive wife, once he has convinced her of the unwomanly character of the suffragette movement to which her heart belongs.

Dinah Craik's romances are a more equivocal response to the Woman Question. Her eponymous heroine in *Olive* (1850) enjoys a successful career as an artist before finding happiness in a conventional marriage with an austere clergyman. *Mistress and Maid* (1862) introduces female characters, who not only possess intelligence, courage, and virtue, but also considerable business acumen. *A Life for a Life* (1859) attacks sexual double standards, allowing, unusually for the time, the fallen heroine to marry her repentant seducer. *A Brave Lady* (1870) supports the measures that would eventually be passed in the Married Women's Property Act (1882). Equally candid, Rhoda Broughton's fiction had the reputation of being sexually provocative, a fact astutely exploited by her publisher George Bentley. The dilemma of love versus duty features in her successful romances *Cometh up As a Flower* (1867), *Not Wisely But Too Well* (1867), *Red As a Rose Is She* (1870), *Goodbye, Sweetheart* (1872), and *Foes in Law* (1900), in which women commonly deny their own desires and happiness, and act out of a false sense of duty toward men they do not love.

Ouida's and Marie Corelli's depictions of women, love, and sexuality were as ambiguous. Paying lip service to both the growing camp of protofeminists and Victorian defenders of love, marriage, and family values, these authors depict sovereign forceful women who find their happiness in patriarchal marriages. Ouida's bestselling novels *Held in Bondage* (1863) and *Under Two Flags* (1867) are flamboyant romantic tales that introduce the aristocratic hero of the later novelette tradition, whose typically Byronic nature and irresistible ways in the boudoir and the battlefield alike, are only surpassed by his singular code of loyalty. The late novel, *The Massarenes* (1897), is a contribution to the debate on women's emancipation. It introduces a rich tradesman's daughter who gives up her independence and marries an aristocrat whose intellectual equal and pecuniary superior she is, but who nevertheless promises to care for her spiritually and financially. In Corelli's romances, base and materialistic love is doomed from the start, and the heroines in *Vendetta* (1886), *The Sorrows of Satan* (1895), and *The Murder of Delicia* (1896) die in disgrace. In contrast, *Thelma* (1887), *God's Good Man* (1904), *The Treasure of Heaven* (1906), *The Life Everlasting* (1911), and *Love and the Philosopher* (1923), celebrate sublime love and marriage. With regard to issues of sexuality, like their literary ancestors, these women novelists mostly portray their heroines as exemplary English maidens who approach the other sex with shy steps and heaving bosoms. Not surprisingly, the first kiss is described as a firework of emotions. The rhetoric of love is generally antirealist, elevated, idealistic, and verbose, as seen in the following passage from Broughton's *Lavinia* (1902):

> As if the words possessed some paralyzing spell over their feet, both of them stop dead short; and, turning round, stare full in each other's faces, conversation shriveling up its thin fabric in that fiery moment; and then—the inevitable happens. The gasping lips draw nearer, nearer, nearer; the idly hanging arms stretch themselves out, enfold, embrace, crush; and, with no apparent initiation on either side, Fate hurls them upon one another's forbidden breasts.

The ideal of marriage as the "natural" place for the independent woman continues well into the twentieth century with novels like Florence Barclay's bestseller *The Rosary* (1909). From the 1880s, however, a different type of woman writer and heroine emerged alongside the romancers. Most of the marriages of George Egerton's heroines in her collections *Keynotes* (1893) and *Discords* (1894), and those of Mona Caird's Hadria Fullerton in *The Daughters of Danaus* (1894) and of Sarah Grand's Beth Caldwell in *The Beth Book* (1897), are devoid of romance. With little sentimentality, the New Woman writers show how women suffocate in loveless marriages that kill their desire for freedom, their spiritual development, and in some cases also their artistic talent. Commonly, **romantic love** is seen as the instrument of women's oppression, and Iota's *Yellow Aster* (1894), Olive Schreiner's *Story of an African Farm* (1883), Mary Cholmondeley's *Red Pottage* (1899), and Ella Hepworth Dixon's *The Story of a Modern Woman* (1894), suggest that women are better off without a man. Despite this overall antiromantic tendency, the realist New Woman writers were, at times, as paradoxical about women and love as the romancers, although in general, more sexually explicit.

With the arrival of a modernist aesthetic, popular female romances were forced into a marginal, derided existence. However, the romantic novel refused defeat. Exoticism replaced the English locale, and this displacement served both as the author's and the heroine's license for sexual freedom. E. M. Hull's desert romance, *The Sheik* (1919) and Ethel Dell's Indian love story, *The Way of an Eagle* (1912), expressed female sexual longing. Elinor Glyn's *Three Weeks* (1907) went even further and celebrated, for the first time, an illicit love affair in which a married *femme fatale*-like princess of a mysterious mid-European kingdom introduces a younger Englishman to the pleasures of sex. This burgeoning eroticism later fed into the industry of mass-produced Mills and Boon and Harlequin romances, in which the ideal of marriage, however, still endures.

Within the last decades, feminist critics have advanced from a simple rejection of romantic fiction as a pernicious ideology, which confirms women's submissive role in a patriarchal society, toward a more productive engagement with the narratives of the genre. They illustrate how psychoanalytical, structuralist, and reader-oriented approaches can help discover the strategies of romantic novels, and explain why they continue to appeal to such a large readership. *See also* Brontë, Charlotte; Gothic Fiction; Novels, Sensation.

Further Reading: Anderson, Rachel. *The Purple Heart Throbs: The Sub-Literature of Love.* London: Hodder and Stoughton, 1974; Moleski, Tania. *Loving with a Vengeance: Mass-Produced Fantasies for Women.* New York: Routledge, 1990; Radway, Janice A. *Reading the Romance: Women, Patriarchy, and Popular Literature.* Chapel Hill: University of North Carolina Press, 1984.

Julia Kuehn

NOVELS, SENSATION. The Victorian sensation novel, a popular literary genre, based on representations of crime, secrets, and transgression, flourished in Britain during the 1860s. The genre initially attracted unfavorable criticism because of its depictions of the darker aspects of middle-class life. As one critic stated in 1863 in *Fraser's Magazine*, "A book without a murder, a divorce, a seduction, or a bigamy, is not apparently considered worth writing or reading, and a mystery and a secret are the chief qualifications of the modern novel." Indeed, the genre was generally perceived as a symptom of modernity, dealing with specifically modern anxieties surrounding the social position of women, marriage, and sexuality. The genre coincided with increasing demands for women's rights, as feminists raised awareness of the social injustices of unequal property laws and the lack of female suffrage. While some women were actively seeking social change, sensation novels often exacerbated fears of **feminism** by depicting desiring and sexualized heroines determined to achieve their goals in ways that disrupted the stability of the middle-class family.

The frank treatment of sexuality, particularly female desire, meant that the sensation novel marked an important stage in the development of the nineteenth-century novel, paving the way for more explicit and detailed treatment of sexual themes in later Victorian and twentieth-century fiction. The most prominent sensation novelists were **Wilkie Collins** (1824–1889), Mary Elizabeth Braddon (1835–1915), and Mrs. Henry (Ellen) Wood (1814–1887), although many other British writers were associated with the genre, such as Charles Reade (1814–1880), Rhoda Broughton (1840–1920), and Ouida (1839–1908). Sensation novelists offered compelling tales of bigamy, illegitimacy, and adultery, combining the titillating details of transgression with fast-paced mystery plots of murder, forgery, imposture, and false imprisonment. However, the most controversial aspect of the sensation novels was its heroines, who walked out of unhappy marriages, committed adultery and bigamy, resorted to forgery, disguise, and even murder to achieve their ends. While sensation novels attracted huge numbers of readers, many conservative Victorian critics, such as Dean Mansell and Margaret Oliphant, testified to the genre's ability to shock in scathing reviews condemning the sensation novel as immoral literature.

Critics have identified Wilkie Collins's *The Woman in White* (1860) as the first example of the sensation genre. The novel's heroine, Laura Fairlie, obliged by her father on his deathbed to marry a man she does not love, finds her husband scheming to seize her fortune. He imprisons her under a false identity in a lunatic asylum. Here, Collins explores marriage as a potential source of misery and imprisonment for women, representing love and desire as the legitimate basis for marriage. When Laura is eventually rescued, she marries her drawing master, Walter Hartright, Collins suggesting that class differences need not be an impediment to a happy union.

Although Collins can be thought of as initiating the sensation genre, it was his two female rivals, Ellen Wood with *East Lynne* (1861) and Mary Elizabeth Braddon with *Lady Audley's Secret* (1862), who promoted the figure of the transgressive, sexually erring heroine as an essential ingredient of the sensation novel. *East Lynne*'s heroine, Lady Isabel Vane, commits adultery and bears an illegitimate child, while the heroine of *Lady Audley's Secret* is a bigamist and murderer. Collins, no doubt, inspired by Wood and Braddon, went on to write other successful sensation novels centered on sexually daring heroines. *No Name* (1862), for example, depicts Magdalen Vanstone, who, on discovering her illegitimacy, disguises herself to marry her father's sick and selfish heir in order to regain her lost fortune. This novel shocked some Victorian critics because Magdalen, instead of being punished for her misdemeanours, went on to live happily, marrying the man of her choice as her second husband. In Collins's next novel, *Armadale* (1866), Lydia Gwilt, a beautiful woman in her thirties with a shady past, schemes and attempts murder in order to gain a fortune. Her thoughts are expressed through her letters, where she openly discusses her sexual attraction to the man she loves, prompting one contemporary reviewer to describe her as "one of the most hardened female villains whose devices and desires have ever blackened fiction." *Armadale* also disrupted middle-class proprieties by depicting Lydia's dubious accomplices, the abortionist, Dr. Downward, and Mrs. Oldershaw, who operates a cosmetics business, which is a cover for a brothel. Collins's determination to explore the underside of British society continued in subsequent novels, including *The New Magdalen* (1873), which depicts a prostitute's rise to respectability and her eventual marriage to a clergyman.

Braddon's long career as a novelist began with her racy sensation fiction, which was in part influenced by the work of French novelists, such as Balzac and Flaubert; indeed, she produced a reworking of the latter's *Madame Bovary* in her 1864 novel, *The Doctor's Wife*. While falling short of Flaubert's explicit depictions of Madame Bovary's sexuality, Braddon's novel offered readers an anglicized version of female desire and discontent in marriage. Henry James, in a review of her novels, indicated Braddon's tendency to explore sexuality when he stated that she "'knows much that ladies are not accustomed to know, but they are apparently very glad to learn.'" Throughout her career, she managed to tread a fine line between *risqué* depictions of sexuality and the world of middle-class respectability. In *Lady Audley's Secret*, the young Robert Audley, meeting his uncle's bride, wonders if he is criminally falling in love with his aunt, while Braddon's next novel, *Aurora Floyd* (1863), depicts a spirited young heroine from a wealthy home, who runs away to make a secret marriage to her father's groom.

Ellen Wood, author of *the* bestselling novel of the Victorian period, *East Lynne*, adroitly used melodrama in her depiction of her "fallen" heroine, Lady Isabel Vane. Bored in her marriage to a respectable lawyer, Isabel elopes with a handsome aristocrat. Repentant, she later returns to her former home in disguise in order to become the governess of her own children, watching her son die without being able to reveal her identity as his mother, and forced to witness the affectionate scenes between her husband and his second wife.

Clearly, sensation fiction was in part a response to the condition of marriage in mid-Victorian Britain, where divorces were difficult to obtain and women were demanding more equality with men. Novelists found sensational potential in the idea of unhappy marriages, sexually bold women, discontented wives, and criminal husbands prepared to rid themselves of wives they married for their money. While most sensation novelists depicted sexual transgression, the resolutions to their novels tended to be conservative —disruptive characters were usually disposed of (e.g., Lady Audley is imprisoned as a mad woman, while Lady Isabel dies repenting her sins). However, despite this, the sensation novel did open up a space for the representation of sexual transgression in British fiction, making characters and situations that had hitherto been deemed "unsuitable" material for a general readership acceptable for middle-class readers. *See also* Gothic Fiction; Novels, Romantic.

Further Reading: Hughes, Winifred. *The Maniac in the Cellar: The Sensation Novels of the 1860s.* Princeton, NJ: Princeton University Press, 1980; Pykett, Lyn. *The Sensational Novel: From the Woman in White to the Moonstone.* Plymouth: Northcote, 1994; Wynne, Deborah. *The Sensation Novel and the Victorian Family Magazine.* Basingstoke and New York: Palgrave, 2001.

Deborah Wynne

NUDE MODELS. Controversy over the use of nude female models in British schools of art reached the House of Commons in 1859 and 1860, when George Hamilton-Gordon, Lord Haddo, Liberal Member of Parliament (MP) for Aberdeen-shire, and son of the former prime minister, George Hamilton-Gordon, fourth Earl of Aberdeen, initiated action against the practice. The issue illuminated the most important cultural trends in mid-Victorian society—an opposition based on morality, and support based on love of the Greek classics. Both ideals were put to test in the arena of politics, which echoed public opinion on many aspects of Victorian culture, including the place of women in society and sexual norms. The commodification of all human products and activities in the world of business proved significant in deciding whether or not to allow the state to sanction female nudity in art education.

The evangelical ethos, first taken up by the middle class, disciplined most of British society by the mid-nineteenth century. For those who followed this ethos, every action had eternal consequences—the world was full of sin, and a word, gesture, **painting**, or novel might place the seed of corruption in the most innocent of souls. Watchfulness for sin was vital not only for one's own redemption, but for national salvation as well.

Fascination with ancient Greece was a Victorian development, while ancient Rome had been the focus of European culture since the Middle Ages. For the Victorians, the Greek classics, or Greats, formed the basis of elite education in England. Victorian authors liked to emphasize their similarity to the ancient Greeks in thought, culture, and moral principles, but rationalized away their profound differences.

The parliamentary aspect of the controversy came into focus on July 25, 1859, when Lord Haddo called attention to the "exhibition of nude living models in Government Schools of Art." He had never seen a more painful or scandalous display than the time he recently visited a government school of art, and accidentally witnessed a life-study session. Haddo brought the subject forward with feelings of shame and disgust, but insisted it was his duty to do so, for "the claims of morality were more important than those of art."

Haddo asked William Ewart Gladstone, chancellor of the Exchequer, if the government intended to assist any training schools by paying for nude female models. Although Gladstone found the subject indecent, he attempted to satisfy Haddo's inquiry by pointing out that state funds were never devoted to nude models, but private expenses might be employed in other ways. While some MPs rejected Haddo, and supported life studies in government-funded schools, and used the ancient Greeks as an example to be emulated, others rose to Haddo's defense, warning that at any instance, if the public funds were used or diverted to pay nude models, it demoralized society as a whole.

European artists had employed female and male models in their own private studios since the fourteenth century, but the public employment of nude models of either sex in state schools of art was a comparatively recent development. In England, women students were not allowed into the Royal Academy until well into the nineteenth century, and until 1893, women were denied the opportunity of studying the nude in a life class. The state Department of Science and Art funded thirty-six local schools of art and design for the working class, and some allowed life classes under strict conditions.

Again, on May 15, 1860, Haddo tried to secure parliamentary approval to force the government to deny funds to such schools. He noted the numerous petitions the Commons had received against the use of female nude models. Haddo believed this "evil and dissolute" employment made it impossible for young Christian men to frequent those institutions, and not be led into acts of debauchery. Richard Spooner, a Conservative colleague, seconded Haddo, and did not think it likely that a dozen male students could look at a naked woman day after day without grievous harm to their morals.

Outside of Westminster, public opinion on the controversy was generally favorable to Haddo, and blended well with other female purity campaigns. Charitable organizations, devoted to the "rescue" of prostitutes, were especially interested in suppressing the employment of women as nude models. Significantly, Lord Haddo was one of the sponsors of such an organization, the London Female Penitentiary, whose patron was Queen Victoria. Before its 1859 annual committee meeting, Haddo prevailed upon the group to petition parliament, condemning the employment of unclothed female models as inimical to the objectives of the organization. The implication of this and many other petitions was that women so employed were also involved in **prostitution**, or at the very least, they were reprobates in need of Christian reclamation.

Home Secretary Sir George Lewis defended the government, asserting that all of the great classical masters gained their expertise through study of the unclothed human form, male and female. C. B. Adderley, a former secretary to the Council on Education, insisted that accurate representations of the human form could not be made without a thorough study of the unclothed figure, and criticized Haddo for misunderstanding the nature of the life class. For Adderley, it seemed paradoxical that Haddo and his allies professed admiration for art, but nevertheless wished to place obstacles in the way of an artist's training. Britain must not fall behind Europe in art and design education, an important element of manufacturing and foreign trade. The Prime Minister, Lord Palmerston, thought Haddo was going too far, making it illegal to study the female form. The motion was defeated.

Such fanaticism about women being employed as nude models was not seen again until the 1880s, when feminists and evangelicals joined in a campaign to condemn the exploitation of women as prostitutes and nude models. The intellectual leader of this mini culture war was J. C. Horsley, a member of the Royal Academy, who deplored not only nude models but nudity in art. For skeptics who do not believe that the Victorian era was one of prudery (excessive regard for sexual propriety), there was also the 1892 legal case of Rudolf Blind, brought to trial for pandering obscenity in his painting of *The World's Desire*. The magistrate dismissed the case after several experts testified in favor of the artist.

Laissez-faire was the business beacon of the middle class, guiding it to prosperity. It was considered to be a doctrine as infallible as the Gospel, and as productive of success in this life as the Gospel was in the next. Along with the evangelical ethos and the Greek ideal, all three Victorian values managed to coexist in equipoise, but with art and freedom of expression there could be disharmony, as exemplified in the Haddo episode. One must emphasize that the commercial value outweighed the religious, using the classical Greek value as support for permitting state funds to help employ nude models in government schools of art and design.

Frank H. Wallis

O

ORGASM. Orgasm is the culmination of a sexual act in which the participant feels an overwhelming sense of intense pleasure. In the male, it is accompanied by ejaculation, the expulsion of seminal fluid. In the female, the experience includes uterine, pelvic, and vaginal muscle contractions without visible fluid.

Ancient beliefs associated female orgasm with fertility from the days of Aristotle (384–322 BCE) and Soranus of Ephesus (c. 150 CE). Some taught that in the female, orgasm was essential for reproduction. Gabriello Fallopio (1523–1562) wrote that when the pleasure is greater, the woman emits seed and suitable material for the formation of the fetus. However, the evidence did not support that association, and the entire question was tricky. Even the existence of female seed was questioned until scientific evidence demonstrated that there was an ovum. Biological science did not progress until the Enlightenment brought anatomical information to the microscope and dissection room. The uterus, clitoris, and ovaries could be studied in minute detail, but there were questions regarding the relationship of **menstruation** to the estrus cycle or "heat," and if orgasm was limited to the human species. The *London Medical Dictionary*, written in 1819, gave *oestrum veneris* as a synonym for the clitoris. Joseph Thomas's *American Medical Dictionary* defined orgasm as eager desire, and referred the reader to *oestrum*. A veterinarian stated that the heat of animals was analogous to menstruation in women. Billings's *Medical Dictionary* of 1890 defined *oestrus* as rut, orgasm, or clitoris. Hence, it is not surprising that so many misunderstandings existed with regard to human sexuality, female physiology, and reproduction.

The nineteenth century was rife with contradictory information. If fertilization required orgasm, and women were expected to bear children, there was the problem of the concept of female desire. A proper woman was not supposed to experience excessive pleasure in the sexual act, and if she did, she might want to deny it for fear of her husband's judgment. On the other hand, prostitutes who probably faked orgasm more than they experienced it, allegedly rarely became pregnant. **Richard von Krafft-Ebing** (1840–1902), a psychiatrist, penned *Psychopathia Sexualis* (1886), a sex manual that underwent at least twelve printings and remained the authoritative work on sexual behavior for almost a hundred years. He wrote that a properly educated physically and mentally normal woman had but little sensual desire, and that a wife accepted intercourse more as proof of her husband's affection than for sensual gratification. Some marriage manuals, such as the one written by **John Kellogg**, taught that sexual pleasure should be minimal, and couples should restrain from activity for better health. Orgasm arrived at from **masturbation** or oral sex was allegedly unhealthy. However, John

Humphrey Noyes (1811–1886), a leader of the Oneida Community, an utopian community that eschewed propagative sex and favored amative sex by advising men to practice coitus interruptus, advised women to experience multiple orgasms. Obviously, he was aware that women could and did have the propensity for pleasure and desire.

In the nineteenth century, as a side effect of the growth of the medical profession, there was a curious attempt to medicalize sexual behavior. If a woman had excessive sexual desire, she was diagnosed as a nymphomaniac. However, excessive was a subjective term often generated by her husband. As an example, one twenty-four-year-old woman who had been married to a man much older was having sexually provocative dreams. She consulted a gynecologist and reported that she fantasized about having sex with any man she met, but did not act on it. She enjoyed sexual intercourse with her husband, but her husband was complaining that he could not perform. The doctor advised her to abstain from sex, limit her intake of meat and **alcohol**, replace her feather pillows and mattress with hair to limit the sensual quality of her bedding, and to take cold enemas and swab her vagina with borax solution to subdue her passions. He advised that if she continued in her "excessive" sexual behaviors, she would be sent to a mental asylum. Another seventeen-year-old girl was taken to her mother's physician, because she had a fit (probably epileptic), but it was thought that she had a "lascivious leer," and her fit was feared to be a demonstration of lust. The doctor diagnosed her to be in a condition of ungovernable sexual excitement, using anthropomorphic characteristics to validate his judgment. In the 1850s, size, shape, and proportions of the features of the skull were believed to be indicative of certain personality types, in hers, amativeness or sexual desire. When the speculum was introduced as a clinical method to examine the cervix and internal tissues of women, immediate concern swept through proper Victorian society that women might become addicted to the pleasure of having the speculum examination.

The boundaries of normal sexual behavior were narrow for women, at least publicly. Masturbation was labeled "self abuse" and harshly punished by parents. The cult of pure womanhood or domesticity may have taught that "ladies" did not have orgasms, and would not want to. A woman's place was in the home, but her true value was in her purity. Virginity and the protection of it acted as a barrier to sexual pleasure before marriage. Purity could be used as a weapon to keep a man under a woman's control, if she remained chaste and refused his advances. If a girl or woman was observed to behave in any way other than the idealized norm, she was subject to drastic measures to eradicate sexual proclivities—the most drastic being the surgical removal of the clitoris, or in certain cases, infibulation (using surgical sutures to close the vaginal opening so that nothing could be inserted). It is unknown exactly how many of these procedures were performed, although recent scholarship suggests they were extremely rare. Women and girls were given bromides, morphine, or barbiturates to dampen or eradicate their sexual desire. Homosexual behavior was likewise regarded as an abnormal avenue to sexual pleasure. In the late nineteenth century, American and British **physicians** began to prescribe orgasm to women as a way of preventing "pelvic tension," believed to result in a multiplicity of mental and physical disorders. Early vibrators were developed as a labor-saving technology to make the task of masturbating female patients less manually taxing.

However, the preponderance of erotic literature and books written by "anonymous" narrating episodes of lust and passionate experiences was characteristic of the nineteenth century. Novels, such as *My Secret Life*, *The Cremorne*, *The Voluptuous Night*, *Flossie*, *The Lustful Memoirs of a Young and Passionate Girl*, and *Rosa Fielding*, described orgasms as something enjoyed by most men and women.

Further Reading: Groneman, Carol. "Nymphomania." In *Deviant Bodies*, edited by J. Terry and J. Urla. Bloomington: Indiana University Press, 1995; Krafft-Ebing, Richard von. *Psychopathia Sexualis*. New York: Paperback Library, 1965; Laquer, Thomas. *Making Sex: Body and Gender from the Greeks to Freud*. Cambridge, MA: Harvard University Press, 1992; Maines, Rachel. *The Technology of Orgasm: "Hysteria," the Vibrator, and Women's Sexual Satisfaction*. Baltimore: Johns Hopkins University Press, 1998; Masters, William H. and Virginia E. Johnson. *Human Sexual Response*. Boston: Little, Brown, 1966; Ruth, Sheila. *Issues in Feminism*. Mountain View, CA: Mayfield Publishing, 1995; Saul, Jennifer. *Feminism: Issues & Arguments*. Oxford: Oxford University Press, 2003.

Lana Thompson

ORIENTALISM. The term "orientalism," most famously articulated by postcolonial theorist, Edward Said, refers to the way in which the study and exploration of non-Western culture builds networks of unequal power relations between West and East, white and nonwhite. "The East" (roughly the area known today as the Middle East, India, and Asia), had long been seen as an eroticized *other* to European culture. The image of the Orient as a space of depraved or uncontrolled sexuality was cemented in the nineteenth century, encouraged by the publication of traditional texts, such as the *Kama Sutra* (translated by **Richard Francis Burton** in 1883), an enormous number of travel narratives by both men and women, and pseudo-anthropological writings on "native" marriage and sexual customs.

A fantasy of exotic excess, in a detail of "The Dance of the Bee," by Vincenzo Marinelli. © The Art Archive/Museo di Capodimonte, Naples/Dagli Orti (A).

The idea of Orientalism, as it is used in postcolonial theory, depends on a Foucaldian notion of the interaction between the construction of knowledge and the workings of power. The study of non-Western cultures, through both academic studies and more popular forms, such as travel narratives, positioned the writer and reader (representing the West) as the active, scrutinizing, authoritative subject, and the East as the passive, knowable object. Indeed, references to "the East" or "the Orient" are in themselves tools of construction, creating, as they do, the idea of a homogenous entity about which generalizations can be made.

The representation of sexuality in Orientalist discourse is intimately tied up with the workings of power in the nineteenth-century imperial context. By defining "the other" of the East as sexually unrestrained, depraved, or abnormal, the West becomes the opposite—the healthy, moral norm. This definition underwrote nineteenth-century imperial rule, as "the East" is constructed envisioned as in need of moral and political guidance. These fantasies of sexual difference and "depravity" appear in various media, from operas, novels, periodicals, pornography, and poetry to **photographs**, postcards, and **painting**s. They permeate both "high" and "low" culture in the nineteenth century, serving both to create an imaginary space of unrestricted sexuality, and to construct ideas of self and home through the creation of an "other."

Nineteenth-century writings about "the East" tend to focus on practices defined as depraved or even illegal by western discourses of love and sexuality, such as polygamy, pre- or extramarital sex, and **homosexuality**. Indeed, the scholar and traveller, Sir Richard Burton posited the existence of a "sotadic zone," a geographical space within which male homosexuality was both common and tolerated by society. Burton's idea provides a telling example of the way in which the self or "home"—the West, is constructed through the construction of the Eastern other. As Burton wrote:

> Within the Sotadic Zone the Vice is popular and endemic, held at the worst to be a mere peccadillo, whilst the races to the North and South of the limits here defined practise it only sporadically amid the opprobrium of their fellows who, as a rule, are physically incapable of performing the operation and look upon it with the liveliest disgust (see http://www.fordham.edu/halsall/pwh/burton-te.html).

The imaginary boundaries of the Sotadic zone thus function to delimit and constrain homosexuality; to distance it from the West; and to construct western masculinities as inherently heterosexual. The East is often feminized, to create a masculinized West, and justify political domination by referring to a naturalized inequality of gender relations. Similarly, nineteenth-century travel narratives that descant upon the lasciviousness and precocious sexuality of non-Western women often compare them with European women, who are thus constructed as "properly" sexually restrained.

However, related to the disapproval and condemnation which permeates these texts is a prurient interest and desire. Orientalist texts and images featuring such scenes as the slave market, the harem, the odalisque, and the dancing girl, all serve to titillate and provide pleasure to the consumer. "Eastern scenes" at Exhibitions and Expositions commonly featured belly dancing by scantily clad women, and brothels capitalized on the imaginary link between sexuality and the East by staging harem scenes for customers. The other side to the construction of an overly sexualized, "depraved," and lascivious culture linked to the East, is the simultaneous construction of a restrained, "healthy," and moral culture associated with the West. Lust and desire—elements seen as distractions and vices—could be projected onto the *other*, leaving the consumer free both to fantasize about these scenes and also to dissociate from them. Orientalism thus provided a kind of "safe" space for fantasies of the kinds of sexuality not allowed at home.

Further Reading: Alloula, Malek. *The Colonial Harem*. Manchester: Manchester University Press, 1986; Burton, Sir Richard Francis. *Terminal Essay: The Arabian Nights 1885*. People with a History at: www.fordham.edu/halsall/pwh/burton-te.html; Said, Edward. *Orientalism*. New York: Vintage, 1979; Schick, Irvin C. *The Erotic Margin: Sexuality and Spatiality in Alteritist Discourse*. London: Verso, 1999; Yeazell, Ruth Bernard. *Harems of the Mind: Passages of Western Art and Literature*. New Haven, CT: Yale University Press, 2000.

Jessica Needle

OTTOMAN WOMEN. Ottoman women's concern with love and sex, and the forms through which this was expressed, took on a new prominence in the nineteenth century as the multiethnic, multifaith empire underwent major periods of reform and accelerated social change. Though many of the formal changes, notably those of the Tanzimat reforms (1839–1876), were directed as men's political and social roles (notably the development of a secular-influenced education system and the palace bureaucracy or civil service), it was widely understood that the ramifications of these innovations were altering women's social roles and the relations between men and women. The advent of Sultan Abdülhamit in 1876 brought a suspension of the Tanzimat constitution, and though the sultan continued, for example, many of the education reforms undertaken by his predecessors, many Ottomans found his reign to be culturally and politically repressive. This was especially so for elite Ottomans involved in the palace bureaucracy and for those prominent in the reformist factions (of which the young Turks were to eventually emerge as the most prominent in the 1908 revolution that reinstated the constitution). In a period noted for Abdülhamit's censorship of the press and his network of spies, matters of love took on a heightened significance as a proving ground for personal freedom. As Duben and Behar (1991) point out, when it was difficult to directly express political demands, the demand to choose affective marriages rather than arranged unions came to stand in for unavailable political liberties—for men and for women. In the politicization of love, the consumption of western (mainly French) literature was seen as a major factor. With elite women now often literate in European languages (owing to the increased numbers of foreign governesses in elite harems, and the attendance of mainly non-Muslim girls at foreign-run missionary schools), the consumption of western romances was sometimes held to be a mixed blessing, making girls dissatisfied with their lot in life and giving them unrealistic expectations.

Commentators from all political perspectives regarded the role of women as an indicator of the general state of the civilization, whether emancipation was seen as a sign of progress or of the decay of valued traditions. Ottomans of all political persuasions also knew that reforms were played out under the eyes of a curious West—whose fascination with the harem was longstanding. The Western Orientalist fantasies of the harem as a space of sexualized excess and depravity bore little relation to its existence as a family domicile, just as the western obsession with polygyny bore little relation to its actual practice, and by the mid-nineteenth century, its rarity. Ottomans were frustrated by western presumptions about the nature of their family life, though rebutting this was often made difficult by cultural prohibitions against discussing the family with outsiders.

Nevertheless, by the second half of the nineteenth century, women themselves were expressing opinions in ever-growing numbers. With increased female literacy, especially in the modernizing metropolises of Cairo and Istanbul, women's cultural and political participation outside the home began to expand. The women's press was active in both cities from the 1890s, and women writers discussed everything from marriage to **fashion** and from politics to domestic science. Well informed about western **feminism**, Ottoman women were not uncritical in their appraisal of Western so-called liberation. But the western model of chosen rather than arranged marriage and self-contained nuclear family living came to be associated increasingly with self-fulfillment and modernity in progressive and elite circles.

What has often, until recently, been overlooked is the extent to which progressive and reformist women were in direct contact with western feminists, not just by reading western sources, but also through networks of personal contacts with western women travelers and correspondence with western activists. This was a two-way exchange in which western women evaluated their own conditions in relation to the lives of Ottoman women. In the mid-century, women in Britain expressed envy that Islamic law, unlike British law, allowed women to own and inherit property, while at the end of the century, the British feminist, Grace Ellison, used to male hostility at home, was astonished at the number of progressive Ottoman men who supported female emancipation as a part of a project of national social emancipation.

In the last quarter of the nineteenth and first quarter of the twentieth centuries, progressive Ottoman women (often but not exclusively Muslim) expounded their views in polemics, memoir, and travel literature written and published in French, German, and English. Specifically challenging western misconceptions about harem life, their books simultaneously intervened in local and international debates about women's rights. Books by women from this period, such as Fatma Aliye Hanum (1862–1936), Halide Edib (1883–1964), and Demetra Vaka (1877–1946), found a market in the West because of the often prurient appetite for harem literature. Nevertheless, their books told of the challenges faced by a generation of women whose lives were often radically different from their mothers'. In the transition that many of this generation experienced from the end of the empire to the advent of the Turkish republic (with its avowedly nationalist and secular project of westward-looking modernization), the sexual politics of love, marriage, and family life were experienced as bewilderingly, but sometimes empoweringly, unstable. The creation of new models of femininity—played out in personal relations and state regulation—was a crucial aspect in the development of regional modernities in the territories that had once been Ottoman. *See also* Imperialism; Islam and Homosexuality; Orientalism.

Further Reading: Duben, Alan and Cem Behar. *Istanbul Households; Marriage, Family and Fertility (1880–1940)*. Cambridge: Cambridge University Press, 1991; Lewis, Reina. *Rethinking Orientalism: Women, Travel and the Ottoman Harem*. New Brunswick, NJ: Rutgers University Press, 2004; Lewis, Reina and Nancy Micklewright, eds. *Gender, Modernity and Liberty: Middle Eastern and Western Women's Writings: A Critical Sourcebook*. London: I.B. Tauris, 2006.

Reina Lewis

P

PAINTING. In nineteenth-century painting, portrayals of relations between the sexes and the rules governing gender expectations were faithfully adhered to from Russia to the United States, and echoed in polite European circles. The doctrine of "separate spheres" was as influential on the subject matter of painting as on the other arts, men being seen as exploring the public world and women as conserving home values. The middle-class Victorian ideal of "The Angel of the House" (the title of **Coventry Kersey Dighton Patmore**'s well-known poem) was as vivid in popular culture as in art: George Elgar Hicks portrays *Woman's Mission*, a triptych of 1863, as being fulfilled by her roles as mother, carer, and helpmeet, respectively, *Companion to Manhood* being the most relevant here. It was applicable as a template for the respectable working class too, as in Hicks's *The Sinews of Old England* (1857), where the humble woman is leaning on, and simultaneously propping up the sinews of her worthy worker husband. This decorum and propriety in manners is portrayed by a robust realism of manner.

The myths of chivalry, especially Arthurian legend, provided a powerful framework —encouraged by the personal interests of Queen Victoria and Prince Albert. Maidens might grow pale, but the knight errant would always ride to the rescue (John Everett Millais, *The Knight-errant*, 1870, or Frank Dicksee, *Chivalry*, 1885). The women could be partially clothed or completely naked so as to make the rescue a moral necessity as well as a matter of safety—preservation of modesty as much as of life.

To the well-known dualisms of madonnas and magdalenes, virgins and whores could be added as a subcategory, that of the unbridled sexual temptress or enchantress. Examples are found in George Frederick Sandys's depictions of the Arthurian sorceress *Vivien* (1863), *Morgan le Fay* (1862–1863), or the Greek *Medea* (1868). Interestingly, Sandys found a social inferior as the ideal model for such cultural Others in the "gypsy girl," Kaomi. Such women could be dangerous and sometimes prove fatal to men, despite any amount of moral armor, as can be seen in Frank Dicksee's late *La Belle Dame sans Merci* (1902, based on John Keats's poem), where the knight spreads his arms in hopeless abandonment, almost in a crucifixion pose. Homeric temptresses inspired much of the later work of John Waterhouse (*Circe Offering the Cup to Ulysses*, 1891, or *Circe Invidiosa*, 1892).

Such stereotypes were to provide moral lessons for contemporary women, should they ever think of transgressing the social or gender boundaries. Even apparently harmless flirtation with male admirers was shown as morally dubious. In three mid-century paintings, the message is explicit. In Frank Stone's *The Tryst* (c. 1850), the suggestion is that of an illicit meeting, with the lovers separated only by a flimsy wooden fence, a symbolic rose dangling precariously from the young girl's hand. Alfred Elmore's *On the Brink* (1865) has a more immediate connotation: the whispering suitor has only to climb over the brink of the window ledge of a brightly lit gambling casino to attain his prize; she, meanwhile, is in a tortured pose, confronted by the symbolic choice between the chaste lily and the passion flower. Edward Matthew Ward's recreation in 1854 of an encounter between the English King Charles II and his mistress Nell Gwynne in the notorious St. James's Park, shows her sitting on a wall, bedecked in finery like the peacock behind her, but as liable to fall as the leaves on the grass. The economic dependence of women on men was taken for granted in nineteenth-century culture, despite, for example, the efforts of Caroline Norton and her circle to gain rights over property, let alone over self. In the third painting of Augustus Egg's narrative trilogy, *Past and Present* (1858), the wife who has betrayed her husband has lost everything—honor, home, and children—and is soon to lose life itself by hurling herself into the river Thames.

"Morgan le Fay: Queen of Avalon," by Frederick Sandys. © Art Resource, NY.

Contemporary "Penitent Magdalenes" were as popular as in Renaissance art. The British Prime Minister, William Gladstone, was not the only middle-class male compelled to rescue fallen women. In Holman Hunt's *The Awakening Conscience* (1854), the kept woman of a middle-class profligate man is seen to have the hope of redemption in her manner, as she rises from his lap into the symbolic sunlight reflected in the mirror behind her. Her conscience has been awakened by the poignant parlor song he has been playing on the piano, "Oft in the Stilly Night," or perhaps by the lines from the poet Tennyson's "The Princess" seen at her feet. In real life, Hunt's efforts to groom Annie Miller, a woman with a doubtful past and therefore perfect casting for his model here, were quite sincere, with marriage in mind. Unfortunately, she reverted to her old ways when he was painting religious scenes in Palestine, and was seen in St. James's Park with a notorious rake.

Thwarted sexuality could provide fruitful subject matter, whether the union is postponed or renounced. In Arthur Hughes's *The Long Engagement* (c. 1854–1859), a curate and his fiancée are kept apart by his poverty, the length of their engagement made explicit by the ivy that now almost obscures her name, "Amy," which he had carved into the tree in the foreground. In Hughes's *Aurora Leigh's Dismissal of Romney (or The Tryst)* (1860), based on Elizabeth Barrett Browning's recently published poem *Aurora Leigh*, the heroine rejects her suitor's proposal in favor of her own poetic aspirations ("I too have my vocation"). In *The Black Brunswicker* (1859–1860) by John Everett Millais, the German soldier bids farewell to his English sweetheart on the eve of the Battle of Waterloo of 1815, where most of the Brunswick cavalry were eliminated, while she holds the door closed, "vainly supplicating him to keep from the bugle call to arms," as Millais expressed it.

Illness and death were a reality of Victorian life, and a near-fatal separation from a suitor was often hinted at in the many paintings entitled *The Convalescent* (by James Tissot, e.g., a French exile to London in the 1870s, whose lover was an invalid). In Tissot's *Bad News: The Parting* (1872), a final separation between the woman and her soldier-lover is suggested. Death was the final separation, of course, and this is commemorated in Dante Gabriel Rossetti's homage to his wife, Elizabeth Siddal, *Beata Beatrix* (1864–1870), where he envisages her as the inspiration for the poet Dante. Ironically, Millais had symbolized the death of a loved one in his illustration to Shakespeare's *Hamlet*, using "Lizzie" as his model for *Ophelia* a few years earlier (1851–1852).

Romantic love could be portrayed in Shakespearian images, such as Dicksee's *Romeo and Juliet* (1883), where the lovers are literally and symbolically wrapped around each other. Married love is seen as dependent on the wife's consciousness of her duties; for example, in Millais's *The Order of Release, 1746* (1852–1853), the Highland woman is shown rescuing her Jacobite husband from English soldiers, but possibly having paid the price of her virtue in order to do so. Rossetti's *The Wedding of Saint George and Princess Sabra* (1857) is a tribute to the romantic ideal of marriage, but William Quiller Orchardson probably depicts the economic realities for many couples in his ironic *Le Mariage de convenance* (1883), where the couple, absorbed in separate thoughts, are symbolically distanced by a long table. Queen Victoria and Prince Albert's apparently blissful relationship was an inspiration for many, though, and is captured in unusually informal royal portraits of the couple by artists, such as Edwin Landseer, surrounded by domestic bliss (*Windsor Castle in Modern Times*, 1841–1845). Though **gender roles** are reversed, in that her rank is higher, Albert is seen as indubitably "the man of the house."

Further Reading: Nead, Lynda. *Myths of Sexuality: Representations of Women in Victorian Britain*. Oxford: Blackwell, 1988; Reynolds, Graham. *Victorian Painting*. rev. ed. London: Herbert Press, 1987.

Sara M. Dodd

PASSIONLESSNESS.   *See* Sexlessness

PATMORE, COVENTRY KERSEY DIGHTON (1823–1896).   Coventry Patmore was an English poet best known for his long poem on marriage, *Angel in the House* (1854–1863). His lesser-known volume, *Unknown Eros* (1864–1878), contains odes marked by startling erotic mysticism. However, the relationship between human and divine passion runs throughout much of his work, from his early poems to his final essays.

Angel in the House, a poem about courtship and marriage, became a best-seller, first, in the United States, and, later, in Britain. Nevertheless, perhaps to its detriment, Patmore persistently revised the text in four editions during the course of three decades. The poem was inspired by Patmore's fifteen-year marriage to his first wife, Emily Augusta Andrews, who died in 1862, and to whom it is dedicated. *Victories of Love* (1863), in which the fictional wife dies, completes the volume. Feminist critics, such as Virginia Woolf have denounced the *Angel in the House* for its sentimental idealization of women. However, the title is supposed to refer not specifically to the wife, but to the spirit of love in Christian marriage. "The Paragon," from Canto 2 of Book 1, ends with the statement, "The nuptial contrasts are the poles/On which the heavenly spheres revolve" (Patmore, *Poems*, 14).

In 1864, Patmore visited Rome, converted to Roman Catholicism, and married heiress and fellow convert Marianne (or Mary Anne) Byles. She raised his six children, and most likely maintained her vow of virginity throughout their marriage. It is probable that her vow, alongside Patmore's favorite daughter Emily's vowed virginity as a sister of the Society of the Holy Child Jesus, and his growing devotion to the Virgin Mary contributed to his turn toward the theme of humanity's virgin marriage with God.

Patmore's preoccupation with virgin marriage is boldly depicted in the *Unknown Eros*. The volume's erotic energy and blend of passionate imagery—both bodily and spiritual—is reminiscent of sensuous Christian mystical literature, to which Patmore was heavily indebted. "To the Body" celebrates the status of the body as the "Little, sequester'd pleasure-house/For God and for His Spouse" (Patmore, *Poems*, 327). "Deliciæ Sapientiæ De Amore," concludes with the image of the elect who are "clad/ With the bridal robes of ardour virginal" (Patmore, *Poems*, 334). Here, celibacy becomes the fullest realization of erotic feeling for God the bridegroom. Other notable sections pertaining to the soul's amorous and celibate union with God include the Psyche odes: "Eros and Psyche," "De Natura Deorum," and "Psyche's Discontent." For Patmore, the Greek mythical characters of Eros and Psyche represent God and the soul, respectively. In "Eros and Psyche," the soul's infatuation with its beloved is exemplified by its desire for mystical pain and suffering: "Kiss, tread me under foot, cherish or beat,/ Sheathe in my heart sharp pain up to the hilt" (Patmore, *Poems*, 341).

Patmore's Christian influences included St. John of the Cross, St. Teresa of Avila and St. Bernard of Clairvaux. Indeed, Patmore and Marianne Patmore translated Bernard's *De Diligendo Deo* and selections from his sermons on the erotic biblical text, the *Song of Songs*. Following Marianne Patmore's death in 1880, the first edition of their translation, *Bernard of Clairvaux on the Love of God*, was completed by her husband and published shortly after in 1881.

In the same year, Patmore married Harriet Robson, who had been his daughter Emily's closest friend and the younger children's governess. In 1883, when Patmore was sixty, their only son was born. In the final years of his life, Patmore developed an attachment to the Catholic aristocratic poet, Alice Meynell. Patmore made public his devotion to the young—and married—woman; praised her in his writing; nominated her for the Poet Laureateship; and even went to the extent of making her husband, Wilfrid Meynell, his confidant. After Alice Meynell put an end to their friendship around 1895, Patmore printed her farewell poem to him in the *Saturday Review*.

On Christmas Day in 1887, Patmore burnt the manuscript of his new prose work, *Sponsa Dei*. This work had engaged his attention for many years, and it was his intention that it be published after his death. Patmore destroyed the work, in part, after taking into consideration the words of caution over its possible publication expressed by his friend, the Jesuit poet **Gerard Manley Hopkins**, who later expressed regret over its loss. The *Sponsa Dei* was considered the flowering of Patmore's thoughts on the bond between bodily and spiritual love, between human and divine union. Nevertheless, much of its substance is said to have survived in his last book, *The Rod, the Root, and the Flower* (1895), published a year before his death in 1896. This slender book is filled with striking quotes and meditations on the powerful relationship between love, sex, and religious experience. Consider, for instance, the assertion, "Lovers are nothing else than Priest and Priestess to each other of the Divine Manhood and the Divine Womanhood which are in God" (Patmore, *Rod*, 115). In this book, Patmore also articulates his concept of the "homo," which refers to the union of male and female not simply with each other but also—like Teiresias—within each individual. For Patmore, this synthesis of dualities, the love between "opposed likenesses" (Patmore, *Rod*, 103), mirrors both the Incarnation and the marriage of Christ with the church.

The enduring association of Coventry Patmore with sentimentality and the *Angel in the House* prevents a full appreciation of his most interesting work, the erotic writings that elucidate his remarkable ideas on God, humanity, love, and sex.

Further Reading: Maynard, John. *Victorian Discourses on Sexuality and Religion*. Cambridge: Cambridge University Press, 1993; Patmore, Coventry. *Poems*. London: G. Bell and Sons, Ltd., 1915; Patmore, Coventry. *The Rod, The Root, and The Flower*. London: The Grey Walls Press, 1950; Reid, J. C. *The Mind and Art of Coventry Patmore*. London: Routledge and Kegan Paul, 1957.

Duc Dau

PENITENTIARIES AND LOCK HOSPITALS. There is little historical evidence that rates of the "great social evils" of the nineteenth century, **prostitution** and venereal disease (VD), were actually increasing. However, factions of the bourgeoisie found them offensive, and demanded that the state take action through legislation and voluntary initiative. VD first appeared in Britain in the late fifteenth century. Early forms were called the Pox, the French Disease, and in Scotland, *grandgore*. Although the connection between syphilis and sexual intercourse was not made until the seventeenth century, discoveries in the scientific community revealed that many diseases were not scourges, but curable or controllable, and public health campaigns to contain syphilis were among the first attempts at social medicine. Nonetheless, syphilis was poorly understood and regarded as vile and loathsome. It was linked to fornication and prostitution and heavily stigmatized. Sufferers were denied admission to Royal Infirmaries and poor law hospitals, and were confined to overcrowded and understaffed wards of workhouses or separate buildings on the grounds of infirmaries. Venereal wards treated both men and women, and by the nineteenth century, evangelical-influenced doctors, and general reformist zeal, came to dominate hospital administration. New charity lock hospitals were established where female venereal patients could be quarantined for longer periods than was possible in other hospitals; however, men were increasingly treated as outpatients. Lock hospitals were named either after medieval houses for lepers or after the French word *loques* meaning rags and bandages. The first opened in England in 1746, in Ireland in 1755, and in Scotland in 1805. Lock hospital patients were poor women who were ineligible for poor relief and unable to provide proof of character; they were presumed to be prostitutes and treated as such. Judith Walkowitz argues that they became the social lepers of the industrial revolution as syphilis replaced leprosy as the symbol of social contagion and disease.

For over 400 years, mercury, in tablet or ointment form, was the principle treatment for syphilis and gonorrhoea. Mercury poisoning was common, and the symptoms—loss of teeth, destruction of the nasal cavity, blindness, and kidney complications—were also described as the symptoms of syphilis. Only state-run lock hospitals had the legal power to detain patients against their will, but all lock hospitals had a penal character. Medical treatment lasted three months and was in tune with the Protestant-dominated culture. Treatment included the careful classification of patients according to marital status, age, number of visits, mercury treatments, solitary confinement, religious education and work in the hospital laundry. A Scottish physician observed that the ideal time to save "unhappy females" was while they were "oppressed with disease, uncertain of life, and looking forward with a tremendous anxiety to another world ... She is convinced; she is changed, and becomes, in place of a burden, a comfort to society."

Lock hospitals were only the first step in the physical and moral rehabilitation of "fallen" women. Owing to the philanthropic work of prison reformers like Elizabeth Fry, the mixing of female prisoners, regardless of age, sex, or type of offence, ended. Reformers demanded nonstatutory penitentiaries, known as female refuges and Magdalene asylums, in order to divert young female misdemeanants, wayward girls, and "fallen" women from the streets, police cells, poorhouses, and prisons. The official purpose of the penitentiaries was to rescue and reform newly "fallen" women and victims of "seduction," not hardened prostitutes or female felons. Sentimentally replicating the religious imagery of Mary Magdalene, the prostitute who had washed the feet of Christ and been reformed, the inmates were called magdalenes, unfortunates, and penitents. The first penitentiaries run by religious orders or philanthropic organizations were London's Magdalene Hospital (1758) and the Lock Asylum (1787), Ireland's Leeson Magdalene Asylum (1766) and Lock Penitentiary (1821), the Edinburgh Magdalene Asylum (1797), and the Glasgow Magdalene Asylum (1815). By 1900, there were over two hundred female refuges throughout the United Kingdom; twenty-three were in Ireland.

Since penitentiaries had no legal power to detain inmates, the administrators favored women in their early twenties who were not pregnant, alcoholics, or diseased, and were of reasonable intelligence and willing to submit to discipline. The majority of inmates were low-rank domestic **servants**, unemployed factory workers, orphans, and homeless teenage girls. Some came voluntarily, but lock hospitals, missionaries, maternity homes, the police, and magistrates referred others. Inmates were expected to stay about two years, but in some cases residency was permanent. The program was strict and the rules numerous. They included obligatory silence, no contact with family and friends, mail censorship, and institutional uniforms. Head shaving and long periods of solitary confinement were also common. A typical day included work, discipline, prayer, bland meals, compulsory silence, and corporal punishment for misbehavior.

Lock hospital and penitentiary operating budgets came from charitable donations and the income generated through inmates' long hours of unpaid labor in laundry and sewing departments. It was assumed that character flaws like laziness and vanity, and not poverty or unemployment, caused prostitution. Therefore, through a regime of hard work, religious education, and discipline, it was hoped that inmates would learn the values of self-sacrifice, chastity, modesty, and sobriety, appropriate for their class position and **gender roles**. Laundry work was favored, because it was imbued with great religious imagery. Through laundry work, sinful women symbolically performed a penance, cleansing themselves of their moral corruption. Penitentiaries promised a "fresh start" to reformed inmates. They tried to return inmates to their families, if possible, or found them employment in domestic service where inmates on probations could continue to be supervised by employers and lady volunteers. Many inmates refused to conform to the rules and discipline and absconded before they were released.

Prostitution and VD rates were seen as pressing social problems. In the late nineteenth century, concern over their spread prompted the passing of the **Contagious Diseases Acts** in the 1860s, and new state-run lock hospitals were designed to control VD through compulsory registration of prostitutes in regulated districts. In areas where the acts were not enforced, municipal police and magistrates had the power to fine women associated with soliciting and public order crimes. Many authorities used their powers to persuade young women to voluntarily enter lock hospitals and penitentiaries rather than face a criminal charge. After the passing of the Industrial School and Reformatories Acts in the 1850s, and the Criminal Law Amendments Acts in 1885, which pertained to the protection of girls and suppression of juvenile prostitution, female penitentiaries became an informal branch of the criminal justice system. These institutions institutionalized the double standard of sexual morality and the distinction between pure and impure women, because women and adolescent girls were more likely to be incarcerated for sexual behavior than men and boys. Magistrates, social workers, rescue societies, and parents used penitentiaries to divert girls in moral danger from the street, prisons, and juvenile reformatories. At the same time, incarceration was used to protect society from corruption and disease.

Further Reading: Levine, Philippa. *Prostitution, Race, and Politics: Policing Venereal Disease in the British Empire.* London: Routledge, 2003; Littlewood, Barbara and Linda Mahood. "Prostitutes Magdalenes and Wayward Girls: Dangerous Sexualities of Working Class Women in Victorian Scotland." *Gender and History* 3 (1991): 160–75; Luddy, Maria. *Women and Philanthropy in Nineteenth-Century Ireland.* Cambridge: Cambridge University Press, 1995; Walkowitz, Judith. *Prostitution and Victorian Society.* Oxford: Oxford University Press, 1981.

Linda Mahood

PHOTOGRAPHS. The daguerrotype, the first practical photographic process, was invented in 1835, and was followed by developments in photographic technology throughout the century. Photography became an integral part of Victorian culture, and played a role in nineteenth-century experiences of love and sexuality. It changed the way in which people saw one another, and the world around them.

The *carte de visite*, a small photographic portrait given to friends and family, became an affordable replacement for the painted miniature as a memento of a loved one. These *cartes* were collected and often kept in albums, and were especially popular in the 1860s to 1880s. The widespread availability of Kodak cameras from 1888 meant that amateur photography became more affordable and simple than ever. Photograph albums held reminders of important family events. It became fashionable to use photographs of loved ones to decorate the home, a practice that demonstrates the emotional significance of photographs.

Sexually explicit and pornographic photographs date from shortly after the invention of photographic technology. These were ordered by post or traded by book and photograph dealers, most notably in London's infamous pornography district, Holywell Street. An 1888 publication entitled *Tempted London: Young Men* noted that "almost every Londoner knows the streets about the Strand where indecent books and pictures are sold," but noted that consumers were often taken in by the implied promise of obscenity only to find that the photographs he has bought "are not worse than may be found in many 'respectable' shops where actresses' portraits are shown" (quoted in Ovenden and Mendes 1973, 45). Indeed, postcards ranging from the humorous or coy to the explicit and extreme were sent through the postal service. Popular genre scenes included women in the private space of the bedroom or boudoir, engaged in activities, such as bathing, dressing, and undressing, being laced into their corsets, and brushing their hair. Other, less-narrative photographs featured partly or wholly nude women reclining on beds or sofas, or simply standing facing the viewer. Men were much less often featured in these erotic photographs, and when they do appear, they almost always play the part of the foil to the woman, even remaining dressed while the woman disrobes, perhaps to function as a surrogate for the (male) consumer. Since modeling for nude or erotic photographs was hardly a respectable occupation, these photographs can be interpreted through the lens of class, as images of working-class or poor women.

In the late nineteenth century, erotic photographs of nonwhite women circulated freely, particularly in the form of postcards. As Malek Alloula notes of postcards featuring Algerian women, "History knows of no other society in which women have been photographed on such a large scale to be delivered to public view" (Alloula 1986, 5). Photographs of this type exploited popular racist attitudes, which attributed excessive sexual desire and a lack of modesty and chastity to nonwhite women. As Alloula argues, the integration of such images into the domestic life of the middle-class West is an act of violent discursive appropriation of the bodies of these women.

Nancy Armstrong argues that the development of pornographic photography had a significant effect on the way in which sexuality was experienced in the nineteenth century, and in particular, the cultural understanding of women, their sexuality and their bodies. According to Armstrong, "fifty years of pornographic photography had reduced the female body to its visible traces, broken it up into various parts, shot those parts from unusual angles, and reconstituted them in albums and stereoscopic sequences, as well as through sheer repetition, to produce a master stereotype—the erotic object itself" (Armstrong 1999, 265). The resulting fragmentation and fetishization effectively produced a new erotic body that was split off from the respectable, middle-class woman, and reconstituted as the "other." Sexuality became understood as something "materially inscribed and therefore visible on the body's surface. What one discovered in viewing the pornographic body was not the sexuality of respectable women, then, but the surface of another body, the body of a class or an ethnic group who 'allowed' their women to be seen" (Armstrong, 265). Photography created a distance between the viewer and the viewed which translated into an experiential distance between subject and sexual object, a distance which followed already existing power imbalances of class, **race**, and gender. *See also* Gender Roles; Orientalism.

Further Reading: Alloula, Malek. *The Colonial Harem*. Manchester: Manchester University Press, 1986; Armstrong, Nancy. *Fiction in the Age of Photography. The Legacy of British Realism*. Cambridge, MA: Harvard University Press, 1999; Green-Lewis, Jennifer. *Framing the Victorians: Photography and the Culture of Realism*. Ithaca, NY: Cornell University Press, 1996; Mavor, Carol. *Pleasures Taken: Performances of Sexuality and Loss in Victorian Photographs*. Durham, NC: Duke University Press, 1995; Ovenden, Graham and Mendes, Peter. *Victorian Erotic Photography*. London: Academy Editions, 1973.

Jessica Needle

PHYSICIANS AND MIDWIVES. Until the nineteenth century, physicians and midwives had different and gendered roles: physicians were male, midwives were female. Midwives could be considered the first health specialists, because they assist at births. They were referred to in the Bible, in Roman and Greek medical texts, and sometimes as wise women. (The word midwife did not appear until the fourteenth century, and comes from the middle English word *mydwyf*, the prefix *mid* meaning "with" and wyf meaning "woman.") The first physicians were either barber surgeons or itinerant doctors, mountebanks, or quacks, often with informal training. Barber surgeons were more educated because, historically, they had guilds that required membership, but the other healers traveled from town to town and sold remedies that held only the promise of a cure. Often their remedies contained opiates or herbs that dulled pain rather than cured the underlying disease.

The university-educated physician evolved from a tradition of natural philosophy, with studies in plant and animal biology and early science. The first medical school in the United States opened in 1765 at the University of Pennsylvania, but women were

Elizabeth Blackwell, ca. 1877. Courtesy of the Library of Congress.

not admitted until the late nineteenth century. Until 1870, women who wanted to become medical doctors were repeatedly denied entrance to Harvard Medical School. However, in Geneva, New York, Elizabeth Blackwell (1821–1910) was admitted to the medical college and graduated in 1849, becoming the first woman medical doctor in the United States. Medical education was not standardized, and ranged from a few months to two years. Some schools had no clinical training, and in others, there were no educational prerequisites, standardized curriculums, or required core courses. Anatomy was often taught in a public venue, and was attended by curious members of the public as well as by students. Training for midwives, although less academic, had a long tradition. Although much of the therapeutic knowledge was folk information, the techniques and understanding of pregnancy, labor, and delivery were well established. Midwives learned from experience, and the profession was often passed down from mother to daughter. A young girl would accompany her mother to assist and observe, thus developing experience in a wide range of situations, and would become better equipped to deliver a baby than any physician.

Although the majority of births were attended by midwives, the barber surgeons also delivered babies occasionally. In the seventeenth century, the Chamberlens, a family of trained barber surgeons who dabbled in midwifery, invented obstetrical forceps. Their closely guarded secret brought them an extraordinary income in exchange for the promise of a fast, painless, safe delivery. They shared their technology only with those who could afford to pay, thus creating an elite cadre of doctors who competed with midwives in a way that appealed to more affluent clients. Midwives were not interested in using forceps because their philosophy did not value speed over nature.

Along with the promise of new technology was the appeal of hospital deliveries. Until monetary value was put on obstetrics, physicians had no interest in delivering babies, and most deliveries were performed in the woman's home by midwives. A schism soon developed based on socioeconomic status. Those who could afford doctors and hospitals were admitted to one section, others continued with midwives. Schools for midwifery were entirely separate from medical schools, and met with resistance for a long time. A new practitioner appeared, albeit one who was met with disbelief and ridicule: the male midwife. They did use forceps and offered an alternative to the traditional female midwife. Upper-class women were attracted to this choice because a male was perceived as stronger and superior to a female.

However, one of the most significant students in the history of gynecology and obstetrics to attend a midwifery school was Ignaz Semmelweis (1818–1865). After graduating from medical school in Vienna, he took a two-month course in midwifery. As medicine became more professionalized, autopsies were performed in hospitals for the purpose of correlating clinical pathology with internal changes. An epidemic called childbed fever developed, and swept through hospitals wherever babies were being delivered. When Semmelweis observed that doctors were going directly from the autopsy suite to the delivery room, he suspected that there was some connection, but without any knowledge of germs or antisepsis, he could not isolate the mechanism of spread. He started documenting the cases of deaths in the physicians' ward, versus those where midwives delivered. Logically, one would have predicted that the less-educated midwives would have more deaths, but his statistics showed that there was more morbidity and mortality in the private ward than in the public. Semmelweis and the physicians were familiar with Lister's carbolic acid solution, recently incorporated in surgical procedures. Semmelweis hypothesized that hand washing with Lister's solution could aid in preventing childbirth infections as well. He began to wash his own hands and instruments before going to the delivery room and convinced a number of other doctors to do the same. The number of deaths was drastically reduced from 12 to 2 percent in the private ward. Unfortunately, politics worked against his life-saving technique, and he was forbidden by his superiors to promote hand-washing. The mentality of the times perpetuated the belief that women's bodies and their normal discharges were so dirty that it did not matter if one washed one's hands or not. It was not until 1861 that Semmelweis published his work which showed that cadaveric fever (sepsis) and childbed fever were the same, proving that the disease that killed women who had gone to hospitals was spread by doctors who failed to wash their hands between patients.

As predominantly male physicians gained acceptance in the gynecological field, the anxieties regarding men having access to women's bodies were allayed by the promotion of a "don't look" mentality. There are pictures of a "proper" gynecological exam where the woman is fully clothed and the doctor's face is turned away. Medical texts stressed the idea of not making eye contact with a woman during an examination. To perpetuate this false modesty, paper and ceramic models were made of pregnant women's bodies so that doctors could learn by looking at models instead of real bodies. Typically, there were few female autopsies performed, and of those carried out, not enough were done on pregnant women for medical students to observe as a matter of curriculum.

In 1910, Abraham Flexner, a secondary school teacher, wrote a report for the Carnegie Foundation that compared medical schools and their curricula. The report was called "Medical Education in the United States and Canada," and it led to improvement in the vastly different requirements for admission to and graduation from medical schools. With these new standards, medical schools produced more educated men and women with backgrounds in the basic sciences. Interestingly, the number of midwifery practitioners shrank until the early 1990s when a renewed interest in the nonmedicalization of childbirth created a demand for an increased number of midwives. Although they never regained their original independent healer status, they remained available as a choice for women who preferred a midwife to a physician. *See also* Pregnancy.

Further Reading: Clausen, Carol et al. "Blackwell, Elizabeth." *That Girl There Is Doctor in Medicine* at: http://www.nlm.nih.gov/hmd/blackwell; Ehrenreich, Barbara and Deirdre English. *Witches, Midwives, and Nurses: A History of Women Healers.* New York: The Feminist Press, 1973; Fee, Elizabeth et al. "Dr. Elizabeth Blackwell." *Changing the Face of Medicine* at: http://www.nlm.nih.gov/changingthefaceofmedicine/physicians/biography_35.html; Thompson, Lana. *The Wandering Womb: A Cultural History of Outrageous Beliefs about Women.* Amherst, MA: Prometheus, 1999.

Lana Thompson

POLYGAMY, AFRICAN. Polygamy is the practice of having more than one husband or wife. In Africa, nearly all marriages were potentially polygamous or, more correctly, polygynous (having more than one wife). **Marriage**, though, represented only one avenue for the exercise of sexuality, since many African societies recognized sexual activity as positive, if subject to restriction. For this reason, polygamy was not only about sex. The links between sexuality and polygamy become clear, though, when we consider issues of fertility, power, and later, **Christianity**. Fertility was a key element of African understandings of sexuality.

Much of our knowledge of nineteenth-century polygamy comes from the work of European colonialists—missionaries, officials, and early anthropologists, who conducted extensive research into African tradition and custom, including marriage and kinship. From this and more contemporary research, it is apparent that polygamy's extent varied considerably. According to observations taken in southern Africa in the 1850s, only 43 percent of men had more than one wife. In Central Africa in 1934, the figure was 14 percent. Rates of polygamy tended to be higher in West Africa, where a 1909 count shows 50 percent of Ashanti men having more than one wife. Generally, only senior men and chiefs had more wives. The rates were likely to be similar for the nineteenth century, though the nature of polygamy changed as different parts of the continent came in contact with European colonization.

Overall, polygamy was not as extensive as Christian missionaries made it out to be. However, a discussion of its extent conflates practice with possibility. Almost any African marriage was potentially polygamous, which represented an ideal with regard to marriage. Equally, though, many men preferred only one wife. An accurate reconstruction of women's views on the issue is seldom possible, given an historical record reliant on male recollection.

The most common explanation for polygamy derives from the way it augmented male status—more wives equaling more power and status. Men (generally older) who aspired to social power accumulated wives to expand their families' or lineages' productive and reproductive capacities. Polygamy, in this way, had a lot to do with acquiring more rights to female fertility. A common African view holds that polygamy results in an increased birth rate.

In those African societies where women's extramarital sexual activity was prohibited, polygamy was also about the control of married female sexuality. Moreover, by limiting younger men's ability to contract sexual relationships and marriage (which happened if they lacked bridewealth—see later), it was about the control of younger male sexuality. Because of this, it might appear that polygamy was an essential feature of patriarchal social formations. However, not all polygamous societies were patriarchal and vice versa.

Another explanation for polygamy also focuses on fertility, though somewhat differently. Here, demographers attribute the practice to a need to promote infant health. Polygamy allowed men to have sex in recognized relationships, while their wives practiced postpartum sexual abstinence and extended breastfeeding. This argument, though, is inflected by confusion around whether it was sex or fertility that polygamy guaranteed for men in such circumstances, as well as assumptions about male sexual entitlement. It is true, though, that in many African societies, sexual abstinence, especially for men, was viewed as having negative effects.

Notwithstanding its often similar rationale, the form that polygamy took across the continent was not constant. While most African marriages required bridewealth (gifts from the groom's family to the bride's in exchange for her labor and fertility), polygamy had additional demands in this area. However, differences in the nature of bridewealth and the control wives had over their bridewealth, as well as the presence or absence of the ranking of wives, meant that not all polygamous relationships were similar.

The presence of Islam also affected the nature of polygamy. Men and women might move through polygamous relationships at different points in their lives. In addition, a fine line existed between polygamy and other forms of male–female relationships like concubinage.

However, polygamy should not be treated as being of anthropological interest alone. During the nineteenth century, it became an increasingly contested site as missionaries, converts, colonial officials, and aspirant nationalists fought over its existence and meaning.

Much of Sub-Saharan Africa's nineteenth-century history is linked to mission Christianity, which found its particular Achilles' heel in polygamy. Both Protestant evangelical and Catholic missionaries were strongly opposed to the practice, tolerance being limited to a few key individuals. Polygamy was, for the missionaries, contrary to the word of God, indicative of sexual immorality, encouraging of adultery, and it also turned women into slaves. Missionaries generally required potential male converts to relinquish additional wives before baptism (in most cases, they recognized women's limited power to exit unwanted marriages). Polygamy thus served as a barrier to incorporation into the colonial social order. The relinquishment of polygamy, together with other sorts of sexual depravity (according to Christian definition) served as a marker of African acceptance in European society. In a few colonies, missionaries influenced the colonial state to the extent that it attempted to prohibit polygamy.

However, toward the end of the nineteenth century, Christian African men began to challenge the missionary view of polygamy (women's lack of power in the colonial context meant they seldom participated openly in these debates). Support for polygamy as well as a desire for religious independence led many Africans to form their own churches, free of European control. In this way, polygamy served as a protonationalist rallying point for aspirant African nationalists. For some of these men, understandings of sexuality contrary to those held by the missionaries were used to challenge the Christian condemnation of polygamy.

Further Reading: Cooper, Barbara M. *Marriage in Maradi: Gender and Culture in a Hausa Society in Niger, 1900–1989*. Portsmouth, NH: Heinemann, 1997; Delius, Peter and Clive Glaser. "The Myths of Polygamy: A History of Extra-Marital and Multi-Partnership Sex in South Africa." *South African Historical Journal* 50 (2004): 84–114; Phillips, Arthur, ed. *Survey of African Marriage and Family Life*. London: Oxford University Press, 1953.

Natasha Erlank

POLYGAMY, AMERICAN.   While "polygyny" is the term properly employed to describe the espousal of one man to several women, "polygamy" was almost universally favored when referring to that practice in the nineteenth century, and is the usage adhered to throughout this article. As one of the most commonly permitted marital patterns in all ages of the world, polygamous marriages were known from the lives of Biblical patriarchs. Christian missionaries and explorers often encountered them in nonwestern societies. Numbers of scholars during and after the Reformation pointed to these instances as evidence that neither scripture nor nature opposed such an arrangement. While a variety of marital configurations were attempted by nineteenth-century reformers, in the West, the taking of a plurality of wives was overwhelmingly a practice associated with The Church of Jesus Christ of Latter-Day Saints or Mormons. They, more than all others of their time, both practiced polygamy and extolled its advantages.

Mormonism's founder, Joseph Smith, Jr. (1805–1844), claimed he was given a divine mandate to restore the truths of earlier dispensations in Judeo-Christian history. This and his practice of sealing couples to each other for eternity provided the basis for marrying multiple women to a single husband. In a revelation given to Smith in 1843, when the young church was centered in Illinois, the faithful were commanded to enter such relationships. Like the ancient patriarch, Abraham, they were promised that their offspring would be as numerous as the stars of heaven, and if faithful, they would continue to reproduce and rule over their progeny in worlds without end. Pursuant to this command, Smith himself took more than thirty women as wives in secret ceremonies. Thirty or so of his closest disciples also married in polygamy. Moral criticism of the practice both in and outside the church, however, contributed to Smith's assassination by an angry mob in June 1844.

Soon thereafter, under the leadership of Brigham Young (1801–1877), thousands made their way to the relative isolation of the Salt Lake Valley in the American West, where they could practice their religion more freely. In 1852, the Saints publicly proclaimed plural **marriage** as an important tenet of their faith. Missionaries defended the system, and church leaders urged all faithful members to enter "the Principle." In addition to claiming divine permission for the arrangement, arguments were made that if sexual intercourse was used only for purposes of reproduction, and lust was banished from the thought of prospective parents, greater health and longevity would follow. The elimination of lustful and romantic feelings between partners also decreased the likelihood, it was claimed, that jealousy would disturb polygamous home life. Polygamy was also said to reinforce patriarchal authority, something Mormons insisted contemporary society desperately needed. Finally, they argued, with a plurality of wives, a man could bring more children into the world than in monogamy, thereby aggrandizing his dominion and glory in the next life.

The proportion of members who entered plural marriage seldom exceeded 30 percent of the Mormon population. Furthermore, even this number gradually decreased after 1860. In addition to the persistence of monogamous sentiments, the general parity of number between the genders assured that plural wifery could never become a practical choice for a majority of Mormon men, and those who did become pluralists, seldom married more than two or three women. Nevertheless, the total number of men, women, and children living in polygamous households during the years of its official approval, undoubtedly amounted to tens of thousands, making it perhaps the largest organized departure from traditional monogamy, excepting religious celibacy, in centuries of Euro-American history.

The contention that polygamy was enjoined as a way to care for excess numbers of women in Mormon society is doubtful. Throughout the nineteenth century in the United States, the sexes were generally equal in number, sometimes even finding males in a slight majority, especially in the American West. However, it is true that women who were marginalized by misfortunes such as **divorce** and widowhood were sometimes taken by men as plural spouses. Despite claims made by apologists that polygamy brought greater domestic happiness than monogamy, divorce seems to have occurred at least three times more often in the families of Mormon pluralists than in Latter-Day Saint monogamous unions. Jealousy, economic distress, and incompatibility were major reasons for such failures.

A federal **law** was passed by Congress in 1862 that criminalized polygamy in United States territories. In the case of *Reynolds vs. United States* (1879), the United States Supreme Court upheld the act, refusing to see it as a violation of the First

Amendment's freedom of religion clause. More coercive federal legislation followed in the 1880s, prohibiting polygamous "**cohabitation**." A flurry of convictions under the statutes sent hundreds of Mormon "cohabs" to prison. Church properties were confiscated and ecclesiastical leaders, nearly all of whom were polygamous, were forced into hiding. Dislocation was so great that by the late 1880s, Mormon spokesmen were insisting that polygamous marriages were no longer performed. This was formalized in 1890, when the church's president, Wilford Woodruff (1807–1898), issued his famous Manifesto, a document subsequently interpreted as providing divine approval for bringing the practice to an end. The United States Congress rewarded Utah with statehood in 1896, an accolade denied in the past chiefly because of the region's peculiar ideas about sex and marriage.

While it took decades following the 1890 manifesto for nineteenth-century Mormon polygamists to pass away, a surprising number of twentieth and twenty-first-century fundamentalists have sprung up, patterning their lives on Mormonism's nineteenth-century teachings. This notwithstanding, fundamentalist charges that the mainline church has apostatized from truths revealed by heaven to their forbearers has little effect in persuading the overwhelming majority of contemporary Mormons to return to earlier sexual and marital ideals. The modern church is thoroughly committed to monogamy and excommunicates all who seek a return to the older, polygamous way.

Further Reading: Daynes, Kathryn M. *More Wives than One: Transformation of the Mormon Marriage System, 1840–1910*. Urbana and Chicago: University of Illinois Press, 2001; Embry, Jessie L. *Mormon Polygamous Families: Life in the Principle*. Salt Lake City: University of Utah Press, 1987; Foster, Lawrence. *Religion and Sexuality: Three American Communal Experiments of the Nineteenth Century*. New York: Oxford University Press, 1981; Hardy, B. Carmon. *Solemn Covenant: The Mormon Polygamous Passage*. Urbana and Chicago: University of Illinois Press, 1992; Van Wagoner, Richards S. *Mormon Polygamy: A History*. 2nd ed. rev. Salt Lake City: Signature Books, 1989.

B. Carmon Hardy

POPULAR SCIENCE. *See* Science, Popular

PORNOGRAPHY AND EROTICA. Pornography and erotica are visual or literary materials that are created with the intent to stimulate sexual arousal. The two words have different meanings as is suggested by their etymology. The word pornography comes from the Greek *pornographos*, meaning writing of harlots. However, erotica or *erōtikos*, also derived from the Greek, means tending to arouse sexual love or desire. All cultures have evidence of sexually explicit material, although the meaning has changed from preliterate to modern societies. Cave art and ancient- or tribal-culture stone, wood, or ceramic images are believed to be more related to fertility or procreational rather than recreational sex.

In the nineteenth century a repressive atmosphere arose regarding the outward expression and sharing of sexual information. As a backlash to this censorship and hypocrisy, erotic literature and art proliferated in a variety of styles. Henry Spencer Ashbee was the epitome of a Victorian gentleman who led a double life. During his lifetime, he collected as much erotic literature as he could find. Under the pseudonym, Pisanus Fraxi (itself a scatological play on words), he published three books: *Index Librorum Prohibitoru: being notes bio-biblio-icono-graphical and critical on curious and uncommon books* (1877), *Centuria Librorum Absconditorum* (1879), and *Catena Librorum Tacendorum* (1885). The latter was a trilogy of lists of prohibited books, lists of historical figures who practiced sodomy or other sexual "perversions," and

HOW A WINE-ROOM SYREN LEARNED THE EXTENT OF A
LOUD YOUNG MAN'S WEALTH—A SUIT OF CLOTHES THAT
WAS NOT SO GOOD AS IT LOOKED.

Pornography masquerading as reportage: "Prostitution," a line
engraving from the *Police Gazette*, 1887. © The Granger
Collection, New York.

descriptions and comments on the available
erotica of his time. He is believed to be the
author of the popular *Walter, My Secret Life*,
originally eleven volumes, containing over
3,000 pages written by an anonymous
author, but condensed to a 640-page publication. The style is similar to that of
Pisanus Fraxi, and the time period and street
names coincide with his lifetime and places
of residence. He is believed to be the author,
because he was in a position both financially
and socially to write about such matters. His
writings are more like a confessional than
constructed to generate prurient interest,
and describe a wide variety of variations in
human sexual behavior, which his contemporaries might not have had the opportunity
to experience. When he died, his collection
numbered over a thousand books of "obscene
and erotica character." In *My Secret Life*, the
author described his own sexual awakening
and observations about women and their
bodies. As he advances in his sexual career,
his writings provide an ethnographic look at
both the nineteenth-century sex vocabulary
and behavior. Some of his most detailed
passages, in the pages that have remained in
publication, involve the succession of events
in convincing or seducing virgins or those ignorant in sexual matters. The more he
experiments, the greater the panorama of behaviors he experiences and observes.
Some of those acts described were illegal if discovered. Homosexual behavior was
known as sodomy, and considered a capital offence until 1828, punishable afterward
by imprisonment.

One of the most dramatic legal pronouncements was against Gustave Flaubert
(1821–1880) and his novel *Madame Bovary* (1857). Emma, the main character has
doubts about her marriage to a doctor. "Before she married, she thought she was in love;
but the happiness that should have resulted from that love, somehow had not come. It
seemed to her that she must have made a mistake, have misunderstood in some way or
other." Nonetheless, she soon recognizes that she is bored, and that there is no passion
in her married life. She becomes sexually involved with a man, and then another, who
does arouse her emotionally. The language in *Madame Bovary* is literate, but the
prosecutors never read the book and refused to quote passages from it because it was too
reprehensible. Instead, they summarized what issues they believed were immoral. First,
they found it disgraceful that a married woman questioned the value of the institution
of marriage. Second, her independent voice and agency was a rarity. Her boredom
with domesticity went against the "cult of pure womanhood" and the standards that
women were supposed to uphold. The idea that a woman would choose to have an
adulterous relationship while married was unacceptable to the moral censors. That
alone magnified the evils of the writing.

Paul Verlaine's *Amies*, a collection of poems and photographs that described bisexual, heterosexual, and homosexual sex was considered "obscene," and a shipment of the material was seized by the French government and destroyed. However, Verlaine was able to republish the material and distribute it. He is the founder of the Symbolist movement, and was referred to as the Prince of Poets. Other French authors of erotica labeled obscene, were Alfred de Musset (1810–1857), who had an affair with George Sand, Théophile Gautier (1811–1872), who was influential in shaping the erotic nature of female vampires in literature, and Charles Baudelaire (1821–1867), who was prosecuted for *Fleurs du Mal*. Friedrich Karl Forberg (1770–1848), an atheist, published *De Figuris Veneris*, a collection of ancient texts describing sexual behavior with illustrations showing group sex, homosexual sex, sex with animals, oral and anal sex, and flagellation. However, the text was in Latin, so that none but the scholarly could understand it. **Algernon Charles Swinburne** (1837–1909) wrote *Lesbia Brandon*, a novel based on the ancient Greek lesbian poet, Sappho. He also wrote poems about **flagellation** and the pleasures associated with masochism. In 1872, the German psychiatrist **Richard von Krafft-Ebing** wrote *Psychopathia sexualis*, a book about sexual perversion or what was considered perversion during his lifetime. Much of the information is in Latin. Often, physicians would hide material in this way to "protect the innocent." Books dealing with sexual physiology were written to inform the public about subjects previously considered too indelicate or mysterious to be understood, and contained coded phrases, such as the solitary vice, referring to **masturbation**, or the social vice, referring to **prostitution**. It is not surprising what with such hazy, ambiguous writings, that novels and explicit descriptions were preferred if one wanted to learn about sexual behavior.

Uncontrolled passion, such as that of *Therese Raquin*, Zola's protagonist in the novel by the same name, and her lover, that leads to the murder of her husband, is punished, in this case by a form of divine retribution that prevents them from enjoying sex because they are overwhelmed with guilt. Honore de Balzac (1799–1850) wrote short stories (*La Contes Drolatiques*) similar to Boccacio's *Decameron*, where pranks and delightful manipulations of amorous situations result in amusing endings. Arthur Schnitzler (1862–1931), a late nineteenth-century physician, who preferred writing to practicing medicine or surgery, wrote poetry, plays, and novellas that dealt with sexual hypocrisy and politics in addition to sexual themes. One play, *Reigen* deals with serial monogamous relationships, and was declared obscene and banned when performed in 1920. Another play, *Traumnovelle*, was made into the 1990s movie *Eyes Wide Shut*.

Erotica of the art world produced a multiplicity of themes. In 1866, Courbet (1819–1877) was commissioned to paint *L'origine du Monde*, a woman's torso seen from the pubic region and stopping above her breasts. The realism of this painting is almost photographic, yet its title invokes subtle humor. *The Sleepers* (also 1866) was considered a startling image of lesbian love. Whereas in previous centuries, naked women in groups of two or three were mythological figures, the nineteenth century provided their contemporaries on canvas. Other popular themes were prostitution, nuns and priests having sex, or consensual flagellation. Felicien Rops's (1833–1898) erotic art dealt with fantasy themes, such as naked women walking pigs on a leash or women suspended Christ-like on crucifixes.

Interestingly, although the subject matter of erotica and pornography of the nineteenth century contains heterosexual sex, homosexual sex, group sex, and forbidden sexual experiences, such as those of religious authority figures with lay people, there are few violent or hateful images. Certain authors believe that it was not until the twentieth century, when women received the right to vote and gained political power that erotica became more pornographic, as a backlash against their independence. It appears that in the nineteenth century, the violations of sexual standards were voluntary and consensual, whereas later pornography was frequently laden with pain, torture, and violence against women.

Further Reading: Anonymous. *My Secret Life*. New York: Blue Moon Books, 1988; Banned Books Online: http://www.my-secret-life.com. Bishop, Clifford and Xenia Osthelder. *Sexualia: From Prehistory to Cyberspace*. Berlin: Könemann, 2000; D'Emilio, John and Estelle B. Freedman. *Intimate Matters: A History of Sexuality in America*. New York: Harper and Row, 1988; Foucault, Michel. *The History of Sexuality*. Vol. 1. New York: Vintage, 1978; Gibson, Ian. *Erotomaniac*. London: Faber, 2001; Marcus, Steven. *The Other Victorians*. New York: Basic Books, 1966; Neret, Gilles. *Erotica Universalis*. Koln, Germany: Taschen, 1994; Homosexuality and the Law in England: www.law.umkc.edu/faculty/projects/ftrials/wilde/wildelawpage.html.

Lana Thompson

PREGNANCY AND CHILDBIRTH. In the era before medical tests for pregnancy, quickening remained the most reliable sign of pregnancy in the great majority of cases. This meant that a good many women remained uncertain about the status of their pregnancy until the fourth month, when they could feel the baby's movements. Although the stethoscope had been invented in 1819, allowing the doctor to hear the fetal heartbeat, most women never visited a doctor during their pregnancies during this period. It was even rarer for women to visit a hospital during pregnancy, with only the very poor resorting there in desperate cases. Wealthy women would visit a doctor in order to have a pregnancy confirmed, or to get advice on behavior while pregnant, since the health of their infants was seen as important to the future of the families to which they belonged. Only royalty had routine medical care throughout the nine months of pregnancy. Because women tended to continue having babies until relatively close to the menopause, multiple births in older mothers were common, and multiparity was a frequent cause of pregnancy loss.

Women were very reluctant to announce a pregnancy prematurely, because crying wolf could result in ridicule. Probably the most famous "pregnancy" of the nineteenth century was that of Joanna Southcott, leader of a religious cult which gained large numbers of followers in the early years of the century. Southcott's miraculous pregnancy at the age of sixty-four, in 1814, was supposed to result in the birth of the second Christ. No baby arrived, and Southcott's subsequent death resulted in the rapid dwindling of the group. Claims of pregnancy could also save the lives of female criminals, or help them to avoid transportation. A pregnant woman convicted of a crime could "plead her belly" to avoid execution, but only from quickening, in order to avoid false and unverifiable claims.

For those women who did consult doctors, bleeding pregnant women remained a popular medical treatment for the first half of the century, and remained in demand longer among the less educated. Antenatal bleeding was believed to rebalance the body's humors, and was also considered to alleviate most of the unpleasant symptoms of pregnancy. Bloodletting was also resorted to in order to ensure that the baby did not suffer from an overindulgent maternal diet. This was part of the "lowering system," dominant in pregnancy care throughout the nineteenth century. It also required pregnant women to eat simple, plain food. This was sometimes taken to the point where affluent women were put on a strict vegetarian diet during pregnancy. The evidence suggests that upper-class women generally welcomed this, as it meant a smaller baby, with a better chance of easy delivery. Among the poor, of course, insufficient diet was not a matter of choice, but of necessity, and was a fact of daily life. Doctors advised that high living impaired fertility as well, arguing that the poor were very prolific. In actual fact, there was no truth in this, as the average **marriage** in the upper classes resulted in eight children, with the middle classes bearing seven live children per marriage. The averagely fertile women, of any class, could expect approximately eight pregnancies in a childbearing span of about eighteen years.

The term "confinement" has led some historians to assume that pregnant women in this period were not seen in public. This was not the case. Aristocratic and affluent women maintained a high social profile throughout pregnancy, going to parties, balls, and other social events. They were advised to live as normally as possible during pregnancy, in the hopes of keeping their spirits up. They normally continued to ride on horseback for exercise and traveled abroad until late in their pregnancies. Those who were confined to the home were constrained because of ill health rather than social decorum. Fresh air was also considered "lowering," providing more evidence that pregnant women were not restricted to the home. Poorer women, of course, continued their work and household duties as usual during pregnancy, as did agricultural field laborers.

The theory of maternal impressions was still widely accepted in the nineteenth century. It was thought that the longings of a pregnant woman, or any sight or event that frightened her, could leave an impression on the baby, usually in the form of a physical deformity or birthmark. Pregnant women were careful, accordingly, to avoid distressing scenes and to moderate their appetites. Both doctors and popular folklore told them that it was important to regulate their emotions in pregnancy, in order to prevent damage to the baby.

There was a widespread belief in the existence of a disorder called "insanity of pregnancy." This was an obstetric theory that linked pregnancy to depression and suicide attempts, which was developed in the 1820s and 1830s, and was often used to defend women accused of child murder, or infanticide. The most dangerous malady of pregnancy was eclampsia, which could be fatal. The symptoms were frothing at the mouth, convulsions, and loss of consciousness, often followed by a speedy death. It was treated with bleeding and laxatives. In any medical emergency during pregnancy, the mother's life was preferred to that of the child. In an era when infant mortality was high even with the best of care, favoring the child's life over the mother's was unthinkable.

Infertile women were flooded with advice and sympathy. Remedies for infertility included mineral water and abstinence from sex. Some women even induced vomiting because it was believed to be a good sign of a healthy pregnancy. Acton thought that women were repulsed by sex during pregnancy, and there is evidence that some women welcomed pregnancy and lactation as a period in which they could legitimately withdraw from sexual activity with their husbands. On the other hand, journals and diaries suggest that some women enjoyed a heightened interest in sex during pregnancy, freed as they were from fear of conception. Miscarriages were assumed to be the fault of the woman, usually because she had overexerted herself or exposed herself to a shocking sight.

In the early nineteenth century, about a third of brides were pregnant at marriage. Evidence suggests that premarital pregnancy was more common in rural than urban areas. Pregnancy that did not result in marriage before the child's birth was considered shameful, and could result in child murder in extreme cases. Given the rudimentary state of medical knowledge, it was very difficult to determine whether a baby had been stillborn or was the victim of infanticide. Some women, especially unmarried mothers who may have attempted to conceal their pregnancy, killed their infants in terror and despair. The corsets worn for much of the period meant that it was possible to conceal a pregnancy if the fetus was small until quite close to full term.

Wealthy women traveled to London to have their babies, where high-quality medical advice could be procured if required. Childbirth was hazardous and women's letters and diaries suggest that many looked forward to it with terror, especially in the first confinement. Labor was often allowed to continue for two or three days, because there was strong faith in allowing nature to take its course. It was considered usual to give birth on one's side with the knees drawn up and (if a doctor was present) with one's back to the doctor, a posture known as Sim's position. Forceps were by far the most common form of obstetric intervention, although an early form of vacuum extractor was invented by James Young Simpson in Edinburgh in the 1840s. Cesarean births were extremely rare, and were only carried out in cases where the pelvis was too deformed for normal childbirth. Doctors found it impossible to stem the hemorrhaging following a cesarean without removing the entire uterus. A study in the 1880s of 134 cesarean operations in Europe, Russia, and the United States, found that the mortality rate for the mother was 56 percent, and that the child almost invariably died. A real danger of any childbirth was sepsis transmission from the doctor to the patient, resulting in the often fatal "childbed fever," actually puerperal fever. Sir James Simpson introduced the use of anesthesia in 1847. **Queen Victoria** is often credited with popularizing anesthesia during childbirth, using it for her labor in 1853, and making it fashionable. Recuperation after childbirth was lengthy, and many women did not leave home until they had undergone the religious ritual of "churching" (which was a service of thanksgiving for the mother's safety), held one to two months after the baby's birth.

Wet nursing was extremely susceptible to changes in fashion over the course of the nineteenth century; at times, even very wealthy and titled women aspired to nurse their own infants. At other times, any woman who could afford it hired a wet nurse. Of course, those infants whose mothers died or could not produce milk required a wet nurse. As the rudimentary feeding bottles available at the time were so unsatisfactory, and the milk supplies were impure, very few infants fed in this manner survived. Women often nursed their children for a very long time in an attempt to space their pregnancies further apart.

Eugenics theory, becoming more popular toward the end of the century, stressed the duty of women in the middle and upper classes to have more children for the good of the **race**. It was thought that poor woman (assumed to be of inferior intellectual and moral standards) were having too many children, while intelligent woman of the wealthier classes were believed to be having too few. Combined with this was a growing horror of hereditary disease that could be passed down from tainted parent to tainted child, weakening both the family and the nation. In the 1890s and after, there was particular concern that men were infecting their wives and their unborn children with syphilis. The social Darwinists were fascinated by pregnancy, and considered fecundity as a female substitute for the intellectual life. Because pregnancy, childbirth, and lactation were considered to be instinctive, it was thought that education was not required in order to live a fulfilled life as a woman. Herbert Spencer argued that reproduction and intellectual development were incompatible, because all of women's energy was required for procreation. He concluded that if women's subordination was necessary for the good of the British race, then women's subordination should be accepted.

Further Reading: Hanson, Claire. *A Cultural History of Pregnancy: Pregnancy, Medicine and Culture, 1750–1900.* Basingstoke: Palgrave Macmillan, 2004; Lewis, Judith Schneid. *In the Family*

Way: Childbearing in the British Aristocracy 1760–1860. New Brunswick, NJ: Rutgers University Press, 1986; O' Dowd, Michael and Elliott Philipp. The History of Obstetrics and Gynecology. New York: Parthenon, 1994.

Susan Mumm

PROSTITUTION. The common expression used when discussing prostitution throughout the nineteenth century in Europe was that it was "the oldest profession," and an inevitable and unpleasant fact of life. Contemporary accounts and much historiography of the subject have tended to treat prostitution as a static and transhistorical phenomenon. However, recent studies focusing on specific countries during defined periods of time, not only demonstrate the historically contingent nature of the trade in purchased sex, but reveal the extent to, and the rapidity with, which massive changes were taking place in the nineteenth century. The most obvious changes concerned official attitudes toward the profession and its regulation, and later in the century, a vigorous critique of this system by feminist and radical campaigners. It would also appear that the sexual marketplace was itself in a constant process of mutation, reflecting the wider processes of economic, social, and ideological transformation occurring throughout the century.

Industrialization, rapid urbanization, the development of new and more efficient modes of transportation, had an enormous impact on existing social structures, taking place at somewhat different stages and at different rates in the various regions of Europe. In some areas, systems based in the family economy had already been largely replaced by wage labor, and in others, this was only beginning to manifest by the later decades of the century. One outcome of these changes, significant for developments in the sex trade, was the influx of the young and unmarried, both male and female, into urban centers in pursuit of waged work. Traditional community practices of control over young adults and their sexuality were thus no longer in operation. In many areas, the young women who flocked to urban centers in search of either industrial or domestic work, were presumed to be all fallen women, since they fitted into no other accepted category.

The nineteenth century saw a major struggle to define and categorize "the prostitute" even though this identity remained, and still is, enormously problematic. Women moved in and out of sex work. If they were engaged in certain trades where the demand for workers fluctuated over the course of year, they might resort to selling themselves during the slack periods. Involvement might also vary over the life course, with young women trading in sex for a few years, just as they might work in a shop or factory, in order to build up a little nest egg prior to settling down in marriage. It was not necessarily a lifetime career choice. Women married to men pursuing occupations that took them away from home for long periods of time, such as sailors, might turn to prostitution during these absences as a means of providing for the family. Domestic **servants** might occasionally go with men for pay, as well as for distraction from the tedium of their lives. Other low-paid female occupations were subject to the temptation to supplement meager wages. Poverty did not provide a simple universal explanation: many impoverished women eschewed the temptations of vice, and observers often noted that, less than absolute poverty, desire for the little luxuries a working woman could not afford formed a powerful motivation.

The profession, if thus it can be designated, itself covered a huge range of differentiated labor, reflecting the social and economic complexities of a commercial and industrialized society. At the top were the grandes horizontales, elite courtesans whose clientele consisted of the wealthy and aristocratic and even royalty. Their power

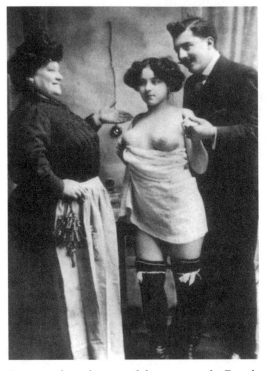

A picture from the turn of the century of a French prostitute with her madame and a client. © The Granger Collection, New York.

of choice over whom they accepted (though for enormous sums of money) was a major factor in their allure. At the bottom were destitute women inhabiting makeshift shelters on the outskirts of army camps, living in parks or on streets and alleys, ragged, malnourished, diseased, verminous, exchanging use of their bodies for paltry sums or a glass of gin. In between were women reflecting the purchasing power and requirements of men at all levels of the social structure. Brothels ranged from sumptuous high-class establishments to production-line versions, in which the inmates might service forty or fifty men a day. Outside brothels, there were women who solicited on the street, or picked up men in bars, cafes, or dance halls; inserted coded advertisements into newspapers and other periodicals; had discreet arrangements with a group of selected customers; and a great range of other possibilities. Women, particularly those who remained in the life, might find themselves in very different positions over the course of the career: usually, though not always, involving a decline in status and conditions as age and disease took their toll.

There were also national differences: for example, in Britain, prostitution was far less institutionalized within brothels than in much of mainland Europe, with most women being independent operators. Several scholars have discerned changes over the course of the nineteenth century in the nature of the trade. With the increasing efficiency of transport, it became a much more international trade, with prostitutes not only moving across European borders, but going to North and South America, and many parts of Asia. In some cases, this was the result of falling into the hands of organized trafficking networks, but it was not uncommon for women to move around on their own initiative to seek out better opportunities (or evade the police). Even those who were trafficked were seldom the decoyed innocents of urban legend. There were women already at least on the margins of prostitution, though possibly persuaded by procurers' misrepresentations about the circumstances they could expect elsewhere.

By the later decades of the century, the number of enclosed brothels had declined, mutating into houses of assignation and accommodation where prostitutes could take their customers in return for rental charges, while much of the trade moved into the more informal atmosphere of bars, cafes, and cigar-divans. Elite brothels increasingly offered facilities for various exotic practices, from **flagellation**, which had long been a common speciality, to variations, such as oral sex, and provision for all kinds of fetishes, in a seductive atmosphere of sophisticated sensuality, a long way from simple provision for male physiological necessities. With the increasing mobility of populations, travel and tourism played a part in the demand for prostitution.

The nineteenth-century prostitute seldom, if ever, wrote her own story, except in the case of certain elite courtesans, but in these cases they were almost certainly complying with the demands of an existing literary genre of "whore biography." Most of the discourses about the prostitute and prostitution were generated by men, and consisted of the fantasies of customers or the perceptions of those who wished to control, if not eradicate, the trade in sexuality. The prostitute was pervasively characterized as lazy. The men who wrote on the subject seem to have been largely unable to conceive what these women did to survive and make a living as work. When women entered the debate, they were philanthropists or reformers, speaking on behalf of other women whom they constructed as the abject victims of male lust. The voices of the women who exchanged sexual favors for money are discernable, if at all, in reported speech, mediated through the preconceptions of the reporter, whether representative of the state, journalist, or moral campaigner.

Most medicosociological observations of "the prostitute" were based on encounters with the lowlier echelons of the profession, the most likely to come to police and medical attention, and associated with wider fears about the "dangerous classes" of society. From French sanitarian reformer Parent-Duchatelet in 1836 (*De la prostitution dans la ville de Paris, considerée sous le rapport de l'hygiene publique, de la morale et de l'administration* was influential and much cited throughout Europe) to Italian criminologist Lombroso in 1893 (*La donna delinquente: la prostituta e la donna normale*), there was an attempt to construct the prostitute as a particular type, distinct from the normal run of womankind, inevitably drawn into the profession, and on that basis to be segregated as much as possible. The British venereologist **William Acton**, however, in spite of being strongly influenced by contemporary French discourses, drew attention to the movement of women into and out of the profession in his 1857 volume *Prostitution Considered in its Moral, Social & Sanitary Aspects*.

Even more shadowy than the prostitute herself is the figure of the client. Who were the men who bought sex, for what reasons, and under what circumstances? There were certain groups known to frequent prostitutes, for example, men in mobile occupations in which marriage was strongly discouraged or forbidden, such as soldiers and sailors. Throughout much of Europe, there was a culture of young men, at least in urban areas, seeking sexual initiation in brothels, and continuing to frequent them in later life. Many men in all social classes were unable to marry for economic reasons, but presumably occasionally able to purchase sexual relief. There is also evidence that married men continued to patronize prostitutes, for a variety of reasons, such as to spare their wives' unwelcome sexual advances or unwanted pregnancies, or to indulge in practices that they could not request in the marriage bed. But, for men in the respectable classes, discretion was of major importance, and this was reflected in the provisions for them, which tend to be less visible to the historian than the lower levels of the sex trade.

Also shadowy, though rather less since they tended to come to the attention of the **law**, were the intermediaries of the profession: the brothel keepers and procurers who were essential to the system and profited by it much more than most of the women themselves. Madams and male brothel keepers occupied an ambivalent position. They were often depended upon by the police to keep the inmates conforming to the conditions under which prostitution was tolerated, and to bring them along for their regular inspections. However, these expectations tended to conflict with the effective commercial operation of brothels.

A number of historians have drawn attention to the rise of homosexual cultures in European urban spaces, accelerated by urban expansion and social mobility of the nineteenth century. While these involved a good deal of mutual and noncommercial same-sex activity, there were also male prostitutes catering to this specialized market, often engaging in blackmail on the side. They were not subject to systems of regulation by moral policing in the same way as female prostitutes, but were affected by various laws relating to homosexual activity, soliciting, public indecency, and vagrancy. Nevertheless, nineteenth-century debates and documents on prostitution focus almost exclusively on female sex workers.

In spite of the rhetorical position that prostitution was an eternal and unchanging problem, officials in many countries during the nineteenth century perceived it to be one that was on the increase and becoming more visible (or possibly more noxious to new standards of respectability and public decency). In the interests of public order and hygiene, most European countries undertook some form of regulation to control the visible manifestations of the sex trade. This was not about actually legalizing prostitution, but establishing certain limits within which the activity would be tolerated and subjected to surveillance. The pioneer in this, much cited as the exemplar by other nations, was France. The mechanism of regulation was applied as administrative practice, on a local and municipal basis, rather than through statutory legislation as a monolithic national structure in France and in several other European nations. Even in countries where national laws were passed (such as Russia), the actual operation of these laws were subject to a good deal of local interpretation and differences of practice.

In the ideal form of this system, prostitutes were to be sequestered within brothels which were to be extremely discreet, not thrusting themselves upon the attention of decent women, children, and young people, and any others who did not fall into that category of those who would potentially frequent brothels for the relief of their physiological urges. Brothels were thus not to display their existence, with no windows onto the public street, and the women were only to go out, if at all, at designated hours.

Many women were resistant to the degree of control and surveillance that working within a brothel involved, as well as the potential for economic exploitation of the inmates by the madam. Many countries, therefore, recognized this reality by instituting a system of licensing, intended to bring women prostituting themselves outside brothels under the purview of the law and into the system of medical inspection. However, many women did not want to have any contact at all with the policing system (since this was rife with extortion and abuse of power), or to be legally identified as prostitutes. Thus, in all countries that had systems of regulation, there was a continuing problem of clandestine prostitution, as well as the casual variety. Police corruption, involving blackmail and bribery, was a common concomitant of regulation.

An argument that was strongly made for regulation was that there was a hygienic benefit in a system that enforced the regular medical inspection of prostitutes for venereal diseases. Even some contemporary observers were skeptical about this, noting the cursory and careless nature of inspections as carried out by the designated police surgeons, the existence of traditional means by which madams could conceal signs of infection in order that women could continue working, and the fact that a woman certified clean could contract VD almost immediately afterward, and infect large numbers of customers before her next inspection. Apart from the dubious accuracy of diagnosis throughout the period (even given rather more careful examinations), the likelihood of a cure during incarceration in hospital was problematic. At best, the system might remove women from circulation during the most infectious stages of syphilis or gonorrhea.

In both Protestant and Catholic countries, there was a tradition of philanthropic provision for the repentant prostitute who wished to leave the profession. However, while authority might concede that women had the right to quit this way of life, this was an individual decision, and the way was seldom easy, usually involving harshly disciplinary magdalene institutions, even if the philanthropists framed their work in terms of rescue. This was conceptualized within religious ideas of the repenting of a sinful way of life, and did not affect the system except at a negligible level.

This changed in the later decades of the nineteenth century with the rise of an abolitionist campaign. This was, at least in principle, not about completely repressing prostitution, but getting rid of the prevailing systems of regulation, which it was claimed effectively enslaved women—a concept embodied in the term "**white slavery**" (which however soon came to be understood as the abduction of unwilling women into a life of shame).

The abolitionist movement originated in Britain where regulation was introduced, in a limited form, in the 1860s, with the passing of the **Contagious Diseases Acts**. These were intended to improve the health of the Queen's forces by enabling the medical inspection of prostitutes, and their incarceration until "cured" in lock hospitals if found to be diseased, in designated port and garrison towns. The selling of sexual services by women to men was not illegal in the United Kingdom. The laws affecting it were phrased in terms of questions of public decency and committing nuisance by soliciting. Women who were doing nothing illegal were, under the Contagious Diseases Acts, being forcibly subjected to painful physical examinations and indefinitely incarcerated on (often suspect) police and medical testimony. The acts aroused considerable antagonism, on religious, civil liberty, class, and gender grounds, leading to a vigorous campaign for their repeal.

A major aspect of this campaign was a protofeminist protest against the institutionalization of provision for the gratification of male lust embodied in the acts, by women already concerned about the oppressive legal position of women, under the leadership of the charismatic **Josephine Butler**. These reformers pointed out the ways in which the policing of prostitution had repercussions for all women, and the way its existence inflected male attitudes toward women throughout society. Their aims soon came to extend beyond simply getting the acts repealed, to advocating a range of other measures that would reduce the exploitation of women in the sex trade, such as raising the **age of consent**, measures against intermediaries, and against trafficking between countries. Reformers made a plea for the revision of society's moral codes, and the substitution of a single moral standard based on that expected of decent women rather than the double standard that punished "fallen" women while excusing the petty sins attributed to male needs.

This new paradigm spread beyond Britain and across much of Europe. Social reformers and radicals were often sympathetic, perceiving the element of class and capitalist exploitation embedded within the existing system. Changing medical understanding of the VDs also played a part in causing doctors and policy makers to cast a critical eye on regulation. Syphilis and gonorrhea remained major public health problems with long-term deleterious effects, and it was recognized by the final decades of the nineteenth century how very pervasive they were throughout society. New ideas about transmission also made it seem increasingly unrealistic to endeavor to control these diseases by surveillance of only one side of the commercial sex transaction. It was also argued that youthful experiences with prostitutes (even if disease-free) did not adequately prepare men for marriage to a respectable woman of their own class.

Nonetheless, measures implemented theoretically to reduce the exploitation of sex workers tended to be punitive and counterproductive in practice. Neoregulationist legislation and administrative practices got rid of the most flagrant and objectionable abuses of the older system without abandoning the underlying structure and assumptions. Many in the burgeoning European **social purity** movement were more interested in suppressing prostitution or at least rendering it invisible than in ameliorating the conditions of women working as prostitutes. *Fin-de-siècle* fears about VDs also influenced attitudes and policies. Various forms of regulation remained in place in numerous parts of Europe well into the twentieth century, although the panic fears of the nineteenth century no longer fuelled debates on the subject. *See also* Penitentiaries and Lock Hospitals, Prostitution Regulated, White Slavery.

Further Reading: Bartley, Paula. *Prostitution: Prevention and Reform in Britain, 1860–1914.* London: Routledge, 1999; Bernstein, Laurie. *Sonia's Daughters: Prostitutes and Their Regulation in Imperial Russia.* Berkeley: University of California Press, 1995; Bristow, Edward. *Prostitution and Prejudice: The Jewish Fight against White Slavery, 1870–1939.* Oxford: Clarendon Press, 1982; Corbin, Alain. *Women for Hire: Prostitution and Sexuality in France after 1850.* Cambridge, MA: Harvard University Press, 1990; Corbin, Alain. *Time Desire and Horror: Towards a History of the Senses.* London: Polity Press, 1995; Finnegan, Frances. *Poverty and Prostitution: A Study of Victorian Prostitutes in York.* Cambridge: Cambridge University Press, 1979; Gibson, Mary. *Prostitution and the State in Italy, 1860–1915.* New Brunswick, NJ: Rutgers University Press, 1986; Harsin, Jill. *Policing Prostitution in Nineteenth Century Paris.* Princeton, NJ: Princeton University Press, 1985; Levine, Philippa. *Prostitution, Race, and Politics: Policing Venereal Disease in the British Empire.* London: Routledge, 2004; Mahood, Linda. *The Magdalenes: Prostitution in the Nineteenth Century.* London: Routledge, 1990; Walkowitz, Judith R. *Prostitution and Victorian Society: Women, Class and the State.* Cambridge: Cambridge University Press, 1980.

Lesley Hall

PROSTITUTION, REGULATED. In the mid-nineteenth century, the policy of trying to eliminate prostitution was replaced by one of trying to control it through regulation. The change in approach began in Paris and spread to other towns in France and abroad. **Prostitution** came to be seen as a necessary evil, essential to maintaining the prevailing moral and social values. Prostitutes provided predatory males with a sexual outlet. Without them, it was feared that the daughters and domestic servants of the middle classes would be at greater risk of being charmed and seduced by roguish males, bringing dishonor to themselves and their families. Regulation, however, should not be confused with legitimization. Prostitutes could not be allowed to live and work like members of any other occupational group. To allow them such freedom would be offensive to middle-class sensibilities and morally corrupting. The purpose of regulation was to push prostitution out of sight and shame those who practiced it. The analogy has been drawn with another unpalatable, but unavoidable feature of urban life that had to be addressed in the nineteenth century. Prostitution could no more be abolished than could sewage. The French approach to both was essentially the same: they had to be managed in such a way as to render them invisible to the middle classes. The similarity in approach is not surprising when one considers the influence in both areas of Alexandre Parent-Duchâtelet. A French doctor with a strong interest in public health matters, his work on the importance of adequate drainage in the growing towns was followed by his immensely influential study *De la Prostitution dans la Ville de Paris*, published in 1836. For the next thirty years, this work provided the definitive treatment of the subject, and its influence can be seen in the regulatory system adopted in the middle of the century in Paris and subsequently in other towns in France and beyond.

The system of regulation, sometimes referred to as the "French system," required all prostitutes (*les filles publiques*) to be placed on a register if they wished to work lawfully.

The authorized prostitute (*la fille soumise*) could fall into one of two categories. One was the woman who lodged in a brothel (commonly referred to as *la fille de maison* or *la fille à numéro*), the other was the woman who worked on her own (*la fille éparse; la fille isolée; la fille en carte*). Both would be issued with a license containing name, date of birth, and physical description of the holder, and sometimes other details, such as records of medical inspections. They had to be produced whenever demanded by the authorities. Brothels and those who ran them were also closely regulated. The Brussels regulations of 1852, for instance, precluded any signs to indicate to passers-by the nature of the premises and prohibited the residents from drawing attention by loitering at the front of the house or in the windows. All prostitutes were required to submit to regular medical inspection. Anyone found to be suffering from sexual infection would immediately be transported to hospital.

The regulations, and the thinking behind them, manifest a concern to prevent the spread of sexually transmitted disease. But the fear of infection was bound up with deeper middle-class anxieties that the prostitute seemed to personify. There was concern at the potential threat to the social order posed by the working classes. By 1880, widespread panic had started to set in about the potential of this disease to topple the middle classes as a result of their sons bringing it home from the brothels and transmitting it across the generations. For Parent-Duchâtelet, in the middle of the century, infection was a corollary of a more fundamental danger, that of moral contamination. The physician's principal function in the regulatory system was to counter this threat and reassert the moral authority of the middle class. To diagnose and treat sexually transmitted infections was to censure the patient with a reminder that the immediate cause of her affliction was the immorality of her conduct. Curing the sick was a secondary consideration. In fulfilling his function, the physician was supported by a regime of regular and compulsory medical examination, with patients being confined to a hospital dedicated to the treatment of prostitutes, or to jail if they refused to comply. At the end of their working lives, there was provision for the prostitutes to be accommodated in a refuge (*maison de relevement*). Above all, this was a system of enclosure that would confine the prostitute to a world sealed off from the rest of society, with the exception of the inspectors who visited regularly to ensure the regulations were being respected.

The measures for regulating prostitution were widely criticized and calls for their abolition, led by the campaigning work of **Josephine Butler**, became more vociferous throughout Europe. The salient defect in the regulations was that, in trying to keep prostitution in check, the burden fell exclusively on the providers of sexual services rather than being shared with their clients. There were different flaws in the system associated with the different categories of prostitute. For the *fille de maison*, the brothel was a place where vulnerable women were subjected to ruthless economic exploitation. The clients' fees would be paid to the brothel keeper who would make a generous deduction to cover the prostitutes' board and clothing allowances before passing on a modest proportion to the women. When they were not physically prevented from leaving the premises, they were housebound by the fact that the only attire in their possession consisted of skimpy garments intended to allure the clients, which would have attracted ridicule and contempt if worn on the street. The patronizing and often contemptuous opinion the authorities had of prostitutes—evident in the work of Parent-Duchâtelet—meant they were unsympathetic to protests by the women that they were being detained, and forced into selling sex against their will. The regulated brothel was thus a precondition for the existence of "**white slavery**."

The law regarding the independent prostitute posed a problem for any woman—irrespective of her occupation—who appeared in public unescorted. Tales abounded of the *police des moeurs* apprehending innocent women, and charging them with working as unregistered prostitutes, without any serious investigation. In accordance with the law, they would be placed immediately on the register of prostitutes. The ignominy for the victim was compounded by being ostracized by friends, family, and employers. As a result, many innocent women were forced into prostitution as the only means left to them of earning any money.

The flaws in the regulationist approach were numerous, and attacked from all sides. The philanthropic opposition of the abolitionist campaign coincided with the self-interest of residents who did not want to see their neighborhood taken over by the sex trade. The resulting public pressure often led local authorities to reject applications for the opening of new brothels. Brothel owners in turn complained about the refusal or inability of the authorities to act against proprietors of unregistered premises. Hotels and cafés that provided "waitresses" and female visitors with a venue to meet and entertain clients avoided the cost of medical inspections and other charges imposed on operators who complied with the law. The financial pressure of being undercut by clandestine competitors combined with another economic factor that can confront all enterprises: changes in consumer preferences meant that the quick, functional visit—which was the stock-in-trade of the regulated brothels—fell out of favor. Instead, clients sought the more relaxed atmosphere for sexual transactions increasingly provided unofficially by the salons and cafés. By the 1880s, the registered brothels were in decline, and with them the system that had evidently failed to regulate their trade.

Further Reading: Corbain, Alain. *Les Filles de Noce: Misère Sexuelle et Prostitution au XIXe Siècle*. Paris: Flammarion, 1982; Parent-Duchâtelet, Alexandre. *De la Prostitution dans la Ville de Paris*. 2 vols. Paris, 1836.

Ian Merrilees

QUEEN VICTORIA (1819–1901). Britain's Queen Victoria was born on May 24, 1819, the only child of Edward, Duke of Kent and Victoria Maria Louisa Saxe-Coburg. Her ascension to the throne was in part due to default; none of her uncles, including King William IV had any legitimate heirs, and thus the throne came to Victoria. She was crowned on June 20, 1837, and ruled until her death on January 22, 1901, the longest reign of any British monarch to date.

Victoria's reign was one of paradoxes, particularly with regard to gender; while Victoria was a woman who was symbolically the leader of one of the largest empires of all time, after marrying Prince Albert she no longer felt that ruling was an appropriate role for women and treated her husband as an equal in all her decisions. Moreover, while Victoria was supportive of extending voting and land-owning rights to the lower classes, she was adamantly against allowing women the vote. Victoria's support for gendered separate spheres and viewing a woman's role as solely domestic led twentieth-century historians to initially view the Victorian period as very proper, traditional, and certainly not sexually explicit. However, as Foucault had repeatedly argued, this perception of the Victorian period is more reflective of modern viewpoints than the actual viewpoints of Victoria's contemporaries, although, famously, she refused to acknowledge that lesbians existed. Sexuality and gender were major issues during Victoria's reign, both in her personal life and in the political actions of the period.

Victoria married Prince Albert on February 10, 1840. Not quite twenty-one years old, Victoria and Albert would have quickly consummated the marriage, as Victoria gave birth to her first child, Princess Victoria, on November 21, 1840. Victoria bore eight other children between 1841 and 1857, suggesting that she and Albert were certainly sexually active. Recently biographers have suggested that Victoria enjoyed sex, and certainly the number of children she bore suggests she was not adamantly opposed to the act as it sometimes suggested of both her and the period. Moreover, there has been some recent suggestion that Victoria felt childbirth interrupted her sex life, something she highly valued as a reflection of her love for Albert. However, her sexual desire was most likely practical as well as enjoyable; the government and the country desired Victoria to provide a male heir to the throne, thereby restoring the "natural" order to the monarchy, which had been exclusively male from Queen Anne's death in 1714. As such, Victoria's actions and desires were ruled as much by her royal responsibilities as her personal wishes.

Outside the bedroom, Victoria also had to address issues of gender in her personal life; while she was Queen of England, she was also a wife, which meant a compromise of power. Lytton Strachey relates an anecdote in which, after a quarrel, Victoria knocked on Albert's door and when he asked who was there, she replied "the Queen of England." Albert denied her entry, and upon him asking her the same question again, she replied, "your wife, Albert" and he opened the door (Strachey, 1921). This instance illustrates the conflict between her role as queen and her role as wife, and the difficulty in balancing the two. However, as previously mentioned, Victoria did not always enjoy her position of power, believing that the woman's role was in the home and by her husband's side; her insistence on mourning for Albert from his death on December 14, 1861, until her own death indicates her womanly devotion.

Victoria's policies on gender were not limited to her own life but extended to her empire as well. She was openly opposed to women's rights and refused to consider that men and women were equal in any way; it is not surprising, then, that women were not allowed to retain their property in marriage until 1882 with the passage of the Married Woman's Property Act. Between the ascension of Victoria and the passage of this act, women suffered through various legislations that were detrimental to their gender, most notably the passage of the **Contagious Diseases Acts** in the 1860s, which allowed for the forcible examination of women suspected to be prostitutes in an attempt to thwart the spread of sexually transmitted diseases. In actuality, these acts degraded women and gave both political and sexual power to men, thereby setting back any progression of gender equality until 1886 when these **laws** were repealed. While women did gain more rights by the end of the Victorian era than they had ever enjoyed before, this was more a natural process than a revolutionary one; Victoria did certainly not assist this evolution in any way.

While women were granted more social and political rights as the century progressed, the sexual freedom of all British citizens was restricted at the end of the century. The Criminal Law Amendment Act of 1885, among other things, raised the age of consent from thirteen to sixteen, strengthened existing legislation regarding **prostitution**, and prohibited homosexual relationships between men (lesbians were excluded from this legislation, allegedly in part because of Victoria's disbelief in **lesbianism**). While the first two aspects of this act would have helped to protect women sexually, the third cause limited the sexual freedom of men; this aspect of the act is still a contributor to legislation regarding sexuality in Britain today.

It is probably this act from the end of the Victorian era which has led people today to believe that the Victorians were prudish, the symbol of this prudery being Queen Victoria. Victoria was certainly traditional in some aspect of her life and policies; she supported the idea of separate spheres for women and condoned sexual activity, but only in privacy and in a traditional, heterosexual manner.

Further Reading: De-la-Noy, Michael. *Queen Victoria at Home*. New York: Carroll and Graf, 2003; Homans, Margaret, and Adrienne Munich, ed. *Remaking Queen Victoria*. Cambridge, MA: Cambridge University Press, 1997; Strachey, Lytton. *Queen Victoria*. London: Chatto and Windus, 1921; Thompson, Dorothy. *Queen Victoria: Gender and Power*. London: Virago, 1990.

Amanda M. Caleb

R

RACE. By the start of the nineteenth century, race and sexuality were tightly intertwined with one another, both read as biologically unassailable facts in which difference—between men and women, between people from different parts of the world—was both natural and hierarchical. To understand the power of these beliefs, we need two major contexts, those of western science and of European imperialism. More perhaps than any other changes affecting the nineteenth century and the Victorian age, the growth of science and the expansion of colonialism helped establish race and sex as key social organizing principles.

Eighteenth-century science had been centrally interested in the classification of the organic world, and this increasing interest led scientists to debate the origins of the human race in language and ideas that went considerably beyond the Biblical account of the creation. Before the eighteenth century, scientists had mostly favored a one-sex model, which minimized bodily differences between the male and female as unimportant, odd as this seems to modern perceptions. In the eighteenth century, as anatomy and physiology grew in stature, scientific knowledge moved toward favoring the more characteristically modern model of two radically different sexes. Likewise in the eighteenth century, scientists increasingly began to wonder whether all humans were descended from the same initial stock or from different regional human stock marked by skin color, hair texture, and other physical differences. Those who believed in the one-race theory of human origins were known as monogenists, while those who favored the idea of separate human species were called polygenists.

Scientific work in this period was heavily influenced by the increased contact with non-European people that developed alongside colonial expansion, and which had brought more and more Europeans into contact with people who behaved in unfamiliar ways and who sometimes looked a little different physically, as well as in dress and bodily decoration. Ship voyages and exploration in the eighteenth century often had botanists and naturalists aboard, their task to collect or describe flora and fauna in new places, including humans. When travelers and explorers encountered peoples with radically different social organizations, they tended to judge their societies by the standards of the Christian west, disparaging them as promiscuous and hypersexual.

The encounter, then, between colonialism and science laid the groundwork for nineteenth-century attitudes to racialized sexuality and sexualized racial thinking in many ways. By the nineteenth century, race and sex had effectively become analogous in science, both deeply enmeshed in hierarchical assessments of worth, of power, and of freedom. Naturalist Charles Darwin's (1809–1882) key text, *The Descent of Man, and*

Selection in Relation to Sex, first published in 1871, applied his now-famous theory of sexual selection to both racial and sexual difference. Darwin used as evidence the work of a Swiss-German scientist, Carl Vogt (1817–1895), who had recently argued that the skulls of men and women varied as greatly as the skulls from different human racial groups, and that those of women and of "Negroid" (meaning African) men were more primitive and child-like. The American physician and anthropologist Samuel Morton (1799–1851) had earlier conducted similar research on cranial difference. His findings, published in his *Crania Americana* in 1839, concluded on the basis of skull size that **Native Americans** were less intelligent than Caucasians (Europeans) and Mongolians (Asians). Ideas about both racial and female inferiority were boosted, then, in the nineteenth century by apparently objective scientific data that relied on the discoveries of colonialism.

These views significantly affected the ways people lived, both in Europe and in the ever-larger colonial world it fostered. Laws, as well as popular opinion, frequently followed the lead offered by science in conflating race and sex, and in seeing in these categories proof positive of natural hierarchies which placed men over women, and whites over every other race of people. Women, as the bearers of children, were key to this vision of an ordered hierarchy. Throughout the nineteenth century, women were defined by their capacity to reproduce, and much of their psychology was reduced to this question. Women were seen as bodies in thrall to their biology, and many in the medical world counseled that stress, an overemphasis on education or too much exercise would endanger women's reproductive destiny. Mental fatigue was understood to shrivel the ovaries, and women were regarded as sensitive and nervous, given to overexcitement, and needing to be shielded from circumstances that might detrimentally affect their capacity to bear progeny.

These alleged dangers only affected women of the "higher" races, however, presumably because, according to the European, people living closer to nature had fewer cares and worries. It was a common and a long-standing belief that "primitive" women had far easier childbirth experiences than their "civilized" sisters, although there was little concrete evidence to support this position. The issue at stake parallels the measuring—of skulls, **brain** size, sexual organs, and the like—that was so characteristic of the science of race and sex in this period. Further from nature, nearer civilization, white women were farther from the animal world, a greater distance from the uncomplicated and animalistic no-fuss giving of birth associated with lower creatures, and therefore bearing the burden of pain. It was the price that the white woman paid for her racial and civilizational superiority.

Women, white and of color, were regarded by scientists—and the public more generally—as closer to nature than men. The evidence of skull size was said to demonstrate their lesser intellect but also, apparently, their greater reliance on and sense of instinct, again aligning them with the less rational creatures of the earth, alongside non-European people. While women's smaller skulls were said to indicate their lack of reason, it was often the size of men's genitals that was said to determine their relationship to reason. The mythical belief that African men as a race had larger penises than those of Europeans was read as proof that they were also governed more by the animal passions than by the definitively human faculty of reason.

One arena where we see this deeply connected racial and sexual determinism at work with far-reaching effects is around the question of interracial sexual relations. Whereas in the eighteenth century, interracial sex had attracted little attention it was, by the nineteenth century, a topic of some considerable anxiety. By the end of the century, marriages and sometimes sexual relations between the races was outlawed, for example, in some of Britain's African colonies and in much of the United States. Prohibition or discouragement of interracial marriage and sex was fueled by a complex host of concerns including fears that "bad" characteristics from "lesser" races would dilute the "good" elements of "higher" races in any offspring of the liaison. Some polygenists believed that mixed-race offspring would themselves be sterile, since they were products of species mixing. Even those who rejected the sterility theory often warned that race mixing would be a recipe for social instability, in which the worst racial features of each parent would be the child's inheritance. Scientists and anthropologists as well as novelists in the late nineteenth century pictured a multiracial dystopia born of an indiscriminate female sexuality.

Fears of interracial sex went well beyond anxieties over the qualities of their offspring. In tropical colonial settings where white settlers lived, the late nineteenth century—and the early twentieth century—saw a series of moral panics around the sexual vulnerability of white women settlers. Black male sexuality was considered by Europeans to be an out-of-control passion, further inflamed by the apparently superior **beauty** of white women. In many colonies, hysteria spread, and black men found themselves needing to take great care when white women were present lest they were accused of untoward sexual behaviors. While in the United States at this time, attention to a white woman might lead to an African-American man's lynching, and, men in some of Britain's colonies could find themselves facing the death penalty for sexually assault on a white woman.

A profound double standard was often at work in debates around interracial sex. While white women who partnered with men who were not white were considered to be depraved, and their black partners might risk their lives, white men's choices of sexual partner attracted far less disapproval. White men living in the colonies without wives were not expected to remain celibate. There was always an assumption that they would seek sexual partners with women from the locale. Many men, and at all social levels, formed what were sometimes known as temporary marriages, living with local women who sometimes bore them children, but in relationships that could easily be terminated at the man's convenience. Prior to the nineteenth century, trading companies working in colonial arenas often encouraged such arrangements as beneficial. Men learned the local language more quickly and earned access to local knowledge that might otherwise have been closed to them. In North America, on the trade routes of the Pacific Ocean, in the Malay Archipelago and in South Asia, men working for companies such as the Dutch East Indies Company had at the very least tacit official encouragement for these liaisons. The Dutch continued to see benefits in these arrangements for most of the nineteenth century, while in British colonies acceptance became more muted, hardening by the end of the century into disapproval, as fears of mixed-race offspring and of men converting to native ways hardened.

As a result of this shift in attitude, a highly successful **prostitution** trade as well as a pornography industry peddling images of "exotic" women were both well established in the European colonies in the nineteenth century alongside the longer-term arrangements of an earlier era. This sex industry catered to the predominantly male population of colonizers whose sexual needs were seen to override any concerns about race mixing. It was also there to ensure a ready supply of women so that men would be less likely to seek same-sex relations with other men. Male **homosexuality** was, in the nineteenth century, commonly dismissed as a deviance typical of people other than Europeans. It was seen both as a sign of inferiority and depravity and as a feminizing weakness among men who could not successfully resist colonial conquest. Even within Europe, the feminized man was considered a failure. Influential British psychologist Henry Maudsley (1835–1918), professor of medical jurisprudence at University College London, wrote in 1874 that what he called "mutilated men" were more like women mentally, while women who were sterile were masculine in their mental habits and their bodily appearance. The association of a "mutilated" man with womanliness had widespread connotations in the colonies, whose men were subjected to British rule. In British India, Bengali men were dismissed as effeminate while men from the Punjab, an area of northern India, which it took the British much longer to conquer, were admired as masculine and martial. Moreover, the weakness of the Bengalis was often explained in largely sexual terms. It was the Hindu custom of marriage at a young age, a fondness for **masturbation** and a general oversexedness that was said to explain Bengali enervation and effeminacy.

Colonial sexualities, whether homosexual or heterosexual, were always threatening. A predilection for the same sex proved the deviance of colonial peoples, while heterosexual behaviors could be dismissed as oversexed and promiscuous. It was the assumption that hypersexuality was the typical condition of colonial people, especially in the tropical and semi-tropical zones, which also made a highly regulated prostitution industry possible. The British and the Dutch, in particular, carefully organized the sex industry in their respective colonies the better to serve their military. The British introduced major legislation in the mid-nineteenth century, which required women working in prostitution to be registered with local authorities and tested for sexually transmissible diseases on a regular basis. A smaller and less encompassing version of this legislation operated in military garrisons and port towns in the British Isles between 1864 and 1886, but the opposition was so ferocious and well organized that the legislation was abandoned in the 1880s. It would be another decade before opponents of regulated prostitution would win a similar ban on the laws in the colonies, and even then unpublicized versions of the **law** continued to operate on a local basis well into the twentieth century. The colonial versions of these acts, known collectively as the **Contagious Diseases Acts**, were far broader in scope than their British counterparts, and affected many more women. While in Britain women were registered under the law only if they were arrested, in many colonies they were either expected to come forward and register voluntarily on the prostitution lists, or the keeper of the brothel where they worked was required to maintain a current list of workers with the authorities. Arrangements such as these would have been politically explosive had they been introduced in Britain where the brothel remained illegal and prostitution was feared as the ultimate immorality. But in the colonies registration was considered acceptable on the grounds that colonial women, already promiscuous and sexual disorderly, would find no shame in admitting to prostitution, unlike their British counterparts. In practice, women everywhere found registration irksome and limiting, and both in the colonies and in Britain sought to get around the requirement.

Throughout the nineteenth century, social commentators and reformers were fascinated by the prostitute, and she frequently became a racialized as well as a sexualized figure. Women working in the sex trade in the capital cities of Europe were frequently seen as a throwback to more primitive human forms. Their bodies as well as their family backgrounds were examined and classified by investigators and they were constantly painted as a group apart from other European women, closer to the natural world and to the lower races biologically as well as socially. Commentators found such women to typify degeneration, and therefore to need careful control and containment for the sake of the public good.

Sex and race throughout the nineteenth century were yoked together to sustain hierarchical ideas that contrasted passion and reason, men and women, "civilized" and "primitive" people, men and women. These distinctions were key social constructs that had profound effects on law, culture, and custom throughout the world. Nineteenth-century sexuality was always shaped by race. Both race and sex were drawn as purely biological and natural categories in the nineteenth century, accessible through description, measurement, and observation. The vast expansion of colonial power that so typifies nineteenth century in Europe intensified this connection, as settlers, civil **servants**, traders, and travelers increasingly encountered people of different habits and practices from those they knew at home. Sexual behavior and custom became one of the most important signifiers of difference between Europeans and other people, and was almost always explained as much in racial as in sexual terms. *See also* Orientalism.

Further Reading: Aldrich, Robert. *Colonial and Homosexuality.* London: Routledge, 2003; Levine, Philippa. *Prostitution, Race and Politics: Policing Venereal Disease in the British Empire.* New York: Routledge, 2003; Nagel, Joane. *Race, Ethnicity, and Sexuality: Intimate Intersections, Forbidden Frontiers.* New York: Oxford University Press, 2003.

Philippa Levine

ROMANTIC FRIENDSHIP. Romantic friendship is the term used to describe intimate friendships between predominantly white, educated women of privileged classes that were prevalent in the United States (and to a lesser extent in Britain) during the nineteenth century. Of varying emotional intensity and longevity, these friendships were characterized by passionate feelings of love and devotion, often expressed in highly romantic language. While some men also formed romantic friendships (most notably, the American Poet Walt Whitman), the term has come to be associated almost entirely with historiographical debates about lesbian identity in the late nineteenth and early twentieth centuries.

The difficulty for scholars is how to interpret the passionate and often sensual declarations of love and longing between women evidenced in letters and diaries in this period. How can we read this desire? What does it mean in this context? To what degree are romantic friendships precursors to contemporary lesbian identity? Should they be understood as specific to a particular historical period during which large numbers of single women were brought together in women's only communities, as for example, the single-sex colleges in the New England region of the United States, where lifelong committed partnerships between women were so common that they were known as Boston or Wellesley Marriages? Or should they be seen as evidence of the high level of tolerance for same-sex intimacy that existed in other periods before the rise of sexological, medical, and psychological theories that were instrumental in shaping the categories of heterosexuality and **homosexuality** with an emphasis on the pathology of the latter? These are the questions that have occupied historians seeking to understand same-sex love and desire in this period.

Although Lillian Faderman was not the first to use the term, her pioneering book *Surpassing the Love of Men* (1981) popularized the concept of romantic friendship and brought it within the purview of lesbian history. Faderman's romantic friendship thesis had two main components: that such relationships were "love relationships in every sense except perhaps the genital, since women in centuries other than ours often internalized the view of females having little sexual passion" (Faderman, 16);

and, that these relationships had been socially accepted and encouraged from the seventeenth century until the end of the nineteenth century when theories about the pathology of same-sex love relationships brought about their "morbidification." Faderman's conception of romantic friendship sparked vigorous discussion (known as the "romantic friendship/**lesbianism**" debate) among scholars who critiqued it for de-sexualizing lesbian identity; for valuing monogamous couples over other women, and for its focus on middle-class women; for not recognizing that the work of the sexologists might provide a framework for women to understand and articulate their same-sex desires; for minimizing women's awareness of the transgressive nature of their same-sex desires and for overstating the degree of social acceptance of romantic friendships. The most enduring legacy of Faderman's work has been the debate over the sexual component of romantic friendships (and implicitly the possibility of sexual relations between women prior to the twentieth century) that has set up a reductive sex/no sex binarism through which all intimate same-sex relationships in this period are viewed and classified. Scholars who wish to deny the same-sex love relationships of certain historical subjects often deploy the notion of asexual romantic friendship to resolve or deflect the specter of the lesbian, while scholars who wish to argue for the sexual component of these relationships cite Faderman as the counterpoint to their own arguments.

Recent scholarship has emphasized the evidentiary aspect of such friendships, arguing that the sources with which we have been left are almost entirely those of literate middle-class women who would have been unlikely to discuss sexual matters in writing. Increasingly "romantic friendship" is seen as only one form of same-sex bonding in this period, which may or may not have included sexual intimacy (however that is defined). Regardless of whether these relationships were sexual or not, they were still perceived as examples of inversion in the sexological literature that helped change cultural attitudes to same-sex love in the last decades of the nineteenth century. *See also* Romantic Love, Lesbianism.

Further Reading: Diggs, Marylynne. "Romantic Friends or a "Different Race of Creatures"? The Representation of Lesbian Pathology in Nineteenth Century America." *Feminist Studies* 21 (1995): 317–40; Donoghue, Emma. *Passions between Women*. London: Scarlet Press, 1993; Faderman, Lillian. *Surpassing the Love of Men: Romantic Friendship and Love between Women from the Renaissance to the Present*. New York: William Morrow and Company, 1981; Smith, Martha Nell Smith. *Rowing in Eden: Rereading Emily Dickinson*. Austin, TX: University of Texas Press, 1992; Smith-Rosenberg, Carroll. "The Female World of Love and Ritual: Relations between Women in Nineteenth-Century America." *Signs* 1 (1975): 1–29; Vicinus, Martha. "'They Wonder to Which Sex I Belong': The Historical Roots of the Modern Lesbian Identity." In Martha Vicinus, ed. *Lesbian Subjects: A Feminist Studies Reader*. Bloomington and Indianapolis: Indiana University Press, 1996.

Sally Newman

ROMANTIC LOVE. The ideal of romantic love as it was understood in the nineteenth-century west developed out of Romanticism in the late eighteenth century. It was closely related to a new form of **marriage**, the love match. Before this era, love did not ordinarily play the deciding role in relationships between women and men, because of the importance of economic considerations. Love was a welcome but not necessary addition to a rational union based on mutual benefit. The kind of love that led to marriage was expected to develop as a reasonable feeling for each other, based not on passion, but on virtues like friendship, companionship, and mutual forbearance for the frailties of the partner. A harmonious friendship founded on respect for the partner and their contribution to the marriage enterprise was what most couples aspired to and could expect. A good marriage was not defined as an emotionally rewarding relationship, but rather as providing economic, social, and judicial protection for women and their children.

Except among the very poor, it was a parental duty to choose suitable spouses for their children, especially for their daughters. Parents focused on security rather than on love, and in much of Europe a dowry given with the daughter was hoped to increase the financial stability of the new partnership. Dowries were not employed in the New World, and in Britain, only the wealthiest demanded "settlements" before marriage, which provided for their daughter's financial security in case of widowhood. Love, it was hoped, would come with years of living together and by habit.

At the end of the eighteenth century, more and more people asked for love as the one and only motive for marriage. Older motives for marriage began to be stigmatized as base and materialistic. This changing emphasis can be seen in literature, in advice literature, and even in sermons preached at marriage. Around the turn of the century, writing on love increasingly opposed business-like considerations when selecting a mate. Love was increasingly thought of as the central and most important element in marriage choice, but many considered love as the sole domain of women, arguing that nothing should be more important for women than love. The English poet Lord George Byron (1788–1824) wrote: "Man's love is of man's life a thing apart, 'tis woman's whole existence." But as time passed it was increasingly assumed that love was desired by both sexes and that marriage without it was sordid. The ideal relationship was a union of souls in marriage.

According to the British sociologist Anthony Giddens, the idea of a love match and the ideals of love in an intimate relationship are rooted in the moral values of **Christianity**. It was based on the idea of giving oneself up to God, when one comes to a fuller knowledge of both God and oneself. Giddens claimed that both men and women tried to fulfill this idea in a relationship. As society became more affluent, more couples could indulge in the luxury of romantic feeling. However, love should not be confused with passion. In the nineteenth century, sex appeal was not a respectable motive for a love match. Much more important were the emotional qualities in a relationship, such as warmth, naturalness, and sincerity. People tried to find a balance between a marriage of convenience and an "impetuous" impassioned love. The latter did not comply with middle-class virtues such as reason and moderation, or with the desire for spiritual union with the partner. Desirable characteristics like seriousness, virtue, and goodness were important conditions for relationship and affinity. Passion was dangerous, as it could temporarily distract from identifying true affinity, and as parental involvement waned, women were increasingly expected to attract suitable men without risking their virtue.

Love and marriage in the nineteenth century was a construct that signaled a passage from a traditional, economically based marriage of convenience toward a modern love match. The ideal form of love in the nineteenth century joined the old model of relationship and added a new conception of love where both sexes were soul partners. Love matches made parental consent unnecessary, because this contradicted the principle of love. As a result, love brought trouble into families and potentially, rebellion of children against their parents: the central problem of many a nineteenth-century novel. Love meant free choice and as time passed this value was more and more often supported by parents, although it inevitably weakened parental authority. Romantic love became a personal goal for many, who wanted this fulfillment in their marriage as well as in their dreams.

Further Reading: Davidoff, Leonore and Hall, Catherine. *Family Fortunes: Men and Women of the English Middle Class, 1780–1850.* London: Hutchinson, 1987; Giddens, Anthony. *The Transformation of Intimacy: Sexuality, Love and Eroticism in Modern Societies.* Cambridge, MA: Polity, 1992.

Ulrike Moser

ROMANTIC NOVELS. *See* Novels, Romantic

S

SADISM AND MASOCHISM.   Sadism and masochism, sometimes called algophilia, are psychological concepts that were developed towards the end of the nineteenth century. Vienese historian and novelist Baron Leopold von Sacher-Masoch (1836–1895) is eponymously remembered for masochism, although he was displeased with the 1890 appropriation by Austrian sexologist, **Richard von Krafft-Ebing** (1840–1902), after one of his patients referred to their submissive desires as masochism. Masoch's novel in which these desires were explored, *Venus im Pelz* (*Venus in Furs*, 1870), has the heroine, Wanda, treat the protagonist like a slave. Masoch's algophilic tastes were not new. Flagellation is found throughout Victorian erotica, usually depicting young women with fleshy bottoms being spanked by strict mistresses and ageing *roués*. Occasionally it is the man who is dominated, a point developed by Algernon Swinburne in some of his poems, such as "Authur's flogging," which describes the whipping of a boy in a manner loaded with homoerotic associations, noting the state of Arthur's bottom as his school master flogged him.

It was **sexology** that reformulated the relationship between sex, pain, and power. Chicagoan psychiatrist, S. V. Clevenger, addressed active and passive sexuality, arguing that in the early history of life, bacteria could combine heritable material either by eating or being eaten. Bacteriophages were considered active; those that "submitted" to being eaten were passive. The "hunger impulse" developed from such primordial desires and, according to Clevenger, so did the sexual impulse. Another American psychiatrist, James Kiernan, applied Clevenger's ideas to the sexual impulse, describing active desires as masculine, and passive desires as feminine. He stressed that these impulses were normal, and indeed were necessary for copulation, but that they could become pathological through exaggeration. This idea was rearticulated up by Krafft-Ebing, who called the two behaviors, when they became extreme, sadism and masochism, in the 1890 edition of his *Psychopathia Sexualis*. There was a general sexological consensus about sado-masochism, but with some dissent. **Havelock Ellis** preferred to think about pain as an erotic symbolism that stimulated sexual deficiency in the patient. He also emphasized that there were normal phases of erotic play deriving from sado-masochism, including kisses, love bites, and the like. He agreed that there was a gendered differentiation of the sexual impulse, with women passive and deriving pleasure from being dominated, and men inclined to dominate. Thus it was difficult for a woman to be a pathological masochist, as it was normal in women except in the most extreme manifestations. He also considered male masochism and female sadism similar in etiology to **homosexuality**, which he considered a form of gender inversion with a

Flogging with a birch branch, an illustration from "Therese Philosophe," the Marquis de Sade's favorite book. © Erich Lessing/Art Resource, NY.

congenital basis. Male sadism, Ellis believed, was the extreme signification of male domination that had to be controlled, as it vitiated his otherwise feminist beliefs in the importance of consensual, non-harmful sex.

Other evidence for the existence of sado-masochistic behavior was sought by ethnologists. Many of these ethnological texts were enrolled by sexologists as supporting evidence, as were historical descriptions of sadistic practices, such as marriage by capture, which was graphically portrayed in Fustel de Coulanges *Cité d'Antique* (1864). In all cases, there was a maintaining of the gendered distinction between sadistic and masochistic behavior, and this historical and cultural evidence did much to support this theory.

Significant sexological developments were made when the distinction was forged between perversions of aim and perversions of object. Perversions of aim included sadistic and masochistic practices, because it was not penetrative sex that was desired, but practices of sexual domination. The Berlin sexologist, Magnus Hirschfeld, stressed this distinction, which had an important impact on the sexual psychology of Sigmund Freud. After Freud, within sexology as well as psycho-analysis, sado-masochism began to be treated not only as a simple paraphilia involving pain, but became emphasized as a personality trait (especially in psycho-analysis) and as a basic phenomenon that was manifest in many other sexual activities. In this vein, another Chicago-based psychiatrist, Harold Moyer, described both lesbianism and bestiality as forms of sadistic behavior, the former being a masculine desire to dominate other women as sexual partners, the latter as the desire to actively seek noncompliant sexual partners and to dominate them. Moyer employed a significantly modified interpretation of sadistic and masochistic behavior that was much more in line with current psychiatric conceptions of the issue. Within psychoanalysis, there was a tendency to utilize the existing sexological categories in a similar way.

Further Reading: Clevenger, S. V. "Comparative Physiology and Psychology." *New Englander and Yale Review*, 49 (1888): 221–22; Ellis, Havelock. *Love and Pain, Studies in the Psychology of Sex.* Vol. III. Philadelphia: F. A. Davis and Co., 1903; Freud, Sigmund. *Three Essays on the Theory of Sexuality.* Trans. by James Strachey. Standard Edition, 1905; Kiernan, James. "Psychological Aspects of the Sexual Appetite." *Alienist and Neurologist* 11 (1891): 188–218; Krafft-Ebing, Richard von. *Psychopathia Sexualis.* Trans. by C. G. Chaddock, Philadelphia: F. A. Davis and Co., 1892; Moyer, Harold. "Is Sexual Perversion Insanity?" *Alienist and Neurologist* (1907): 193–204.

Ivan Crozier

SCIENCE, POPULAR. Sensitized to a specific discourse in the Romantic Age, Victorians continued and expanded the passionate public discussion of love, albeit with new undertones that changed over time while society continued to pay tributes to more rigidly defined **gender roles.** In contrast, they seemed to exclude sex from public debate. In fact, sexuality appeared in many more areas of Victorian discourse than was generally assumed in earlier studies of the period. One of these areas was popular science. Its bulky literature dealt with aspects of natural history or, as the century progressed, with emerging specialized disciplines such as biology, chemistry, geology, astronomy, and physics. In this way, the genre provoked a more lively and diversified debate in a number of forums. For one, popular science attracted attention to a great variety of subjects previously considered unsuitable for public discussion, including emotions and procreation. Second, as part of a general expansion of education it reached out to a larger public that was more socially and culturally heterogeneous than ever before. Third, the way sex and love figured in popular science drew from at least three sources, adding new facets to the debate: from science itself, from the methods and style of the more general debate on these issues, and from the stylistic and linguistic idiosyncrasies of presenting scientific knowledge popularly. The publication of evolutionary theory strongly affected popular science, introducing new concepts of love and sex and a new way of talking about them. However, some of the traditional concepts and methods of presenting them persisted.

In the first decades of the nineteenth century, popular science expounded variations of love, influenced by the dominating ideas of natural theology. According to William Paley (1743–1805), nature followed a divine plan and provided a source of morality and proof of the existence of a benign god. To love nature meant to love God. Publications on biology, being thematically closest to the issues of the emotions, promoted this concept of love. But other disciplines such as geology, chemistry, physics, meteorology, and astronomy employed the same interpretation. Popular science, writing about aspects of every one of these specialising sciences, carried this specific idea of love into new fields. Thus, moons, planets, fragments of stars orbiting around a sun or a bigger planet were depicted as tied by a feeling of belonging or of love. The fusion of chemical elements, of two atoms of hydrogen and one of oxygen producing water, was supposedly guided by an attraction akin to love and culminating in the creation of something new, the birth of a water molecule. The formation of rocks or clouds, the workings of magnetism and electricity, the whole breadth of chemical reactions or the emergence or collapse of stars: all this could be presented as governed by a feeling of love mirroring the bond between two people. It gave expression to God acting through nature.

Some of these approaches survived well into the second half of the century, even well into the twentieth, as books such as Henry Farquhar's *Nature's Story. Science Talks to Young Thinkers* (1895) or Agnes Giberne's *This Wonder World* (1913) testify. Nonetheless, the general tendency in popular science writing was to become more matter-of-fact. The image of love as the moving force of processes in animate and inanimate nature was used much more sparingly, mostly, though not exclusively in texts written for the younger generation. Books on biology, particularly on man, approached the subject from a point of view expounded as scientific. For advocates of Darwinian theory, love appeared as an in-built element of the natural world, "the happiest feat of **evolution**" (Graham 1881, chapter III, 4), and the logical consequence of the evolution of man. In contrast to the Social Darwinist focus on the struggle for existence, widely read popularizer Arabella Buckley (1840–1929), for instance, depicted "self-devotion and love" (Buckley, 353) as the law of life—at least for the more complex life forms. The meaning of life could not be reduced to its own reproduction and preservation, but lay in the evolution of a certain principle, in the progress of sympathy and love. To Buckley, this had qualified mammals to become the "Winners in Life's Race."

As for sex, at least a certain segment of popular science literature was read as a source of information. Adolescents turned to books on anatomy or health to garner some knowledge on sex. Girls or women found in them details about procreation, though human sexuality was either left out or cloaked with metaphorical language which highlighted love or duty as the prime forces in the preservation of a species.

Darwinism changed popular science writing on sexuality. According to natural theology, sex or rather procreation followed an order from God, and was part of a divine plan. Darwinist theory transformed it into a characteristic of a struggle for existence. However, the dividing line between different ways of dealing with the issue in popular science did not run between pre- and post-Darwinian texts but between those primarily written for or consumed by the lower, and those written for and read by the middle classes. In line with other elements of popular culture, the former tended to be more graphic, more outspoken, less inhibited by conventions. The latter carried the bourgeois Victorian imagery of male and female into the popular presentation of nature, in an attempt to educate the young of the middle and all age groups of the working classes. The most influential scientist to do so was Charles Darwin (1809–1882) himself, who introduced middle class gender roles into science when he formulated his theory of sexual selection. It expounded the idea of women as "less eager than the male" (Darwin, chapter VIII), as sexually less active and inferior to men. It went well with the ideal of the chaste woman, afterwards popularised in a plethora of books on medical and psychiatric subjects as a scientific fact. Books of this kind were staple fare with generations of mainly middle class readers before **Havelock Ellis**, the pioneer of **sexology**, began to offer a general readership new and scientifically valid approaches to the subject at the turn of the century. At that time, contemporaries had already entered on a debate whether to have more or less information on sexual matters. To know little about sex was approved of, particularly in women whose ignorance of certain facts was idealised. Others favored a lack of carnal knowledge as evidence to a higher degree of civilization.

Contrary to this debate and the idealization of ignorance, knowledge expanded as more and more details were discussed in the continually growing bulk of literature, in the medical and biological books, and in those on other areas of science. In the latter half of the century, books on astronomy, physics, chemistry or any of the other new disciplines could draw too from the new frame of reference that, with some popularizers, replaced the imagery of natural theology: the concept of sexual reproduction underlying evolution. Writers accepting this interpretation rejected the romanticized elaborations on sex of an earlier period and replaced them with matter-of-fact descriptions offered in technical language, supposed to underline the scientific character of a text. On the whole, however, the use of such metaphors in popular science texts, other than biological or medical, tended to decrease toward the end of the period.

Popular science then contributed to a process that gave love and sexuality a greater prominence in nineteenth-century public discourse. The subjects were not only broached more often, but given new aspects and introduced into new contexts, so that a more elaborate imagery or even completely new images developed. In consequence, it supplemented the tendency to render the ideas of love, and to a lesser degree of sex, a Victorian household word.

Further Reading: Buckley, Arabella Burton. *Winners in Life's Race or The Great Backboned Family*. London: Edward Stanford, 1892; Darwin, Charles. *The Descent of Man and Selection in Relation to Sex*. London: Murray, 1871; Graham, William. *The Creed of Science. Religious, Moral, and Social*. London: Kegan Paul, 1881; Mason, Michael. *The Making of Victorian Sexuality*.

Oxford: Oxford University Press, 1994; Russett, Cynthia Eagle. *Sexual Science: The Victorian Construction of Womanhood*. Cambridge, MA: Harvard University Press, 1989; Schwarz, Angela. *Der Schlüssel zur modernen Welt. Wissenschaftspopularisierung in Großbritannien und Deutschland im übergang zur Moderne (ca. 1870–1914)*. Stuttgart: Franz Steiner, 1999.

Angela Schwarz

SENSATION NOVELS. *See* Novels, Sensation

SERVANTS. In the nineteenth century, domestic service reached its numerical peak, due in part to the fast growth of the middle class in Europe and North America. All middle class families aspired to employ at least one servant. Professional families believed that two or three servants were essential to familial comfort. The very wealthy employed vast armies of servants: the Duke of Westminster employed over 300 at his home in Cheshire, and at this level the upper servants would have their own servants. However, multiservant households were the minority; two-thirds of servants found themselves the only employee of the household. In Britain, most servants were natives of the United Kingdom; in the United States there was a color divide, with a substantial minority of black Americans employed as servants. Domestic service was the largest employer of American blacks in late nineteenth century, and they comprised 30 percent of all servants in the United States in the 1890s. Other sources of servants for America were Ireland and Europe, including Scandinavia. In Australia, the transportation of female prisoners meant that the line between servant and a slave-like condition could be blurred: convict women were assigned to households as servants without any right of refusal or freedom to leave their employment before the period of assignment was over. In any country, servants had few legal rights, and the ease with which they could be dismissed meant that they were vulnerable to sexual harassment by their employers, as well as exploitation of other kinds. Servants' only defence was to leave their posts, and most servants in the nineteenth century changed jobs regularly. Posts were numerous and servants with good references could change jobs at relatively short notice.

Servants were ordinarily single, and young; many entered service at the age of twelve or thirteen. Married servants were frowned on, except for the small minority of butler/housekeeper couples found in some large households. Servants who married secretly continued to live in and kept their change of status to themselves; disclosure would mean immediate dismissal. This meant that service, for most, was a transitional occupation for the young and unskilled, engaged in only until marriage. Youth, inexperience, and isolation combined to make general servants vulnerable in a number of ways. In an era when street **prostitution** was endemic in most cities, and where chaperonage was taken as a sign of modesty, young female servants were sent into street at night where they could be propositioned.

It was difficult for servants to engage in courtship, and in Britain, their age at marriage was significantly higher than the average for the working class. General servants, working alone in the household, would come into contact with very few men other than the assistants of the tradesmen who supplied the house with necessaries such as groceries, baked goods, and meat. Restrictions on their going out (a half-day of freedom a week was considered generous) meant that their social opportunities were severely restricted. Most households in the United Kingdom enforced a "no followers" rule, meaning that servants were not allowed to openly engage in courtship. This forced them either into social isolation, or compelled them to engage in clandestine courtship, with the dangers associated with secret relationships with relatively unknown men.

225

In multiservant households, flirtation and romance with the other servants was a possibility, but it was equally difficult to avoid unwanted attentions. If affection was not returned, the tension between servants could become unbearable. All of these factors combined to ensure that servants' choice of partner was severely limited by class and situation.

The domestic architecture of nineteenth-century homes could add to sexual tension. Large families meant that servants were crammed into spaces in the basement and the very top of the house, in segregated areas away from family traffic. Servants often did not have locks to their doors, because in theory the mistress of the house had the right to inspect them at any time. This made it easy for the master, a son of the house, or another servant, to demand sexual favors. Some manuals for servants advised them to barricade their doors at night. Same-sex servants often shared rooms. This minimal privacy was a great hardship associated with domestic service, and was often cited as a reason for leaving the occupation.

The nineteenth-century house was a claustrophobic environment. It was hard for families to hide their own sexuality from their omnipresent servants, and it was common for servants to provide the key testimony in divorce cases. Because it was commonly believed that working-class women were less modest than their middle-class counterparts, servants could be seen as a threat to family purity. Aboriginal and black servants were even more vulnerable to sexual exploitation within the family, because of popular beliefs about their "natural" licentiousness.

Any servant unlucky enough to become pregnant was dismissed instantly without a reference, meaning another post would be very difficult to obtain. Servants often attempted to conceal pregnancy, and hoped that their families might take in their illegitimate child, since it was obviously impossible for them to raise the child in their employer's house. This made servants especially vulnerable to baby farmers, who would contract to care for infants in return for money, often a high proportion of their wages. There were a number of scandals in the nineteenth century regarding the abuse, and even murder, of infants entrusted to baby farmers.

Further Reading: Butler, C. V. *Domestic Service.* New York: Garland, 1980, reprint of 1916 ed.; Huggett, Frank. *Life below Stairs.* London: John Murray, 1978; Higman, B. W. *Domestic Service in Australia.* Melbourne: Melbourne University Press, 2002; Horn, Pamela. *The Rise and Fall of the Victorian Servant.* London: Sutton, 2004.

Susan Mumm

SEX CRIMES. *See* Murder and Sex Crimes

SEX EDUCATION. Sex education encompasses all forms of shaping the knowledge of children and adolescents about sexuality. At the beginning of the nineteenth century, it was generally assumed that children were not curious about sexuality. They were considered to be sexually "innocent." The middle classes saw the sexual innocence of their children as being under threat through indecent talk of **servants** or other members of the lower classes, school friends, and the like. The working classes and their living conditions, in a world which became industrialized, were perceived as being immoral in their behavior and hence as a threat to morality in general and the innocence of children in particular. Therefore, middle-class children had to be shielded from any form of premature sexual knowledge that would contaminate their innocence. This was especially important for girls since it was thought to be the task of their future husband to awaken them sexually when entering **marriage**.

Although the experience of working-class children and adolescents might have been quite different due to the cramped living conditions and a much lower average marriage age, working-class parents did not talk more openly about sexuality than parents from the middle classes. Children living in the countryside at least could have gained some sort of sexual knowledge from observing nature. But, when asking their parents about sexuality children from all classes often received evasive answers referring them to the stork or gooseberry bush. With regard to adolescents and their emerging sexual feelings, parents were advised to teach them to moderate their sexual urges through self-control and a reasonable lifestyle which followed dietary rules, such as avoiding spicy food, **alcohol**, nicotine and coffee, and which included a lot of exercise and cold baths for sublimation.

One issue that had already emerged at the beginning of the eighteenth century still caused major concern among clerics, pedagogues, parents, and **physicians** in the nineteenth century, namely **masturbation**. It was the antimasturbation campaign that brought the young's sexual behavior into the center of debates on sex education. By the beginning of the nineteenth century, the discourse on masturbation had become a medical discourse. Medical textbooks as well as advice literature described the horrible effects of masturbation, a disease that could lead to bodily decay, insanity, and eventually to death. Parents and teachers could choose between a broad range of advice literature on how to detect this bad habit in their children, and what to do to distract and stop them from masturbating. To combat self-abuse, as masturbation was called at the time, different types of devices were available to make it impossible for children to touch their genitals, including erection alarms and appliances to keep girls from spreading their legs. In the worst cases, physicians suggested and even occasionally performed surgical procedures such as the removal of the clitoris (clidoridectomy), blistering, and cauterization of the penis. These drastic procedures for preventing masturbation were based on a concept of human physiology that saw the body as a closed energy system, which must not be weakened through excessive loss of seminal fluids, energy, and vitality. In their fight against masturbation, however, pedagogues and physicians saw themselves confronted with a dilemma they could not solve. By teaching children not to masturbate they precisely informed them about masturbation and the practices involve, thereby actually contributing to the spread of the behavior they wanted to eradicate.

In the second half of the nineteenth century, in many European countries the "silence" on sexual matters was increasingly questioned. Among the first who discussed sexuality in public were the women and **social purity** movements who began to criticize openly the double moral standard regarding male and female sexuality. In England, the **Contagious Diseases Acts** of the 1860s which aimed at controlling prostitutes and thereby stopping the spread of venereal diseases (VD) in the British military, caused vociferous protest from women's and social purity organizations, because the acts penalized women but not men. During the last decades of the nineteenth century, the women's movements in many European countries propagated the idea that the young should receive some form of instruction on sex and morality from their guardians, be these teachers, priests, physicians, or respectable women and men. Articles, pamphlets, and books were published in increasing numbers to provide parents with advice on how to educate their daughters and sons on sexual matters. Some of this literature was aimed at children as readers. These publications in general differed in content and moral tone in relation to the gender and class of their intended audience and the background (e.g., clergy, medical profession, social purity movement, women's movement, teachers, and so on) and gender of their authors.

Advice books, some of them written for the young, included *The Human Flower* (1894) and *Baby Buds* (1895), both by Ellis Ethelmer, the pseudonym the radical feminist Elizabeth Wolstenholme Elmy and her husband Ben Elmy both used. Another example was a widely distributed and influential book by the retired American Lutheran minister Sylvanus Stall entitled *What a Young Boy Ought to Know* (1897). It saw several editions and translations (e.g., into French, German, Spanish, Italian, Swedish) and started a series of similar sex advice books, including *What a Young Girl Ought to Know* (1897), written jointly by Stall and the physician Mary Wood-Allen, who published several further sex education and advice books for girls and young women.

In Germany, additional impetus for dealing with sex education came from the life and sex reform movements, as well as from the youth movement. The topics discussed around the turn of the century ranged from **homosexuality** and masturbation, the declining birth rate and population politics, to **birth control** and **abortion**. The most important issue was the spread of VD, which attracted the attention of medical practitioners, public health administrators, the social purity movement, and the women's movement. Public health educators soon recognized that they could not warn against VD without discussing sexual matters with the young. Among the first to support sex and moral education of the young in Germany was a small group of women who criticized the double moral standard and fought state regulation of **prostitution**. The Abolitionists, as they called themselves, propagated a sexual morality equally valid for men and women and urged to morally educate the young at an early age, at the latest when they were leaving school. By the turn of the century, Abolitionists organized first talks for pupils at schools, which were given by physicians who warned the young about the health consequences of immoral behavior and admonished them to take seriously their sexual responsibility toward themselves and the coming generation. These early sex education lessons often started with explaining reproduction by referring to birds and bees, but sometimes did not stop there and also mentioned issues of human reproduction.

By the end of the century, sex education had become a "burning contemporary issue," as the Berlin sexologist Ivan Bloch phrased it. Several discourses had stimulated this new interest in sex education. The debate about the effects of pornography, for instance, drew the attention of pedagogues to the young's sexual behavior and morality. By the turn of the century, sex education had become an important topic of public debates. Although some representatives from the churches still contested this, the general consensus was that giving children the right to information on sexual matters would not only guard them against moral traps and contracting VD, but also prepared them for marriage and reproduction.

Further Reading: Hall, Lesley. "Birds, Bees and General Embarrassment: Sex Education in Britain, from Social Purity to Section 28." In *Public or Private Education?*, edited by Richard Aldrich, ed. London: Woburn, 2004; Nelson, Claudia. "'Under the Guidance of a Wise Mother': British Sex Education at the Fin de Siècle." In *Maternal Instincts: Visions of Motherhood and Sexuality in Britain, 1875–1925*, edited by Claudia Nelson and Ann Sumner Holmes. London: Macmillan, 1997; Sauerteig, Lutz D. H. "Sex Education in Germany from the Eighteenth to the Twentieth Century." In *Sexual Cultures in Europe: Themes in Sexuality*, edited by Franz Eder, Lesley Hall, and Gerd Hekma. Manchester: Manchester University Press, 1999.

Lutz D. H. Sauerteig

SEXLESSNESS.   The terms sexlessness (United Kingdom) and passionlessness (United States) refer to the notion, prevalent in the nineteenth century, of women's inherent lack of, or incapacity for sexual desire. This sexual ideology has been linked to the rise of Evangelical Protestantism and Romanticism in Europe and the United States during the early decades of the nineteenth century. Historians regard these twin movements as a reaction against enlightenment sexuality, which had become associated with the excessive pursuit of pleasure.

While differently conceived, the emphasis of both movements effectively placed women's sexual passivity at the center of their value systems. The cult of domesticity promoted by evangelical religion stressed the place of women within the home as wife and mother. As historian Nancy Cott argues "the evangelical view, by concentrating on women's spiritual nature, simultaneously elevated women as moral and intellectual beings and disarmed them of their sexual power. Passionlessness was on the other side of the coin which paid, so to speak, for women's admission to moral equality" (Cott 1978, 228). This view co-existed easily with the "idealization of love, and particularly of woman, that was central to the Romantic quest" (Porter and Hall 1995, 32).

Debates in women's history have focused on the degree to which the notion of women's passionlessness reflected cultural attitudes and/or influenced behavior at different times during the century. Some scholars have argued that women would have internalized the idea of passionlessness to such an extent that they would have rarely been capable of experiencing sexual passion in their relationships. Others have argued that letters and diaries left by a range of women in this period shows that many women experienced sexual passion and enjoyed intimate physical relations with men prior to and after marriage. The situation for female same-sex relationships has been more difficult to ascertain, as the debate over **romantic friendship** and **lesbianism** illustrates.

Historians are generally agreed that any straightforward assertion about women's sexuality founders in light of the complexities involved in interpreting textual sources from this period. Reading these sources requires scholars to be sensitive to their own assumptions about what might constitute evidence of sexual desire. As Karen Lystra has argued, the emphasis on "purity" in letters and diaries cannot be read simply as asexuality, but must be read in the context of a social and cultural world where the secular and religious could be co-extensive. Recent scholarship has emphasized women's agency in using the notion of passionlessness for a variety of purposes of their own. These range from a desire to reduce family size, to escape from the demands of marriage and family responsibilities, as an assertion of moral selfhood for African American women after slavery, and as proof of women's higher moral status than men in the fight for women's rights. As Cott argues, "the serviceability of passionlessness to women in gaining social and familial power should be acknowledged as a primary reason that the ideology was quickly and widely accepted" (235).

Further Reading: Cook, Hera. *The Long Sexual Revolution: English Women, Sex, and Contraception, 1800–1975.* Oxford and New York: Oxford University Press, 2004; Cott, Nancy. "Passionlessness: An Interpretation of Victorian Sexual Ideology, 1790–1850." *Signs* 4 (1978): 219–36; Faderman, Lillian. *Surpassing the Love of Men: Romantic Friendship and Love between Women from the Renaissance to the Present.* New York: William Morrow and Company, 1981; Lystra, Karen. *Searching the Heart: Women, Men, and Romantic Love in Nineteenth-Century America.* New York: Oxford University Press, 1989; Porter, Roy and Lesley Hall. *The Facts of Life: The Creation of Sexual Knowledge in Britain.* New Haven, CT: Yale University Press, 1995.

Sally Newman

SEX MANUALS. A sex manual was a book or pamphlet written to inform young people approaching puberty and newly married people about sexual maturation, the changes in their bodies, and their relation to the ability to procreate. The manuals of the nineteenth century contained equal parts of anatomy, physiology, and hygiene, usually with warnings about the harmful effects of **masturbation** and tobacco. The attention given to **birth control** and woman's sexual response were either minimal or nonexistent.

One of the first manuals written for women was Richard Carlile's (1790–1843) *Every Woman's Book* (1826). In jail at the time of its publication, convicted for criticizing government brutality in a newspaper called *The Republican*, he had a reputation for giving free rein to the expression of controversial political and social issues. He felt strongly that women should have a right to vote and practice birth control. In this first sex education text published in England, he wrote of ways to limit the number of children. In 1831, Robert Dale Owen (1801–1877), an editor of the *Free Enquirer*, a newsletter for free thinkers and radical intellectuals, published the first book in the United States on contraception and advice on sexual matters. It was called *Moral Physiology; or, a Brief and Plain Treatise on the Population Question*. The *Free Enquirer* went on to publish a variety of articles on marriage and the rights of women. Fanny (Frances) Wright (1795–1852), co-author of the *Free Enquirer*, gave talks on family limitation at a time when women did not speak to mixed audiences. Like **Josephine Butler** (1828–1906), she defied the typical conventions of her social milieu. In a society where women were subordinate politically, socially, and occupationally, sexuality was contained within these larger social issues because without a political voice, women could not make decisions that controlled their lives. Without learning to read, women could not learn about their own bodies and without training, some women found **prostitution** the only way to survive. Ignorance regarding sex also facilitated the spread of venereal disease. When ignorance of sexual passion was present, moral and physical disease followed. Wright promoted the virtue of reason over the virtue of unrealistic purity.

As Owen and Wright continued to promote their ideas, a backlash was growing among the wider, Protestant-dominated culture, where they were referred to as the "anti-Christ." Promotion of birth control was distorted by conservatives as advocacy of prostitution. The controversy regarding contraception related to ideas of original sin and woman's punishment for Eve's transgression. If one were to free woman from her god-given burden, what would keep her from becoming promiscuous? The belief was that women needed to be controlled by men because they were too weak to control themselves. Religion, aided by the traditional patriarchal family structure, fought to prevent the spread of knowledge of sexual matters through written material.

The titles of sex manuals are inviting. Many combine a biologic formal title with a less technical explanatory subtitle. Frederick Hollick's originally titled *The Origin of Life in Plants and Animals* was revised and reprinted as *The Marriage Guide* (1850). His other works were *The Male Generative Organs in Health and Disease* (1849) followed by *The Diseases of Woman, their Causes and Cures, Familiarly Explained* (1855). His manual for married women, entitled *The Matron's Manual of Midwifery and Childbirth* was written in 1848.

Medical Common Sense (1858), by Dr. Edward Bliss Foote, gave advice on contraception to married couples. A sex manual written in 1869 reinforced the belief that a woman needed no sexual gratification. Women only submitted to their husbands to please them and if it were not for the desire to become pregnant, women would prefer to do without sex altogether. Other manuals advised restraint and continence, because the authors believed that all sexual excitement was physically harmful, whether it was masturbation or intercourse. The best-known sex manuals regarding sexual abstinence were written by **John Harvey Kellogg** (1852–1943) whose philosophy regarding health was founded on the beliefs of the Seventh Day Adventists. After becoming a doctor, he became the administrator of the Battle Creek Sanitarium. He advised circumcision for all boys to prevent masturbation, but without the use of anesthetic because the pain would be connected with punishment and have a salutary effect on the youth's mind. For girls, he recommended the application of pure carbolic acid to the clitoris. His early sex manuals were concerned with diet, exercise, and keeping the colon clean with a focus on enemas and bowel health. Since he was a celebrated doctor, his books sold well and contributed to the belief that sex robbed the male body of power with each loss of sperm.

All sex information, regardless of context, was temporarily hijacked by an anxious postal clerk by the name of **Anthony Comstock** (1844–1915). He had come from a family of fourteen children and rather than sympathize with the plight of his mother, he began a crusade, first against contraception which later expanded to include opposition to any information about sex at all. He put all sexual information in one category, the obscene, and was able to convince **law** makers to pass the Comstock Act (1873), which prohibited any material of a sexual nature to be carried by the U.S. mail. In 1868 in England, obscenity was a crime because it was believed to deprave and corrupt those minds open to immoral influences but in the United States it was not. Comstock, with the backing of the YMCA, sought to have similar legislation in New York State. At the public hearing, Comstock produced a collection of pornography, contraceptive devices, and abortifacients, alleging but never proving that they had been sent in the mail. A shocked Congress amended the criminal code to prohibit the transportation of every obscene, lewd, lascivious and filthy book, which included sex manuals and legitimate medical information regarding prophylaxis of venereal disease.

The Comstock Act was impossible to enforce uniformly. Although it created hardships, most infringements were not pursued through the courts. By the turn of the century in both North America and Britain, birth rates were in steep decline, obvious proof that the contraceptive advice in sex manuals and availability of condoms, pessaries, and diaphragms had begun to be disseminated, although the poorest families were to remain without reproductive control for at least another generation. *See also* Censorship; Anthony Comstock.

Further Reading: D'Emilio, John and Estelle B. Freedman. *Intimate Matters: A History of Sexuality in America*. New York: Harper and Row, 1989; Hayes, A. *Sexual Physiology of Women*. Boston: Peabody Medical Institute, 1869; Hollick, Frederick. *Dr. Hollick's Complete Works*. Philadelphia: David McKay, 1878; Horowitz, Helen Lefkowitz. *Rereading Sex*. New York: Alfred A. Knopf, 2002; Kellogg, John Harvey. *Plain Facts for Old and Young: Embracing the Natural History and Hygiene of Organic Life*. Burlington: I.F. Segner, 1877; Kellogg, John Harvey. *Treatment for Self-Abuse and its Effects, Plain Facts for Old and Young*. Burlington: F. Segner & Co., 1888; Kellogg, John Harvey. *Ladies Guide in Health and Disease*. Des Moines, IA: W. D. Condit & Co., 1890.

Lana Thompson

SEXOLOGY. The discipline of sexology, though not the term itself, dates from the second half of the nineteenth century. The word "sexology," a Latin-Greek hybrid describing the study of sex, originated from the German *Sexualwissenschaft*, which was first used in 1907 by the dermatologist and sex researcher Iwan Bloch (1872–1922). Sexology differs from erotology insofar as it focuses upon the theoretical rather than the practical aspects of sexuality. The advent of sexology in Britain and continental Europe was made possible by a number of related factors, including the French physician B. A. Morel's influential concept of physiological and psychological "degeneration," the medical profession's growing interest in **homosexuality**, and the public's concern over the proper relationship between men and women. During its early phases in the Victorian period, sexology was generally viewed as a somewhat radical and morally questionable field of study.

Among the first sexologists was the gay German lawyer Karl-Heinrich Ulrichs, who coined the term "Uranism" (for homosexuality) in a series of twelve pamphlets (1864–1879). His neologism derives from the Greek word *Uranus* (Heaven) and refers to a distinction Plato draws in his *Symposium* between earthly (Pandemian) love and heavenly (Uranian) love—the former existing between men and women, the latter between men. Blending ancient mythology with contemporary biology, Ulrichs explains how human beings are divided before birth into three categories: male, female, and "urnings" (male homosexuals) or "uringin" (lesbians). In Ulrich's opinion, male and female homosexuals are those with the biology of one sex and the sexual instinct of the other; thus, he describes an urning as a "female soul in a male body." Because Uranism is inborn, natural, and healthy, he contended, laws against it ought to be repealed. His views were shared by the Austrian-Hungarian writer Karoly Maria Kertbeny, who in 1869 first used the term "homosexual" in an anonymous pamphlet addressed to the Prussian Minister of Justice.

Perhaps the best-known practitioner of sexology was the Austrian psychiatrist **Richard von Krafft-Ebing**. Krafft-Ebing at once maintained the accepted wisdom of his period and sought to advance it through evolutionist theory. He believed, as did most of his contemporaries, that **masturbation** was dangerous, and that it was implicated in mental illness and sexual pathology. Yet he also subscribed to the more progressive notion that defects in the nervous system were responsible for disease, and he claimed that while some "perversions" were innate and others acquired, even those of the latter type could not manifest themselves in individuals whose nerves were sound. His opinion on the primary function of sex—to reproduce—logically led to his judgment that any sexual practices not conducive to reproduction were unnatural.

Krafft-Ebing's case studies of unconventional sexuality were collected in his *Psychopathia Sexualis* (1886), in which he analyzes homosexuality, **fetishism**, sadism, and masochism. To categorize these variations, he either uses the terms devised by others or develops his own. He borrows "homosexuality" from Kertbeny and "fetishism" from the French psychologist Alfred Binet, while deriving "sadism" from the Marquis de Sade (who took pleasure in giving pain), and "masochism" from Leopold von Sacher-Masoch (who enjoyed receiving it). Krafft-Ebing also discusses satyriasis, nymphomania, **necrophilia**, incest, and pedophilia, mostly from a legal point of view.

Krafft-Ebing hoped that *Psychopathia Sexualis* would assist other **physicians** in treating the sexual difficulties of their patients and enable the courts to cope more thoughtfully with diverse sexual practices. Because his book was read not only by professionals but also by the general public, however, its most significant effect may well have been to help make alternative sexuality a topic of widespread discourse and debate. *Psychopathia Sexualis* also influenced the forensic psychiatry practiced in continental Europe during the early twentieth century.

Another significant late-Victorian sexological text is *The Evolution of Sex* (1889) by Patrick Geddes and J. Arthur Thomson. Unlike *Psychopathia Sexualis*, *The Evolution of Sex* focuses on mainstream sexuality and is especially concerned with "the divergent

evolution of the sexes" as expressed in "the preponderating passivity of the females, and the predominant activity of the males." Geddes and Thomson argue that men's often-destructive "katabolic" nature expends energy, while women's nurturing "anabolic" temperament conserves it. They also claim that "[m]an thinks more, woman feels more." These sex-based dichotomies apply to even the lowest forms of life and are immutable; hence, "What was decided among the prehistoric Protozoa cannot be annulled by Act of Parliament." Because the sexes are "complementary and mutually dependent," men and women ought to cooperate more fully; furthermore, women ought to play a larger role in public life if the human species is to progress toward higher levels of civilization.

In *Love's Coming of Age* (1896), Edward Carpenter draws upon the work of Geddes and Thomson. While he accepts the differences between the sexes as biologically determined, he believes that men and women should not be "two groups hopelessly isolated in habit and feeling from each other." Moreover, he claims that male dominance jeopardizes civilization, and that female influence is a necessary counterbalance. Carpenter is more original when arguing for sex as a means of unifying two people rather than simply reproducing the species. Himself a gay man and the author of the pamphlet *Homogenic Love and its Place in a Free Society* (1894), Carpenter also discusses homosexuality in a section entitled "The Intermediate Sex." Here, he argues that those of the "Uranian type" are often fit and healthy, and that they might well "have an important part to play in the evolution of the **race**."

Havelock Ellis, ca. 1918. Courtesy of the Library of Congress.

Carpenter's progressive attitude toward sexual diversity is shared by **Havelock Ellis** in his seven-volume *Studies in the Psychology of Sex* (1896–1928). In the first volume, Ellis contends that sex is "the central problem of life," describes the deleterious effects of silence on this crucial topic, and promises to present his research and conclusions "in that cold and dry light through which alone the goal of knowledge may truly be seen." Using medical, anthropological, biological, literary, and autobiographical sources, Ellis investigates the wide range of sexual practices with grace, conscientiousness, and objectivity. His books are remarkable for both their sober tone and their willingness to challenge commonplace assumptions about topics such as masturbation.

Developing from the work of Ellis and other pioneers, sexology flourished during the first decades of the twentieth century. Most activity in the field occurred in Berlin, where the *Zeitschrift für Sexualwissenschaft* (*Journal of Sexology*) was published in 1908; the Society for Sexology took shape in 1913; the Institute for Sexology was created in 1919; and the International Meeting for Sexual Reform on a Sexological Basis was convened in 1921.

Further Reading: Bland, Lucy and Laura Doan, ed. *Sexology in Culture: Labelling Bodies and Desires*. Chicago: University of Chicago Press, 1999; Bland, Lucy and Laura Doan, ed. *Sexology Uncensored: The Documents of Sexual Science*. Chicago: University of Chicago Press, 1999; Bullough, Vern. L. *Science in the Bedroom: A History of Sex Research*. New York: Basic Books-HarperCollins, 1994; Porter, Roy and Lesley Hall. *The Facts of Life: The Creation of Sexual Knowledge in Britain, 1650–1950*. New Haven, CT: Yale University Press, 1995.

Jamil M. Mustafa

SEXUAL PLEASURE. *See* Orgasm

SLANDER, ENGLISH LAW. The ecclesiastical courts of the Church of England administered a system of **law** quite separate from the common law. Until the middle of the nineteenth century, the ecclesiastical courts had jurisdiction in respect of several subject matters over the whole population of England and Wales. One of these subject matters was sexual slander.

There is a distinction in English law between libel (defamation by written words) and slander (defamation by spoken words). All libels and some kinds of slander were actionable in the common law courts, and in such cases the jurisdiction of the ecclesiastical courts was excluded. But an imputation of sexual misconduct (adultery or fornication) was not actionable at common law unless it caused actual financial loss, and it was this kind of slander that remained, until 1855, within the jurisdiction of the ecclesiastical courts.

A suit for defamation in the ecclesiastical courts was instituted and controlled by the plaintiff (claimant), but did not lead to an award of money damages. It was regarded in ecclesiastical law as a "mixed" suit, partly for the benefit of the plaintiff, and partly to control and punish the misconduct of the defendant. The order against an unsuccessful defendant was that he or she should perform "penance," which required a formal apology to the plaintiff, and five or six of her friends if she and they chose that they should be present, usually in the vestry room of the parish church. The defendant was also ordered to pay the plaintiff's costs, which could amount to a substantial sum. Ecclesiastical procedure was cumbersome and expensive, and costs of £20 or £30 were not unusual in a disputed case.

Orders of the courts were enforced by imprisonment for contempt of court, and a number of persons were imprisoned for ignoring the initial summons, or for refusing to perform penance or to pay costs. Imprisonment occurred in about twelve cases each year, and in some cases, where the defendant lacked the means to pay, imprisonment lasted for an indefinite period.

The cases brought to the ecclesiastical courts were of various kinds, and cannot easily be classified. Some arose out of insulting words used in the course of argument, typically calling a woman a "whore." Even where the words were mere insult, and could not be understood to impute actual unchastity, they were punishable in the ecclesiastical courts. Other cases involved the spreading of rumors, which could be very harmful, and could ruin a woman's chance of a good marriage.

An example of the latter kind of case occurred in 1849. Sarah Sharpe, an innkeeper's daughter, unmarried at the age of forty-one, was engaged to be married to Thomas Fowler, aged forty-five, who gave his profession as "contractor," and was described as a "gentleman" in the plaintiff's claim. Evidence in the ecclesiastical courts took the form of written depositions, and the depositions of six witnesses were given in support of the plaintiff's case. Joseph Rea, like Sarah Sharpe's father, an innkeeper, said that Thomas Dauncey, the defendant, had observed to him that, if the intended marriage took place "Fowler would not have a very prudent girl." Dauncey said that this was a common report in the village (Stonehouse, Gloucestershire), and that he himself had "been with her" several times (taken to imply sexual intercourse), and that he could tell him the day. He said that it was reported that an eighteen-year-old girl, Elizabeth, who had lived with Sarah Sharpe and her parents until her recent death, though supposed to be Sharpe's niece, was really her illegitimate child. Dauncey, who was a shoemaker, said that he had often made shoes for Elizabeth, and that Sarah Sharpe had always paid for them. He also said that she had had a miscarriage in consequence of her association with a man called Blanche. Rea repeated all this to Fowler and two weeks later, when Fowler and Dauncey met at the inn, Fowler asked Dauncey to go into another (presumably private) room, where Dauncey repeated the allegations, adding that Sharpe was "anything but a virtuous woman." Fowler himself gave evidence and said that he had decided to break the Slander, English Law engagement on account of the rumors about Sharpe's chastity, though this was not, he said "wholly in consequence of the defendant's statements: he had heard things from other quarters quite sufficient to induce him not to marry the plaintiff, whatever his intentions might once have been." He said that he thought Sarah Sharpe's character was injured by the defendant's words, but added that "her character was spoken lightly of, as far as I can now learn, previously to the commencement of this suit." Rea thought that her character was not injured by the defendant's words, which suggests either that her reputation was already damaged, or that Dauncey was not credible.

Evidence was also given by four near relatives of Sarah Sharpe. Her brother John, on hearing that Dauncey had defamed his sister's character, sought him out and demanded an explanation from Dauncey, who, according to John's evidence, at first refused to answer the questions but then said that he "had better let the matter drop, else there would be a damned sight more come out, and he (Dauncey) would expose the whole buggering family." He added, "she is a damned thundering whore, and damn me if I have not got down the day of the month when I made her a whore." According to John Sharpe, Dauncey said that he would have married her himself "if it had not been for the character he had heard of her and of her general bad conduct." Another brother, Edward, and his wife, gave evidence, saying that they were the true parents of Elizabeth, though not giving any very persuasive explanation of her having resided from the age of three with her aunt and grandparents. These witnesses were supported by a sister, Mary Hadley, who claimed to have been present at Elizabeth's birth. All four witnesses said that Elizabeth was Edward Sharpe's daughter, and the last three said that they had seen the plaintiff at frequent intervals throughout her adult life, and had never known her to be pregnant.

The depositions show how important to an unmarried woman, and to her relatives, was her reputation for chastity, and how strong was her interest in a good marriage. Thomas Fowler took it for granted that if she had been imprudent, as alleged by Dauncey and others, she would not be a suitable wife. John Sharpe evidently considered it his duty to confront Dauncey on behalf of his sister and to remonstrate with him as to the injustice of defaming her. He did not consider it surprising that Dauncey, as well as Fowler, should have broken off engagements on account of rumors of his sister's unchastity. The case also illustrates the different attitude to a man's reputation for chastity: Dauncey was not reticent, nor expected to be so, in acknowledging his own part in Sarah Sharpe's unchastity. Such unconcern with a reputation for chastity was quite common among men, but by no means universal. About 10 percent of the defamation cases were instituted by men. Sharpe's suit was successful. Sentence was given against Dauncey, requiring the formal apology (penance) and payment of costs of £12. Unlike some plaintiffs, Sarah Sharpe insisted on actual performance of the penance, and, on Dauncey's refusal he was imprisoned, and spent six months in jail.

As demonstrated in this case, the ecclesiastical courts did not receive oral evidence. With a few exceptions evidence in defamation cases took the form of written depositions taken in private by an officer of the court (the examiner). Only at the very end of the court's jurisdiction was a statute enacted that permitted the use of oral evidence, and some use was made of this in 1854 and 1855.

There were certain points to be made in favor of the system of written depositions. It was convenient for witnesses, who could make an appointment with the examiner, at a mutually suitable time, and did not have to wait, perhaps away from home, while the trial proceeded. Where the witness could not travel evidence might be taken by commission at any convenient place. Since witnesses did not have to be accommodated during the trial, some observers thought that the ecclesiastical procedure was cheaper, but against this consideration had to be set the actual cost of preparing and copying the depositions. More substantively it was argued that, particularly on delicate matters a witness was less frightened and embarrassed, and more likely to reveal the truth, when examined in private. Cross-examination in open court, it was said, was more a test of the advocate's skill than of the reliability of the witness: a sensitive and experienced examiner could discover the truth in private more effectively than a common law advocate in the adversarial atmosphere of the courtroom. It was also said that the ecclesiastical courts, not having power to commit for contempt in the face of the court, would find it difficult to maintain order and decorum in hearing oral evidence.

But the arguments against the system of written depositions were very strong, and eventually they prevailed. Too much depended on the attitude and ability of the examiner, which varied greatly. Some examiners merely read the allegation or interrogatories to the witness, but others explained and rephrased them, and put questions of their own in order to probe for the truth. The difference between sympathetic and unsympathetic questions could obviously affect the answers, and since neither the judge nor the parties' lawyers were present at the examination, there was no effective way of assessing the tone in which the questions were asked and answered, or the demeanor of the witness. Evidence was often taken down in the third person, so that the precise words of the witness were not recorded, and it was therefore difficult to tell, in cases of a non-answer, ("and further to this article the witness knoweth not to depose") whether, if untrue, it was a matter of contempt (for refusal to answer) or perjury (for giving false evidence). Perhaps most important, not all the witnesses' words could be recorded: hesitations, rephrasings, repetitions, questions asked by the witness, introductory speech, and intermediate conversation were all omitted, so that the end result was not so much the witness's written evidence, as a partial record of an oral examination.

Cross-examination was possible only be written questions (called "interrogatories") prepared in advance. This was a very inferior mode of cross-examination, because all the questions had to be framed in ignorance of what evidence the witness was to give in chief, and in ignorance of answers to previous questions. The effectiveness of interrogatories depended entirely on the examiner, who might or might not press the witnesses for pertinent answers. Thus one ecclesiastical lawyer complained that "The witnesses ... by some means have evaded giving Answers to the Interrogatories in some material points ... When they are speaking of the utterance of the defamatory words they swear point blank; but when they are pushed as to the particulars they answer they know not or they cannot say."

There was a real danger of gross error, because the examiner might not know the details of the case, and there was no one present to set him right. In the evidence to the royal commission of 1832 the case was mentioned of a witness who had deposed in a case involving a will to the execution of entirely the wrong document. In another will case in Norwich, the witness was deaf, and misunderstood the deposition when read over to him, only realizing that it was erroneous in crucial respects when he happened to see a copy of it three months later. Another weakness was that general denials were often permitted of specific allegations. For example, in a Chester case the whole of the witness's answers to quite specific interrogatories was, "she saith that referring to what she has deposed she can only further answer & depose in the negative to each and every matter interrogated." In another case in the same diocese a witness's full answer was "that she cannot depose as to any matter or thing thereby interrogated." The lawyers framing interrogatories attempted to guard against this sort of answer by including such directions as "let the witness be most strictly interrogated as to the above facts," or "the [examiner] is respectfully requested to obtain a clear and distinct answer to the latter part of these interrogatories, as the answers thereto may be the subject of a criminal proceeding hereafter." The inclusion of such requests itself indicates that the proctor had no effective control over what occurred in the examiner's office.

About 3,000 defamation cases were instituted in England and Wales in the forty-year period between 1815 and 1855. The frequency varied considerably from one diocese to another, mainly because in some dioceses the officials of the ecclesiastical courts took active steps to discourage defamation suits. Though the number of suits was not large, there is evidence that social attitudes were influenced by knowledge of the law. Most people knew, in general terms, that it was illegal to call a woman a whore, and the evidence shows that many women were aware that the use of the word, or its equivalent, gave them significant legal rights. Ninety percent of the cases were instituted by women, mainly belonging to the middle or lower income groups.

By the nineteenth century, the defamation suit had come to seem obsolete for a variety of reasons. The notion of Church of England courts exercising jurisdiction over the whole population came to seem anomalous in an increasingly pluralistic society. The truth of the words spoken was not a complete defense, and this feature of the law attracted some criticism as a restraint on free speech. Most importantly, imprisonment was an excessive punishment for use of insulting words spoken hastily in the heat of argument, and many (although not all) of the cases were of this kind. The prevailing opinion, reflected in a royal commission report in 1832 was that the jurisdiction of the ecclesiastical courts should be removed, but that there should be substituted a new minor criminal offence of sexual slander. The latter suggestion was never implemented.

In 1853, a woman in South Wales was summoned to appear in court for calling her neighbor, in the course of a quarrel, "a whore and a damn whore, too." She ignored the summons, and was committed to prison for contempt of court. When she had been in prison for ten months her case was taken up by a local lawyer, and a statute was enacted in 1855 abolishing the defamation jurisdiction of the ecclesiastical courts. The consequence was that an imputation of unchastity by spoken words was no longer amenable to any legal process unless it caused actual financial loss.

The ecclesiastical defamation suit, though obsolete and anomalous in several respects, and sometimes oppressive, yet served a social purpose that was useful to women in many cases, and to women of modest means, and that gave them an independence of action not found in other branches of English **law**. In some cases the motive of the plaintiff was to vindicate her reputation, in others to punish the defendant. The abolition of the jurisdiction was perceived as leaving a gap, and in 1891 a statute was enacted (the Slander of Women Act) to give jurisdiction in cases of sexual slander to the common law courts, but only in favor of women.

Further Reading: Helmholz, R. H. *Select Cases on Defamation to 1600.* London: Selden Society, 1985; Sharpe, J. A. *Defamation and Sexual Slander in Early Modern England: The Church Courts at York.* Borthwick Papers, no. 58. York: Borthwick Institute, 1980; Waddams, S. M. *Sexual Slander in Nineteenth-Century England: Defamation in the Ecclesiastical Courts, 1815–1855.* Toronto: University of Toronto Press, 2000.

Stephen Waddams

SOCIAL PURITY. The term "social purity" referred to a loose coalition of nineteenth-century organizations that sought, through a variety of anti-vice crusades, to regulate and "elevate" public standards of morality. Social purity campaigns surrounding the moral policing of **prostitution**, incest, **masturbation**, drink, sex education, and the censorship of obscene forms of literature and entertainment took place on an international scale throughout the United States, the United Kingdom, Canada, and Europe, each exhibiting their own distinctive national emphases. In Britain, vigilance work had taken place since the eighteenth century with the "Societies for the Reformation of Manners," but the social purity movement, in its most systematic and organized form, arose out of the mid-nineteenth-century campaign to repeal the **Contagious Diseases Acts** (1864–1869), which legislated for the compulsory medical examination of any women suspected of engaging in prostitution.

The eradication of prostitution and the demand for a single standard of sexual morality, with its distinctive emphasis upon an equivalent male sexual chastity, remained the mainstay of British social purity activism. Bolstered by the collapse of state-regulated prostitution in the early 1880s, purity workers began to initiate their own agenda of sexual reform through the criminal legislature. A proliferation of diverse organizations such the Social Purity Alliance (1973), the Moral Reform Union (1881), the Gospel Purity Alliance (1884), the White Cross Army (1883), and the Church of England Purity Society (1883) were united in their motivating impetus—evangelical Christianity—and, initially, in a common political goal of raising the age of sexual consent from thirteen to sixteen years. This was achieved with the successful passage of the Criminal Law Amendment (CLA) Act in 1885, and was in large part attributable to the public outcry caused by William Stead's sensationalist series of articles on juvenile prostitution published in the *Pall Mall Gazette* in July 1885 entitled "The Maiden Tribute of Modern Babylon." Stead's journalistic accounts, questionable as they were, provided huge momentum to existing anti-vice work. The CLA Act may have succeeded in raising the **age of consent**, but, more controversially, it enshrined stronger penalties for brothel-owners and greater police powers of entry and arrest to the police. In order to enforce the working of the Act, Stead established the National Vigilance Association (NVA), which was to become the central coordinating vehicle for social purity activism throughout the 1880s and 1890s. Its Executive Committee was composed of leading feminist reformers such as **Josephine Butler** and Millicent Fawcett, as well as prominent religious orators such as Catherine Booth, Ellice Hopkins, and the Methodist Percy Bunting. Under the organizational abilities of its secretary William Coote, the NVA boasted 300 local vigilance branches by 1888.

Social purity's preparedness to utilize criminal legislation and increasingly interventionist methods of vice control, such as enlarged powers of police surveillance and the forcible suppression of brothels, represented a dramatic shift away from previous libertarian reform strategies. Purity reformers regarded the **law** as an educative vehicle through which God's kingdom would be ushered in on earth and, the moral regeneration of society achieved. A defining feature of the movement, therefore, was its attempt to infuse society with improved levels of sexual respectability. This was achieved through the mass dissemination of moral prescriptive literature among the clergy, rescue workers, and district visitors for use with poorer families. These didactic tracts were frequently melodramatic, misinformed and plagued by class limitations. Discontinuities between middle-class ideologies of adolescence and the social reality of working-class childhood undoubtedly prohibited social purity reformers' awareness of the actual sexual development of their "charges." This resulted in a sometimes repressive surveillance of working-class behavior. It would be wrong to assume, however, that social purity advocates were solely concerned with the sexual habits of the working classes. Young middle- and upper-class men at public school were also the targets of sustained antimasturbation campaigns generated by members of social purity organizations issuing apocalyptic warnings concerning the "solitary vice." Here, the message of male self-control and bodily self-discipline reflected wider concerns about British national destiny and imperial progress.

In historiographical terms, social purity has been depicted as the high watermark of Victorian antisensualism. According to Edward Bristow's germinal work *Vice and Vigilance: Purity Movements in Britain since 1700* (1977), for example, the social and psychological impact of social purity was overwhelmingly negative. During a period in which modern sexual theory was in its nascent stages, purity reformers retarded the development of more liberal, educated attitudes by perpetuating beliefs that "sex was a nasty appetite to be curbed by faith, cold water and lessons in good citizenship" (Bristow 1977, 127). Such an analysis fails to appreciate the feminist critique of the sexual double standard contained within purity agitation. While many feminist historians, such as Judith Walkowitz in her classic work *Prostitution and Victorian Society* (1980), have been equally uncomfortable with social purity's more interventionist and repressive approach towards prostitution, others, such as Sheila Jeffreys, have depicted female purity activism as a politics of revolutionary **feminism**, whose assault against male sexual immorality compared favorably with the sexual philosophies of the most militant feminists. Similarly, the work of Lucy Bland demonstrates how purity women's moral policing of public entertainment may be interpreted as a form of feminist vigilantism that which sought to defend the rights of women to traverse public spaces without fear of male interference or attack.

Ultimately, as Alan Hunt has pointed out, the *fin-de-siecle* movement for social purity is best understood, not in any complacent denunciatory sense or indeed as a quaint caricature of the epithet "Victorian," but in terms of wider social anxiety theories about sexuality, youth, and gender. And, also in and the way in which even seemingly conflictual discourses such as religion and medical science may combine forces at certain moments in the history of moral panic to exercise a powerful "normalizing" influence on the construction of sexual identities.

Further Reading: Bland, Lucy. *Banishing the Beast: Feminism, Sex and Morality, 1885–1918*. Harmondsworth: Penguin, 1995; Bristow, Edward. *Vice and Vigilance: Purity Movements in Britain since 1700*. Dublin: Gill & Macmillan, 1977; Hunt, Alan. *Governing Morals: A Social History of Moral Regulation*. Cambridge, MA: Cambridge University Press, 1999; Jeffreys, Sheila. *The Spinster and her Enemies: Feminism and Sexuality 1880–1930*. London: Pandora, 1985; Mort, Frank. *Dangerous Sexualities: Medico-Moral Politics in England since 1830*. London: Routledge, 1987; Pivar, David. *Purity Crusade: Sexual Morality and Social Control, 1868–1900*. Westport, CT: Greenwood, 1973; Valverde, Mariana. *The Age of Light, Soap and Water: Moral Reform in English Canada, 1885–1925*. Toronto: McClelland & Stewart, 1991; Walkowitz, Judith. *Prostitution and Victorian Society: Women, Class and the State*. Cambridge, MA: Cambridge University Press, 1980.

Sue Morgan

SPERMATORRHOEA. The disease concept of *spermatorroea* was the product of the medical profession's efforts to pathologize the normal and natural phenomenon of nocturnal seminal emissions. Belief in the existence of a disease called "spermatorroea" spread throughout the medical world following the publication of *Des Pertes Séminales Involontaires* by Claude-François Lallemand (1790–1853). Evidence for medical concern with nocturnal seminal emissions can be found in earlier works, such as Tissot's *A Treatise on the Diseases Produced by Onanism*, but Lallemand's work had greater success in convincing the medical world that "the emission of semen without copulation" or "involuntary seminal loss of every kind" if left untreated, inevitably resulted in physical debility, wasting, insanity, epilepsy, and eventually death. The very construction of the word *spermatorroea* was an obvious and deliberate lexicographical analogy with other disease names such as *gonorrhea*. This had the effect of reinforcing the classification of spermatorrhœa among the venereal diseases, that is, diseases arising as a consequence of "impure" or "excess" sexual activity.

The etiology of spermatorrhoea was understood to be **masturbation**, which was believed to damage the seminal vesicles, resulting in a life-threatening involuntary discharge. Not only was the involuntary loss of semen considered a disease, but spermatorrhoea was also seen as the cause of a myriad of other fatal diseases and mental disorders. In addition to being deadly, spermatorrhoea was believed to be extremely common. Consequently, the treatments devised to cure this condition were correspondingly severe.

The most common treatment for gonorrhea in the nineteenth century, a course of urethral injections of silver nitrate, was also employed to treat spermatorrhoea, but by the early twentieth century, treatment for spermatorrhoea became increasingly extreme and mutilating. Castration, vasectomy, and circumcision were among the most common drastic surgical methods used to halt the nocturnal flow of semen.

Belief in the existence and importance of spermatorrhoea continued well into the twentieth century, especially among the American medical profession. While the concept of spermatorrhoea was never formally disproved, medical interest in it waned over time, as reflected in gradual decline of studies on the topic published in the professional medical literature. In the popular medical literature aimed at the American public, however, dire warnings about the harmful consequences of both masturbation and seminal emissions could be found as late as the 1920s.

Further Reading: Darby, Robert. *A Surgical Temptation: The Demonization of the Foreskin and the Rise of Circumcision in Britain.* Chicago: University of Chicago Press, 2005; Glick, Leonard B. *Marked in Your Flesh: Circumcision from Ancient Judea to Modern America.* Oxford: Oxford University Press, 2005.

Frederick Mansfield Hodges

SPINSTERS. Spinster is the term for unmarried women used from the seventeenth century. As a group they attracted unprecedented attention during the later decades of the nineteenth century when Victorian society was consumed by the so-called "problem of surplus women." This view was epitomized by English industrialist W. R. Greg in his influential article "Why are women redundant?" (1862), where he argued that the "unmarried constitute the problem to be solved, the evil and anomaly to be cured" (Poovey 1988, 2). Recent scholarship has suggested that the numbers of single women in the United Kingdom were actually much higher during the seventeenth century than the nineteenth. Why then was the spinster considered such a serious social problem in the later period?

Scholars have isolated several factors that coincided mid-century in Britain and in the later decades of the nineteenth century in the United States. The mid-century decades were the first years during which Britain's population could be measured by comparative census reports. Spinsters became a distinct social group that could be tracked when marital status was included as a separate question in the 1851 census (1880 in the United States). Between the United Kingdom censuses of 1851 and 1861, two changes stood out as significant: one was the "surplus" of women to men, and the other a doubling of the numbers of single women in the course of the decade. These figures exacerbated neo-Malthusian concerns of overpopulation (the reason for the census being introduced initially in the United Kingdom) and fears for the "future of the species." Perceived as excess to the population on one hand, spinsters did not fulfill their duty to provide imperial subjects for the nation on the other. The significance attached to these figures in Britain and the United States reflects cultural anxieties specific to each country but one factor common to both (aside from industrialization) was women's increasing agitation for suffrage, and for the same opportunities to work and education as men. In the United States the issue of education for women was largely responsible for changing attitudes about spinsterhood (previously known as "Single Blessedness"), as higher numbers of the early generations of college-educated women remained single than those who did not attend college. These figures were used to support medical theories linking education with serious health risks for women and were specifically targeted at single women. The debates over spinsterhood crystallized anxieties about women's place in society. Women working outside of the private sphere challenged Victorian domestic and sexual ideology that presented women as the keepers of the hearth whose natural instincts were fulfilled in the dual roles of wife and mother. This is not to suggest that the "crisis of single women" was entirely about ideology. There were serious social issues caused by increasing numbers of single women seeking work that needed to be addressed, as the English women's advocate **Josephine Butler** (1828–1906) argued in *The Education and Employment of Women* (1868). Butler argued for the recognition of the economic difficulties facing single women in a society that allowed them minimal access to education and work opportunities. The professions open to women were limited (teaching, nursing, domestic service) and severely oversubscribed, with the result that wages were low and barely covered living expenses.

Lack of sources about the experiences of working-class women makes it more difficult to know whether they stayed single by choice when they had to work out of necessity, but we do know that working-class women emigrated to the colonies in larger numbers than middle-class women. Whether to pursue a better marriage market (the male/female ratio was drastically reversed in the colonies), or improved work opportunities or both, hundreds of thousands of single women left Britain during the course of the nineteenth century.

For a small number of middle-class women, remaining single was a choice made for many different reasons including the desire to pursue a vocation, undertake meaningful work and/or for independence from men, marriage or children. Many such women formed committed partnerships with other women or joined women's only communities such as the Settlement House movement or the sisterhoods who provided the foundations for support and friendship networks. These communities encouraged single women to view themselves as productive members of society because of their spinsterhood. Women revalued the terms of their singleness, embracing chastity and purity as emblems of their higher purpose and as a defense against the charge of abnormality or inversion that was increasingly attributed to single women in the early decades of the twentieth century.

Further Reading: Chambers-Schiller, Lee Virginia. *Liberty, a Better Husband: Single Women in America, the Generations of 1780–1840.* New Haven, CT: Yale University Press, 1984; Hill, Bridget Hill. *Women Alone: Spinsters in England, 1660–1850.* New Haven, CT: Yale University Press, 2001; Kranidis, Rita S. *The Victorian Spinster and Colonial Emigration: Contested Subjects.* New York: St. Martin's Press, 1999; Poovey, Mary. *Uneven Developments: The Ideological Work of Gender in Mid-Victorian England, Women in Culture and Society.* Chicago: University of Chicago Press, 1988; Vicinus, Martha. *Independent Women: Work and Community for Single Women, 1850–1920, Women in Culture and Society.* Chicago: University of Chicago Press, 1985.

Sally Newman

STOKER, BRAM (1847–1912).   Bram Stoker became famous due to the publication of *Dracula* in 1897. Dracula is the most overtly sexual character in the novel but if the two heroines, Lucy and Mina, are seen as the Count's victims, the reader is however invited to read a subtext where female desire (in Lucy's case at least) is expressed in more or less explicit terms around four key scenes: the letter to her friend Mina, her "draculaization," her infanticides, and the final impalement.

As one of the many narrators—*Dracula* is a polyphonic novel—Lucy writes to her friend and confidante Mina, a letter out of the men's knowledge and reach, entrusting her with her secret: she has had three proposals in a row (the figure THREE is in capital letters) which cannot but boost her coquette's ego, despite her protest to the contrary as she knows Victorian decency demands modesty in a woman. Lucy's oxymoronic declaration is the stylistic expression of her Victorian dilemma: she is caught between desire and morals and her confession to Mina violates the dominant patriarchal code. Lucy is one of the New Women derided by Mina—the epitome of Victorian morality— and her textual rebellion only paves the way to her sexual one. The vamp is but a budding vampire. For Lucy, men are interchangeable, though valuable, items (the later blood transfusions prove her right). Her "crying like a baby" is the bodily expression of her protests, as if she were claiming her innocence at the very moment her only desire is to lose it.

Lucy's wish: "Why can't they let a girl marry three men?" will be fulfilled later when all her suitors give their blood in turn to save her. Lucy's body becomes a battlefield between Dracula and the men of the "Crew of Light" (as the group of men call themselves), as if Stoker, fearing any possible homosexual reading, had to interpose a woman between all the men. Lucy is an easy prey for Dracula who breaks the monotonous monogamy she will be doomed to, once married to Arthur. Dracula is the exotic/erotic lover, the "odd one in" who establishes a vaudevillesque situation in the legitimate (or almost legitimate) couples: Lucy and Arthur first, then Mina and Jonathan. Once Lucy has been vampirized by the Count, she becomes openly sexual in her prayer to Arthur: "Come Arthur, come," which he finds as difficult to resist as Jonathan with the three she-vampires in Dracula's castle. Arthur is saved at the last minute by Dracula's antithesis, good Doctor Van Helsing, the leader of the Crew of Light. Lucy, the former sleepwalker, has become a dangerous streetwalker, and, like the three she-vampires, a body-snatcher whose victims are young children whom she kills and whose blood she sucks in a perverted inversion of the maternal relation.

The repeated injections resemble mini penetrations anticipating the final drastic impalement, but prove unable to defeat Dracula. Lucy's first death is only a simulacrum as it gives back her **beauty**. Death suits her. Lucy has sold her soul to the devil, and

Dracula promises the resurrection of the body. Dead Lucy is not Lucy but only a monstrous, vampiric, sexual double. Her dilemma is her in-betweenness, between life and death, angel and devil.

Since she has become a devil, the men's love for her has also turned into sheer hatred. Van Helsing urges Arthur to kill her. Lucy must die twice for the Crew of Light to claim her as one of their own, one "of God's true dead." Her impalement is aimed at re-erecting the barriers between life and death, good and evil, men and women. But Lucy's fiancé is also cast as Othello: a man who perceives himself wronged by a passionate woman and consequently uses violence to reassert the patriarchal gender code (Pope, 76). Lucy the witch will be impaled by her own future husband in a scene where the men are turned into savage beasts thirsty for the blood of one to whom they have given so much.

If sexual intercourse can never take place before or out of wedlock, it does in death, on "the bridal bier" (to quote Victor Frankenstein when the Monster has just killed his bride). Arthur literally breaks or tears Lucy's heart to pieces (like Frankenstein with the Monster's bride) to reestablish order among chaos. Only death will give her back her human dignity. But if Dracula is a serial killer, the men also are murderers who kill in the name of God and morality. The scene can be read as a collective rape. Arthur's alternatively falling and rising arm is strongly evocative of sexual intercourse and his ensuing exhaustion resembles postcoital relaxation. At the end, Lucy recovers her serenity, the true Lucy replaces the false one, the angel has expelled the demon, the virgin supersedes the whore and Lucy at last performs the etymology of her name. The beauty is at last sleeping for good.

Dracula's choice of Lucy as an ideal prey is not accidental: Lucy was ready to be vampirized, as the only way out from the Victorian demands of a patriarchal society that forbids sex for women, but society does win in the end with the defeat of Dracula himself and all his accomplices.

Further Reading: Stoker, Bram. *Dracula. New Casebooks* edited by Glennis Byron. London: St. Martin's Press, 1999; Pope, Rebecca A. "Writing and Biting in Dracula." In *Dracula. New Casebooks* edited by Glennis Byron. London: St. Martin's Press, 1999: 68–92.

Claire Bazin

SWINBURNE, ALGERNON CHARLES (1837–1909). Algernon Charles Swinburne was one of the most controversial literary figures of the Victorian period. His first collection of poetry, *Poems and Ballads Series 1*, caused outrage on its publication in 1866 due to the frank sexuality of its subject matter. Like the sensation novel of the early 1860s, which put middle- and upper-class domestic sexuality under the microscope, Swinburne's volume was also exploratory, although his choice of topics went far beyond anything treated by the novelists. Inspired in part by the greater license of French writers, especially the infamous *Les Fleurs du mal* (1857) by the poet Charles Baudelaire (1821–1867), Swinburne interrogated the darker side of sexuality, sexual love, and emotion in poems, which, among other things, featured **lesbianism**, **necrophilia** and sado-masochism. Particularly galling to his critics was the fact that subjects generally considered beyond the pale were celebrated in verse, which showed a brilliant mastery of poetic form. Swinburne's superb metrical capability, fluent lyricism, and consummate craftsmanship challenged the convention that only low, coarse, and reprehensible forms of expression could communicate matter deemed dubious or morally improper. *Poems and Ballads 1* is also notable for its emphasis on female sexual power. Its notorious succession of *femme fatales* features the goddess

Venus, Lucrezia Borgia, Dolores and Faustine to name but a few. However the volume's most important female figure is the Classical Greek poet Sappho who appears in both "Anactoria" and "Sapphics." Swinburne venerated Sappho's verse and, in "Sapphics," a poem written in the meter she made famous, he sees her as the sexually aberrant "outsider" poet whose poetry simultaneously charms and repels mainstream heterosexual society. As such, she is his muse and sister-poet, and a type he conspicuously emulates. *Poems and Ballads 1* would prove influential for poets writing after Swinburne both in terms of style and content, in particular the poets of the *fin de siècle* such as Arthur Symons, Ernest Dowson, and Oscar Wilde who relished the opportunity to describe sexual feelings and experiences conventionally proscribed. However, none of these writers' verses would ever raise the storm generated by Swinburne's volume.

Swinburne, the eldest of six surviving children, was born on April 5, 1837 into an aristocratic High-Church family. His father Captain (later Admiral) Charles Henry Swinburne and his mother Lady Jane (*née* Hamilton) settled at East Dene on the Isle of White where Swinburne spent his childhood and developed his love of swimming and the sea. As a child, he quickly showed a keen interest in literature, in particular poetry. His mother, a gifted linguist, taught him Italian and French. Aged twelve, he entered Eton College where he later won the Prince Consort's Prize for Modern Languages. However, the larger part of his formal schooling was in the classics, which dominated the public school curriculum at this time. Like other public schools, Eton maintained discipline by flogging. The experience of being flogged at school was a *rite de passage* for most middle- and upper-class men and, in some cases, engendered a sexual fixation on corporal punishment. In Swinburne's case, it seems to have been responsible for his enduring sexual obsession with pain and **flagellation**. In 1854, he left Eton and in 1856 entered Balliol College, Oxford. While at Oxford he devoted much time to extending his reading and writing poetry, as well becoming a member of the Old Mortality Society, an intellectual group founded by his close friend, John Nichol, who encouraged his rejection of **Christianity**. At Oxford, he also met the Pre-Raphaelites William Morris, Edward Jones (later Burne-Jones), and Dante Gabriel Rossetti **painting** the walls of the Oxford Union and began important friendships with all three.

Swinburne left Oxford in 1860 without taking his final examination and moved to London where he published his verse-plays as the collection *The Queen Mother and Rosamond*. The next five years were spent perfecting his verse. Critics now believe that during his youth Swinburne had fallen in love with his cousin Mary Gordon who seems to have shared his interest in flagellation. However, in 1864, after traveling in Italy, he learnt of her engagement to Colonel Disney Leith. This early disappointment may have colored a number of poems in *Poems and Ballads 1* which deal with the pain of the abandoned male lover, a relatively unusual subject in poetry which traditionally has focused more on the emotions of the abandoned woman. In March 1865, Swinburne published his highly acclaimed classical verse drama *Atalanta in Calydon* and, in November, *Chastelard*, a verse play about Mary, Queen of Scots, one of his idols, and her lover, the French poet Chastelard. Both these works foreshadow the themes of *Poems and Ballads 1*, the later play in particular with its eponymous masochistic hero and fatally alluring heroine.

Swinburne's only known sexual relationship was a brief affair in 1867 with the actress and poet Adah Menken which was most probably unconsummated. He frequented a flagellant brothel in St. John's Wood in 1868–1869. Otherwise, his sexual impulses seem to have found vent in *risqué* conversation and letters shared with male friends, and in a cache of poems about schoolboy floggings. During the 1870s, he suffered increasingly poor health due to alcoholism but was eventually rescued from an untimely death by his friend Theodore Watts (Watts-Dunton after 1896), a solicitor and literary critic who took him off to recuperate in Putney. There the two friends moved into No. 2 "The Pines," where Swinburne lived peacefully for the rest of his life, protected by Watts, who weaned him off his dependence on **alcohol** and kept him out of the way of his more disreputable acquaintances. He died on April 10, 1909.

After *Poems and Ballads 1*, Swinburne's poetry was much less sexually provocative, although he never managed to shrug off his early notoriety. His energies were redirected towards political goals, in particular the reunification of Italy, which he celebrated in his *Songs before Sunrise* (1871). *Poems and Ballads 2* (1878) is very different from its earlier namesake, striking a predominantly elegiac and wistful note. The figure of Sappho as muse and sister-poet returns in the remarkable poem "On the Cliffs," from *Songs of the Springtides* (1880). Many Swinburneians believe the poet's best work to be his Arthurian epic *Tristram of Lyonnesse* (1882), which tells the legend of the fatal romance between the harpist and singer, Tristram, and Iseult, the wife of King Mark of Cornwall. The poem illustrates Swinburne's mature thinking on the nature of love and is also remarkable for its beautiful and passionate description of the couple's lovemaking in the woods near Tintagel. The quality of Swinburne's later verse is uneven and the best pieces such as "A Nympholept" and "The Lake of Gaube" tend to be explorations of the rhythms and energies of the natural world. His prose criticism was highly influential and a number of early pieces such as his 1862 review of Baudelaire's *Les Fleurs du mal*, his essay "Notes on the Designs of the Old Masters at Florence" (1868), and his analysis of the paintings and prose of his friend, the Jewish homosexual painter Simeon Solomon (1871), all show a marked interest in the common ground shared by pain and pleasure. Also noteworthy are his novels: the epistolary *Love's Cross Currents* (1905), a brilliantly witty overview of upper-class sexual intrigue, later published uncensored as *A Year's Letters* (1974), and the unfinished and somewhat fragmentary *Lesbia Brandon*. His letters, edited by Cecil Lang and more recently Terry Meyers, show his particular, often disconcerting vein of sexual humor, which is notable in his exchanges with the widowed Mary Disney-Leith with whom he resumed correspondence in later life.

Further Reading: Maxwell, Catherine. *The Female Sublime from Milton to Swinburne: Bearing Blindness*. Manchester: Manchester University Press, 2001; Maxwell, Catherine. *Swinburne. Writers and their Work*. Tavistock: Northcote House, 2005; McGann, Jerome. *Swinburne: An Experiment in Criticism*. Chicago: University of Chicago Press, 1972; Rooksby, Rikky. *Swinburne: A Poet's Life*. Aldershot: Scolar Press, 1997; Swinburne, Algernon Charles. *The Swinburne Letters*, edited by Cecil Y. Lang. 6 vols. New Haven, CT: Yale University Press, 1959–1962; Swinburne, Algernon Charles. *Major Poems and Selected Prose*, edited by Jerome McGann and Charles Sligh. New Haven, CT: Yale University Press, 2004; Swinburne, Algernon Charles. *Uncollected Letters of Algernon Charles Swinburne*, edited by Terry Meyers. 3 vols. London: Pickering & Chatto, 2005.

Catherine Maxwell

T

THEATER. One of the most popular and widespread forms of entertainment in the nineteenth-century, theater encompassed a variety of genres including historical drama, farcical comedy, and pantomime. But, melodrama in all its guises (nautical, domestic, gothic, sensation) ruled the stage for much of the century. Scholars have argued that the continuous popularity of *Macbeth*, *King Lear*, *Richard II*, and *Romeo and Juliet* over other Shakespearean plays in this period was largely due to their similarities with the subjects, style, and form of popular melodrama (often violent emotional or generational family conflict). Melodrama was a highly adaptable form that could be tailored to suit contemporary concerns, as the immense popularity of W. H. Smith's temperance play *The Drunkard* (1844) and the stage production of Harriet Beecher Stowe's *Uncle Tom's Cabin* (1852) in the United States indicates. The popularity of melodrama in this period has been theorized as giving a voice to the powerless (working classes, women, slaves, and migrants), as providing moral certainty in a period of enormous social change primarily wrought by industrialization and urbanization, and as satisfying fantasies of the triumph of good over evil regardless of seemingly insurmountable obstacles. Cultural critic Elaine Hadley has even suggested that the melodramatic mode characterizes the broader nineteenth-century culture. Scholars no longer view melodramatic plays as embarrassing remnants of a naïve theater, but as texts that can be read for the cultural values and preoccupations of different decades of the nineteenth century.

Among the themes dealt with in these plays are the evils of child labor, working conditions, the role of women, familial conflict, illegitimate children, **prostitution**, adultery, the temptations of vice, alcoholism, poverty, the corruption of the upper classes, cultural differences, assimilation, women's suffrage, the essential nobility of the American Indian (United States), and the "street Arab" (United Kingdom) and the abolition of slavery, to name only the most prominent examples. As melodrama turned to the domestic sphere it became the "ideal genre for the narration of a woman's personal story and therefore the perfect vehicle for a popular actress" (Hadley 1995, 133). For example, in Britain the hugely successful stage production of the popular novel *East Lynne* (1863), which featured a "fallen women" who died tragically having learned the error of her ways, was a staple of the oeuvre. This may have coincided with the increasing numbers of women entering the theatrical profession (a massive rise from 310 in 1841 to 6,443 by 1901) where they could, almost uniquely in this period, expect to be remunerated at similar rates to their male counterparts. While melodrama continued to be used, most notably by the Melville brothers in their backlash plays against the emancipation of women (e.g., *The Worst Woman in London* 1899) and in the spectacular or sensation melodramas of Irish playwright Dion Boucicault (1822–1890) which used mechanical innovations in stagecraft to replicate realistic sets, historians of the theater discern a shift in the last decades of the century toward the realistic portrayal of social issues.

Characterized by the plays of Henrik Ibsen (1828–1906), Anton Checkhov (1860–1904), and George Bernard Shaw (1856–1950), the new drama was concerned with the complexities of real life, rather than what was increasingly viewed as the contrived plots and sentimentalism embodied in melodrama. The *fin de siècle* theater also saw the rise of the "problem play" most particularly associated with the work of Arthur Wing Pinero in Britain (1855–1934) and James A. Hern in the United States (1839–1901) whose "fallen women" plays *Margaret Fleming* 1890, *The Second Mrs Tanqueray* 1893, and *The Notorious Mrs Ebbsmith* 1895 dealt with the social and emotional consequences of adultery by women. The focus of much of this decade was on women's sexuality, emancipation and changing role in society, anxieties that often surfaced in farcical comedies such as Pinero's *The Amazons* 1893, and Sidney Grundy's *The New Woman* 1894.

British and American theater shared many of the same actors, plays, and playwrights—a cultural exchange that was facilitated by the new steamship route across the Atlantic—but there were also significant differences, and often tensions between the theatrical cultures of both countries over the course of the century. English actors Fanny Kemble Butler (1809–1893), Ellen Terry (1847–1928), Henry Irving (1838–1905), and American actor Charlotte Cushman (1816–1876) found transatlantic fame while others, famous in their homeland, found notoriety overseas. William Charles Macready (1793–1873), the English actor had earlier toured successfully (and without incident) in the United States, but his appearance in Macbeth at the Astor Place Opera House in New York (1849) resulted in a riot in which twenty people were killed and hundreds were injured. Scholars have attributed this incident to anti-British feeling among Irish immigrants exacerbated by the inadequate British response to the Irish Potato Famine (1845–1849), growing nationalism (Native Sons of America and the Order of United Americans were involved), as well as the bitter professional rivalry between Macready and the American actor Edwin Forrest (1806–1872) whom the rioters demanded take the stage instead. This was the worst of several riots that took place in theaters in Boston and New York between 1825 and 1850 and reveals the theater as the site in which national cultures were performed both on- and offstage. Forrest had recently toured in Britain with fellow actor Charlotte Cushman but had been savaged by reviewers for his "slowness of enunciation which, we have heard, is customary in the United States" (Merrill 2002, 87). The acting style that had made him famous in the United States as an exemplar of the heroic, independent American character was viewed in Britain as parochialism, but perhaps also represented the emergent nationalism of a former colony. In contrast, Lisa Merrill argues that Charlotte Cushman was successful in Britain largely because of her nationality, which allowed her performances to be interpreted outside of the gender and class conventions that bound English actresses. Cushman's physical and emotional expressiveness (unusual for a female actress) was perceived as evidence of a "masculine intellect" rather than a lack of feminine "charms of form and feature" as one contemporary reviewer put it. The perception of masculinity was further heightened when Cushman appeared in "breeches" parts, such as the role that made her one of the most popular romantic figures of the nineteenth-century stage, that of Romeo in Shakespeare's *Romeo and Juliet*.

During the nineteenth century, women commonly performed "breeches" roles as young boys and young men in a range of different settings including the "principal boy" of

pantomime tradition. After the theater, the most widespread appearance of women in breeches was the music hall where male impersonators such as Vesta Tilley (1864–1956) and Annie Hindle (c. 1847) were tremendously popular. The tight-fitting male clothing revealed women's bodies in ways that contemporary dress did not, and scholars in the past have considered the phenomenon to be entirely aimed at exciting the appreciation of male audience members. In fact as recent scholarship has shown, stars like Cushman and Hindle attracted a large and devoted female spectatorship. Hindle received "mash notes" from women who addressed her as both sir and madam: "she once compared billet-doux with Henry J. Montague, the matinee idol of Wallack's Theatre, and her admirers all women, far outnumbered his" (Senelick 1993, 91–92). This suggests that the spectatorial pleasures for female audience members could range from wanting to be, be desired by, and/or desire the cross-dressed woman on stage. The phenomenon of breeches roles for women, and indeed the massive popularity of Cushman's Romeo may seem difficult to understand from the distance of more than a century, but what this attests to are the specific historical circumstances in which nineteenth century theater developed. It was not until the later decades of the nineteenth century that distinctions between same-sex and different-sex love relationships were defined as the

Vesta Tilley dressed in men's clothing, New York, 1906. Courtesy of the Library of Congress.

basis for a person's identity, suggesting that audiences could experience a wide range of hetero-/homoerotic desire within their cultural milieu. Indeed, it seems that we are just beginning to uncover the complexities of theater culture in the nineteenth century.

Further Reading: Bank, Rosemarie K. *Theatre Culture in America, 1825–1860.* Cambridge and New York: Cambridge University Press, 1997; Booth, Michael R. *Theatre in the Victorian Age.* Cambridge and New York: Cambridge University Press, 1991; Davis, Tracy C. and Ellen Donkin. *Women and Playwriting in Nineteenth-Century Britain.* New York: Cambridge University Press, 1999; Law Fisher, Judith and Stephen Watt. *When they weren't Doing Shakespeare: Essays on Nineteenth-Century British and American Theatre.* Athens: University of Georgia Press, 1989; Hadley, Elaine. *Melodramatic Tactics: Theatricalized Dissent in the English Marketplace, 1800–1885.* Stanford, CA: Stanford University Press, 1995; Merrill, Lisa. *When Romeo Was a Woman: Charlotte Cushman and her Circle of Female Spectators.* Ann Arbor: The University of Michigan Press, 2002; Powell, Kerry. *The Cambridge Companion to Victorian and Edwardian Theatre.* Cambridge and New York: Cambridge University Press, 2004; Senelick, Laurence. "Boys and Girls Together: Subcultural Origins of Glamour Drag and Male Impersonation on the Nineteenth Century Stage." In *Crossing the Stage: Controversies on Cross-Dressing,* edited by Lesley Ferris. London and New York: Routledge, 1993.

Sally Newman

TROLLOPE, ANTHONY (1815–1882). Anthony Trollope was an English novelist whose personal life ran along conventional lines, with no breath of sexual scandal, but he was not unworldly or intolerant of the foibles of others. His fiction exemplifies this open-mindedness.

Crushing family debts and deaths forced him to follow in the footsteps of his mother, Frances Trollope née Milton (1779–1863), a successful author, rather than in those of his father, Thomas Anthony Trollope (1774–1835), an unsuccessful barrister. His fear of scandal and dislike of hypocrisy kept Trollope's private life free from sexual dalliances. During his adolescence, his mother was absent for several years, traveling with a male artist (Hervieu) and a radical feminist (Frances Wright), and the family was later compelled by bailiffs to flee the family home and escape to Belgium. Not surprisingly, Trollope preferred, in his adult life, to seek sanctuary in a respectable Victorian marriage, which, unlike that of other famous nineteenth-century novelists, was long and happy. Rose Trollope née Heseltine (1820–1917) was his primary literary advisor and editor as well as his devoted wife. His strong memory of the premature deaths of several of his siblings and his father encouraged him, unlike many Victorians, to limit his family to two boys, born just a year apart early in the marriage. His friendship with the young American feminist and writer Kate Field caused him middle-aged "heart-flutterings," but Trollope remained a loyal husband, and Rose sensibly accommodated this patronage. To the end of his life a "reverent" Anglican worshipper, Trollope never lost his tolerance toward others who, less fortunate than he, sought unions outside marriage. He stayed a friend to George Henry Lewes (1817–1878) and George Eliot (1819–1880), frequenting their soirées, yet mindful enough of the world's opinion not to have Rose accompany him. Eliot's Sundays "at home" were legendary to young men wishing to worship the "great secular teacher," but no woman holding a social position would dare attend. Trollope's tact in these matters extended to his ability to take people as he found them. He even sent his Australian grandson to the school run in Margate, Kent, by Dickens' erstwhile mistress, Ellen Wharton Robinson née Ternan (1839–1914) (and her clerical husband), having airbrushed her past notoriety. As far as his nuclear family was concerned, though, Trollope was not amused to learn, on returning from Australia to visit his son Frederick James Anthony (1847–1910), that his older son Henry Merivale (1846–1926) had fallen in love with a woman described variously as an actress, a "woman of the streets" and a prostitute. Playing the Victorian father to perfection, Trollope swiftly despatched Henry to join his brother in Australia, hoping that the heat of that continent would conversely cool his passion. It did.

Anthony Trollope, ca. 1865. Courtesy of the Library of Congress.

Being a model Victorian in his private life did not prevent Trollope from demonstrating in comic fiction his understanding of the vagaries of human nature when it came to sex. Every one of Trollope's fictional narratives, told in his forty-seven novels and forty-two short stories, thrums with the beat of human emotions, sexual and otherwise. Not having the burden of post-Freudian obsession with sex, nor having the impediment of strict Victorian orthodoxy to matters of the flesh, Trollope shows that human behavior is motivated by complex impulses, of which sex is one. Other impulses, both negative and positive, drive the full range of his characters— from villains to heroes. These impulses include greed, ambition, hate, guilt, jealousy, envy, love, compassion, desire, and devotion. No one is so wicked that he or she does not have a redeeming feature. But sex is never absent, for he sees it as natural and healthy.

Although Trollope was proud to assert in *An Autobiography* (1883, 146) that "no girl has risen from the reading of my pages less modest than she was before," he also once said publicly (cited in Mullen with Munson, 263) that, as a novelist, he was morally bound "to teach ladies to be women and men to be gentlemen," for he believed that carefully nurtured daughters were overprotected from worldly knowledge. This is why he was prepared to tackle taboo subjects such as adultery, **bigamy**, premarital sex, **divorce**, **illegitimacy**, **prostitution**, and even, by allusion, syphilis, and **homosexuality**. More than once did an editor of a journal serializing his works object to Trollope's bold references to breasts and breast-feeding and his equally "vulgar" relish in describing passionate kisses between betrothed couples. Careful reading of his fiction often surprises us as to how much Trollope actually says about sex, as he claimed to be "afraid of nobody except God and Mudie" (Mullen and Munson 1996, 338), on the latter of whom he was dependent, since Mudie's circulating libraries could make or break a writer, and he was a strict censor.

Generally, critics have not focused much on Trollope's attitude to sex, since his fiction encompasses such a huge number of topics. While most studies remark on Trollope's surprising openness to human love and sexuality, commenting on his inclusion of mistresses, prostitutes, and sexually erring clerics, they nonetheless conclude that he endorses Victorian orthodoxy: sex should be within and confined to marriage. One commentator, Margaret Markwick, has argued that Trollope's ultimate adherence to the status quo is just a blind to conceal his *risqué* allusions to all manner of carnal responses. She even suggests that Trollope tells us when Plantagenet Palliser, future prime minister and model of moral rectitude, has his first erection. While speaking to the married Lady Dumbello and possibly contemplating a future liaison with her, "[i]t seemed as though a new vein in his body had been brought into use, and that blood was running where blood had never run before." As further evidence, Markwick cites John Millais's illustration of Palliser in *The Small House at Allington* (1864), standing stiffly and awkwardly before the lady in question with his hands crossed over his crotch (Markwick 1997, 78–79). Most critics, however, admit to Trollope's private jokes and occasional coarse remarks—from a Victorian's perspective—but do not see him in quite so daring a light.

Acts, sexual or otherwise, interested Trollope far less than human motives and reactions. He deplored violent reactions to sexual misbehavior, providing powerful images to encourage tolerance. Louis Trevelyan (*He Knew He Was Right* [1869]) drives his wife from him and himself insane, jealous of his wife's perceived, but not actual, adultery. To enact revenge, Mrs O'Hara (*An Eye for an Eye* [1879]) murders the seducer of her daughter, sending herself too into insanity. But the Vicar, Frank Fenwick (*The Vicar of Bullhampton* [1870]), horrified by Carrie Brattle's plight as well as attracted by her beauty, persuades her father to reclaim her from prostitution. And Burgo Fitzgerald (*Can You Forgive Her?* [1865]), a hopeless reprobate, treats a starving prostitute to a meal, simply from compassion. Trollope illustrates the delights of connubial sex and the dangers of extramarital sex, but advocates compassion, not punishment, for sexual misconduct.

Further Reading: Durey, Jill Felicity. *Trollope and the Church of England.* Houndsworth: Palgrave-Macmillan, 2003; Glendinning, Victoria. *Trollope.* London: Hutchinson, 1992; McMaster, Juliet. *Trollope's Palliser Novels.* London: Macmillan, 1978; McMaster, R. D. *Trollope and the Law.* New York: St. Martin's Press, 1986; Markwick, Margaret. *Trollope and Women.* London: Trollope Society, 1997; Mullen, Richard and James Munson. *The Penguin Companion to Trollope.* London: Penguin, 1996; Terry, R. C., ed. *Oxford Reader's Companion to Trollope.* Oxford: Oxford University Press, 1999.

Jill Felicity Durey

VICTORIA, QUEEN OF GREAT BRITAIN.   *See* Queen Victoria

VIRGINITY.   Virginity was a complex issue in the nineteenth century. It had a high cultural value (especially for marriageable women of the property-owning classes) and was held to be a particular virtue in the Roman Catholic Church; all Christian denominations advocated premarital virginity for both men and women. However, life-long virginity was frequently the object of scorn or at least suspicion, and by the end of the century freethinkers publicly advocated premarital sexual activity.

Virginity was expected for marriageable women of the propertied classes, partly as a way to ensure that property would be inherited by the husband's children; however, there is some evidence that engaged couples could involve in some sort of sexual exploration that stopped short of intercourse. In Roman Catholic countries, a convent education for girls was meant in part to protect their virginity until marriage. Virgins were often categorized as nonsexual; it was not until the second half of the nineteenth century that medical doctors began to realize that ovulation in women was not dependent on coition, and that in fact virgins did ovulate. The emphasis on female virginity (which was also thought to be manifested in a disinclination for marital sexual activity) had certain advantages for women: it could allow them to avoid the consequences of premarital sexual relations, to establish close friendships with women, and to practice a form of **birth control** within marriage.

The visual celebration of virginity came in the ceremony that marked the end of virginity, as by the second half of the nineteenth century women in western cultures began to adopt white (symbolizing the purity and virginity of the bride) as the preferred color for their wedding dress. When **Queen Victoria** wore a white dress for her 1840 marriage to Prince Albert, the **fashion** was set.

Societal emphasis on female virginity meant that at least some women dreaded their wedding nights. The double standard was very much in effect, and men of the propertied classes had more opportunities to lose their virginity before marriage than did their female peers, especially as the number of brothels rose in European and American cities. However, at least some (and perhaps many) men of the propertied classes—especially middle-class men—entered marriage as virgins, and, some evidence suggests, as perplexed by the sexual act as their new wives were. The image of the virginal male—otherwise known as the life-long bachelor—could also be a liberating one, as in the stories of James Fenimore Cooper.

Premarital virginity was rather less important, as a rule, for working-class women, some of whom engaged in casual **prostitution** to supplement their incomes or to replace their incomes during bad economic times. Female **servants** were notoriously vulnerable to the advances of their employers or fellow employees. By the beginning of the modern period, sexuality had become more important to the self-identity of working-class males in western cultures, and thus the age of the loss of virginity dropped from the mid-twenties to the late teens, especially for urban men.

Some middle-class men fetishized the virginity of working-class girls and young women; one of the most famous examples is that of **"Walter,"** the otherwise anonymous author of *My Secret Life*. In 1885, W. T. Stead, the editor of the *Pall Mall Gazette* (London), published a four-part series, "The Maiden Tribute of Modern Babylon," purporting to describe how young virgins were kidnapped and sold into prostitution either at home or abroad.

While all Christian denominations valued premarital virginity, the Roman Catholic Church placed a special value on vowed virginity as a way to imitate the lives of both Jesus and the **Virgin Mary**, both of whom Roman Catholics believed to have been life-long virgins. Religious orders offered both men and women an opportunity to choose vowed virginity, although anticlerical campaigns were a feature of the Second and Third Republics in France and in Bismarckian Germany. As Roman Catholic missionary orders spread to Asia, Africa, and the Pacific, they attracted native recruits, who were not, however, treated as equals until the twentieth century. In this period, Anglo-Catholics introduced religious orders for men and women into the Church of England. Besides some short-lived brotherhoods, only a few brotherhoods were established. Sisterhoods were far more successful: at least sixty-five Anglican sisterhoods were established from 1845 to 1900. Besides spiritual growth, religious life offered women opportunities to avoid the dangers of childbirth and the inconvenience of being subservient to a husband or a father, as well as opportunities for useful work. Protestants, however, rejected vowed virginity as a pagan holdover that threatened the family. A frequent complaint was that priests and nuns were not, in fact, celibate but were rather hypersexual: celibacy was imagined as a way to lure unsuspecting women into the confessional, and convents were imagined both as places of debauchery (as in Maria Monk's *Awful Disclosures of Hotel Dieu Nunnery of Montreal* [1836]) and as the prisons of unhappy women.

Virginity was not, however, an absolute value, as the ridicule directed at "spinsters" showed. Throughout the century, social and political radicals such as communists and some socialists, who advocated "free love" and saw marriage as a form of legalized prostitution did not place a high value on virginity for either men or women. At the end of the century, sexual radicals also rejected virginity as a special virtue.

Further Reading: Singleton, John. "The Virgin Mary and Religious Conflict in Victorian Britain." *Journal of Ecclesiastical History* 43 (1992): 16–34; Pope, Barbara Corrado. "Immaculate and Powerful: The Marian Revival in the Nineteenth Century." In *Immaculate and Powerful: The Female in Sacred Image and Social Reality*, edited by Clarissa W. Atkinson, Constance H. Buchanan, and Margaret R. Miles. Boston: Beacon Press, 1985.

Carol Marie Englehardt

VIRGIN MARY. The Virgin Mary, both the religious symbol and the Biblical figure, received a great deal of attention, positive and negative, official and popular, in the nineteenth century. This was partly because, more than in any earlier period, the figure of the Virgin Mary became a means of identifying one's religious allegiances. Further fueling the interest was the resemblance between the traditional image of the Virgin Mary—the sinless virgin mother—and the dominant western ideal of womanhood in this period.

Within the Roman Catholic Church, the Virgin Mary had long been a focus of both popular devotion and theological interest. Both forms of attention increased in the nineteenth century, as the hierarchy and laity became more enthusiastic about Marian devotion. The most important theological pronouncement was the papal declaration that the Virgin Mary had been conceived without sin. On December 8, 1854—the day that had been celebrated as the Feast of Mary's Conception—Pope Pius IX issued *Ineffabilis Deus*, which declared that the Virgin Mary had been given this unique favor in advance of, but in recognition of, the merits of her son. Although Roman Catholic tradition had represented Mary's conception as occurring by means of a kiss between her parents, *Ineffabilis Deus* did not suggest that the means of Mary's conception had been extraordinary. This new dogma was declared by the pope alone rather than by a council of the church. It was supported by most but not all of the bishops; a few believed the timing to be inopportune. However, most Roman Catholics greeted the declaration with enthusiasm, and it quickly became part of the liturgy. This declaration, which paved the way for the declaration of the dogma of the Assumption of the Virgin Mary in *Munificentissimus Deus* (1950), has been interpreted as a papal reaction against modernity, but it had been gaining popular support since John Duns Scotus had first articulated a convincing rationale for it in the early fourteenth century.

While traditional forms of devotion, such as the Rosary, remained popular in the nineteenth century, a new, more controversial, form of public devotion emerged: visiting the locations of, reading about, or purchasing objects related to the reported apparitions of the Virgin Mary. The first such apparition was in Paris. In 1830 Catherine Labouré, a Sister of Charity, reported seeing several visions of the Virgin Mary in her convent on the Rue de Bac. In one of the later visions, the Virgin Mary appeared standing on a globe, surrounded by the words, "Oh Mary, conceived without sin, pray for us who have recourse to thee," and with beams of light radiating from her; reportedly a voice commanded the nun to have a medal representing this vision struck. Within a decade, millions of copies of this medal were owned by Roman Catholics throughout the world. (This representation of the virgin became the standard one, even being reported by later visionaries at Lourdes and Pontmain.) Other apparitions followed; the most famous included those at LaSalette, France (1846), Lourdes, France (1858), Marpingen, Germany (1876), Knock, Ireland (1879), and Pontmain, France (1871). Although the Roman Catholic Church never officially approved any of these apparitions, and some of the visionaries later retracted their testimonies (and then retracted the retractions), the Roman Catholic faithful flocked to these sites as a way to express their religious beliefs and even, in the case of Marpingen, to demonstrate their opposition to the government.

Marian devotion was traditionally associated with the Roman Catholic Church, but beginning in the 1830s two new groups within the Church of England—Ritualists and Tractarians—began to practice limited forms of Marian devotion as a way of declaring their membership in the universal Catholic Church and, they said, to make the Church of England's liturgy warmer, and thus more able to retain the allegiance of those who might otherwise convert to Roman Catholicism. These two groups, who jointly became known as Anglo-Catholics, were extremely hesitant about developments such as the Immaculate Conception that they thought had a tendency to elevate Mary above God.

In response to Roman Catholics' more frequent invocations of the Virgin Mary as well as to the growing presence of Roman Catholics in Protestant cultures such as England and the United States, some Protestants began to reverse the tradition of paying little attention to her. In sermons, periodical articles, public speeches, and even works of fiction, they denounced Marian invocations as nonscriptural practices that interfered with the worship of God, and even compared Marian devotion to the worship of ancient goddesses. The declaration of the Immaculate Conception gave them a specific opportunity to repeat these charges, as well as to criticize the doctrine's lack of scriptural basis. This harsh public attitude represented a change from previous practice; many of the reformers had either held the Virgin Mary as a model of Christian behavior or had generally ignored her.

Nineteenth-century Protestants' unique contribution to the debate was to question the traditional belief in Mary's eternal virginity, which dated from the early church and was affirmed by the major reformers, including Martin Luther, Ulrich Zwingli, John Calvin, and John Wesley. While in the nineteenth century some agnostics, atheists, and deists argued against the virgin birth, this belief was generally maintained among Christians. However, in the nineteenth century, some Protestants began to declare that Mary and Joseph had had children of their own. This representation of the Virgin Mary was intended to limit Mary's exceptionalism, and thus devotion to her, as well as to argue that her life provided no support for clerical celibacy. Protestants did not, however, question the virgin birth, which (following Augustine) they maintained was necessary for Jesus to be sinless.

Although devotion to the Virgin Mary continued into the twentieth century, Protestant controversial writings became less frequent by the end of the century, as Roman Catholics became better assimilated into Protestant cultures and as the rise of secularism made Christian denominations more interested in emphasizing similarities rather than differences.

Further Reading: Pope, Barbara Corrado. "Immaculate and Powerful: The Marian Revival in the Nineteenth Century." In *Immaculate and Powerful: The Female in Sacred Image and Social Reality*, edited by Clarissa W. Atkinson, Constance H. Buchanan, and Margaret R. Miles. Boston: Beacon Press, 1985; Singleton, John. "The Virgin Mary and Religious Conflict in Victorian Britain." *Journal of Ecclesiastical History* 43 (1992): 16–34.

Carol Marie Englehardt

"WALTER". "Walter" is the pseudonym of an anonymous individual who wrote *My Secret Life*, first published in the late 1880s but banned for 100 years. This confessional-style book begins when the author is manually masturbated by his nursemaid at age eight, and continues to fill eleven volumes with the **evolution** of his sexual experiences for over 100 chapters. The original 2,360 pages have been cut and rearranged so that much of the text is missing and of the twenty sets originally published, only four survive. Consequently, the available popular versions consist of only one volume of approximately 650 pages.

Henry Spencer Ashbee (1834–1900), an affluent collector of erotica, had the opportunity to travel and enjoy a variety of experiences and is thought to be "Walter" for a number of reasons. His worldview sees people from the top down rather than portraying them sympathetically as equals or as victims of economic duress. The descriptions of place, although general, correspond to his environment and lifestyle. The vocabulary and point of view is that of an upper-class Victorian. Most of the women described in the book are either **servants** or prostitutes, types that a person of means would be able to employ or hire. There are references to "low" people, indicating a class consciousness on the part of Walter.

The book advances from his first sexual experience to his ignorance of female anatomy, and how he tries to see the shape of a vagina, after the nursemaid leaves him alone momentarily, with his nine-month old sister. He is obsessed with the desire to learn about the act of sexual intercourse and the appearance of female genitalia. With his cousin, he spies on women who are urinating in hopes that he will see their "cunts."

Some of the language used in *My Secret Life* is anachronistic, yet typical of nineteenth-century erotica. The words "cunt" and "quim" are used instead of vagina; "motte" refers to the pubic area or mound of Venus. Both the Biblical (and misapplied) term "onanism," and the crude "frig" are used to describe **masturbation**. "Gamahuche" is oral sex and a "Lapunar" is a house of **prostitution** or brothel, and a "Paphian" is a prostitute. The word "prick" is used instead of penis, "arse" instead of "ass," and "spunk" instead of seminal fluid. Menstruation is referred to by the medical term, "catamenia," and the more common, "courses." He appears to be in awe of female biology and often remarks at the "self-cleansing" property of the vagina after intercourse, or how a woman's sexual organs return to normal after her period and childbirth.

Throughout the book, he describes each woman's genitalia in detail and states that even though he loves the sexual experience, he also loves the woman who provides it to him. He describes a vivid dislike for anal sex after an intense experience, so much that he never returns to the street or the house where he experienced it. Although the book is considered pornographic, crude, and perhaps obscene by some, it does lend insight to the important matter of sexuality in a time period that is ostensibly repressive. His straightforward language is in stark contrast to the typical hypocritical, polite, and flowery words of his century. Although he states in one part that when one writes about a secret life, one must not omit anything and that he is not ashamed of anything, he states in another part that if he gives too many clues, it may give the reader information about the actual people and since he discussed his adventures with friends and relatives at his clubs, much of his manuscript must be destroyed.

Further Reading: Anonymous. *My Secret Life*. New York: Blue Moon Books, 1988; Foucault, Michel. *The History of Sexuality*. Vol. I. New York: Vintage, 1978; Gibson, Ian. *Erotomaniac*. London: Faber, 2001; Mirsky, Maya. Critique. *My Secret Life*. www.etext.org/Zines/Critique/article/mysecretlife.html; Ockerbloom, John Mark. Banned Books Online at http://www.my-secret-life.com.

Lana Thompson

WHITE SLAVERY. The late nineteenth-century "white slave traffic" consisted of tricking young women into sex slavery in brothels where they were held against their will and compelled to undertake **prostitution** without adequate remuneration. The term was borrowed from references earlier in the century to women's low-paid work in clothing sweatshops, but by the 1870s had become a term applied only to the sex industry. The white slave trade agitation is one of the classic moral panics of the late nineteenth century, and produced a vast quantity of literature as well as significant political action in Britain, Europe, and the United States.

The term entered popular consciousness in the late 1870s, when the British moral reformer **Josephine Butler** began to publicize claims that English girls were being lured abroad under the promise of respectable work, only to find themselves confined to brothels and compelled to work as prostitutes. The traffic arose as a byproduct of opportunity, as women increasingly seized opportunities to work and travel outside England. As the continent became more familiar to British women, it became possible for the more adventurous to envision moving there for work, or to enhance their life chances. A number of women were trafficked there, often tempted by promises of jobs in hotels or bars, or by promises of marriage to the trafficker, who normally posed as a businessman. The white slave trade agitation received substantial support in 1880–1881, when twelve brothel-keepers were convicted of offences against the Belgian *Code Penal*, for confining English women and forcing them into prostitution. At about the same time, anxiety began to be expressed about trafficked women in Canada and the United States, although in both countries the popular movement did not become prominent until the early twentieth century. Anxiety about "white slaving" did not subside until after First World War.

The Victorians drew a deep demarcation between trafficked victim and prostitute, which allowed them to express sympathy for victims while condemning voluntary prostitution; unsurprisingly, the stories recounted by English girls to their rescuers always protested their complete innocence. No woman who knew she was going to work in the sex trade was considered to have been trafficked by most nineteenth-century commentators. Even if she were lied to, taken to a location where she did not wish to work, confined against her will, enmeshed in debt bondage, and beaten, the fact that she had consented to sex outside of marriage removed her from all hope of sympathy.

Conventional ideas of sexual purity actually worked to the advantage of the procurers. Because the Victorians' false theology viewed prostitutes as uniquely debased, and "fallen" to an extent that simply was not possible for a man, no matter what his crime might be, it was possible for women to internalize the view that they were hopelessly cast out from decent society, including their families of origin. Women who seemed dissatisfied with their conditions as sex workers or who showed an inclination to leave, could be beaten. However, it was far simpler, and probably more effective, to threaten women with exposure, which could mean telling her family and friends that she had voluntarily consented to prostitute herself. Police collusion, real or imagined, also made women afraid to leave, believing as they did that the police would simply return them to the brothel, which indeed, under French and Belgian law, they were obliged to do.

Successful traffickers could enjoy high profits and continuing income from the same workers at very low risk to themselves. Until the scandals of the 1880s, convictions were rare, sentences were short, seldom more than a month or two, and fines were often levied instead. One of the commonest strategies was the lure of a good job on the other side of the Channel. The offer of work abroad as a barmaid or hotel employee was especially common, as it made the woman willing to travel without question. A few registry offices appear to have operated, in part at least, as fronts for trafficking. Some appear to have been genuinely dangerous places for a friendless woman to frequent. Two women interviewed in different Belgian brothels testified that, having applied for work at the same Brussels *bureau de placement*, the owner seduced or raped them, and then placed them in brothels, pocketing the trafficker's fee.

After providing transport to the country of destination, the women were subsequently charged exorbitant amount for transport, subsistence, and clothing, creating serious debt-bondage, which they were told they would have to pay back through their labor as sex-workers. Conditions in Belgian and French brothels added to the sense of imprisonment, both on the part of the sex-workers themselves and their advocates. Due to a concern to avoid street solicitation, brothels were kept locked from the inside, and the registered women were not permitted to go out alone, again to avoid nuisance to passers-by. Municipal

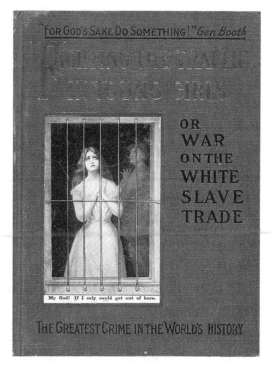

One example of a number of books published around the turn of the century warning young girls of the white slave trade. Courtesy of the Library of Congress.

regulations held that the women were compelled to wear costumes provided by the proprietor, meaning they were too scantily clothed to decently appear in public. The inhabitants were charged for their bed and lodging, and they would be returned to the brothel if they left before discharging their debts, effectively keeping them in a form of debt-bondage.

It is clear that "white slaves," in the Victorian sense of virginal innocents, were in a minority among these trafficked women. Most may have had, at the very least, a strong suspicion about the nature of the work, but were unaware of the debt they would be incurring, which would both immobilize them and also prevent them from saving money. Women who ended up in an unsavory foreign brothel, far worse than they had anticipated, felt that they had nowhere to turn. If a brothel paid its inmates extremely poorly or not at all, it was necessary to lock the women in to keep them from leaving. English women, unaware of the insistence on public order in the Belgian system of regulated prostitution, were appalled by the appearance of these brothels, finding that they looked like prisons, with barred and darkened windows. Sex work in these conditions was not glamorous or exotic. Women were ordinarily kept in nightdresses all day, were not allowed to refuse clients, and could, especially when new to the brothel, have to service long queues of men, and were never permitted to refuse a client, no matter how drunken, violent, or diseased. The majority of them were sold on from one brothel to another. The abolitionists thought this was to make them harder to trace, but it is more probable that after a few months each woman's novelty waned with a particular brothel's clientele, meaning she would be sold on to another establishment, increasing her debt burden. In the lowest class of brothels, the madam or her representative collected the money from the client at the outset of the transaction, so the prostitute would have no chance of holding back some of the payment. She would receive only as much as the brothel-keeper saw fit. Many claimed under oath to have received nothing at all.

Those women, whether or not they had been prostitutes in Britain, had certainly been trafficked in the modern understanding of the term. They were locked in, paid little or nothing for their sex work, and could be sold on to other establishments until their debts were paid off. Butler emphasized that an offence against the liberty of a prostitute was as great a crime as an offence against the liberty of a respectable woman; an idea that her society found hard to accept. Josephine Butler argued that the liberty of a prostitute was as valuable as her own, but she was in a tiny minority in her time. Most abolitionists, although they worked with her and appreciated her genius for popularizing a subject, divided trafficked women into guilty and innocent categories as confidently as the rest of their society.

The root cause of the traffic was not some perverse continental preference for British women, but English Law and the nature of the French and Belgian legal systems. Regardless of the age of consent, the continental regulations prohibited women from working as prostitutes under the age of twenty-one. The United Kingdom was unique in providing no protection of any kind for girls aged over twelve, except for heiresses, for whom a special exception was made. English Law with relation to procuring made a bad situation worse. Procuring was an offence to English Law only if committed in England. Obtaining women abroad and trafficking them to England was not punishable; nor could English courts punish traffickers outside their jurisdiction. By the end of 1880, even the most skeptical of government officials admitted that sex trafficking existed and that nine-tenths of procuration cases involving British subjects escaped detection. Furthermore, they agreed that English Laws should be tightened up to reduce its frequency. While the British government leisurely drew up new legislative proposals, the Maiden Tribute scandal forced them to immediate action.

The British government authorized two official investigations of the white slave trade in the nineteenth century. The police sent to the continent to investigate the trade reported to the Home Office that few of the English women in brothels were held against their will. Concern with the soundness of the police investigation led to the appointment of T. W. Snagge, a respected barrister, to carry out a second investigation.

Snagge's report concluded that the traffic in women and girls was real, and although not a torrent, it remained a worrying and completely unacceptable trickle. Like Butler, he felt that both innocent women and others deserved help. His conclusion was that the practices he had uncovered did indeed constitute a slave trade: girls were lured abroad on false pretenses, and detained in brothels against their will.

In the 1880s, a number of antitrafficking organizations were set up in England with close ties to European reformers, including the Minor's Protection Society, the Belgian Traffic Committee, and the Central Vigilance Society, all of which eventually merged with the National Vigilance Association. By 1885, the moral climate had changed so much that the *Times* rejoiced when an agreement was signed between the Belgian and Dutch governments for the suppression of the traffic in young women, a traffic whose existence the newspaper would certainly have denied a decade earlier. While the traffic was in abeyance by this date, it never died out entirely and was subject to revival at intervals as traffickers came and went, or served prison sentences. It also shifted from country to country as police commitment to suppression waxed and waned.

In 1899, the National Vigilance Association (NVA) was active in encouraging the establishment of National Committees in countries affected by the white slave trade. Committees for the Suppression of the White Slave Traffic were established in Argentina, Austria, Belgium, Canada, Denmark, Egypt, France, Germany, UK, Holland, Hungary, Italy, Norway, Portugal, Russia, Spain, Sweden, Switzerland, Turkey, and the United States. A major goal of the National Committees was to pressure governments into passing **law**s against procuration; at this time, most countries had laws punishing women convicted of prostitution but no measures that would assist in the prosecution of traffickers. The first international congress was held in London in June 1899, with 120 delegates in attendance. Later congresses were held in Frankfurt (1902), Paris (1906), Madrid (1910), and London (1913), before the First World War intervened. Their findings and recommendations formed the basis of national and international legislation against trafficking, including the very effective measures adopted by the League of Nations in the interwar period.

Further Reading: Bristow, Edward. *Vice and Vigilance: Purity Movements in Britain since 1700.* Dublin: Gill and Macmillan, 1977; Corbin, Alain. *Women for Hire: Prostitution and Sexuality in France after 1850.* Cambridge, MA: Harvard University Press, 1990; Mumm, Susan. "Josephine Butler and the International Traffic in Women." In *Sex, Gender, and Religion: Josephine Butler Revisited,* edited by Jenny Daggers and Diana Neal, 55–72. New York: Peter Lang, 2006.

Susan Mumm

WIDOWHOOD. The nineteenth-century widow was in **law** a *feme sole*, a woman who had absolute control over her property, person, and movements. She could buy property in her own right, make contracts, and pursue court actions. This meant that she had more autonomy than either wives or unmarried daughters living with their parents. In fact, with the exception of the franchise, her legal position was identical to that of an adult male.

Contrasting strangely with the legal dignity and independence of the widow was her place in Victorian popular culture, where widows were the butts of many ribald jests, usually linked to their presumed sexual insatiability. In popular culture the widow was a disquieting liminal figure, sexually experienced but manless. This combination was disturbing and was often dealt with by reducing these women to ridicule. One commonplace joke was that a woman married the first time to please her family, the second time to please herself.

Widows, especially young widows, were expected to remarry, once the intense grief of their early bereavement was past. Those who had inherited their former husband's property or business were very attractive marital targets. Until the 1870s a man who married a British widow became the owner of all her assets at the moment of marriage, including those bequeathed by a former husband.

Widows of recent standing could ordinarily be distinguished by their mourning garments. The mourning wear industry was a major **fashion** influence during the period and widows were its primary customers. Even the poorest women aspired to wear something black to signify their widowed status, even if it was no more than a black handkerchief wrapped around the wrist. Among more affluent women, mourning wear was elaborate and extensive: at one point, it even ascended to the level of special mourning undergarments, including a padded chest protector to allow the bereaved woman to beat her breast with dramatic effect but without hurting herself. Middle- and upper-class women wore variations of mourning wear for two years in Britain; famously, **Queen Victoria** stayed in mourning for Albert for the remainder of her very long life. Social life was severely restricted for elite and middle-class women during the earlier phases of widowhood. A woman still in mourning was not supposed to be courted or receive suitors: the black garments and protracted mourning rituals cut her off from the world of attraction, sexuality, and reproduction. They also protected grieving women from inappropriate social behavior of many kinds.

Of course, not all women waited two years to marry again, nor were all heartbroken by the loss of their husbands. One of **Anthony Trollope**'s most famous characters, Mrs. Greenow in *Can You Forgive Her?* was a widow keen to remarry, preferably someone younger and more attractive than her elderly and wealthy first husband. Her accelerated period of mourning and the unseemly courtship of the affluent widow is one of the comic themes of the novel. If a woman remarried while still in mourning, the second ceremony was ordinarily small and private. It was considered correct to come out of mourning at the time of a second marriage.

Historians have argued that only a tiny minority of nineteenth-century widows were financially secure enough to enjoy their independence. Very wealthy women would have had settlements made on them at the time of their marriage, which ensured their financial comfort in the case of widowhood. Middle-class women, ordinarily completely uneducated in financial matters, could find themselves in desperate straits if their professional husbands had been completely dependent on their earned income. Few could have hoped to save enough from their earnings to support their wives for years, perhaps decades, after their own death. If their husbands had failed to ensure their lives for a sum sufficient to support their widows and children over the longer term, there was no alternative for these widows but work. These women normally had not been trained in anything that would allow them to undertake well-paid posts. The classic resort of the undercapitalized widow was sending their children to a cheap boarding school, and then seeking work as a governess. Others tried to establish small private schools, or resorted to needlework or the grudged generosity of relatives. Working-class widows without assets found themselves working as cleaning women, untrained nurses, or as domestic servants. For many, the only way out of poverty was to risk a second marriage.

Further Reading: Curran, Cynthia. *When I First Began My Life Anew: Middle-class Widows in Victorian Britain*. Bristol, IN: Wyndham Hall Press, 2000; Hellerstein, Erna O. et al., ed. *Victorian Women*. Stanford, CA: Stanford University Press, 1981.

Susan Mumm

WOMEN IN THE MEDIA. The nineteenth-century British press publicized five major perceptions of women: the lady, the laborer, the criminal/prostitute, the "domestic economist," and the "New Woman." One of these was the exemplar, but all were significant because the medium was so influential in the Victorian age. As autodidacts throughout the era and compulsory education after 1870 increased readership and faster printing processes and abolition of paper, advertising, and stamp duties reduced prices, periodicals became the chief means of public communication. They multiplied dramatically, from elite reviews and London dailies to miscellaneous magazines and penny newspapers that saturated the kingdom. Although the public wondered whether serials confirmed or shaped opinion, no one doubted their capacity to do either better than other venues. Situating female identity in a press of great variety and growing reach magnified sexuality as a subject.

Early in the century, reporters of both sexes expanded their coverage of women as part of a larger story. The onset of industrialism moved the nation to a position of international preeminence at the same time that it eroded traditional bases of stability. If people did not know their "natural" places, change would destroy, not enhance British civilization. Since women were a large segment of the population, they and men had to understand what being female was. While journals were an obvious agency to circulate definitions, both men and women journalists had trouble clarifying an identity that crossed economic and religious lines among others. The discussion of the "Woman Question" was at best perplexing, at worst polemical. Its language demonstrates the complexity of the issue of how human equality and sexual diversity intersect.

The oldest construct, the lady, appeared in magazines such as the *Ladies' Cabinet*, *Ladies' Monthly Museum*, *Ladies' Pocket Magazine*, *London and Paris Ladies' Magazine*, *Magazine of the Beau Monde*, *New Monthly Belle Assemblée*, *World of Fashion*, and *Young Lady's Magazine*. The label dated from the eighteenth century, when the *Lady's Magazine* was born, and originally referred to the aristocracy, although the upwardly mobile soon commandeered it. Costume and beauty gazettes, designed to honor this version of being female, actually demeaned it. In a discourse of dependence, they marginalized the lady by infantilizing her and trivializing her activities, ones that merely verified the wealth of father or husband. Columnists introduced her as a juvenile striving to acquire "accomplishments" that fit a feeble **brain** for **marriage** and preserved limited energy for childbirth. Pages on "finishing" sanctioned a process intended to convey a veneer of culture and the habits associated with good breeding that culminated in an outcome idealized by commentators. They explained that at sixteen, with her training complete, this girl wore the latest gowns to the right parties where she cast subtle sexual lures in order to hook a mate. Her guides, who promised that a wife basked in the envy of her single friends and the adoration of her indulgent spouse, thereby testified that the authentic woman was essentially a child.

Gradually, more general miscellanies, from the *Penny Satirist* to the *Foreign Quarterly Review*, decried a model in which attire destroyed a woman's body and minutiae, her mind. Hostile scribes alleged that the lady relieved her boredom by imagining ailments, by gossiping in public, and by drinking in private; satisfied her ego by being obstinate, and gratified her libido by reading romantic novels or having extramarital affairs. By 1850, the majority of observers announced that this prototype was obsolete in a capitalist world.

At the same time that the lady was the star in expensive serials, many other noticed her purported social opposite, the woman worker. This depiction was never absent from the papers, surfacing first in the cheap and often reformist unstamped tribunes begun before 1815. Supplementing their voices were those in costly publications such as *Blackwood's Edinburgh Magazine* and the *Quarterly Review*, the specialized press, including the *Journal of Health* and *Journal of Education*, and the professional, such as the *Journal of the Statistical Society of London*. Irrespective of bent, everyone agreed that this genre of womanhood was inappropriate because it bolstered the ranks of rebels or weaklings and undermined national assertions of morality.

The characterization of the worker, like that of the lady, put women at the periphery but overlooked other commonalities by concentrating on class rather than on gender. For example, the 1860s journalistic brouhaha about infanticide, whether it was murder or justifiable homicide to avoid starving a child, popularized the pretense that the act never occurred except among the poor. Likewise, the paragraphs about spousal battery and debilitation from multiple pregnancies singled out laborers. Stories designed to spur improvements in employment reinforced the notion that women of any rank were incapable of managing their own lives. Journalists customarily pictured the worker as an obvious victim, the lowest of a subsidiary social grade, and they expressed dismay when she acted contrarily. They castigated her for reacting to abuse the way that men responded, by drinking, fighting, swearing, or having random sex. Writers were quick to comprehend that degradation could spawn the criminal and the prostitute, the antitheses of a womanhood of subordination.

Most analysts saw female lawbreaking as doubly abnormal, violating both social and sexual conventions. The criminal challenged "place" and proclaimed "independence" in ways that the lady and the worker did not. Social commentators therefore welcomed imprisonment as an opportunity to "reform" the criminal, to teach her authenticity, a theme that the *Reformatory and Refuge Journal*, for instance, was happy to emphasize. Convicts would learn values appropriate to and skills sufficient for domestic service. These jobs offered reintegration into the folk and occasions to meet suitable mates and to practice proper wifely conduct. Skeptics who alerted that cooks and maids, with little money and mobility, would not escape the harassment of mistresses and the rape of masters not only strengthened the perception of woman as victim but also failed to discredit domesticity.

The "domestic economist" was the favorite interpretation of being female in Victorian magazines. It was the epitome, the one which the press advertised most, from the 1830s when the middling classes, whose notions it mirrored, become consequential in society. This stereotype centered womanhood in the home. The media emphasized that the hearth was a woman's sphere as the bigger one beyond was a man's but never specified what precise powers attached to her governance. Enthusiasts published in the numerous women's monthlies, such as the *Christian Lady's Magazine*, *Domestic Journal*, *Englishwoman's Domestic Magazine*, *Family Economist*, and *Female's Friend*, and in the religious press, from the mediocre *Christian's Penny Magazine* to the stately *Church of England Magazine*. All declared that the domestic economist was neither frivolous nor vicious but efficient. She was not man's idol or prey but his equal because she was useful, in her proper station doing her proper tasks. Since men were clearly busy in public, her orbit was private, supervising the home and rearing children. With these duties, she would have no hours in which to be sick, no inclination to sin.

Popular culture lauded those who accepted or aspired to this role and scorned those who did not. Few fans of the domestic idyll noticed that it dignified chores otherwise disdained because they connoted poverty and, more crucially, that it transformed marriage from a sexual union with a person to an asexual bonding with a building. Instead, serials celebrated the cloistering of wives because it gave husbands a womblike retreat where they could recuperate from their battles with other men. The wife, by maintaining a routine, supposedly anchored her spouse as he rode the cosmopolitan economic and political rapids. To authenticate this paradigm, chroniclers, especially the religious, resorted to Biblical evidence. They advised her to submit absolutely to a husband's directions. She should cultivate humility to the point of abnegation of personality, emblematic of her legal loss of identity in marriage. Submission was necessary because defiance repeated the offense of Eden with all its deleterious effects. To compensate for this prior offence, she should be his redeemer spending time in the prayers and charitable deeds that atoned for his transgressions and presumably inhibited her susceptibility to new temptation. The papers thus expanded womanhood to encompass guilt for manhood's sins.

Press iconography of the "housewife" was bizarre when it underscored one aspect of this identity, namely, maternity. Although a constant of most models was that every female was potentially pregnant, the journals printed nothing about the specifics of conception. The frequent articles alluding to her as a "vessel" minimized her function in reproduction and implied that sexual ignorance protected society from the indiscriminate intercourse that might sabotage male status and property. Extolling motherhood within marriage also decertified celibacy as well as infidelity. Organs such as the *British Mothers' Journal*, *Mother's Friend*, and *Mother's Magazine* issued veiled warnings about the implications of unsavory behavior while they proclaimed the benefits of mothering. How a person not trusted to make decisions for herself could superintend the young was not a favorite topic in this discourse. Still, some commentators consistently recorded that being a domiciliary was as unsatisfactory as being a decoration or a drudge. The round of dull errands, broken only by church and volunteerism, apparently made middle class melancholia as dangerous as aristocratic *ennui*. Raised at home to stay at home, this woman had few reprieves. By the 1850s, radical writers on **prostitution** had begun to suggest that it was the extension, not the contradiction, of this style of being female.

Prostitution was synonymous with deviance in every press perception of womanhood. Sexuality was certainly not a subject that Victorian papers missed. In the pornographic, such as the *Exquisite*, and the scandal-ridden, as the *Fly* and *Town Talk*, stories and sometimes illustrations broadcast its delights. However, in the majority of media outlets, from the *Daily Telegraph* to the *Spectator*, *Meliora* to the *Magdalen's Friend*, prostitution connoted the worst form of sexuality, one beyond the control of a male. As prostitution became more visible, so did news about it. An object of repugnance to mothers for whom female and asexual were synonymous, the prostitute had few champions in the press. Even those sympathetic to her situation were uneasy because they considered her a seducer. They revered deathbed renunciation because it ended the real problem and documented the worth of asexuality. Acknowledging that this scenario was unusual, reporters settled for confinement to asylums that would modify inmates psychologically and tutor them for work or wedlock. Essays, daring in the 1850s, but less explosive after the *Pall Mall Gazette's* exposé of the exploitation of juveniles, argued that the "social evil" would last until women themselves campaigned for its abolition.

If the endless columns on prostitution did not lead to its demise, they did indicate that it was the most insidious result of readying women only for matrimony in a time of urbanism and **imperialism**. Therefore, from the late 1850s onward, a dramatically different theory of being female emerged. Genuine women, their mentors enlightened by papers such as the *English Woman's Journal* and the *Victoria Magazine*, defined themselves and directed their own destinies. This concept, which harkened back to papers of the French Revolution, had almost vanished from the press by 1830. It echoed in the short-lived *Isis* of 1832 and the longer-running herald of utopian socialism, the *New Moral World*, but its resurrection in the *Westminster Review* was critical because powerbrokers read and sometimes penned this quality serial. In 1851 Harriet Taylor Mill, collaborating with John Stuart Mill, wrote that Paradise was neither near nor likely for females. She asserted that circumstances were not unique, that men had long discriminated against women and had defended their deeds as prize or punishment, both deserved. From this heritage, Taylor Mill insisted, women had to liberate themselves, not on gender but on human grounds. What she contemplated was that once free, her sex would determine its own identity.

Emancipationists, the precursors of the "New Woman," assumed that rationality was open to both sexes, so editors who spotlighted this category of womanhood soon found themselves embroiled in debate. Followers of Taylor Mill contended that teaching women to think logically and to act decisively would win them admiration in a world that treasured self-reliance. Enemies, exemplified by a famous *Saturday Review* series, argued that if women became confident, assertive, and ambitious, like men, only two results were possible. The mutation would shatter social harmony or would force men into effeminacy. The choice between chaos and a female future measured by a male past widened the media war of words.

Even the battle, everyone believed, was corroboration that sexual metamorphosis had commenced. A female victory would result in male impotence unless people immediately and completely rejected this form of womanhood. Men's attacks were sometimes patronizing, such as when Charles Dickens's *All the Year Round* asked whether M.D. stood for medical doctor or my dear. This text and myriad others demonstrate how much the new order disturbed men. Simultaneously, serials featured the female panic that accompanied male unease. As most men denounced a destiny of deference, many women endorsed it. Reporters hinted that women were frightened of independence because they lacked the training necessary to act as adults. Because of the breadth of the opposition, most general gazettes could conveniently relegate the emancipated to the class of the "peculiar" that again put women on the sidelines.

Opponents of women's emancipation need not have worried. Self-governance, some pundits predicted, would be more exhausting than exhilarating. Without reorientation of the marital relationship, they warned that the "New Woman" would have two options, the toil and tensions inherent in combining matrimony and career or the contempt attached to spinsterhood. After 1870, both comprehensive and women's journals underlined that women had greater access to education, however hard the fight to secure it, more job opportunities, and fewer legal restraints. Stories also associated better health with physical exercise, but were divided on the primary purpose of wellness, whether for women themselves or for their progeny.

Headlines however went to suffrage, notably after 1890, when the reasoning of the *Women's Suffrage Journal* and its kin gave way to more strident journalism by and about women. Whether female voters would purify elections or endanger democracy was less important to journalists than how their national citizenship would affect societal roles. The core of their often-heated wrangling was the meaning of suffrage: was it the ultimate symbol of social disintegration or the ultimate resolution of female identity? If the answer to the "Woman Question" was as unclear in 1900 as in 1801, certainly perceptions about women had shifted over the decades. The importance of having the first mass media actively engaged in this discourse about the majority of the population cannot be overestimated.

Further Reading: Adburgham, Alison. *Women in Print: Writing Women and Women's Magazines from the Restoration to the Accession of Victoria.* London: George Allen and Unwin, 1972; Beetham, Margaret. *A Magazine of Her Own?: Domesticity and Desire in the Woman's Magazine, 1800–1914.* London and New York: Routledge, 1996; Kanner, S. Barbara. "The Women of England in a Century of Social Change." In *Suffer and be Still: Women in the Victorian Age,* edited by Martha Vicinus, 173–232. Bloomington and London: Indiana University Press, 1972; Shattock, Joanne and Michael Wolff, ed. *The Victorian Periodical Press: Samplings and Soundings.* Leicester: Leicester University Press, 1982.

E. M. Palmegiano

WOODHULL, VICTORIA CLAFLIN (1838–1927). Victoria Woodhull was an advocate for women's social and sexual rights following the American Civil War. A woman of humble origins, born into a large, itinerant family on the Ohio frontier, Woodhull challenged 1870s cultural politics on many fronts. She was the first woman to run for president of the United States, the first (along with her sister Tennessee Claflin) to open a stock brokerage firm on Wall Street, and the first to command a wide popular audience for her radical views on marriage and sexuality.

Woodhull became notorious for advocating "social freedom," a polite euphemism for a philosophy, denounced by critics as "free love," which advocated reform in marriage or even the abolition of marriage altogether. Her radical newspaper, *Woodhull & Claflin's Weekly,* became a forum for wide-ranging discussion about women, sexuality, dress reform, socialism and other unconventional ideas. In her most celebrated speech, "The Principles of Social Freedom" (1871), she dismissed marriage as "legal prostitution." Before an audience of 3,000, she challenged women to denounce the hypocrisy that condemned prostitutes for the informal exchange of sex for money, when many marriages involved a similar, if slightly more formal, economic transaction. "I honor and worship that purity which exists in the soul of every noble man or woman," she said, "while I pity the woman who is virtuous simply because a **law** compels her." In fact, she argued, the law itself fostered dishonesty and hypocrisy in marriage. "Social freedom," for Woodhull, was the only solution to the tyranny that kept women trapped in sexual slavery, whether in **marriage** or prostitution. "The sexual relation must be rescued from this insidious form of slavery," she said. "Women must rise from their position as ministers to the passions of men to be their equals." To achieve this goal, Woodhull demanded a "single sexual standard for all."

The speech and particularly Woodhull's depiction of marriage as "legal prostitution," aroused critics, who saw her as promoting the destruction of family life. Newspapers excoriated her extreme statements as "advocating harlotry." Political cartoonist Thomas Nast depicted her with horns and wings, reminiscent of the demon Apollyon in

"Get thee behind me, (Mrs.) Satan!," 1872. A woman carrying 2 children and a man holding bottle of rum on her back, and speaking to winged woman who is holding a sign reading, "Be saved by free love" (representing suffragist Victoria Woodhull). Courtesy of the Library of Congress.

265

John Bunyan's Christian fable, *Pilgrim's Progress*, holding a sign reading "Be Saved by Free Love"; a young mother in the drawing, burdened with a drunken husband and countless children, responds "Get thee behind me, Mrs. Satan! I'd rather travel the hardest path of matrimony than follow your footsteps." Her vocal defense of social freedom alienated some women's suffrage allies, including Susan B. Anthony, while international socialists, including Karl Marx, struggled to disassociate their movement from such radical sentiments.

Supporters, by contrast, saw Woodhull as a compelling spokeswoman for women's rights to social and economic equality; many radical spiritualists shared her desire to make marriage less "tyrannical" for women. They created a new political party, called the Equal Rights Party and nominated Woodhull for president in May 1872, with civil rights advocate Frederick Douglass (without his consent) as her running mate. Ridicule in the popular press caused her to be evicted from her home, and cost her some of her more moderate followers. In retaliation for what she saw as social hypocrisy, Woodhull decided to expose one of the period's most beloved religious leaders, celebrated Brooklyn pastor Henry Ward Beecher, for alleged adultery with Elizabeth Tilton, the wife of his colleague Theodore Tilton. Self-appointed public censor **Anthony Comstock** had Woodhull arrested for sending an "obscene" publication (the exposure issue of her paper) through the mails. The ensuing legal struggle crippled her financially, temporarily suppressed her newspaper, and destroyed her Wall Street firm.

Woodhull defied Comstock's efforts to silence her, and capitalized on growing public concerns over his **censorship** activities. She took her version of the Beecher-Tilton scandal on the road, and launched a highly successful series of lecture tours from 1873 through 1876, in which she championed the single sexual standard. Woodhull's lectures brought the details of the Beecher-Tilton scandal to a national audience, and generated lively debate about contemporary standards that criticized women, but forgave men, for the same behavior. She and her family, particularly her sister Tennessee and her daughter Zula Maud, proved adept at working the lecture circuit, bringing the Woodhull phenomenon to big cities and small towns in the north and west, the Pacific coast, and even, in spring 1876, to the south. Her successful tours gave Woodhull the financial means to keep her paper and the scandal before the public, and encouraged her to take the show to England in 1877, where she lectured for some years before marrying wealthy banker John Biddulph Martin in 1883. In her five decades in England, she moderated her radical views. Like other sex radicals in the 1890s, she turned to biological, rather than environmental, theories to explain social problems, and became an active promoter of eugenic thought until her death in 1927.

Further Reading: Fox, Richard Wightman. *Trials of Intimacy: Love and Loss in the Beecher-Tilton Scandal.* Chicago: University of Chicago Press, 1999; Frisken, Amanda. *Victoria Woodhull's Sexual Revolution: Political Theater and the Popular Press in Nineteenth Century America.* Philadelphia: University of Pennsylvania Press, 2004; Horowitz, Helen Lefkovitz. *Rereading Sex: Battles over Sexual Knowledge and Suppression in Nineteenth-Century America.* New York: Knopf, 2002.

Amanda Frisken

Bibliography

Ballhatchet, Kenneth. *Race, Sex and Class under the Raj: Imperial Attitudes and Policies and their Critics, 1793–1905*. London: Weidenfeld and Nicolson, 1980.

Barnhart, Jacqueline Baker. *The Fair but Frail: Prostitution in San Francisco 1849–1900*. Reno: University of Nevada Press, 1986.

Barret-Ducrocq, Francoise. *Love in the Time of Victoria*. Harmondsworth: Penguin, 1991.

Berger, M. "Imperialism and Sexual Exploitation: A Review Article." *Journal of Imperial and Commonwealth History* 17 (1988): 83–98.

Bland, Lucy. *Banishing the Beast: Feminism, Sex and Morality*. 2nd ed. London: I. B. Taurus, 2002.

Bland, Lucy and Laura Doan. *Sexology Uncensored: The Documents of Sexual Science*. Chicago: University of Chicago, 1998.

Bleys, Rudi C. *The Geography of Perversion: Male-to-Male Sexual Behaviour Outside the West and the Ethnographic Imagination, 1750–1918*. New York: New York University Press, 1995.

Bristow, Edward J. *Prostitution and Prejudice: The Jewish Fight against White Slavery 1870–1939*. New York: Schocken Books, 1983.

Bullough, Vern and Bonnie Bullough. *Women and Prostitution: A Social History*. Buffalo, New York: Prometheus Books, 1987.

Butler, Anne M. *Daughters of Joy, Sisters of Misery: Prostitutes in the American West 1865–90*. Champaign: University of Illinois Press, 1985.

Carlton, Charles. *Royal Mistresses*. London: Routledge, 1990.

Carmen, A. and Moody, H. *Working Women: The Subterranean World of Street Prostitution*. New York: Harper & Row, 1985.

Cohen, B. *Deviant Street Networks: Prostitution in New York City*. Lexington, MA: Lexington Books, 1980.

Connelly, Mark Thomas. *The Response to Prostitution in the Progressive Era*. Chapel Hill: The University of North Carolina Press, 1980.

Cott, Nancy F. "Passionlessness: An Interpretation of Victorian Sexual Ideology, 1790–1850. In *A Heritage of Their Own: Toward a New Social History of American Women*, edited by F. Nancy and Elizabeth H. Pleck, 162–81. New York: Simon and Schuster, 1979.

D'Emilio, John D. and Estelle B. Freedman. *Intimate Matters: A History of Sexuality in America*. New York: Harper & Row, 1988.

Gay, Peter. *The Education of the Senses: The Bourgeois Experience, Victorian to Freud*. New York and Oxford: Oxford University Press, 1984.

Gibson, Mary. *Prostitution and the State in Italy, 1860–1915*. New Brunswick, NJ: Rutgers University Press, 1986.

Gilfoyle, Timothy J. *City of Eros: New York City, Prostitution, and the Commercialization of Sex, 1790–1920*. New York: W. W. Norton & Co., 1992.

Goldman, Marion S. *Gold Diggers and Silver Miners: Prostitution and Social Life on the Comstock Lode*. Ann Arbor: University of Michigan Press, 1981.

Harsin, Jill. *Policing Prostitution in Nineteenth Century Paris*. Princeton, NJ: Princeton University Press, 1985.

Hall, Catherine. *White, Male and Middle-Class: Explorations in Feminism and History*. New York: Routledge, 1992.

Hall, Lesley. History of Sexuality. Social Science Information gateway Website: homepages. primex.co.uk/~lesleyah/webdoc3.htm.

Hill, Marilyn Wood. *Their Sisters' Keepers: Prostitution in New York City, 1830–1870*. Berkeley: University of California Press, 1993.

Hyam, Robert. *Empire and Sexuality: The British Experience*. Manchester and New York: Manchester University Press, 1990.

Jalland, Patrica and J. Hooper. *Women from Birth to Death: The Female Life Cycle in Britain, 1830–1914*. Brighton: Harvester Press, 1986.

Laquer, Thomas W. *Solitary Sex: A Cultural History of Masturbation*. New York: Zone Books, 2003.

Mahood, Linda. *The Magdalenes: Prostitution in the Nineteenth Century*. London: Routledge, 1990.

Maines, Rachel P. *The Technology of Orgasm: Hysteria, the Vibrator, and Women's Sexual Satisfaction*. Baltimore: Johns Hopkins University Press, 1999.

Mason, Michael. *The Making of Victorian Sexual Attitudes*. Oxford: Oxford University Press, 1995a.

Mason, Michael. *The Making of Victorian Sexuality*. Oxford: Oxford University Press, 1995b.

Maynard, John. *Victorian Discourses on Sexuality and Religion*. Cambridge: Cambridge University Press, 1993.

McLaren, Angus. *Birth Control in Nineteenth Century England*. London: Croom Helm, 1978.

McLaren, Angus. *The Trials of Masculinity: Policing Sexual Boundaries, 1870–1930*. Chicago: Chicago University Press, 1999.

Mendus, Susan and Jane Rendall. *Sexuality and Subordination: Interdisciplinary Studies of Gender in the Nineteenth Century*. London and New York: Routledge, 1989.

Mumm, Susan. "Not Worse than Other Girls: The Convent-Based Rehabilitation of Fallen Women in Victorian Britain." *Journal of Social History* 29 (2006): 527–47.

Pearsall, Ronald. *The Worm in the Bud: The World of Victorian Sexuality*. London: Sutton History Classics, 2003.

Russett, C. *Sexual Science: The Victorian Construction of Womanhood*. Cambridge, MA: Harvard University Press, 1989.

Sommer, Matthew H. *Sex, Law, and Society in Late Imperial China*. Stanford, CA: Stanford University Press, 2000.

Stone, Lawrence. *The Road to Divorce: England, 1530–1987*. Oxford: Oxford University Press, 1990.

Szreter, Simon Fertility. *Class and Gender in Great Britain, 1860–1950*. Cambridge: Cambridge University Press, 1996.

Walkowitz, Judith R. *City of Dreadful Delight: Narratives of Sexual Danger in Late-Victorian London*. Chicago: University of Chicago Press, 1992.

Weeks, Jeffrey. *Sex Politics and Society: The Regulation of Sexuality since 1800*. London: Longman, 1989.

Index

Boldfaced page numbers indicate main entries.

Abolitionists, 228
Abortion, 3–4
Acton, William, 5–6, 86
Adolescence, 6–9
Adultery and fornication, 9–11
Age of consent, 11–13
Age of Consent Act, 110
Agriculture, 13–15
Albert, Prince, 211, 212
Alcohol, 15–17
Alloula, Malek, 191
Anthropology and sexuality, 17–20
Armadale (Collins), 59–61, 175
Armstrong, Nancy, 191
Art. See Nude models; Painting

Baartman, Saarti, 17
Bancroft, Herbert, 18–19
Bartlett, Adelaide, xvii
Bastardy. See Illegitimacy
Beauty, 21–23
Berkeley, Theresa, 86
Besant, Annie Wood, 23–24, 31–32
Bestiality, 25–27
Beth Book, The (Grand), 98
Bigamy, 27–29
Binet, Alfred, 84–85
Birth control, 23, 29–30
Blackwell, Elizabeth, 192
Bloch, Iwan, 20
Bowdler, Henrietta, 41
Bowdler, Thomas, 41
Braddon, Mary Elizabeth, 174, 175

Bradlaugh, Charles, 23, 30–32
Brahmans. See Hinduism
Brain, 32–33, 130
Broadsides. See Newspapers and broadsides
Brontë, Charlotte, 34–35, 142
Brothels, 86. See also Prostitution
Broughton, Rhoda, 172, 173
Brown, Isaac Baker, 55
Büchner, Georg, 140
Buckley, Arabella, 223
Burton, Richard Francis, 17–18, 35–37, 181
Butler, Josephine, 37–39, 64, 65, 258, 259
Byford, William Heath, 101

Carpenter, Edward, 233
Carter, Robert Brudenell, 100
Catholicism, 52. See also specific topics
Censorship, 40–45, 164
Chamberlain, Lord, 43–45
Charcot, Jean-Martin, 114
Chen Sen, 49
Chien Lung, 49–50
Child abuse, 45–47. See also Domestic violence
Childbirth. See Pregnancy and childbirth
Child labor, 6–7
Child marriage, 109–10
Child prostitution, 39, 47–48. See also White slavery
China, 48–50

Ch'ing dynasty, 49
Christianity, 50–54; social thought and, xvii
Circumcision, 5, 54–56, 119–20
Clevenger, S. V., 221
Clitoridectomy, 54–56
Clothing. See Fashion
Cobbe, Frances Power, 71–72
Cohabitation, 57–59
Collins, Wilkie, 59–61, 174, 175
Comic opera. See Gilbert and Sullivan
Communal societies, 89–91
Comstock, Anthony, 61–62, 231
Comstock Law, 43, 62, 231
Consent. See Age of consent
Constable, John, 77
Contagious Diseases (CD) Acts, 5–6, 39, 62–65, 207, 212, 227
Contraception. See Birth control
Coram, Thomas, 88
Corelli, Marie, 172–73
Cosmetics, 22
Courtship, 65–66
Criminal Law Amendment (CLA) Act, 8, 36, 37, 45, 47, 212, 238
Cross-dressing, 50. See also Theater
Cross-gender roles, 167
Cushman, Charlotte, 247, 248

Dance/dances, 67–68
Darwin, Charles, 78–80, 85, 102, 103, 213–14, 224
Dauncey, Thomas, 234–35
Defamation. See Slander

Dennett, John, 26
Divorce, 53, **69–71**, 170
"Domestic economist", 261–63
Domestic servants. *See* Servants
Domestic violence, **71–73**
Dracula (Stoker), 242–43
Dress. *See* Fashion

Education, 6–7, 83
Edwin, xvii
Ellis, Havelock, 26, **74–75**, 102,
    103, 136, 221–22, 233
Erotica. *See* Pornography and
    erotica
Etty, William, **75–78**
Eugenics theory, 202
Evil Genius, The (Collins), 61
Evolution, **78–80**

Factory girls, 8
Faderman, Lillian, 217–18
Fashion, **81–83**
Faulkner, Thomas, 67
Feminism, **83–84**. *See also* Grand,
    Sarah; Linton, Eliza Lynn;
    Women
Fetishism, **84–86**
Flagellation, **86–87**
Flaubert, Gustave, 198
Fornication. *See* Adultery and
    fornication
Foundlings, **87–89**
Free-love communities, **89–91**
French system. *See* Prostitution,
    regulated
Freud, Sigmund, xviii, 46, 114, 222
Friendship, romantic. *See*
    Romantic friendship
*Fruits of Philosophy,
    The* (Knowlton), 31, 32

Galton, Francis, 80
Gardner, Augustus K., 100
Geddes, Patrick, 232–33
Gender roles, **92–93**, 167. *See also*
    Feminism; Linton, Eliza Lynn;
    Women, in the media
German literature. *See* Literature,
    German
Giddens, Anthony, 219
Gilbert and Sullivan
    (comic opera), **93–94**

Gilchrist, Alexander, 76, 77
"Girl of the period," 8
"Girl of the Period, The" (Linton),
    138
Gladstone, William Ewart, 176
Gonorrhea, 240
Gorham, Deborah, 48
Gothic fiction, **94–96**
Grand, Sarah, **97–99**
Greg, W. R., 63
Grimms' fairy tales, 140
Gynecological manuals, **99–101**

Haddo, Lord, 176, 177
Haggard, H. Rider, 124
Hardwicke's Marriage Act of 1753,
    156
Hardy, Thomas, **102–4**
Harems, **104–6**
Heavenly Twins, The (Grand),
    97–99
Heine, Heinrich, 140
Hermaphrodites, **106–8**
Hermaphroditus, 106
Hicks, George Elgar, 184
Hindle, Annie, 248
Hinduism, marriage in, **108–11**
Hirschfeld, Magnus, **111–12**
Hollick, Frederick, 230
Homosexual, origin of the term,
    113
Homosexuality, 36–37, **113–15**,
    131–32, 181, 232; anthropology
    and, 17–19; in China, 49–50;
    in fiction, 96; Havelock Ellis
    on, 74–75; Islam and, 126–27;
    and the law, 134
Hopkins, Gerald Manley,
    115–16
Hopkins, Jane Ellice, **116–18**
"Housewife," 263
Hughes, Arthur, 185
Hunt, Holman, 185
Hutchinson, Jonathan, **118–20**
Hyam, Ronald, 123
Hysteria, 100

Illegitimacy, **121–23**. *See also*
    Collins, Wilkie
Imperialism, **123–26**
Insanity. *See* Madness
Interracial sex, 215

Intersex. *See* Hermaphrodites
Islam and homosexuality, **126–27**

James, Henry, 175
Jane Eyre (Brontë), 34, 96
Jesus Christ, 115

Kanyadana, 110
Kellogg, John Harvey, **129–30**,
    231
Knowlton, Charles, 30, 31
Koniangas, 18
Krafft-Ebing, Richard von, 25, 86,
    130–32, 136, 137, 161, 178,
    221, 232

Labouchere Amendment, 36–37
Ladies' Association for the Care of
    Friendless Girls (LACFG), 117
"Lady" construct, 261–62
Lallemand, Claude-François, 5,
    240
Lamarck, Jean-Baptiste, 78
Lamarckianism, 78
Law, **133–34**. *See also specific topics*
Leadbeater, Charles, 24
Lesbianism, 96, **134–37**. *See also*
    Homosexuality; Romantic
    friendship
Lewis, Matthew "Monk," 95
Libel, 234
Linton, Eliza Lynn, **137–38**, 172
Literature, German, **138–42**
Lock hospitals. *See* Penitentiaries
    and lock hospitals
Lombroso, Cesare, 161
London Foundling Hospital, 88–89
Love: "at first sight," **142–44**; in
    marriage, **144–45**; romantic,
    218–19. *See also specific topics*
Lydstrom, Frank, 25

Madame Bovary (Flaubert), 198
Madness, **146–48**, 161, 201
Magnan, Valentin, 114
Malthus, Robert, 29
Malthus, Thomas Robert,
    148–152
Marriage, xvii, **152–55**, 265;
    Christianity and, 51–53;
    irregular, **156–57**

Mary, Mother of Jesus. *See* Virgin Mary

Masochism. *See* Sadism and masochism

Massage, uterine, 100

Masturbation, 100–101, **157–59**, 227; circumcision to prevent, 54, 55

Matrimonial Causes (Divorce) Act, 70

Media: women in the, 261–65. *See also* Newspapers

Menmonia community, 90

Menstruation, **159–60**, 168

Mental illness. *See* Madness

Merrill, Lisa, 247

Midwives and physicians. *See* Physicians and midwives

Mill, John Stuart, 103

Millais, John Everett, 185, 186

Mitchell, S. Weir, 147

Modern Times, 90

Moll, Albert, 25–26

Morel, Bénédict, 113

Mormonism, 195–96

Morris, Robert, 56

Moyer, Harold, 222

Murder and sex crimes, **161–63**

Muscular Vegetarianism, 129–30

Music halls, **163–65**

Musset, Alfred de, 26

My Secret Life ("Walter"), 255–56

Native Americans, **166–68**

Necrophilia, **168–69**

Newspapers and broadsides, **170–71**. *See also* Media

"New Woman," 261, 264

Nichols, Mary Gove, 90

Nichols, Thomas, 90

Novels: romantic, **171–73**; sensation, **174–76**

Nude models, **176–77**. *See also* Photographs

Obscenity. *See* Censorship

Oneida community, 90

Orgasm, **178–79**

Orientalism, 127, **180–81**

Ottoman women, **181–83**

Ouida, 172

Owen, Robert Dale, 30, 230

Painting, **184–86**. *See also* Nude models

Paragraph 175, 112

Parent-Duchâtelet, Alexandre, 208, 209

Parent-Duchatelet, Jean-Baptiste, 136–37

Passionlessness. *See* Sexlessness

Patmore, Coventry Kersey Dighton, **186–88**

Pederasty, 37

Penitentiaries and lock hospitals, **188–90**

Perversions, 131. *See also* Krafft-Ebing

Photographs, **190–91**

Phrenology, 33

Physicians and midwives, 100, **191–93**

Physiognomy, 21

Pi Yuan, 49

Place, Francis, 150

Ploss, Hermann, 19

Polygamy: African, **193–95**; American, 28, **195–97**; Christianity and, 51

Popular science. *See* Science, popular

Pornography and erotica, xvii–xviii, **197–200**. *See also* Nude models, Photographs

Postpartum depression, 201

Pregnancy and childbirth, **200–202**

Prostitution, 117, 124, 188, 189, **203–8**, 216, 238; child, 39, 47–48; in China, 49; lesbianism and, 136–37; in the media, 261, 263–64; regulated, 5, **208–10**. *See also* White slavery

Psychiatry. *See* Krafft-Ebing; Madness

Psychoanalysis, 114. *See also* Freud

Psychopathia Sexualis. See Krafft-Ebing

Purity. *See* Social purity

Queen Victoria, **211–12**

Quianlong Emperor. *See* Chien Lung

Race, 124, **213–17**; beauty and, 22

Radcliffe, Ann, 95

Ramé, Maria Louise. *See* Ouida

Rape, 162; marital, 72. *See also* Child marriage

Religion, xvi–xvii

Remarriage, 52, 109, 111

Romance novels. *See under* Novels, romantic

Romantic friendship, 135, **217–18**

Romanticism, 139

Romantic love, **218–19**. *See also* Love

Rossetti, Dante Gabriel, 143, 186

Rural society. *See* Agriculture

Sadism and masochism, 86–87, **221–22**

Said, Edward, 127

Sandys, George Frederick, 184, 185

Sappho, 244

Sayre, Lewis, 55

Schlegel, Friedrich, 139

Schnitzler, Arthur, 141

Schools, 6–7

Science, popular, **222–24**

Semmelweis, Ignaz, 192–93

Sensation novels. *See* Novels, sensation

Separation. *See* Divorce

Servants, 66, **225–26**

Sex crimes. *See* Murder and sex crimes

Sex education, **226–28**

Sexlessness, **228–29**

Sex manuals, **229–31**

Sexology, 221, **231–33**

Sexual abuse, 45–47. *See also* Child prostitution; White slavery

Sexual identity, 115

Sexually transmitted diseases (STDs). *See* Contagious Diseases (CD) Acts; Venereal disease

Sexual pleasure. *See* Orgasm

Shakespeare, William, 41, 43

Sharpe, Sarah, **234–35**

Shastras, 108–10

"Shiahng gung", 50

Simpson, James Young, 202

Sims, Marion, 99–100

Slander, English law, **234–37**

Smith, Joseph, Jr., 196
Social purity, **238–39**
Societies for the Prevention of
    Cruelty to Children (SPCCs),
    45, 46
Sodomy, 17–19, 162
Southcott, Joanna, 200
Spermatorrhoea, **240**
Spinsters, **240–42**
Statutory rape. See Age of consent;
    Child marriage
Stead, William T., 171, 238
Stoker, Bram, **242–43**
Stridhan (women's separate prop-
    erty), 110
Surgery, 99–101, 107
Swinburne, Algernon Charles,
    243–45
Syphilis, 5, 6, 188. *See also*
    Contagious Diseases (CD) Acts

Tardieu, Ambroise, 25
Taylor Mill, Harriet, 264
Thackery, William Makepeace,
    xv–xvi
Theater, **246–48**; censorship in,
    41, 43–45
Theatres Act of 1843, 43
Theosophy, 24
Thomson, J. Arthur, 232–33

Tilley, Vesta, 248
Trafficking. *See* White slavery
Transgenderism. *See* Cross-gender
    roles
Transvestitism, 50
Trollope, Anthony, 65,
    248–50

Ulrichs, Karl-Heinrich, 113–14,
    232

Vegetarianism, 129–30
Venereal disease (VD), 188, 189,
    206, 240. *See also* Contagious
    Diseases (CD) Acts
Verlaine, Paul, 199
Victoria, Queen. *See* Queen
    Victoria
Victorians, xv, xvi
Virginity, **251–52**
Virgin Mary, **252–54**

Walpole, Horace, 94–95
"Walter", **255–56**
Warren, Josiah, 90
Wedekind, Frank, 141
Wells, Thomas Spencer, 101
West, Charles, 55
Westermarck, Edward, 19

Westphal, Karl, 85,
    113–14
White Cross Army (WCA),
    117
White slavery, 39, 45, 46, 209,
    256–59. *See also* Child
    prostitution; Prostitution
Widowhood, **259–60**
Wollstonecraft, Mary, 83
Woman in White, The (Collins),
    59, 60, 174
Women, 83–84; in the media,
    261–65; suffrage and
    emancipation, 264 (*see also*
    Feminism). *See also*
    specific topics
Wood, Ellen, 174, 175
Woodhull, Victoria Claflin,
    265–66
Wright, Fanny (Frances),
    230

Xin Yue Zhu Ren, 49

Yeazell, Ruth Bernard, 104,
    105
"Youth problem," 7

Zuñi, 167

About the Editor and Contributors

Nancy Fix Anderson is professor of history at Loyola University, New Orleans. She is the author of *Woman against Women in Victorian England: A Life of Eliza Lynn Linton* (1987) and many articles on Victorian women and the family. She is currently working on books on Annie Besant and on Victorian sports.

Claire Bazin is a professor at Nanterre (Paris X) University, France. She is the author of two books on the Brontës—*La Vision du Mal chez les Sœurs Brontë*, (1995), and *Jane Eyre: Le Pèlerin moderne* (2005)—and of many articles on the same subject. She has also written on New Zealand author Janet Frame.

Danielle Bertrand is a graduate of the University of Ottawa, Canada. She is currently working in the Faculty of Arts at the Open University, United Kingdom.

Mary Block is an assistant professor of history at Valdosta State University, Valdosta, Georgia. She is completing a book on the history of rape law in the nineteenth-century United States.

Barbara Brookes is professor of history and head of department at the University of Otago, Dunedin, New Zealand. Her research interests lie in the intersections between the history of women and the history of medicine. In her most recent book, *Sites of Gender: Women, Men and Modernity in Southern Dunedin, 1890–1939* (2003) co-edited with Annabel Cooper and Robin Law, she explores how gender structured health status, leisure opportunities, and expectations of marriage.

Alyson Brown is a senior lecturer in history at Edge Hill College of Higher Education. She has researched extensively on the history of crime and punishment, specifically on child prostitution and abuse and upon penal history. She has published many articles and chapters and also *Knowledge of Evil: Child Prostitution and Child Sexual Abuse in Twentieth Century England*, co-authored with David Barrett (2002) and *English Society and the Prison* (2003). Her edited book is *Historical Perspectives on Social Identities* (2006).

Amanda M. Caleb teaches at the University of Sheffield. Her research interests include *fin de siècle* popular fiction, sex, and sexuality in the Victorian period and the intersections between science and literature in the Victorian period. Publications include: "Hysterical Heredity: The Implications of Female Inheritance in *The Legacy of Cai, Interdisciplinary Essays on Wilkie Collins* (2006) and "Monsters Manufactured: Vivisecting the Scientist in the British Fin de Siècle," *Journal of Commonwealth Studies* (2006). She is currently working on editing a collection of interdisciplinary essays on science in nineteenth-century Britain.

Ivan Crozier is a lecturer in the Science Studies Unit at the University of Edinburgh. His main areas of interest are the history of sexology and the history of forensic psychiatry.

Robert Darby is an independent scholar and freelance writer from Canberra, Australia, with a particular interest in history of sexuality and cultural fashioning of the body. He is currently the review editor for *H-Histsex* and part of the Humanities Online Project at University of Michigan. His recent publications include: *A Surgical Temptation: The Demonization of the Foreskin and the Rise of Circumcision in Britain* (2005).

Duc Dau teaches at the University of Western Australia. Her research interests include poetry, theology, the body, erotica, and philosophies of love. She has published articles on Seamus Heaney, Gerard Manley Hopkins, and celibacy and virgin marriage in Tractarian poetry.

Sara M. Dodd is an associate lecturer and faculty manager in the Arts Faculty of the Open University, United Kingdom. Her publications have been mostly on nineteenth-century art, specializing in women artists and their education. She lectures on art history.

Lisa Downing is a reader in French Discourses of Sexuality at Queen Mary, University of London. She is the author of several books and articles on representations of nonnormative sexualities in literature, film, and theory, including *Desiring the Dead: Necrophilia and Nineteenth-Century French Literature* (2003). She is co-editor (with Dany Nobus) of *Perversion: Psychoanalytic Perspectives/Perspectives on Psychoanalysis* (2006).

Jill Felicity Durey is an associate professor at Edith Cowan University, Perth, Western Australia. Her current research interests are in marriage and genetics in the nineteenth-century novel, including *Realism and Narrative Modality: The Hero and Heroine in Eliot, Tolstoy and Flaubert* (1993) and *Trollope and the Church of England* (2002).

Carol Marie Englehardt is associate professor of history at Wright State University, Ohio.

Natasha Erlank is an associate professor in historical studies at the University of Johannesburg, South Africa. She works principally on African and colonial history, and her research interests include gender, religion, and nationalism in Southern Africa.

Kyle E. Frackman is a Ph.D. candidate in German and Scandinavian Studies at the University of Massachusetts Amherst. His research focuses mainly on German and Austrian boarding school literature of the late nineteenth and early twentieth centuries.

Amanda Frisken is an assistant professor in the American Studies Department at SUNY College at Old Westbury. Her research highlights the intersections between media production and social activism, in conjunction with the emergence of modern American culture. In her recent book, *Victoria Woodhull's Sexual Revolution: Political Theater and the Popular Press in Nineteenth Century America* (2004), she examines the impact of one of United States' most unusual public figures, the first woman to run for president. Currently, she is working on a book about the rise of sensational media at the end of the nineteenth century.

Ginger Frost is an associate professor of history at Samford University. She is the author of *Promises Broken: Courtship Class and Gender in Victorian England* (1995), numerous articles on legal/social history, and a book-length manuscript on cohabitation in the nineteenth century. Her future projects will concern Victorian childhood and illegitimacy.

Lesley Hall is an archivist at the Wellcome Library for the History and Understanding of Medicine and an honorary lecturer in the history of medicine at University College, London. She has published extensively on issues to do with gender and sexuality in the nineteenth and twentieth centuries. Her most recent book is the anthology *Outspoken Women: Women Writing about Sex 1870–1969* (2005). Her website is at www.lesleyahall.net.

B. Carmon Hardy is emeritus professor of history at California State University, Fullerton. He specializes in American Intellectual History, American Religious History, and American Constitutional History. For the last dozen years, his research has focused intensively on the Mormon polygamous experience. His most recent work on the subject, *Doing the Works of Abraham: Sources of Mormon Polygamous Thought and Practice*, is presently at press and due to be published by the Arthur H. Clark Co.

Frederick Mansfield Hodges, Ph.D. (Oxon), is a medical historian.

Laurie Jacklin is a Ph.D. candidate at McMaster University, Canada, specializing in the history of medicine.

Louise A. Jackson is a lecturer in modern social history, economic and social history, School of History and Classics, at the University of Edinburgh. Her research interests include: histories of gender, crime, policing, and child welfare. Her publications include: *Child Sexual Abuse in Victorian England* (2000); *Women Police: Gender, Welfare and Surveillance in the Twentieth Century* (2006).

Praveena Kodoth works at the Centre for Development Studies, Trivandrum, India. In research, she has engaged with questions of gender in the context of institutional change and in the development process in Kerala, South India and has drawn on historical and anthropological perspectives. At present, she is writing on contemporary articulations of gender in negotiations of marriage in Kerala.

Max Kramer is a Ph.D. candidate at Columbia University. At present, he is finishing his dissertation entitled "*The Poetry of Inversion. Queer Metaphor in Arthur Rimbaud, Stefan George, and Federico Garcìa Lorca.*" He is presently a guest professor at Sarah Lawrence College. He has delivered various papers on the subject of homosexuality and nineteenth-century literature, on Rimbaud, George, Lorca, and on the influence that western conceptualizations of same-sex sexuality have in Muslim-majority societies. His publications include a review of Wanda Klee's *Leibhaftige Dekadenz* in the Romanic Review, an article on the German poet Stefan George in the *Encyclopedia of Erotic Literature*. He is currently working on an article entitled "The Gay Advance

in the Muslim World: Liberation or New Colonialism?"

Julia Kuehn is an assistant professor in English at the University of Hong Kong. Her research interests lie in nineteenth- and twentieth-century literature and culture, with particular focus on popular writing.

Isaac Land teaches history at Indiana State University. His book project concerns masculinity and maritime culture.

Jean-Marie Lecomte is a lecturer at Nancy University (France). His research interests and publications include late Victorian literature and film studies (late silent cinema, the birth of the talkies and the semiotics of film dialog).

Philippa Levine teaches at the University of Southern California. Her research interests include race, sexuality, and the prehistory of eugenics. Previous publications include: as editor, *Gender and Empire: Oxford History of the British Empire Companion Series* (2004), *Prostitution, Race and Politics: Policing Venereal Disease in the British Empire* (2003), and *Feminist Lives in Victorian England. Private Roles and Public Commitment* (1990, 2004).

Reina Lewis is a professor of fashion studies at London College of Fashion, University of the Arts, London. She is the author of *Rethinking Orientalism: Women, Travel and the Ottoman Harem* (2004), *Gendering Orientalism: Race, Femininity and Representation* (1996) and co-editor, with Sara Mills, *Feminist Postcolonial Theory: A Reader* (2003) series co-editor, with Teresa Heffernan, *Cultures in Dialogue*, reprint facsimile editions with critical introductions of western and middle-Eastern women's travel writing.

Donna Loftus is a lecturer in history at The Open University with research interests in the industrial and urban culture of Victorian Britain. Recent publications include "The Self in Society: Middle-Class Men and Autobiography" in David Amigoni, ed. *Life Writing and Victorian Culture* (2006) and "Capital and Community: Attempts to Democratize the

Market in Mid-Nineteenth-Century Britain" *Victorian Studies* (2002).

Linda Mahood is an associate professor in the Department of History at the University of Guelph, Ontario, Canada. She holds a B.A. from the University of Saskatchewan and an M.Litt and a Ph.D. from Glasgow University. Her publications include: *The Magdalenes, Prostitution in the Nineteenth Century* (1988); *Policing Gender, Class and Family: Britain, 1850–1945* (1995); and co-editor with Bernard Schissel, *Social Control in Canada* (2000) as well as articles in: *Gender and History, The Journal of the History of Sexuality, Women's Studies International Forum, Canadian Journal of History, Voluntary Action: The Journal of the Institute of Volunteering Research, History of Education*.

Helen Mathers is a research fellow at the University of Sheffield and associate lecturer at the Open University. She has a longstanding research interest in Josephine Butler and has published several articles about her, including a major study of her evangelicalism published in *Journal of Ecclesiastical History* in 2001.

Christopher Matthews teaches at Washington and Lee University in Virginia. He has published essays in *Victorian Studies* and *Nineteenth-Century Literature*. At present, he is at work on a book-length study of male heterosexuality in the literature of mid-nineteenth-century Britain.

Catherine Maxwell is a reader in Victorian Literature, at The School of English and Drama Queen Mary, University of London. Her research interests lie in nineteenth-century English poetry and the literature of the Victorian *fin de siècle*, with special reference to gender, aesthetics, vision, and the visual. She is the author of articles on various nineteenth-century writers (including Browning, George Eliot, Ruskin, Shelley, Christina and Dante Gabriel Rossetti, Swinburne, Hardy, and Vernon Lee) published in various edited collections and in periodicals such as *Victorian Poetry, English Literary History, The Review of*

English Studies, and *The Yearbook of English Studies*. Her most recent articles are "Vision and Visuality in Victorian Poetry," *The Blackwell Companion to Victorian Poetry*, ed. Richard Cronin, Antony Harrison, and Alison Chapman (2002); "Vernon Lee and the Ghosts of Italy," *Unfolding the South: Nineteenth-century British Women Writers and Artists in Italy 1789–1900*, ed. Alison Chapman and Jane Stabler (2003); "It once should save as well as kill: Dante Gabriel Rossetti and the Feminine," *Outsiders Looking In: The Rossettis Then and Now*, ed. David Clifford and Lauren Rousillon (2004); and "Swinburne: Style, Sympathy, and Sadomasochism," *The Journal of Pre-Raphaelite Studies* (2003).

Ian Merrilees is senior lecturer in European Union Law at Leeds Law School, Leeds Metropolitan University. His research interests include contemporary European law and the history of legislation relating to sex and marriage.

Sue Morgan is principal lecturer in gender history and head of the School of Cultural Studies at the University of Chichester. She has published widely on modern women's history and religious history. Her publications include: *A Passion for Purity: Ellice Hopkins and the Politics of Gender in the Late-Victorian Church*" (1999), *Masculinity and Spirituality in Victorian Culture* (2000) co-edited with Andrew Bradstock, Ann Hogan, and Sean Gill, the single edited collection *Women, Religion and Feminism in Britain, 1750–1900* (2002), and *The Feminist History Reader* (2006).

Ulrike Moser is a Ph.D. student in the Department of Economy and Social History of the University of Vienna. She also works as a freelance journalist for *Profil*, an Austrian independent news magazine and *Trend*, an Austrian economy magazine. At present, she is completing her Ph.D. thesis on *Herzensbildung. Education, Moral Values and Sexuality in the Diaries of Young Women of the Middle Class in the Late 19th Century*. She is interested in women's history, especially between the French Revolution and First World War with a strong focus on love, sexuality, and morality in autobiographical sources.

Susan Mumm is dean of Arts and Sciences at Mount Saint Vincent University, Halifax, Canada. She conducts research into women's philanthropic communities, people trafficking, and alternatives to family structures for women. At the time that this Encyclopedia was being compiled, she was head of the Department of Religious Studies at the Open University, Milton Keynes, Buckinghamshire.

Jamil M. Mustafa is an assistant professor in the English Department at Lewis University, where he teaches courses and conducts research in nineteenth-century British literature, Gothic fiction, and the horror film.

Jessica Needle is a postgraduate student in English and Cultural Studies at the University of Western Australia. Her research interests include sexuality, gender, consumerism, class, and imperialism.

Caryn E. Neumann is a lecturer in history at the Ohio State University. She is also past managing editor of the *Journal of Women's History*.

Sally Newman is completing her Ph.D. in the Centre for Women's Studies & Gender Research at Monash University. Her dissertation focuses on the textual representation of lesbian desire and the historiographical complexities of archival research for the lesbian historian. Her work has appeared in *Hecate*, *Journal of the History of Sexuality*, and *Women's History Review*.

E. M. Palmegiano is a professor of history at Saint Peter's College, New Jersey, and a past president of the American Journalism Historians Association. She has written four books and over thirty articles and papers on the nineteenth-century British press as well as numerous reviews in scholarly journals. She serves on the editorial boards of the *Encyclopedia of American Journalism*, *Journalism History*, and *Media History Monographs*. At present, she is working on a book-length study of press

perceptions of journalism and journalists in the Victorian era.

Jody Pennington is associate professor in media and culture studies in the Department of English, University of Aarhus, Denmark. Educated at Georgia Southwestern College and the University of Aarhus, he has published articles and presented papers on various aspects of film and popular music, as well as American constitutional law.

Richard Phillips teaches cultural geography and postcolonial criticism at Liverpool University. His publications include: *Mapping Men and Empire: A Geography of Adventure* (1997); *De-Centring Sexualities: Politics and Representations Beyond the Metropolis* (co-edited, 2000), and *Sex, Politics and Empire: A Postcolonial Geography* (2006).

Elizabeth Reis is an associate professor in women's and gender studies and history at the University of Oregon. At present, she is writing a book called *Impossible Hermaphrodites: Intersex in America, 1620–1960*.

Angelique Richardson is a senior lecturer at the University of Exeter. She has published widely on nineteenth-century literature and culture and is the author of *Love and Eugenics in the Late Nineteenth Century: Rational Reproduction and the New Woman* (1993).

Fang-Fu Ruan (Ph.D., M.D., ACS, ABS) is a professor at FAACS and is a visiting professor at The Institute for Advanced Study of Human Sexuality, San Francisco and The Graduate School of Human sexology, She-Te University, Kaohsiung, Taiwan.

Lutz D. H. Sauerteig is Wellcome Trust University Award Holder and lecturer in history of medicine at Durham University, School for Health. He has widely published on the history of public health and venereal disease policy in England and Germany. At present, he is researching the history of sex education in England and Germany between the 1880s and 1970s. He is also working on a comparative history of sex education in England and Germany (1880s to 1970s) and editing together with Roger Davidson a volume on *Shaping Sexual Knowledge: Sex Education of the Young in 20th Century Europe and North America. A Cultural History.*

Karen Sayer teaches at Leeds University, Trinity & All Saints. Her research falls within those elements of culture and society, especially gender relations and nineteenth-century constructions of femininity that cut across boundaries such as rural/urban, nature/culture, and the relationship between the "ideal" and the "real," "representation" and "reality." She has published two monographs on rural women: *Women of the Fields: Representations of Femininity in Nineteenth Century Rural Society* (1995); and *Country Cottages: A Cultural History* (2000), and related articles.

Angela Schwarz is a professor in modern history at the University of Duisburg-Essen. She has published books and articles on popular science in Britain and Germany, political, social, cultural, and media history. She has recently published *Der Park in der Metropole* (2005), which turns to the connection between urban growth and the creation of public parks in Europe and the United States.

Derek B. Scott is professor of music at the University of Salford, Manchester, UK. His research interests include: music, culture, and ideology. He is the author of *The Singing Bourgeois* (2nd ed., 2001), *From the Erotic to the Demonic: On Critical Musicology* (2003), and editor of *Music, Culture, and Society* (2000). He is also a composer.

Jessica Ann Sheetz-Nguyen is professor of history at Oklahona City Community College.

John C. Spurlock is professor of history and chair of the Division of the Humanities at Seton Hill University. In addition to his work on free love, he is co-author (with Cynthia Magistro) of *New and Improved: The Transformation of American Women's Emotional Culture* (1998). His present research deals with adolescent sexuality during the twentieth century.

Stephen K. Stein teaches a variety of courses in American history and military history at the University of Memphis. His first book *From Torpedoes to Aviation: Washington Irving Chambers and Technological Innovation in the New Navy* is forthcoming from the University of Alabama Press.

Lana Thompson is an independent scholar with research interests in sex, deviant behavior, and sexuality in the Renaissance, history of anatomy, medicine, gynecology; forensic anthropology, intersections of religion and science, witchcraft, and the pancultural worship of cats. She is the author of *The Wandering Womb: A Cultural History of Outrageous Beliefs about Women* and "Bodies from the Darkside: Anatomical Paradoxes in the Renaissance."

Stephen Waddams is a Goodman/Schipper professor of law at the University of Toronto. He is a graduate of the University of Toronto (B.A. 1963, LL.B., 1967), Cambridge University (B.A., 1965, M.A., 1969, Ph.D., 1994), and the University of Michigan (LL.M., 1968; S.J.D., 1972), and a fellow of the Royal Society of Canada. He has been a visiting fellow at Jesus College, Oxford, 1981–1982, All Souls College, Oxford, 1988, and Clare Hall, Cambridge, 1996. He is the author of about 100 published articles, notes, reviews, and essays, mainly on contract law, and of the following books: *Products Liability* (4th ed., 2002); *The Law of Contracts* (5th ed., 2005); *The Law of Damages* (4th ed., 2004); *Introduction to the Study of Law* (6th ed., 2004); *Law, Politics and the Church of England: the Career of Stephen Lushington 1782–1873* (1992), *Sexual Slander in Nineteenth-Century England: Defamation in the Ecclesiastical Courts, 1815–1855* (2000), and *Dimensions of Private Law: Categories and Concepts in Anglo-American Legal Reasoning* (2003).

Frank H. Wallis is an independent scholar and writer, now concentrating on British expansionist policy in India, 1838–1849. His publications include *Popular Anti-Catholicism in Victrorian Britain* (1993).

Deborah Wynne is now a senior lecturer in nineteenth-century literature at the University of Chester. She is the author of *The Sensation*

Novel and the Victorian Family Magazine (2001). She has published on a range of authors, including Dickens, Ellen Wood, Elizabeth Gaskell, and Jane Austen and film.

Dan Vyleta is an assistant professor at ECLA (Berlin) and junior research fellow at Fitzwilliam College, Cambridge. His research interests include the history of "modernity," especially the history of crime, criminology, and of antisemitism in the nineteenth and twentieth centuries. His recent publications include: *Crime, News and Jews* (2006); "The Cultural History of Crime." In Stefan Berger, ed. *A Companion to Nineteenth-Century Europe, 1789–1914* (2006).